ABOLITIONIST FROM VIRGINIA

Life and Times of Moncure Daniel Conway

1832–1907

Moncure Daniel Conway

ABOLITIONIST FROM VIRGINIA

Life and Times of Moncure Daniel Conway

1832–1907

by
Clara Marburg Kirk

Edited and Foreword
by Donald Kirk

HERITAGE BOOKS
2023

HERITAGE BOOKS
AN IMPRINT OF HERITAGE BOOKS, INC.

Books, CDs, and more—Worldwide

For our listing of thousands of titles see our website
at
www.HeritageBooks.com

Published 2023 by
HERITAGE BOOKS, INC.
Publishing Division
5810 Ruatan Street
Berwyn Heights, MD 20740

Cover photos and photos within the text are
courtesy of Encyclopedia Virginia

International Standard Book Number
Paperbound: 978-0-7884-2732-9

In memory of

Fanny Dulaney Moncure Marburg

1868-1958

Moncure D. Conway

Moncure Daniel Conway in his garden

TABLE OF CONTENTS

Foreword

This book reflects considerably more than an interest generated by Moncure Daniel Conway's place in a family tree of Virginia and Maryland ancestors. It represents an effort on the part of Clara Marburg Kirk, my mother, at linking the life of this preacher-author with the 19th-century American literary figures whose work she and my father, Rudolf Kirk, taught and researched for more than 40 years, mostly as members of the English Departments at Rutgers University and Douglass College. The author to whom they were most devoted was William Dean Howells, an esoteric name to Americans today but a giant of the late 19th century – and a friend, confidante and source of inspiration for Moncure Conway.

Before turning to the life of Conway in the 1960s, my parents wrote and edited a dozen books and numerous articles, several of them important commentaries on the life and work of Howells. Among Clara Marburg Kirk's best-known works were *W.D. Howells and Art in His Time* (1965) and *W.D. Howells, Traveler from Altruria, 1889-1894* (1962), both published by Rutgers University Press, as well as a biography, *William Dean Howells* (Twayne, 1962), co-authored with my father. For years my parents interviewed Howells contacts and relatives and rummaged through obscure files, traveling from the place of his upbringing in Ohio to libraries in Chicago, New York and Boston, connecting his early life in the Midwest to the days of his greatest success as an editor and author in the elitist east.

My mother's turn to Conway represented a logical diversion after the years of work on Howells. The story of Conway and numerous other Virginia ancestors was deeply ingrained in her subconsciousness as a result of tales passed on mainly by her mother, my grandmother, Fanny Dulaney Moncure Marburg, to whose memory this book is dedicated. Other family members, notably my mother's older sister, Frances Marburg Zeigler, but also their brother, Edgar Marburg, and younger sister, Anita Marburg Lerner, delighted in passing on the tradition. I have vivid memories of tales told by my grandmother as well as my mother, aunts and uncle of a pantheon of Virginians. Their names, beginning with that of Robert "King" Carter, are part of the legacy of the Tidewater region as well as American history from colonial to Civil War times to the present.

Clara Marburg Kirk never clearly defined why she immersed herself so deeply in Conway as her final focal point of scholarly endeavor. One reason, however, may be that he represented a noble divergence from the mainstream of Virginians in both his work and views. Another no doubt was the connection between Conway and Howells. In any case, her interest in Conway was an extension of the earlier research she and my father conducted on Howells.

As the title word "abolitionist" indicates, Conway was a southerner who deeply opposed slavery in all its forms. What makes his crusade all the more interesting, from a personal family viewpoint, was that it brought him into close touch with my father's ancestors in the staunchly anti-slavery community of the Society of Friends in Sandy Spring, part of Olney, Maryland, then as now out Georgia Avenue from the District of Columbia.

Students of history can find a legacy of both these communities in their religious institutions, living memorials of the people who once worshipped in them -- and still do today. Go down Interstate 95 from Washington, on south through Alexandria and the suburban Virginia sprawl a few miles, and you eventually reach Stafford County, home of Aquia Church, in whose graveyard lie the remains of members of the Moncure, Conway and numerous other Virginia clans, many of them interrelated. Or drive past the Olney Theater in Maryland, and you come upon the Friends Meeting House next to another graveyard bearing the names of Brookes, Kirks, Farquhars, Stablers and others from my father's side. For a greater understanding of the Quaker community and traditions, you might spend a few hours at the Sandy Spring Museum, on the same road in a home known as Tall Timbers before the last of its Brooke and Stabler occupants passed away in the 1980s.

The story of Moncure Conway if anything is more relevant today than it was when my mother researched and wrote it in the 1960s. It is possible to link this abolitionist figure with present-day theologians, some of them bearing similar messages of peace and reconciliation, others more interested in sowing seeds of division and discord. The scenes that Conway saw, in which he participated, from Cincinnati to Baltimore to Boston to New

York, Washington and London, are moments in a rich history that goes on in today's racial struggles. It is a source of pride that Moncure Conway should have espoused the just cause of a weak, oppressed and, as the book makes clear, often terrorized and brutalized black minority at a time when his views were far from popular in the region where he first waged the good fight. His courageous stand placed him in conflict not only with many of his peers but also with some of his relatives.

My mother's research and writing on Conway might have been entirely lost had I not discovered it in a box in the attic of my home in Washington. Although she managed to complete the entire manuscript, including footnotes and bibliography, she lost the energy to find a publisher and left it along with notes on her other scholarly work before passing away in 1976. It was not until after my father died 13 years later in San Marcos, Texas, where my parents retired from Rutgers to teach at Southwest Texas State, now Texas State University, and spent the last years of their lives, that this material came my way as executor of the estate.

Readers will note some politically incorrect usages in the manuscript – a reflection of the times in which my mother lived and wrote. Blacks are called "Negroes," and the words "gay" and "gaily" bear no relationship to what has come to be known as a term of identity. Doubtless there are other examples of words and terminology that have fallen from fashion or changed meaning. Deleting or editing such language, however, would serve no real purpose. Many words that are now in vogue will be interpreted in quite different ways generations hence. Once we begin altering manuscripts, we risk a process of rewriting that may do more to distort than to "correct" or "update" the inner sense and point.

Thus, Clara Marburg Kirk's study of Moncure Conway stands on its own, as she wrote it. It is a glimpse into the life and times of a man to whom prejudice of any kind was anathema many years before others in his Virginia milieu had the heart to echo the same sentiments. His words live on in the pages of his own books and articles, most of which are long forgotten. They are quoted extensively here as a reminder of the origins and evolution of the most turbulent drama in our country's history -- one that remains very much a work in progress.

For bringing this story to life and light so many years after it was written, I am indebted to the editors at Heritage Books,

Leslie Wolfinger and Debbie Riley, as well as a number of Conway descendants, notably Dan Chichester, who extended his hospitality in visits to Glencairne farm outside Fredericksburg, Virginia; Conway Zeigler, for his indefatigable research into family records; Ted Marburg, for his assistance at critical moments; and Susanne Tomlinson, friend and editor, who also pored over the manuscript.

Donald Kirk, Washington

Preface

This study of the life and times of Moncure Daniel Conway is written by a member of the same Virginia tribe into which Moncure was born. "Uncle Richard" and "Aunt Mary," of Stafford County, are my great-grandparents, known to me by hearsay when, as a child, I was released from the restraints of winters in Philadelphia and allowed to run barefoot around "Glencairne" for long summer months. My great-grandfather's "office," where Moncure as a boy had the privilege of reading, was still standing. The chief justice himself, his wife and many of his descendants were buried in a small family plot on the edge of the sloping cornfields. The slave quarters had been torn down, except for the portion known as "the summer kitchen." We children played "Pussy-Wants-A-Corner" among the trees on the lawn of Glencairne with our grandfather (also a judge) exactly as described by Conway in his *Autobiography*: *Memories and Experiences of Moncure Daniel Conway.*

Curiously, my husband's great-grandfather, Roger Brooke, of Sandy Spring, Maryland, is also included by Conway in his *Autobiography*. He was the old Quaker patriarch who welcomed the visitor from Virginia when, one Sunday morning in 1851, he tied his horse to a tree and entered the Friends' Meeting House of Sandy Spring. Roger Brooke invited the young stranger home to dinner and, in reply to Conway's questions about the obvious prosperity of "the neighborhood," said, with a smile, "It may be because we pay wages to our laborers." Conway realized that, for the first time, he was speaking with an acknowledged abolitionist.

These personal facts are only worth mentioning because they indicate why I was drawn to study the ideas of this free-thinker from Virginia, who was like the uncles and aunts I knew, but different. He was different largely because he was more sensitive than those among whom he lived to the problem of the Negro, and what it would mean many years later to the whole country.

Moncure Daniel Conway as a young man

Introduction

This is the story of the education of a young abolitionist of Virginia, Moncure Daniel Conway, and his growing comprehension of the complex problem of races. Born in 1832 to an old and established family of Stafford County, Virginia, he journeyed from his well-loved village to the North, where he experienced his "second birth." In Concord, Massachusetts, he became the friend of a group of abolitionists, Ralph Waldo Emerson, Amos Bronson Alcott, Henry David Thoreau, William Henry Channing and many others, who were to change his way of thinking so profoundly that he could never again live in Virginia.

Beginning his career as a Methodist circuit-rider, Conway soon discovered the limitations for him of this group and adopted the views of the New England abolitionists. Upon his graduation from the Harvard Divinity School in Cambridge, he accepted a call from the First Unitarian Church of Washington, D.C., hoping to carry the message of abolition to the South. Having listened for several years in Boston to the sermons of Theodore Parker, the orations of William Lloyd Garrison and Wendell Phillips, young Conway, then aged twenty-two, was unprepared for the confusion on the question of slavery which he found in Washington.

Though loved by his generally pro-slavery congregation, Conway's resignation was accepted when he was called to the First Congregational Church in Cincinnati. Emerson, Bronson Alcott, Parker, and other abolitionists were frequent lecturers in this city, which was the first station of the underground railroad for escaping slaves on their way from Kentucky to Canada. Conway was soon more interested in launching a new journal, *The Dial*, than in delivering the orthodox sermons demanded by his flock. Again his resignation was welcomed by a tearful but relieved congregation.

Responsive to all the winds of thought of this day, Conway followed *The One Path* (the title of his earliest book on "The Duties of the North and South"), open to thoughtful men in a world of mixed races and continued to preach and write in

Cincinnati, Washington, Concord, and elsewhere, on the problems of race culminating in the Civil War.

Conway's repeated thought was, first emancipate the slaves throughout the country, since slavery was in itself a wrong, and then consider further adjustments, both economic and social, that would necessarily follow. *The Rejected Stone: or Insurrection vs. Resurrection* (1861) and *The Golden Hour* (1862) were widely read and reviewed at the outbreak of hostilities, as were Conway's editorials in his anti-slavery journal, *The Commonwealth.* The central idea of these various exhortations was that "The Golden Hour will not wait on us to the measure of our own moral cowardice." Conway frequently expressed his doubts concerning the delaying policies of Lincoln, who seemed to him not to avail himself of "the rejected stone," justice. "'We should not be in haste to determine that radical measures are necessary,' says the president. True, but we should be as much without rest as without haste, for no hour will bear to have its task put off upon another hour. The present hour offers us a peaceful victory through emancipation."

When Conway left for England in 1863, at the behest (as he supposed) of the abolitionists, he did so with the full intention of winning the British to the support of the cause of the anti-slavery movement. During his first few months, Conway spent his time successfully preaching and lecturing throughout England. Convinced that he had the backing of the American abolitionists, he threw himself into an ill-considered attempt to mediate the Civil War and bring it to a speedy close. Instead, he brought down the wrath of many of his American supporters - notably that of William Lloyd Garrison – and confused his British audiences. Stunned by the effect of his efforts, Conway retreated to Venice for several months, and, on his return to London, accepted the pastorship of a liberal congregation of free-thinkers at South Place Chapel, London, where he remained for many years, freely commenting on the events of the country from which he felt exiled.

Conway's earliest presentation of the slavery question to the English began with an essay written originally for *The Commonwealth*, "Benjamin Banneker, The Negro Astronomer," 1862. This was followed by *Testimonies Concerning Slavery*, 1864. Conway's autobiographical account of his own contact with slavery as a growing child in Virginia proved so popular that he reduced a portion of the small book (reissued in 1865) to an essay. The *Testimonies* was, however, never reprinted in the United States. Neither the North nor the South was in the mood at that time to read such advanced views concerning the problem of races. Many essays on the American abolitionist and the rights of Negroes, before and after the Civil War, appeared during the next two decades in *Fraser's Magazine*, in *The Fortnightly Review*, as well as in magazines and newspapers in America.

Crucial as the question of slavery seemed to Conway, it became, as his knowledge of science and anthropology deepened, only one aspect of the larger question of the rights of man as defined by Thomas Paine. Just as Conway had slowly come to an understanding of the injustice toward Negroes among his own people, so he had gradually grown to realize that the rejection of the thought of Paine was attributed to the desire on the part of slaveholders and cotton manufacturers not to heed the warning of Paine's essay, "African Trade in America." Conway's *Life of Thomas Paine* (1864) is his monumental contribution to an appreciation of a misunderstood philosopher who defended the rights of men of all races. Paine was to Conway the first man to speak out boldly against slavery in this country.

Conway began his "Reminiscences," as he first thought of calling his *Autobiography*. in New York, July 1897, at the suggestion of his wife, Ellen Dana Conway, in whose memory he dedicated his memoirs. Because of the illness of his wife, Conway had resigned from South Place Chapel in May 1897 and had returned to New York, where Mrs. Conway died the following Christmas. Though actively engaged in many other projects during the next few years, Conway worked intermittently on his "Memories and Experiences" (the subtitle of the *Autobiography*) until its publication three years before his death.

Even after the loss of his wife, Conway, in retelling the events of his life, depended on "the joint memory" on which he had leaned for so many years, making use of "a sort of journal" left by Ellen Conway among letters to her friends and relatives. He also frequently referred to "several journals" of his own and an accumulation of letters from "many valued friends in America and Europe." Most of these journals, letters, drafts of sermons, and articles, which were also used in writing the *Autobiography*. are in twenty-eight boxes in the library of Columbia University. On this material we have drawn, with the permission of Columbia University and the owner of the copyright of the Conway manuscripts.

It is clear that Conway, in preparing his *Memoirs and Experiences* at the end of his life, turned to his printed works in books and pamphlets. These he himself assembled in as nearly complete form as he could and deposited at the Library of Congress in Washington, where they now are. Many of the printed essays and books began as vehement sermons or newspaper articles, aimed at what he considered the major problem of the day, slavery. The circumstances under which they were written are described in his *Autobiography*.

The present study recounts the experiences of a young man, brought up in a slave-holding Virginia family, who turned from his traditions early in life to embrace the larger thought of his day. He himself claimed that, far from repudiating the attitude of his family toward slavery, he was, in fact, restoring it to that of a still earlier generation. "I was born of people opposed to slavery," he wrote of his "unorthodox forebears," in the first chapter of his *Autobiography*, "and when in my twenty-second year my role seemed to many Virginians that of the Prodigal Son, it was the new proslavery Virginian who was the Prodigal, while my part was that of the father at home mourning for the wanderer."

Peter Humstead, an old slave belonging to Conway's grandfather, never wearied of telling the boy of the terrifying blizzard through which he drove the thirty miles to Falmouth and back to fetch the doctor the night the child was born. By the time he became a man, Conway was caught up in an even more frightful storm, that of the Civil War. We are still dealing with the destruction left in its wake, in terms not unlike those suggested by Conway well over a hundred years ago.

One might well ask why the seventy-odd books by Moncure Daniel Conway, and the uncounted contributions to magazines and newspapers – to say nothing of sermons issued as pamphlets – why this mass of material, much of it bearing in one way or another on the question of race, has never been fully examined and placed in its proper framework. The answer is simple: Southerners are not drawn to a writer who deserted their side of the battle-line; northerners can hardly credit the fact that a spokesman from Virginia could have spoken out against slavery with a clearer voice than most of their own abolitionists. Both southerners and northerners find it difficult to understand how, at the same time, Conway continued to love the South and denounce slavery. And, finally, what American, after the disastrous Civil War was ended, could take seriously a critic of Abraham Lincoln? More of an idealist than a politician, Conway was convinced, by an earlier Emancipation Proclamation, war might have been averted. Whether he was right or wrong, the steps by which this many-sided Virginian came to his conclusions are well worth retracing. They lead us back to the origin of the questions concerning the social and political relations of races with which we are faced today.

To comprehend the issues as Conway himself understood them, we are basing our study largely on Conway's own writing, both printed and in manuscript. This we have supplemented by material drawn from newspapers, journals, letters of the period. Scholars of a later day might see quite clearly the dilemma in which Lincoln found himself when he became President of a divided country; to a vehement young preacher from Virginia, imbued with the idealism of the abolitionists, the focus was very different. Though Conway lived until 1907, his thoughts on the place of the Negro in American society both before and after the Civil War were fully expressed by 1875.

Conway's understanding of the problem of the Negro led him ten years later to begin "the long and arduous task" of writing *The Life of Thomas Paine*, whom he called "the first American abolitionist." This two-volume study is still considered the standard work on Paine. When it appeared in 1892, the alumni of Conway's alma mater, Dickinson College, invited him to give their annual address, and, to his surprise and pleasure, conferred on him the degree of D.H.L, doctor of humane letters.

The Life of Thomas Paine was translated into French in 1900, for the voice of the defender of the "Rights of Man" had been heard in the French Revolution, as well as the American. To Conway, who had slowly come to understand the part Paine played in the early days of the American republic, it became apparent that, had the framers of the Constitution heeded Paine's warning, experienced in his essay, "African Slavery in America," the Civil War would have been averted.

Though Conway's effort to stop the war was a political mistake, his presentation of the problem of the Negro in terms of the "Rights of Man" is a permanent contribution to our concept of American democracy. To quote the titles of Conway's most well-known books – *The Golden Hour*, which he hoped would follow the emancipation of the Negro, has not yet come to this country, for *The Rejected Stone* of justice still lies across *The One Path* to national unity, as it did all those years ago when this young missionary from Virginia traveled the familiar rough road known to us today.

CHRONOLOGICAL TABLE
Moncure Daniel Conway

March 17, 1832: Born in Middletown, Stafford County, Virginia. Son of Walker Peyton Conway and Margaret Daniel Conway.

1842: Fredericksburg Academy. Visit of Charles Dickens.

1847: Dickinson College, Carlisle, Pennsylvania.

1848: Home with fever. Visit to Richmond. Wrote for The *Democratic Recorder*, Fredericksburg. "Outaliski's Revenge," reprinted in *New York Herald*. Returned to college. Wrote for the Richmond *Examiner*.

1849: Founded *The Collegian* at Dickinson College. Graduated. Class Orator. Joined Southern Rights Association in Fredericksburg. "Young Virginia." Read law with Colonel William Fowke Phillips in Warrenton, Virginia. Home with chills and fever. Read Emerson, wrote to him.

1850: Returned to Warrenton. *Free Schools in Virginia* reviewed by Horace Greeley in the *New-York Daily Tribune*, September 7, 1850. Gave up law and became Methodist minister. Circuit Rider, Rockville Circuit, Maryland. Visited with Friends of Sandy Spring, Maryland.

1851: Letter to Emerson, November 4. Letter from Emerson, November 13.

1852: Death of brother Peyton. Appointed to Frederick Circuit. Maryland. Honorary M. A. degree awarded at the Dickinson College Commencement in June. Resigned as Circuit Rider. Home.

1853: Harvard Divinity School. Visited Concord, attended Emerson's lecture on "Poetry" at Divinity School.

1854: Anthony Burns case. Graduated from Harvard Divinity School. Minister, First Unitarian Church, Washington. Trip to Falmouth. Threatened by mob. Preached in Charlottesville, Va. Visit to Emerson, in Concord. Visit to Whitman in Brooklyn.

1856: Preached sermon, "The One Path: or the Duties of North and South." Horace Greeley sent resume to *Tribune* (January 26). Reproof from Church Committee. Trip to New England to raise money for the Church. (*Tribune* letter, May 29, 1856.) Joined the Republican Party. October 5, asked to resign his ministry. Became Minister of the First Congregational Church of Cincinnati.

1857: Emerson lectured in Cincinnati. Second visit with Whitman in Brooklyn.

1858: Published *Tracts for To-day*. Conference of Western Unitarian Churches. Visit to Antioch College, Yellow Springs, Ohio. Married Ellen Davis Dana. Visit to Concord, Massachusetts.

1859: "The Natural History of the Devil." Emerson lectured in Cincinnati. Lincoln in Cincinnati. Split in First Congregational Church. Trip to New England. Birth of son Eustace.

1860: Edited *The Dial*, January-December. *The Rejected Stone.*

1861: Birth of son Emerson.

1862: January 27, lectured at Smithsonian Institution, Washington. June 29, last sermon in the First Congregational Church of Cincinnati. Escorted Conway slaves to Yellow Springs, Ohio. *The Golden Hour*. In August, moved to Concord, Mass. First issue of *The Commonwealth*, September 1862.

1863: Member of anti-slavery delegation from Boston to confer with Lincoln. January 25, addressed the Senate on "The Unrecognized Gift of God to America." April 11, sailed for

England. The Mason-Conway affair. Visited the Howellses in Venice. September 13, first Discourse at South Place Chapel, Finsbury. Arrival of family. Resigned as editor of *The Commonwealth*, continued weekly letters.

1864: Became regular minister at South Place Chapel. Death of son Emerson. Began weekly letters to the *Round Table*. *Testimonies Concerning Slavery*. London.

1865: Birth of son Dana. Speech of the Negro before The British Association for the Advancement of Science.

1866: Lecture tour, Scotland and England. Contributions to English journals.

1867: Trip to Paris. Last letter to *The Commonwealth.*

1868: Trip to Central Germany and Austria. Birth of daughter Mildred. Journeys through Wales and southern England.

1870: War correspondent, the New York *World*, in Franco-Prussian War. *The Earthward Pilgrimage*. Letters to *Cincinnati Commercial*.

1875: Extensive lecture tour in the United States. Guest of W. D. Howells in Boston. Return to London in March.

1883: Trip around the world. Visit with Conway family in Fredericksburg, Virginia.

1884: Returned to London. Death of Walker Peyton Conway. Resigned from South Place Chapel.

1885: Returned to America.

1886: Death of Dana.

1892: *The Life of Thomas Paine*, 2 vols. Degree of L.H.D., Dickinson College.

1893: Returned to South Place Chapel as minister.

1897: Left England because of illness of Ellen. Death of Ellen Dana December 25.

1898: Conway visited London and took up his residence in Paris.

1900: Publication of the French edition of *The Life of Thomas Paine.*

1904: *Autobiography: Memories and Experiences of Moncure Daniel Conway.* 2 vols.

1906: *My Pilgrimage to the Wise Men of the East.*

November 15, 1907: Death of Moncure Daniel Conway in Paris.

Chapter I
Conway House

Moncure Daniel Conway was born on March 17, 1832, in a "lonely corner" of Stafford County, Virginia, fifteen miles from the village of Falmouth.[1] The child was brought in his second year to a large farm on the outskirts of the hamlet called "Inglewood," which burned almost to the ground on a "tragical day" in 1838. The charred ruins and the surrounding orchards, flower gardens and hedges remained in the family, however, for the property lay between the farms of several well-loved relatives. One of the cousins continued to teach the neighborhood children in a small "office" left standing near the remains of the two-storied house that had been the home of the Conways. To the school of cousin Elizabeth Gascoigne the boy "Monc" walked with his older brother Peyton as soon as he was old enough to cross the fields separating the new home in the village from the old home in the country.[2]

Moncure was six years old before he came to live in Conway House, a substantial mansion built several generations earlier by a gentleman from Holland who had papared the drawing-room with scenes from his native Rotterdam, showing women washing their clothes in the canal, children playing along the sides, and barges passing by the towered town. This wall-paper remained until the house was turned into a war hospital, 1862-1865. Conway House stands today in a grove of old trees a little back from the road by the side of the Rappahannock River, a square, red-brick dwelling, once the largest residence in Falmouth. Behind it are the remains of the flower and vegetable gardens, the foundations of outhouses, and slave-quarters, and beyond these, a series of steep terraces, relics of the fortifications built to defend the town against the Indians in 1675.

Falmouth was originally a stockade in the wilderness, built to protect the neighboring white settlers from all sorts of dangers. True to its military tradition, it was the first area in Virginia a hundred years later to raise a company against Great

Britain, a distinction still commemorated when Conway was a child by a parade of little boys in blue and white, armed with wooden guns.

The Washington farm bordered on Falmouth, and here George Washington spent his youth, probably attending the small school in the village, and certainly enrolling at the Fredericksburg Classical and Mathematical Academy as an older boy. At the age of ten, Conway, too, walked with the contingent of boys from Falmouth across the bridge to Fredericksburg Academy. Monc was the youngest in the group of boys from "Hogtown," the name given Falmouth by the scholars of Fredericksburg. Shy, homely, excitable, and proud, he had to struggle as best he could by the side of his older brother in the fights between the boys of "Hogtown" and those of "Sheeptown" (Fredericksburg). The exchange of epithets caused no serious altercations, but an accidental blow from a "bandystick" (hockey stick) on Conway's right eye made it necessary for the boy to lie in a darkened room for a while and be treated with leeches. Conway never completely recovered from this accident.

Conway did not understand why Fredericksburg, the younger but more prosperous town across the Rappahannock from Falmouth, was called "Sheeptown," but it was all too evident why Falmouth was named "Hogtown." Though twenty or more handsome homes of the gentry were visible on neighboring hilltops, the road through the town was muddy or dusty, according to the season, and pigs did roam the lanes and take their noon-day naps under the high steps of Mr. Basil Gordon's general store. Monc remembered his neighbor, originally a poor immigrant from Scotland, as the most picturesque man in the neighborhood. Garbed in knee-breeches, shoe-buckles, long dress-coat, and wearing a powdered wig and queue, Gordon would hasten down the road to oversee his small shop even after his flour mill had made him the richest man in that part of Virginia.

Not far from the store and the mill was another equally important building, known as "Captain Pickett's," where Negroes were sent by their cruel masters to be whipped for unspecified causes. Though his parents warned their children not to loiter near Captain Pickett's, Monc remembered well the unsmiling captain and the cries of the sufferers whom Conway never actually saw. Years later Conway returned to the village and found the dilapidated town stocks still visible in the churchyard (they had formerly stood by the door of the church), but the old whipping-post was concealed in the constable's office. Captain Pickett, he learned, had hanged himself.[3]

It was known to Monc, even as a child, that slave dealers quietly purchased slaves in the neighborhood, usually from the quick sales of old estates, and transported them to the deep South. All the sales were affected surreptitiously, for it was generally considered disreputable for a gentleman to do business with a slave-dealer. "Hiring-day" in Falmouth was for the purpose of renting to neighbors the slaves who had grown too numerous to be kept on the estate.[4] The very word "slave" was not used by these county families as far as the child Monc knew. Negroes were either "free Negroes" or "servants." With no thought of the feelings of the "servants" in the large kitchen of Conway House, Monc enjoyed declaiming in their midst his favorite school speech, ending with "Give me Liberty or Give me Death," and he basked in the hearty applause and loving exclamations of his colored friends. Moncure, his three brothers, and younger sister were always on affectionate terms with the Negroes and their families, for it was the Negroes who helped the children, black and white together, with their projects – the raising of poultry or pigeons, the planting of a small watermelon patch or the mending of a fishing rod. As far as Monc could see, the little colored children were never mistreated; he envied them, for they seemed to have nothing to do but play and roam the countryside.

Charles Humstead, a brilliant young mulatto boy, was the guardian of the Conway children on their two-mile walk across meadows and over brooks, to school near the "Inglewood" farm. Armed with a long stick to kill water-moccasins along the way, Charles sang songs, told stories and set his snares for foxes and rabbits. Charles was the son of Monc's first nurse, Maria Humstead, whose boundless affection and ringing laughter Conway never forgot. "Come, Monc, 'fess your faults!" was her notion of sufficient discipline for her white child.

However, when Charles, age seventeen, in a moment of high spirits and idleness, set fire to an old, deserted firehouse in Falmouth, there was no alternative (except possible capital punishment) to selling the boy to a plantation in the far South. Charles was the only slave ever sold by Conway's father; he was never heard from again, though Moncure made a search through the South for him after the War.[5]

Moncure's parents, Walker Peyton Conway, and his wife, Margaret Eleanor Daniel Conway, treated their servants with the utmost kindness, for they were Methodists, and believed that colored people as well as white had immortal souls. But the elder Conway, as owner of the local cotton mill and presiding justice of Stafford County, had a special obligation toward law and order in Falmouth, a gathering-place for the county. Here, on Saturday nights, the country-folk, both black and white, poured in from neighboring farms to partake of Falmouth's whisky. Conway himself was a "total abstainer," but he appealed in vain to his fellow magistrates to regulate the flow of strong liquors.

The "poor whites," as they were sometimes called (the term was forbidden in the Conway family), were probably the descendants of convict labor sent over to this country from Great Britain, who found themselves displaced "squatters" with the advent of slavery.[6] Expert in fishing and hunting, they made good soldiers when the Civil War gave them social status; with the freeing of the slaves, they had a chance to earn a living. Since many of the gentry became, after the War, as poor as the poorest whites, the phrase "poor white" was no longer heard – at least in Conway's family.

Walker Peyton Conway was a tall, handsome man, gay in his youth and fond of card-playing and dancing. How a popular and worldly lad, born to an old, established county family, and bred in the Episcopal Church, could have been "converted" at a Methodist camp meeting to a religion requiring two sermons as well as Sunday school every Sunday, a rigid curtailing of social pleasures, as well as a distinct loss in "gentility," is difficult to understand. Perhaps the influence of his young wife, Margaret, whom he married on May 28, 1829, might partially explain the Calvinistic tone of the religious beliefs of the pair. Margaret Daniel, also by birth an Episcopalian, related to many of the colonial families of Maryland and Virginia, had lost both parents while still a child and had been raised by a loving but firm Presbyterian aunt.

More important still is the fact that at the time of the marriage of the Conways, the Episcopal Church, at least in Overwharton Parish, had fallen to such a low ebb in its fortunes that not one of the three churches, Potomac, Aquia, or Cedar Church in Falmouth, held regular services. At the same time, the Baltimore Methodist Conference was actively sending preachers throughout the country, "converting" the country folk by rousing camp meetings attended by both Negroes and whites, among them young Walker Peyton. When his father, John Moncure Conway, heard that his son had succumbed to what seemed to him merely vulgar fanaticism, a scene ensued that permanently divided his large family into two camps, Methodist and Episcopalian, for five of his thirteen children followed the lead of their brother. Peyton Walker's wife was glad to embrace the new religion since it was akin to the Calvinism with which she was familiar, and her son remembered her quoting with a merry laugh the old Negro hymn,

I never foun' no peace nor res'
Till I jine the Methodess.

Grandfather Conway, for forty-seven years clerk of Stafford Courthouse, soon forgave his children for their religious aberration and continued to welcome them and their numerous families to large gatherings at his country home, "Erleslie," near the Courthouse. The child Monc remembered strolling before breakfast with his grandfather and his dog through the well-kept farm that stretched for a mile behind the house. His grandfather, after he abandoned his queue, continued to wear on all occasions a blue dress-coat with brass buttons, a ruffled shirtfront, and an enormous white cravat drawn through a large gold ring.

Monc remembered, too, the stately grandmother, seated under a tree in queenly fashion on summer evenings while several of her daughters served a supper of griddle-cakes and molasses, bonny-clabber and preserves, to an uncounted number of grand-children in a nearby arbor. The grandmother (Catherine Storke Peyton) was tall, humorous and beloved. To her grandchildren she was a story-book character, for she always wore a snowy white turban, like a crown, to which a fresh rose was pinned with a ruby clasp. Though good manners and a genuine sense of democracy forbade the children from any expression of pride in ancestry, they were quite aware of the fact that the parents of their grandmother were Dr. Valentine Peyton and Mary Butler Washington, a cousin of George Washington, and that this ancient pair still resided a few miles from Stafford Courthouse, at "Tusculum," noted for its festive hospitality to many Virginia dignitaries. They were familiar, too, with the large engraving of Conway Castle in Wales, which an ancestor of Grandfather Conway had brought to the colony in 1640 and now hung in his office in the Courthouse.

Driving back to Conway House from these excursions to Stafford Courthouse, a boy could curl up in a corner of the big, round carriage and dream away the fifteen miles that separated home from "Erleslie." Though Monc could feel the contrast between the households, he found no difficulty in relating to both the Episcopal and the Methodist way of living. Episcopalians, it was clear to him, took a more lenient attitude toward sin and damnation than that which he had heard expressed at home. His grandfather Conway, for example, a graduate of William and Mary, respected for his learning, had observed to a more orthodox relative as the two sat together on the wide veranda of "Erleslie," "I cannot believe that the father of mankind would send any human being into this world knowing that he would be damned."

Grandfather Conway's remark was greeted with silence, but the listening boy never forgot either the comment or its reception. Nor did this honored grandfather, though a vestryman of Aquia Church, feel that it was necessary always to attend the services held in the old family church down the road from "Erleslie." One Sunday morning, when John Conway was leaving his office to walk home to dinner, he saw a man with a pack on his back roughly shoved out the door of the only Inn at Stafford Courthouse because the stranger had spent his morning walking around the country lanes instead of attending church. Conway immediately invited the "Sabbath-breaker" to dine with him, and found his guest so interesting that he kept him at "Erleslie" for several days. The man was Amos Bronson Alcott, and the incident was told to Moncure by Alcott himself when, years later, he lived for a time in Concord.[7]

Neither grandfather nor grandmother Conway ever talked to Moncure about church-going or prayers, but it was apparent to the boy that the religious atmosphere of "Erleslie" was not like that of his home in Falmouth. When services at Aquia were suspended because of lack of attendance, and the Methodists filled the Courthouse itself with a large congregation, the elderly

Conways without commenting simply ceased to go to any church. How differently things were managed at home!

The basement of Conway House was arranged for prayer-meetings held there twice a week. James Petty, tailor and preacher, usually conducted the meetings. Many years later the whole scene came back to Conway with the clarity of such early experiences. "I find the scene engraved in my memory," he wrote in *Autobiography: Memories and Experiences of Moncure Daniel Conway:*

> ....this fine intellectual father of mine, accustomed to preside over courts, and the refined elegantly dressed lady beside him, surrounded by poor, dusty, patched people, of whom some could hardly read. My father had no interests to subserve by this devotion to an humble faith, no clients to gain, no votes to seek; his office was not elective, his interests were all the other way, for the preachers were supported and the meeting-houses built mainly out of his purse. Some of those gathered in the basement he had picked up out of the ditch. They looked up to him with reverence, but in humility he surpassed them all. Somehow I to this day think of my handsome father's appearance as noblest when seated among those dingy and illiterate people.

The dreary little boy was probably seated near his mother, and the visionary world evoked by the hymns was far from dead.

> My mother was musical and had a fine soprano voice [he wrote]; I too developed early a taste and some voice for singing. It was through the beautiful Methodist hymns that religious feeling reached me. As I sang in the basement second treble to my mother, I dreamed of the distant beauties of Palestine, though the cedars of Lebanon were thick on our Falmouth hills, and no rose of Sharon ever equalled those of our garden. The wondrous Judas-tree at our door, and our fig-trees, myrtles, fireflies, meadows, crystal streams, all materials of a paradise were around me while I sang of things far off and never to be attained.[8]

Margaret Conway was always called upon, after her husband, to pray, and this she did with such simple eloquence that, in the absence of her husband, she was often asked to conduct the meeting. Her fervor and purity of heart were reflected in the fact that she put aside an hour every Sunday afternoon for the children of the house, white and black together, to teach them the catechism and to read to them stories from the Bible. Reports of these gatherings leaked out, however, together with the rumor that Mrs. Conway was teaching the colored children to read, which was clearly illegal. The mixed lessons ceased, for reasons unexplained to Moncure.[9] Nor did the boy understand why one of the slaves,[10] age about twenty, asked him, a boy of ten, to teach him to read in one of the wood-cellars, in exchange for a beautiful necktie, the first "mannish thing" Monc ever wore.

Dedicated to Methodism as the elder Conways were, they did not subscribe to the ignorance and superstition that seemed to accompany followers of their religion, both black and white. When the seventeen-year locust filled the woods, the fields, and the gardens of the neighborhood, each wing was thought to be marked with a large W foretelling War, and, indeed, news of the Mexican War soon filled the village. The comet of 1843 caused such a sensation that crowds flocked into Mr. Petty's tailor-shop beseeching him to pray for them against the approaching Judgment Day.

Haunted houses, ghosts, witches, serpent-lore (Monc was sure the Devil was a snake) filled the imagination of the growing boy, even though his parents were impatient of all superstition. Overcome by tales of lights seen in the windows of a large, empty house across the river, Monc ventured to mention the matter to his father who looked up from the papers he was studying, and murmured, absent-mindedly, "Jack o' Lantern, probably," leaving Monc to wonder who Jack was and what kind of lantern he carried. Knowing that to his parents all forms of superstition were "vulgar," he asked no questions but, instead, suffered that night from a vision of hobgoblins whirling him through the midnight sky. This, too, he kept to himself, but he listened with attention to family comment on the young Methodist who thought she suffered from "the unpardonable sin" and the "sister" who was reported to have achieved "entire satisfaction".

"Watch Night," as it was kept in the basement of Conway House, filled those crouching on the floor with undefinable emotions. A moment before midnight all knelt together, including the servants, and while kneeling sang a hymn to the New Year:

Come let us anew
Our journey pursue,
Roll round with the year
And never stand still till the Master appear.

His adorable will
Let us gladly fulfil,
And our talents improve
By the patience of hope, and the labour of love.

Often amused by the way their simple neighbors took religion, and still oftener saddened by their backsliding, the elder Conways, through the church they had chosen, faithfully pursued their mission in the county. The Methodist Church was, indeed, the only temperance organization in the neighborhood, and the only one more interested in charity and humanitarian effort than in dogma. Neither his parents nor his aunts had any idea how the little boy in their midst was hanging on the words of the preachers -- most of whom stayed overnight at Conway House -- nor the feeling stirred in him by the hymns concerned with worldliness, sin, and death. Since Moncure went swimming, fishing, and hunting with his brothers and the boys from the village, they hardly realized that he took quite literally such hymns as the following:

The world is all a fleeting show
For man's delusion given:
Its smiles of joy, its tears of woe,
Deceitful shine, deceitful flow,
There's nothing true but heaven.
I'm a pilgrim, and I'm a stranger,
I can tarry, I can tarry but a night.

Our life is a dream;
Our time as a stream
Glides swiftly away.

Oh, tell me no more of this world's vain store,
The time for such trifles with me now is o'er.

Hark from the tomb a doleful sound:
My ears attend the cry:
"Ye living men, come view the ground
Where you must shortly lie!"[11]

The high point of the year was, of course, the Methodist Camp meeting, held in a forest behind Conway House, lasting for a week. Around a great clearing, built like an amphitheater, rows of benches were arranged to seat at least a thousand people. A dozen or more preachers, sent out by the Baltimore Conference, sat on the raised platform, in front of which was a large enclosure for the "mourners." Tents were pitched among the trees for the various families moving in from the county for the "grand barbaric picnic," as Conway called it, where horse-trading, whiskey, and love-making were nicely mixed with piety. Three sermons a day, each followed by a prayer-meeting, were only preludes to the scenes of the evening, when strings of small lanterns hung from tree to tree, and the thrilling chorus of hymns was heard rising from the congregation as the preachers walked about the platform shouting, "Now is the accepted time!" and "Call upon him while he is near!" Not infrequently, the singing was interrupted by a scream from one struggling with Satan, and then by shouts of "Glory!" "Hallelujah" as a Brother led down the forest aisle a repentant sinner to the "throne of grace."

Curiosity often prompted Moncure to mingle with his colored friends behind the platform, for "there the Negroes received such crumbs of grace as fell from the white "table." There were no mourners among these worshippers, he observed; all were in "ecstasy," having long ago been "converted". Untroubled by dogma, most of the Negroes were both Baptists and Methodists, preferring the "total immersion" practices of the former and the hymn-singing and "ecstasy" of the latter.

Moncure was often a quiet observer of the ceremony of the colored people which took place on a sandy point of the river, opposite his home. Dressed in white cotton, they moved in the Sunday morning sunshine, singing softly as they walked to the river's edge where a white minister performed the rite. The newly baptized were then embraced by their relatives, and all filed slowly down the road, singing as they went. White converts were immersed separately, but there were few of them and the ceremony was unimpressive by comparison with that performed for the Negroes.

Moncure as a child actually saw no cruelty toward Negroes in his home or in any homes he visited, though he heard rumors that made him suspect later that Negroes were not infrequently mistreated. To be sure, the Negro children were occasionally whipped in the Conway household, but no more severely nor more frequently than were the white children. News of a man in a respectable family, a certain Captain B., who had beaten a slave so brutally that he later died, filled the Conway family and their friends with horror.[12] Walker Peyton Conway attempted to bring the master of the slave to justice, but he failed because only slaves had witnessed the thrashing, and the word of a slave carried no weight in any court.

Moncure himself was present on an occasion, the memory of which was never effaced from his mind, when the same Captain B. brought to Stafford Courthouse four female slaves and accused them of attempting to poison him. The owner presented no evidence of any kind, and it became all too clear either that his own cruelty had caused the attempted murder or that he wished to have the unmarketable women executed so that he could collect the money for them that the county would be obligated to pay him. The women were acquitted, but the owner seized them by the wrists and ankles, bound them to the back of his cart, ordered the driver to go on, while he lashed the bare backs of the women with a rawhide whip until the wagon disappeared at the bend of the road. The muttering crowd of onlookers made no move to stop the man, and perhaps had not the power to restrain him from the abuse of his "property." But the boy who witnessed the scene and asked no questions never forgot.

This was the same boy who was so afflicted when an ugly duckling he was nursing back to health near the kitchen stove was bitten to death by a rat that he never again desired to have another pet. Instead of enjoying an actual dog, Moncure shed tears over "Keeper in Search of his Master," the story of a lost dog, found in the family library. Not popular among the village boys where his handsome older brother was a leader, Conway lived in a story-book world of his own, peopled by characters from *The Child's Own Book*, the *Arabian Nights*, *The Pilgrim's Progress*, and Maria Edgeworth's *Moral Tales*. These he found on the shelves of his room, in among the old medical books of his grandfather Daniel. The Bible, too, was on the shelf, and Conway was encouraged to memorize long passages to be recited in Sunday school in exchange for red and blue tickets for the purchase of pretty little volumes supplied by the Methodist Book Concern.

This practical trafficking in religious books seemed to Conway burdensome, making Sunday school far less fascinating to him than the hours he spent listening to the literary discussions between his mother and his cousin Elizabeth Daniel of Richmond, who brought with her the latest word on Charles Dickens, Walter Scott, Lord Byron, Robert Southey, Thomas Moore and many other current writers not by any means beyond the range of this Episcopalian family turned Methodist. Moreover, the numerous uncles, aunts and cousins in Richmond had no concern with Methodism. They belonged to the more sophisticated society of a Southern capital where literature, music, card-games and law were more interesting than religion. The charming Cousin Elizabeth thrilled the ten-year-old Conway by inviting him to correspond with her. Their letters were concerned with books rather than with religious doctrine, for Elizabeth and all her family, except for the Falmouth branch, were, of course, Episcopalian, and accepted their religion without comment. Moonlight evenings on the "crystal Rappahannock," when the ladies strummed guitars and the men played their flutes and all sang together Moore's verses and old Scottish songs, seemed to the small boy, crouching among the billowing skirts of his cousins, a taste of pure bliss.

Several visits with brother Peyton to the home of his mother's uncle and aunt in Richmond gave the boys an experience in worldliness. Uncle Peter V. Daniel, a justice of the United States Supreme Court, was noted for his learning and eloquence. His wife (daughter of Edmund Randolph, first attorney-general of the United States) presided over a household that seemed to Conway the last word in splendor. Here the boys met for the first time John Moncure Daniel, the orphaned son of their mother's older brother, who had been taken into the family of his great-uncle Peter. Cousin John, some years older than the boys, took them about to see the wonders of Richmond, while his cousins, Elizabeth, Anne and Peter, introduced their little Methodist visitors to a pack of cards -- the first they had ever seen -- and taught them to play "seven-up." Except for an occasional lecture on astronomy or zoology, accompanied with magic-lantern slides, or a memorable trip to the Town Hall of Fredericksburg to hear a famous singer, or a stolen glimpse under the tent of a travelling circus, these brothers knew little of "sinful amusements" and made the most of their visits to the larger world of Richmond.

Though the village of Falmouth afforded no public amusement whatever, except perhaps the Methodist Camp meetings, a boy starved for beauty remembered the rest of his life certain traditional customs still maintained in his neighborhood. For example, a group of "Buy-a-broom" girls, dressed in gaily colored costumes, used to wander from door to door with their worthless little brooms, singing a tune that Conway as an old man could hum:

Buy a bro-o-m, buy a bro-o-m!
Buy a bro-o-m, buy a bro-o-m!
O buy of the wandering Bavarian
A Broom[13]

To the child who willingly gave up his pocket-money, this troupe of singers was as good as an opera, beautiful, graceful, and strange.

Until the puritanical spirit of Methodism put an end to the annual Tournament and Ball of Stafford, the children looked forward with eagerness to the gathering of gaily caparisoned steeds on the lane by the Rappahannock. Here youths from neighboring counties tilted for the victor's wreath and knelt before the Queen of Love and Beauty, who, surrounded by her maids of honor, surveyed the scene from a high platform in true Sir Walter Scott manner. Such medieval reminders of traditions brought to Virginia several hundred years earlier from England gradually disappeared but not until they had left an impression on the imaginative child, responsive to both sides of his mixed inheritance.

The Fredericksburg Classical and Mathematical Academy to which Conway boys were sent maintained its connection with an older tradition as best it could. Thomas Hansen, the principal, taught Greek and Latin to the sons of the old Virginia families, leaving the other more modern studies to his two assistants. Public education for either white and black was unknown at that time, the Academy being maintained by St. George's Episcopal Church of Fredericksburg. Conway, the youngest "scholar" among the two hundred boys who attended the school, won high marks in Latin and Greek though he never enjoyed the classics until he discovered his grandfather Daniel's English translations of Virgil's *Aeneid* and Ovid's *Metamorphoses* on the shelves at home and then devoured them with delight. Not infrequently, when "Old Tommy" Hanson discovered his youngest pupil poring over a book at recess that he supposed to be Caesar or Virgil, he discovered it to be a novel by the new writer, Charles Dickens, of whom Hanson was hardly aware.

A one-day visit of Dickens to Fredericksburg in 1842 resulted in the only flogging Hanson ever found necessary to inflict on his star pupil, and this he was later to regret. Since Conway's Methodist family had for years laughed and wept together over the tales of "Boz" (in spite of the general disapproval of novel-reading), the parents had approved the boy's suggestion that he ask his teacher's permission to leave school in time to see the great man descend from his coach at Farmer's Hotel for lunch. However, when Moncure stood silently beside Mr. Hanson's desk awaiting an opportunity to speak, the principal, engaged in scolding another student, motioned him away. Moncure returned to his desk, but instead of taking his seat, jumped through an open window seven or eight feet from the ground and arrived at the hotel just in time to gaze upon his idol. A dead silence greeted him on his return to school; since Conway was too dazed by the experience to speak, there was nothing for it but to endure without a murmur the inevitable switch. The "dear, old master," when he finally learned the true circumstances, treated Conway for the remaining five years in the Academy with a special affection and praised him before the whole school when Moncure left for college at sixteen.

The law courts of Fredericksburg and Stafford County, and the legal discussions carried on by visiting lawyers around the table of Conway House gave Moncure a more "lasting education" than the Academy could furnish. Walker Peyton Conway was not only the leading Methodist of the neighborhood and the owner of the local cotton-factory but also presiding magistrate of the county and constantly consulted in his home on legal matters.

Walker Peyton's father had also been educated for the bar and was for many years clerk of the court; two of his sons, John Moncure and Eustace, were prominent lawyers, and his eldest daughter (Mary Butler Washington Conway) married Richard Cassius Lee Moncure, afterwards Chief Justice of Virginia. Since most of Moncure's vacations were spent at "Erleslie," the home of his grandfather Conway, the boy had ample opportunity to attend court sessions at Stafford Courthouse. To glimpse the shadowy face of the criminal between the bars of the small jail beside the courthouse door, and to hear one of his uncles argue either for or against the accused man before his intense and serious neighbors, was not only theater enough for Moncure but also a lesson in effective speaking and logical thought never to be forgotten.

Uncle Richard Moncure, commonwealth's attorney for Stafford County, made a lasting impression on the boy and was later described as Judge Stirling in Conway's novel, *Pine and Palm*.[14] This beloved uncle presided over "Glencairne," which was to the Conway children a second home. The comfortable mansion was not more than two miles from Conway House and near the new school built by Uncle Richard and Moncure's father for their numerous flock of children. Simple, playful, and affectionate in family relations, Uncle Richard was unrelentingly firm in legal affairs, and so conscientious in the discharge of his duties that he was known throughout the district as "Honest." He refused to accept a case unless he was convinced that it was just, a fact that was so well known that his acceptance of a case was usually considered equivalent to a court decision.

Many legends have gathered around this courageous lawyer who, as chief justice of Virginia, gave a minority opinion of a famous case concerning slaves that cost him his position and gave him a place in legal history. A certain Mrs. Coalter granted freedom to her slaves in her will, with the proviso that if they did not desire to be free they might choose their own masters.[15] Since the clause giving the slaves this choice was not, in pre-Civil War days, valid in Virginia, the husband of Mrs. Coalter's heir argued that the whole will was thus rendered invalid. The Court of Appeals sustained the contention, and the Negroes, to whom Mrs. Coalter had frequently promised freedom, remained in slavery until they were freed by the Emancipation Proclamation. Against the aroused feeling of southerners, Chief Justice Moncure wrote a strong minority report now accepted by judicial opinion even in Virginia.[16]

To Conway as a boy Uncle Richard was the old friend and confidant who allowed him to read his law books in his little "office," a small building near the large house, and who inquired about the boy's studies at the Academy, his schoolmates, his tastes in reading. Though the senior warden of St. George's Church, Uncle Richard never discussed religion with his Methodist nephew; nor did he ever allude to the change when Conway became a Unitarian. Uncle Richard's benign tolerance of all religions did not mean that he was not a devoted churchman; neither he nor his Methodist brother-in-law saw any reason why Moncure should not occasionally accompany his cousins in the family carriage to St. George's in Fredericksburg, though he was supposed to be a lamb of another flock.

The contrast between this handsome church and the Methodist conventicle, a one-room wooden structure, where the droning hymns were led by an old man with a tuning fork and a cracked voice, was all too evident. Except for the Conway family, and Uncle Eustace, the sparse congregation was poor and ignorant; there was no choir and no organ; the women wore drab gowns and bonnets somewhat like those adopted by the Quakers. "Father Cobler," an aged local carpenter, usually preached the sermon, but he was deprived of this privilege by his Methodist congregation after his marriage to a widow who possessed slaves. Reminded of the beliefs of his sect, he manumitted the slaves and continued his preaching.

What a blessing it was that there was no Christmas service among the Methodists! On that day Conway was allowed to take his place in a red-cushioned pew with his more elegant cousins in the old colonial church festooned with sweet-smelling evergreen. He listened with rapture to the Christmas hymn, "While shepherds watched their flocks by night," sung, it seemed to him, by angels from above. To the amusement of his family, Conway, at the age eleven, declared himself an "organ Christian" and was permitted by his parents to race to St. George's, the instant the Methodist service ended, in time to join in the closing hymn. Painfully precocious in matters of beauty and style, Conway suffered increasingly from his connection with "Liberty Corner," where the Methodist chapel stood, and envied his cousins "their sparkling worldliness and their indifference about their souls," and the privilege of attending St. George's Episcopal Church!

Fortunately for Moncure, his sister Mildred also inherited from their mother a taste for music. A piano was installed in Conway House and a teacher was engaged for the younger sister, who shared his knowledge with her brother. Moncure lost no time in procuring a hymnal from St. George's and quickly learned to play "Gloria in Excelsis," "Nativity," and all the other hymns in the book; soon his Methodist family was fervently singing the old Episcopal hymns from a hymnal which included ballads and songs from Scotland and Wales.

In 1841 the Methodist built a trim new church - again, without an organ - and turned over to the Negroes their old chapel. Soon afterwards, St. George's, where the Washingtons had worshipped a hundred years earlier, was replaced by the present structure. Conway retained from his childhood something of the self-examining social concern of his Methodist family and something of the beauty-loving, worldly sophistication of his Episcopalian relatives. From both groups he learned a humane and even affectionate attitude toward Negroes, which in no sense precluded an assumption that the institution of slavery was, in fact, a part of the order of the universe.

Another conflict in the attitudes of his elders had to do with the political views of Grandfather Conway (who was a Whig), and his father, who, as a Democrat, had once represented Stafford County in the Virginial legislature. Naturally, Conway, at the age of eight, considered himself one of the Democratic boys of Falmouth, and threw his fagots on the blazing bonfire with enthusiasm when Martin Van Buren, an aristocratic New Yorker, ran for a second term as President in 1840. He was defeated by the Whig candidate, William Henry Harrison, because, the boys concluded, Harrison's campaign insignia, a log cabin, was emblazoned everywhere. Though of an old Virginia family, he had lived briefly in the West, and "that log cabin was the ace with which the Whigs triumphed in our country."

Harrison died one month after his election and was succeeded by John Tyler, who was soon at odds with Henry Clay over the question of a second national bank. When Clay was nominated by the Whigs for president in 1844, he had expected that the Democrats would again nominate Martin Van Buren. However, by then, another national issue of tremendous importance had arisen, the annexation of Texas, which Van Buren opposed, as did Clay. However, President Tyler signed the annexation into law four days before he left office in 1845.[17] The Democrats, fortunately, had chosen as their candidate James K. Polk, an ardent believer in "manifest destiny" and the annexation of Texas.

That this westward movement to new territory would involve the questions of whether or not slavery should be extended occurred to few southerners in 1845 --- certainly not to the thirteen-year-old Monc, who was only surprised to see on the wall of Grandfather Conway's office a framed letter written to him by Henry Clay, and to realize that his father, or the other hand, had supported Polk for president.

Soon after his fifteenth birthday, Conway joined his brother at Dickinson College in Pennsylvania. On the college campus, which was apparently peaceful, Conway was soon to discover that the question of slavery demanded an answer as it did in Virginia. The conflicts latent in the boy's religious and political inheritance were not resolved until years later - if, in fact, they ever were. But at Dickinson he came to understand the significance of his hitherto unexamined belief in the rightness of slavery; for the first time he met those who took the opposite position.

Chapter II
Dickinson College and After

In the latter part of March 1847 Conway traveled up to Dickinson College, in Carlisle, Pennsylvania, with his brother Peyton, and was put at once in the sophomore class. By June he was admitted into the junior class, the youngest member of the group.

Dickinson College was just the place for the Conway boys; not only was it a Methodist institution, but the student body was recruited largely from Maryland, Virginia, and other Southern states. As far as Moncure could remember in later days, there was not a single abolitionist in the student body and very few among the faculty. The thought that slavery might one day be abolished had, in fact, never occurred to either of the Conway brothers, nor to many of their elders.

Though Dickinson College was oriented toward religion, as were most colleges and universities of that time in this country, the aim of the professors was not to turn out preachers but rather to develop "leaders of men." Rhetoric, oratory, debating, clear writing, and concise thinking were stressed by a group of superior teachers, who found in young Conway an apt and eager student. He joined the debating society, wrote humorous skits to be read aloud in Chapel, and made a name for himself as one of the outstanding Saturday nights "declaimers," orating on such subjects as, for example, "The Philosophy of Language."

So susceptible was Conway to the persuasive flow of language, that he remembered to the end of his life a professor who preached in Chapel on the text, "What a coronet of brilliants around the brow of Charity." (I Cor. xiii). The boy understood, however, that the thought of the speaker was more important than the flowers of rhetoric. From his professor in logic he heard again the lesson he had already been taught by his lawyer-uncles, that "the object of all eloquence is to carry one's point;" anything that distracts from the issue at hand is the reverse of genuine eloquence. Truth might be found in all forms of writing; the professor of logic even told the boys to search it out in "imaginative literature, especially fiction." To the amazement of his Methodist students, their professor urged them to discover the kind of fiction that aimed at telling the truth. "And, gentlemen," he added, "whatever people may say against novels, such a work is always worth reading."[18]

The teacher who actually changed Moncure's thinking was a certain Dr. John McClintock, professor of Greek. McClintock was not only a teacher who could make his students love Greek literature but also a scholar and writer of whom the college was proud.[19] There was wild excitement, therefore, when it was learned that McClintock had become involved in a riot that had caused the death of a slaveowner from Maryland who had come to Carlisle in quest of three runaway slaves.

The facts of this forgotten case are as follows: Professor McClintock, on the afternoon of June 2, 1847, casually walked across the courthouse square, and, learning of the trial of the fugitive Negroes then in progress, entered the court and listened. When the case was decided against the Negroes, McClintock stepped up to ask the judge whether he was acquainted with a law just passed that he thought might have been the means of acquitting the Negroes. Learning that the judge knew nothing of it, McClintock left the courtroom with the intention of returning to his home for a copy of the new law. As he crossed the square, he observed a white man raising a stick over the head of one of the Negroes. McClintock quietly said, as he passed near the victim, "If you are struck apply to me, and I will see justice done you." By the time McClintock returned, a riot had broken out around the Negroes in the course of which their owner had been fatally shot. McClintock remained entirely detached from the scene and turned toward his home, pausing once to find out whether or not the slave-owner was likely to recover, and again to protect an elderly Negro woman.

As McClintock recalled the scene,

> Near the Court-house corner, I saw two men holding and apparently abusing an old negro woman. I asked if they had authority. The woman jumped towards me and threw her left arm round me. I released myself, and then told the officer that if he arrested the woman wrongfully, he did it

> on his own responsibility and I should see justice done to her. The woman said that she had done nothing, but only attempted to get her old man out of the melee, for fear he should be hurt. The officer said he saw her strike. I then asked, 'Did you see her strike?' He said hesitatingly, 'At least I saw her raise her hand to her head,' and then I think he let her go. In a short time after I returned home.[20]

The excitement among the Dickinson College boys that followed the news of these events was intense. Moncure and Peyton, like most of the other pro-slavery southerners, started at once to pack their trunks for home. President Robert Emory summoned the student body to chapel on the evening of June 2 to caution them against any reckless action. The southerners, however, met together the next day to decide alone what their attitude towards an overtly anti-slavery professor should be. Suddenly, in the midst of their stormy meeting, appeared the serene Dr. McClintock. He merely walked to the front of the room as though he were about to conduct his usual class in Greek and explained to the boys, without any apology or undue emphasis, exactly what had happened the previous afternoon. Then McClintock descended from the platform, walked rapidly down the aisle and out of the door, leaving the boys in a state of respectful silence.

After brief consultations, several seniors drew up resolutions of entire confidence in Dr. McClintock, which were signed by the ninety boys gathered in the room and taken at once to the local paper for publication. Conway had never before seriously considered the question of slavery; he was amazed by the calm moral force of Dr. McClintock, who was content to rest his case on simple truth. For the first time, Conway questioned the institution he had taken for granted. Could his professor's stand be the just one, and the assumptions of his Virginia family and friends, humane though they apparently were, unjust and abusive?

Fortunately for the study of Greek at Dickinson College, the court trial of Dr. McClintock took place during the summer months. When the students returned in the fall it was to find their teacher triumphant against a conspiracy of pro-slavery politicians who had tried in vain to have McClintock put into prison. Witnesses appeared to testify that McClintock had himself been in the group responsible for the murder of the slave-owner, and from their perjured testimony that accused was rescued only by the evidence of two lawyers, themselves pro-slavery men, who testified that McClintock was standing on the side of the square quietly talking to them at the time of the murder.

The fact brought out in court against his teacher, that "McClintock was the only white man by the Negroes," came to seem to Conway, when he read over the newspaper accounts in the fall, a noble tribute "At least in Carlisle there was one white man concerned for the Negroes. The cruelty of one slaveholder attempting to seize his runaway slaves with the connivance of those who calmly watched the scene suddenly seemed to the boy to outweigh all the tales of benevolent masters on which he had been nourished. "It would not have been easy at that date," remarked Conway later, "to find a professor in any American college willing to shield Negro slaves."[21]

The questions raised in the mind of Conway by this dramatic confrontation of attitudes in regard to slavery affected subconsciously his allegiance to the religion of his family. When he returned to college in September 1847, he listened with more attention to the discussion carried on between a junior named Willard, the single college "infidel," and the group of boys who plied him with questions. Conway himself never asked a question, but he sought out Willard for country walks and private talks. The influence of this intriguing friend, who at no time tried to shake his religious beliefs, can be seen in a sentence from a skit Conway wrote, "Dura Studentis," that was read aloud in Chapel in the autumn of 1847. Rhetorical as were his words, one can catch the skepticism in the declamation of the fifteen-year-old author:

> The Mahometan system of forcing into the moral corpuses of bored students the principles of natural and revealed religion – virtue and all – is got in vogue. Though he (the Junior) be an infidel here he is forced to give utterance to the clearest and most conclusive arguments in favour of Christianity, and – though unwilling – is forced to become either a convert or a hypocrite.[22]

Such passing thoughts, however, by no means prevented Moncure, early in 1848, from experiencing "conversion" to

Methodism, the religion of his father and mother. Not only did he realize that the family at home would rejoice when they learned that he had "experience religion," but he also perfectly understood that the college, too, expected all of its leading students to come, sooner or later, to the "mourners bench." Indeed, here in Carlisle, in contrast to Fredericksburg, the "learned and polite" belonged not to the Episcopal. Church but to the Methodist. When Conway heard that a revival meeting was about to take place in the town, he resolved in his room beforehand that he would get his lessons early in the afternoon and attend the evening session. "I myself had very little feeling or conviction of anything. But I was resolved never to stop from that moment until I enjoyed religion in my heart, if there was such enjoyment to be had."[23] Feeling satisfied by the sense of peace he experienced on the first Sunday of the revival, he formally "professed religion" on the third Sunday, January 16, 1848.

A month later, on February 16, 1848, Conway wrote in his diary, "Took a walk with Willard." In the same period – perhaps to counteract the influence of the college infidel – Conway taught a Sunday-school class, sang in the choir of the Methodist Church, and became an active member of the temperance society. The inner conflict, apparently, was too much for the boy; the result was that Moncure spent his sixteenth birthday in bed with chills and fever after his devoted but puzzled father traveled up from Falmouth to escort him back to the quiet life of Conway House. "Pa concluded to 'carry me back to Old Virgini'," he wrote in a journal of his religious "conversion."[24]

On their journey through Baltimore, father and son were visited in their hotel by a certain Rev. Dr. T. E. Bond, then famous for his articles in the *Christian Advocate and Journal* and *The Methodist Quarterly Review*, the most influential Methodist publications. From his bed, the feverish boy took in the import of the lengthy conversation he overheard between Bond and his father. The question of slavery had in 1844 divided the Methodist Church. The Baltimore Conference, as represented by Bond, was making a mighty effort to hold the church together in a firm stand against slavery despite the rising pro-slavery sentiment of the Methodists of northern Virginia who were on the point of joining the seceding group, the "Methodist Church South."[25] Bond realized that the position of the Methodists of northern Virginia depended on the elder Conway. Moncure knew as he listened, though his father was against slavery as an institution, he would never actively support the anti-slavery forces, for politically he was necessarily tied to his pro-slavery state. Having come to understand the injustice of slavery through the stand of Dr. McClintock, what could Moncure make of the ambivalent position of his father? In the next few years his father's anti-slavery convictions beneath his political pro-slavery acquiescence became clear to him, but not before he was drawn into the circle of a younger generation of Virginians who were arguing the question of slavery on different grounds.

During Moncure's enforced five-month vacation, the question of slavery took on a larger political dimension as a result of the termination of the Mexican War in March 1848 and the nomination by the Whigs of General Zachary Taylor for the presidency.

With the acquisition of vast new territory in the West, the question as to whether or not the new land should be free-soil became the pivotal point of the campaign waged during the summer between Taylor, the hero of Buena Vista, though he remained vague as to the expansion of slavery, and Senator Lewis Cass of Michigan, the Democratic candidate, who was equally vague on slavery and undecided as to the Mexican War. The fact that a vigorous group of anti-slavery Democrats in New York refused to support Cass threw the nomination to Van Buren and split the party so that New York gave its vote to Taylor. Just as the elder Conway, though opposed to slavery by conviction, could not wholeheartedly give his support to the northern Methodists, so now as a delegate to the Democratic National Convention, he gave his support to the nomination of Cass.

In the summer of 1848, Moncure had an opportunity "to study things not taught in academy or college," for his lawyer-uncle, Eustace Conway, invited him to join him in his buggy for a tour of the courts in Stafford, Prince William and Fairfax counties. Since the presidential campaign was in full swing, court was usually adjourned for the day after the morning session. At two o'clock the courthouse bell was rung and the neighborhood gathered in a nearby grove to hear political speeches by well-known congressmen and lawyers. Conway responded with all his heart to the brilliancy of the oratory, but he firmly held to his

Democratic allegiance, for nothing in his talks with uncle Eustace or his father had led him to doubt that slavery should be extended to the new territories.

After hearing an address by Congressman George H. Pendleton of Ohio, who presented the free-soil position of the Whigs, Conway wrote in his diary, "Mr. Pendleton is certainly one of the finest political speakers I have ever heard, -- he possesses great fluency, much ingenuity, and ready wit. His speech was delivered beautifully -- declamation unexceptional -- but his arguments specious."[26]

With equal enthusiasm, the sixteen-year-old boy, still not recovered from his undiagnosed illness, listened with rapt attention to the eloquence of visiting Methodist preachers sent out by the Baltimore Conference to the increasingly important new Methodist Church of Fredericksburg, where the division in the church was being thrashed out. One Sunday morning, a certain Norval Wilson appeared in the pulpit, upholding the antislavery position of the Baltimore Conference. This tall, thin, middle-aged man, with a receding chin and beaked nose, charmed the half-sick boy on the hard bench before him by the sheer intellectual power gleaming from the preacher's pale grey eyes. Wilson's head was small, his face thin, his movements awkward, "but never did preacher speak to my inmost soul like this man."

> He was almost inaudible when beginning his sermon, and his voice never rose to a high pitch; but as he proceeded his eyes kindled with a strange fire, his tremulous tones came as if from aeolian chords in his breast, and my heart lay like a charmed bird in his hand. There was no rhetorical trick, no sensational phrase, none of the stock stories of the pulpit, but convictions personally and profoundly thought out and uttered with few gestures and self-forgetting simplicity. His mission was to the individual heart; his word came from the depth of his heart, and deep answered unto deep. Our eyes at times filled with happy tears. When the enchantment ceased I longed to clasp his knees.[27]

A nearer influence on the mind of Conway than either political orator or Methodist minister was that of his fascinating older cousin, John Moncure Daniel, who visited at the Conway home in early April. Though the elder Conway frowned upon "the seductive cynicism" of his brilliant nephew, the younger Conway not only drank in every word of his cousin but also assiduously followed the *Richmond Examiner*, to which "John M. Daniel" was contributing literary and political articles. Having been sent to Richmond to study law with his great-uncle Peter, John had spent most of his time reading extensively in the large English, French and Classical library of his distinguished uncle. By the time he visited the Conways, John had given up law in favor of literature and had become owner and editor of the *Richmond Examiner*.

"John M. Daniel's paper," as the *Examiner* soon became known, was undoubtedly the most important journal of opinion of the South at that period. Several of the poems of Edgar Allan Poe first appeared in the *Examiner*; Thomas Carlyle's pamphlet, "The Nigger Question" (omitted from the American edition of his *Latter-Day Pamphlets*), was published in Daniel's paper; in these columns Southern readers first read extracts and reviews of such Northern writers as Poe, Ralph Waldo Emerson, Nathaniel Hawthorne, Theodore Parker, and others. The editor's views were expressed with acid wit and intemperate partisanship -- a tendency that involved young Daniel in several duels though he had no skill in weapons.[28] Perhaps as a result of the instability of his temperament and his fondness for duels, Daniel never married; his paper in the summer of 1848 was discussed in every corner of the state. In Falmouth, Moncure not only read and digested the contents of this dazzling sheet but resolved in his heart to imitate his romantic cousin.[29]

A golden opportunity offered itself when Moncure's uncle, Judge R.C.L. Moncure of Glencairne, then running for the Virginia legislature, asked this seemingly idle boy to act as clerk of the election, April 27, 1848. Uncle Richard had no desire to enter the legislature; doing so entailed sacrificing his own legal practice, but he was urged to run in order to serve on a committee then revising the Virginia code. The Whigs nominated as his opponent Charles Francis Suttle and made a great though unsuccessful effort to defeat Richard Moncure. The young clerk of the election thought he might add to the $2 paid him for his services – the first money he had ever earned – by writing a satiric squib on the event for the Fredericksburg paper, The *Democratic*

Recorder. His little piece, "Richard is himself again," duly appeared in the paper, under the pseudonym "Stafford." Delightful as it was to see himself in print, Conway was amazed and alarmed to learn that the Whig youths of Falmouth were prowling the streets and lanes armed with horsewhips, hunting for "Stafford." Moncure, in May Day of that year in bed again with chills and fever, thus avoided his pursuers.

Once having tested authorship, especially of the anonymous variety, Moncure entertained himself for the remainder of the vacation by slipping poems, stories, satires and essays into the box of the Fredericksburg *Democratic Recorder* under the pseudonyms of Cleofas II, Alphonso III, Scholarship, and so on. These he read aloud to his twelve-year-old sister, always winning her approval and promise of secrecy. One of his tales, "Outaliski's Revenge," a "true" story of an Indian tragedy, appeared in the *Recorder*. It was reprinted in *The New York Herald* as a genuine legend, though Moncure later admitted there was no foundation whatever for the tale.

As the summer wore on, the presidential campaign between Lewis Cass and Zachary Taylor became more vociferous and, of course, inspired Moncure's satirical pen. Taylor refused to come out against the northern demand for the restriction of slavery in the new states. For the sake of victory, which Cass failed to win, Conway and his young friends felt that they must "fire the Southern heart, irritate it against the North, and sow tares like the devil." In other words, Conway resolved to write and speak for the extension of slavery in the new states of the West.

When Conway returned to college in the fall, mended in health but somewhat demoralized in his political views, he threw himself once more into the life around him. But now, after his five months in the South, he aimed his Saturday declamations against the Whigs in the audience. Though all was couched in the gayest good humor, Conway spent so much of his time laboring over his political orations that his studies suffered. Furthermore, John Moncure Daniel had asked him to write for the *Richmond Examiner*. Hence many of his afternoons were spent searching out subjects for ridicule in the town of Carlisle such as the hovels in which the free Negroes in the North lived or the drinking habits of northern youth.[30] Conway also learned from the northern youths whom he was satirizing the satisfactions of both alcohol and tobacco. Caught in a blizzard, he tells us, he and a friend stopped for a night at a country inn, where they were warmed by whiskey punch. "This," he adds, "was my first taste of anything alcoholic, and after that I took my first cigar -- without a qualm, moral or physical."[31]

Fortunately, the defeat of Cass in November 1848, made Conway withdraw his thoughts from politics and turn them instead to literature. Works by Johann Wolfgang von Goethe, William Henry Channing, George Sand and Nathaniel Hawthorne, whom Conway had learned to know through his cousin John, were not to be found in the library of Dickinson College. On the shelves of his college library, however, he found Poe, Henry Wadsworth Longfellow, William Cullen Bryant, Washington Irving, James Fenimore Cooper, William H. Prescott and a long row of English novels. The result, in the spring of his senior year, was five articles in the Fredericksburg paper on "Old Writers of Fiction."

Conway also established early in 1849 *The Collegian*, a journal that lasted until spring vacation, as a platform not only for his own essays and stories but also for those of other students and for several assistant professors of the college. In the course of the spring, Conway fell in love with the seventeen-year-old sister of the president; she, however, was too sensible to consent to a betrothal. He delivered the commencement oration on "Old Age" and after graduation returned to his corner of Virginia. An exuberant seventeen-year-old, he was none the worse for having spent his last night in college moping under the window of his beloved, who was peacefully asleep.

Like all young southerners of the day, Conway assumed, on his graduation, that he would enter political life. Though college had taught him that there were many people in the world who questioned the institution of slavery, he himself could not imagine a world without slaves. He soon discovered a lively group in Fredericksburg called "Young Virginia," organized "to promulgate the philosophical, sociological, and ethical excellence of slavery." Pamphlets and articles were being written in support of slavery by local ministers, lawyers, eminent judges, and even by the president of Randolph-Macon College. The more moderate anti-slavery views of his father began to seem old-fashioned to his son, especially when he discovered that his uncle Eustace

Conway, now a judge, was the personal friend of John C. Calhoun, who was becoming more extreme in his advocacy of "Southern Rights" and secession. Zachary Taylor's hints, in his campaign speeches for the presidency, that he might not support slavery were enough to prompt Conway to write satiric articles about him for the *Richmond Examiner.*

A few months after Conway's graduation, a Southern Rights Association was formed by half a dozen youths in the office of a Fredericksburg lawyer.[32] Conway, present at the meeting, was flattered to be asked to act as secretary. Conway had attended the gathering surreptitiously, for he knew his father's views. The elder Conway, however, quietly asked his son while riding with him to Stafford Courthouse to tell him what had transpired. After listening to Moncure's account, his father remained silent for a few moments, then said, "Don't be the fool of those people! Slavery is a doomed institution."[33] Moncure received the comment with amazement, for this was the first anti-slavery remark he ever heard made by his father, or, indeed, by anyone else in his circle of relatives and friends.

Moncure had noticed -- but had never mentioned the fact -- that his father and his uncle Eustace had found themselves on opposite sides in the Methodist dispute concerning slavery. His father did not forget his conversation with Dr. Bond but refused to take a public stand against slavery; Uncle Eustace, on the contrary, supplied the money to build a Southern Methodist Church in Fredericksburg that was definitely pro-slavery. Both brothers were lay-readers, each in his own Methodist Church; the question was never discussed at home, and Walker Peyton and Eustace remained close friends. Their differing attitudes toward slavery, however, helped to hasten the break in the Methodist Church of northern Virginia in the years before the Civil War.

Aware of the underlying currents of feeling among his family and friends, the restless young Conway, who had been corresponding with John Moncure Daniel since the visit of his older cousin in the summer of 1848, turned to him for guidance on the subject of slavery. To the consternation of his family, Conway merely disappeared in March, 1850, traveled to Richmond and asked his cousin for a permanent position on the *Richmond Examiner*. Daniel sensibly replied that he would give him a place on the paper only if he had, in fact, resolved to break with his family and follow journalism as a career. This Conway, now eighteen, was not prepared to do. Instead, he sent word to his family as to his intention to return and settled down for a few days in Daniel's library.

The shelves of Daniel's private library contained the works of Baruch Spinoza, Georg Wilhelm Friedrich Hegel, Immanuel Kant, Goethe, Johann Gottlieb Fichte, Ludwig Feuerbach, Charles Fourier, Victor Cousin, Jean-Jacques Rousseau, Voltaire, Francis Bacon, Alexander Hamilton, Emerson, Theodore Parker and many others. Moncure, who had for some time been fascinated by his misanthropic cousin, studied with interest the marginal notes he found in his books. Here was a man who at once subscribed to the belief that "all men are created free and equal" but who stood up for slavery in the columns of the *Richmond Examiner*. Not given to moderate statement, Daniel wrote in an editorial, for example: "We hold that Negroes are not men, in the sense in which that term is used by the Declaration of Independence. Were the slaves men, we should be unable to disagree with Wendell Phillips."[34]

Louis Agassiz's theory of the diversity of origin of the various races of men, and the inferiority of the African, were then becoming known in the South, and these Daniel carefully explained to his young cousin. Moncure accepted with enthusiasm this justification for slavery and felt as though he had now been freed to pursue the political career to which he aspired. Cousin John further dazzled Moncure by urging him to write for the *Examiner* and by introducing him to the men who shared these new "scientific" ideas concerning Negroes. Moncure noticed that nearly all of these leading citizens were secessionists dreaming of a great empire made up of the southern states, freed from the North and supported by Cuba, the West Indies, Mexico, and South America. Moncure was fairly carried away by these concepts. However, his more sober uncle, Eustace Conway, then serving in the legislature and living in Richmond, persuaded the boy to return to his home and family.

To the surprise of his son, Walker Peyton Conway greeted him on his return to Conway House with one of his rare bursts of anger. Still worse, his father immediately made arrangements to send his son to Warrenton, far from Richmond, to read law with Colonel William Fowke Phillips, a learned lawyer and clerk of

Fauquier County. Conway was to live at the Colonel's home and act as his deputy clerk when not reading his *Blackwood's Magazine*. The elder Conway had long cherished the hope that his mercurial son would at last settle down and become a Methodist minister. Deeply pained by the secessionist influence under which Moncure had fallen, he now digested his disappointment and hoped only to hustle him away from the contagion of his cynical cousin to a remote corner of Virginia where he might possibly be turned into a lawyer

Even while preparations for young Conway's exile were in progress, an invitation came to him from "a number of gentlemen of Fredericksburg" to lecture in the Town Hall on any subject he might choose. On the evening of March 1, 1850, the eighteen-year-old Moncure addressed a large audience of "the finest people," among whom, no doubt, were his father and mother, on the subject of "Pantheism." Though few in the crowded auditorium knew the meaning of the word, all were charmed by Moncure's comparison of the Trinity with the three primary colors blended into one light.

Alexander Pope, at least, received a round of applause when Conway quoted the couplet:

All are but parts of one stupendous whole
Whose body Nature is and God the soul.

After this minor triumph, a lawyer in the audience warned the speaker against making himself unpopular by speaking "above the vulgar comprehension." However, two days later the Methodist minister of Fredericksburg gave him "a certificate of church-membership" with the prophetic remark, "St. Paul before he preached tarried three years in Arabia -- now Warrenton may be your Arabia." Conway lingered in his Arabia only a little over a year, in the course of which he experienced his second "conversion" – this time to the cause of abolition. His "conversion," however, was not immediate.

A copy of the most recent *Richmond Examiner* was, of course, tucked into his portmanteau when, on March 4, 1850, Moncure traveled to Alexandria, and thence, by coach, to Warrenton. An entry in his journal reads: "Read in the coach, from the *Richmond Examiner*. 'The Great Stone Face, '--the writer of it, Nathaniel Hawthorne, is a striking writer." Not only was Moncure following the thought of his cousin through the *Examiner*, he was also on the lookout for subjects he himself might use for his own contributions to the paper.

Hardly had Conway settled into Colonel Phillip's comfortable home, presided over by his widowed sister and his two daughters, than news of Daniel Webster's famous speech in support of the Compromise of 1850 brought forth vehement discussion. A young Methodist preacher, also living in the Phillips' household, read the speech aloud in the drawing room two days after it had been delivered in Congress on March 7, 1850. "Heaven's, what a Titan is Webster! I should like to see his dust subjected to chemical analysis after he's dead,"[35] wrote Conway in his diary.

He soon learned from his *Examiner* that the speech had stirred resentment both in the North and in the South – in the North because the compromise promised a still more effective fugitive slave act, in the South because California was to be admitted as a free state and New Mexico and Utah were to be allowed admission into the Union with or without slavery as they should decide. John Moncure Daniel printed Theodore Parker's attack on Webster's address in the *Examiner* and did not hesitate to call Webster an "elephantine coward."[36] Though Conway was later to find himself opposed to the Compromise of 1850 because of its support of the Fugitive Slave Act, he now opposed it as a fire-eating southerner who wished to see the balance maintained between pro-slavery and anti-slavery states.

Most of the able lawyers whom Conway met in the office of Colonel Phillips were ardent Democrats such as the uncles and cousins with whom he had been reared in Falmouth and Fredericksburg. One of these associates, Robert Eden Scott, however, proved to be a Whig, already known to Moncure as a political opponent of his Uncle Eustace. As a member of the Virginia legislature, Eustace Conway had, in 1848, introduced resolutions hostile to the Wilmot Proviso, which ruled that any territory acquired from Mexico should be forever barred from slavery. The "Conway resolutions" affirmed that any such agreement would justify the secession of the slave states from the Union. Scott led the party opposed to these resolutions, and, as a result, was defeated in the next election. On March 25, 1850, Scott, again a candidate for office, addressed an audience at the courthouse of Warrenton, in the course of which he warned that any attempt to set up a southern confederacy would certainly end in ruin.

Conway came later to realize that Scott's position was both courageous and in the best tradition of Virginia. At the time, Conway was still a member of "Young Virginia" and wrote up Scott's address for the *Richmond Examiner* with satiric flings at the speaker in the tone he knew would meet the approval of the editor. Though Conway was charmed by the personality of this tall, handsome man, who, at the risk of his political career, fought the battle against the secession of Virginia, it never occurred to him that Scott's position might be worth serious thought.

Conway was still the romantic youth unable to reconcile his new experiences with his old political views. Under Colonel Phillips' watchful eyes he carefully copied his assigned legal documents and rapidly read through his law books like a boy disposing of his daily lessons. Since his tasks were light, there were two or three days of the week when there was nothing for the homesick law student to do. On Sunday afternoons he often climbed to the gallery of the empty church and played on a little organ, his sole companion being an elderly Negro sexton who shared with Conway his love of music and gladly blew the bellows for him.

A certain Rebecca Green in a nearby county was an occasional solace for this lonely boy, for she played the piano with skill and introduced him to Beethoven, Mozart and Weber. One piece, "Musetto de Nina," inspired him to write "Confessions of a Composer," a romance now unfortunately lost. "O my poor dead self -- aimless, morbid, passionately longing for it knew not what, -- pass to thy tardy cremation!"[37] wrote Conway many years later when he perused his old diaries and manuscripts. This mourning youth was not left in his melancholy condition very long, however, for six weeks after his arrival in Warrenton he was again subject to chills-and-fever and obliged to return to Falmouth for a few weeks of rest.

Finding himself once more among the familiar surroundings of his old home, Conway picked up his long-neglected flint-lock gun and wandered alone along the banks of the Rappahannock River, hoping to recover some of his old boyish pleasure in hunting. At the same time, he put into his bag a discarded copy of *Blackwood's Magazine*, not knowing whether gun or journal would be the better weapon against his listless moodiness. At the top of the first hill the boy took a little-used dirt road leading to a clear spring, from which he drank from a folded leaf as a cup. There he sat admiring the scenery, vaguely meditating his future, with no impulse either to read or shoot. The thought of becoming for life a country lawyer was distasteful to him. But what was he to do?

Presently, through the underbrush, appeared two naked mulatto children, a boy and a girl of about seven or eight, in quest of water for the tin cans they were carrying. Conway talked a few minutes with these "pretty statuettes of bronze," whose minds he found as attractive as their bodies, but equally unclothed, without "a stitch of knowledge." The children disappeared as mysteriously as they had come, leaving Moncure to meditate on the condition of the Negro race in America from which these beautiful, neglected children had sprung. Who was their father and what was their future?

Forgetting his gun, Conway reached for *Blackwood*, an old issue, dated December 1847. [38] There he found an unsigned contribution, entitled "Emerson," until then hardly more than a name to him. The article proved to be a compilation of selections from Emerson's essays, loosely connected by interpretive sentences. The first extract his eyes fell upon was from "History." The paragraph that seemed to "fix itself in [him] like an arrow" began:

> It is remarkable that involuntarily we always read as superior beings. Universal history, the poets, the romancers, do not, in their stateliest pictures – in the sacerdotal, the imperial palaces, in the triumphs of will or of genius - anywhere make us feel that we intrude, that this is for our betters; but rather it is true that in their grandest strokes, there we feel most at home. <u>All that Shakespeare says of the king. yonder slip of a boy that reads in the corner, feels to be true of himself.</u>[39]

Whatever in the words of Emerson moved him so deeply he never knew, but he spent the rest of the April afternoon meditating on Emerson's phrase, "true of himself." What "self"? The self that was studying to be a country lawyer? The self that took pleasure in writing clever articles in favor of slavery? The self that shot small birds for recreation? Some sort of "spiritual crisis" took place in Moncure as he gazed at the vault of the sky, making him profoundly discontented with his former selves. An old legend he had heard as a child of a shipload of English skylarks brought over by Governor Alexander Spotswood and set free in the meadows of Stafford came to mind. He remembered once having caught the note of a marvelous bird that ascended swiftly to the sky. Could this have been one of the governor's birds? His elders smiled when he rushed home with the news and convinced the child that no skylark could have survived a hundred and fifty years. "But it was no fancy that now in my mature life Emerson had set free in my heart a winged thought that sang a new song and soared – whither?"[40]

When Conway went home in the late afternoon, he laid aside his gun forever, and walked across the river in quest of Ralph Waldo Emerson's *Essays* in Chester White's bookstore in Fredericksburg. The clerk offered him Emerson's *Arithmatic* and was willing to send for a copy of *First Series*, which Conway was reading with his usual enthusiasm when cousin John Moncure Daniel several weeks later came for a visit. Conway jotted in his diary after this visit:

> We got to talking of Emerson. He asked me which of his writings I liked best. I said I had read few, but of those I had been most fascinated by the Essay on Love. He said he liked that better than any other. 'It should not,' he said. 'be called an essay nor a treatise, nor anything of that sort; there is no name for so divine a thing, - no even poem. It is more like a fine glorious strain of music. The heavens are opened in it, and you see everything."'[41]

Southern "fire-eaters" though they were, these two young Virginians were responsive to Emerson's New England voice, not knowing where it would lead.

Chapter III
"Free Schools in Virginia"

Several weeks before Conway returned to Warrenton for his second year, he stood on the platform of the Fredericksburg station and listened to his uncle Eustace deliver on behalf of the town a speech of homage to John C. Calhoun. The senator from South Carolina was returning to Washington for the last time. Eustace Conway and the aged secessionist were in complete agreement that the South should secede rather than accept a subordinate position in the Union -- which was in their eyes by no means sacred. Moncure shared with his uncle and the weary old fighter for states rights a belief that the price paid for Union was too high.

Conway in later years never changed his views. The grounds of his mistrust of an enforced union between North and South, however, were drastically altered by his experiences in compiling and publishing his first small book, *Free Schools in Virginia.* Beginning the year with no thought of seriously questioning the pro-slavery assumptions of the men he admired, he ended it an avowed anti-slavery advocate who thought the slaves should be emancipated at once even at the risk of destroying the Union. The compiling and writing of his pamphlet on *Free schools in Virginia* brought about Conway's second "conversion," this time to the cause of the Negro. The steps by which he came to this position were slow and painful.

Conway stopped off in Washington for a few days on his return trip to Warrenton in May 1850 to hear the senatorial debates then in progress concerning the much-discussed Compromise Bill. Hardly past his eighteenth birthday, he felt his political responsibilities as secretary of the Southern Rights Association of Northern Virginia and also special correspondent of the *Richmond Examiner*. From his place in the Visitors' Gallery, he sought out the faces of those who, in defending the bill, became "victims on the altar of the great idol – the Union." He listened with deep interest to the speeches of Daniel Webster, Henry Clay and others, sadly taking note of the empty seat of Calhoun, "the greatest of Southerners." He perceived, to his surprise and bewilderment, aroused Southern feeling against the bill as voiced paradoxically by indignant states-rights senators in accord with that of a smaller group of northern abolitionists. To Conway, it seemed that a Union held together by such an "Omnibus Bill" as that supported by Webster would only breed confusion and violence -- as indeed it did.

A restless and troubled young man boarded the stagecoach for Warrenton to return to his tiresome duties as Colonel Phillips' deputy clerk. As he left Washington, however, he picked up a volume of essays by Horace Greeley and Horace Mann, and soon found himself drawn into "a great world where people were cultured, well to do, and engaged with manifold schemes for the improvement and happiness of mankind."[42] Conway was already acquainted with Greeley's *New-York Daily Tribune*, the liberal newspaper of New York. He was particularly moved now by Horace Mann's "Report on the Schools of Massachusetts," included in his volume of essays. Conway was well aware of the painful contrast between Virginia and Massachusetts in their educational plan. Only eleven of the nearly 150 counties of Virginia maintained any semblance of public education even for white children. Boys in the families of the gentry had to acquire a classical education in private schools usually maintained by local churches; girls were taught only the rudiments at home. Small wonder that Massachusetts, which had established public education when it first became a colony, had forged ahead of Virginia, economically and culturally. Now the North seemed to be planning to seize control politically as well.

Conway, as he rode through the rolling hills of northern Virginia, thought of his many horseback rides through this beautiful, fertile, healthful countryside, and of the poverty-stricken whites whose hovels, crowded with children, seemed to bear wordless evidence of the economic ruin brought about by "free labor" in a slave state. Not infrequently during his first year in Warrenton Conway had dismounted and talked with these children, who, it was not difficult to see, were growing up in complete ignorance and hopeless poverty. The debased faces of their parents bespoke the same poverty of mind and body.[43] Perched on his seat in the Warrenton stagecoach, Conway now and again looked up from Mann's "Report" and glanced at the "deplorable condition" of the lonely cabins and the neglected farms glimpsed through the windows of the coach. Why not attempt to write a "Report" on the state of education in Virginia, similar to that of Mann's on Massachusetts, and thus begin a campaign for free school in his own state? An effort to enlighten the minds of the ignorant white people of Virginia (obviously nothing could be done to educate the black man!) might, indirectly, ameliorate the condition of the Negro by elevating the white race to a higher concept of its responsibilities.

Conway had become aware, during his first months in Warrenton, of a difference in the treatment of Negroes in the northern country of rolling hills and large estates from that he had known in the Tidewater section. Though he had persuaded himself, under the influence of his cousin John, that Negroes were subhuman, he was nevertheless not prepared to find that in Warrenton and the surrounding area they were treated with a brutality quite unfamiliar to his young eyes. If the Negroes were mere brutes, what could be said for the white men of all classes, who corrupted and abused the Negro women? Completely without the protection of the law, Negro men were unable to defend their women, for anyone who should make the attempt would be either lynched or sold.

"It is certain," wrote Conway looking back over these scenes a few years later, "that the licentiousness, cruelty and suffering appertaining to Slavery at that time were so shameless and fearful, that they turned the stomach." When Conway discussed these matters with Colonel Phillips and other associates in Warrenton, he was told that such evils were found in every society; that in time the "scientific" view of the Negro as an inferior species would be reflected in new and better laws separating the races; that in the meanwhile the thing to do was to reform the white man through education that would elevate him above such bestiality. This last suggestion recurred to Conway's mind as he studied Mann's "Report" on his way back to his duties in Colonel Phillip's office. By observing the relation of the races and urging the establishment of free schools in Virginia similar to those in Massachusetts, Conway believed he could "cut the tap-root of all the evils of society," including slavery.[44]

With such a project in mind, Conway found his second year in Warrenton anything but boring. All his spare moments were devoted to the assembling of statistics on the ignorance of the people and the resulting social waste; on the proportion of uncleared, undrained land to the small area of available farms; on the unexploited mineral resources close at hand. In the evenings the young clerk assembled and organized his material, hoping to place his "Report" before the state convention, meeting in the fall to revise the code of laws of Virginia. Uncle Richard Moncure, he knew, would be one of the chief movers for reform, and on him he thought he could count. His studies carried him far afield, for they drew to his attention the whole question of the granting of free-homes to settlers in the West, then being discussed in Congress as the homestead question. Senator Dodge of Iowa was the champion of this dream, and Conway saw the possibility, if the law should pass, for the "poor whites" of Virginia now living on exhausted farms to move westward to more fertile areas.

After passage of the Omnibus Bill in the summer of 1850, a dinner was arranged for Virginia's two senators, James Murray Mason and Robert M.T. Hunter, in appreciation of the services of these two men on behalf of the bill.[45] They were accompanied by a certain renegade Quaker, Ellwood Fisher, author of a pamphlet written to prove that the South had been kept poor by its union with the North and advocating the separation of the two.[46] All three men made speeches proposing that local clubs be organized to acquaint the people with the idea of secession. After the meeting, the senators, and Conway, repaired to the home of Colonel Phillips for "tea."

Here the unfortunate young deputy clerk ventured to lay before the guests his two favorite ideas, that of homesteading in the West and free schools for Virginia. He was shocked to discover that his ideas were greeted with sneers and he himself treated with disdain! Hunter, a modest and intelligent man, argued against the Homestead Act, which he thought would soon upset the balance between pro-slavery and anti-slavery territory. Mason grew particularly vehement in speaking against the education of the white "masses," predicting that such a movement would bring down to the South many other offensive northern "isms." Conway listened in silence, all the more determined to continue work on his pamphlet. He realized that he was more interested in the education and improvement of the people of Virginia, including the Negroes, than in the petty politics these men represented.

Conway dedicated his spare time that summer to gathering statistics on the eleven counties of his state that had made at least a beginning in establishing free schools for white children. By September, as an opening gun in his single-handed campaign, he wrote a letter to the *New-York Daily Tribune* setting forth his proposals. To his amazement, Horace Greeley answered him in an editorial in the *Tribune* of September 7, 1850. "Never will Virginia's White children be generally schooled until her Black ones shall cease to be sold. Our friend may be sure of this."[47]

Greeley's editorial reached Conway in the midst of the feverish preparation of his pamphlet, for the State Convention of Virginia was to meet in Richmond one month later. The editorial simply served to make him ply his pen more furiously. Transcribing Greeley's entire column into his pamphlet, he addressed himself to his imagined readers with this peroration:

> Men of Virginia! Are you dumb to such words as these? Yes. But this is not the truth in the matter; we can have Common Schools, and that too, co-existent with Slavery. Read the Reports from our Counties which have adopted Free-Schools and successfully, Mr. Greeley!

A carefully analyzed and tabulated abstract of the School Commissioners' Reports on the eleven counties with some form of "free education" followed, together with the more "cheerful" excerpts Conway was able to find among the "doleful records" of the counties with a minimal form of public education. "No remarks," written in the report by the vast majority of the counties of the state, meant those areas had made no effort to provide any form of education. After several pages of rhetorical defense of "universal education," it soon became evident that the author meant "universal" only for the white portion of the population. "Society," wrote Conway, "is a bundle of relations: whatsoever, whether remotely or otherwise, affects one atom of the system, disturbs the whole mass." Perhaps because of Greeley's editorial, Conway threw in a few sentences concerning Negro education:

> We have amongst us a race who are prohibited education by law -- I mean the free Negroes. Of course it is thought best; but I would ask any one who knows anything about the statistics of crime in Virginia, if the largest proportion of it is not from them? There is no more lawless set in the Commonwealth.

Conway then proceeded to show how Massachusetts had established in 1647 free education for both white and Indian children from the earliest days of their settlement at Plymouth Rock in 1620. "But alas!" wrote the author, "what was the course of those who landed at Jamestown thirteen years before? Darkness lived long with them; and, in truth, their children have scarcely seen any dawn." While free-schools were being established in Massachusetts, Virginia, under governors sent out by the British, was kept ignorant. In 1671 Sir William Berkeley proudly declared in his report to the Crown: "I thank God, there are no free schools nor printing. and I hope we shall not have these hundred years; for learning has brought disobedience, and heresy, and sects into the world, and printing has divulged them, and libels against the best government. God keep us from both!"

That Massachusetts had forged ahead of Virginia seemed to Conway not difficult to understand. The Free School system is clearly "the very best promotion for the State's prosperity." This lack of schools, Conway concluded, "is the only thing that is weighing us down beneath the level of other states. Like men with night-mare we are striving to rise or go on, or avoid some indefinite evil; if some hand do not awake us, we die."[48] The nightmarish evil with which Conway was struggling was, as Greeley had pointed out, slavery. One is not surprised to read in Conway's diary for September 16, 1850, "Was taken sick while writing a pamphlet on Education."[49]

As usual, Moncure found an amiable uncle to help him. Paid $50 by the writer himself, Samuel Greenhow Daniel, editor and owner of the Fredericksburg *Democratic Recorder*, printed five hundred copies of the essay for his nephew. The title page reads:

Free Schools
in Virginia

A Plea of Education, Virtue and Thrift vs. Ignorance, Vice and Poverty

Let There be Light [The Bible]

By Moncure Daniel Conway

Recorder Print.
Fredericksburg, Virginia,[50]
October, 1850

Conway dedicated the document "To the State Convention of 1850" with these words:

> Gentlemen: Trustful that you will 'hear me for my cause,' which is that of our State and our Humanity according to my earnest conviction, I dedicate these pages to you 'with whom is all our hope.'

Conway mailed copies of his booklet to every teacher, preacher, lawyer, newspaper man or public servant whose address he could find, and he saw to it that a copy was placed upon the desk of members attending the State Convention for revising the State Code. A few personal letters were received by the author; otherwise, the pamphlet was completely ignored except for those who attacked it. The "poor whites," of course, could not read, and, in any case, showed no desire for education; the so-called educated whites had reasons of their own for not seriously considering the ideas expressed by this simple-minded young idealist. He was "expecting echoes where there were no hills," he later admitted.[51] Though Conway quietly went about his daily task as deputy clerk of Warrenton, his disappointment was deep. As he admitted several years later:

> I cannot express the grief I felt at the hands of the leading men and journals of the State. I was virulently attacked as an effort to introduce into the South the worst phase of New-England society -- as the effort to make a 'mob-road to learning.' The poor whites, it was plainly declared, must be kept ignorant; for if they were educated, they would revolutionize Southern society.[52]

In his *Autobiography*, Conway observed of the failure of his pamphlet that "the social, physical, and financial conditions of Virginia at the time were little comprehended by me, in my nineteenth year."[53] He could hardly have been expected to understand that the moment had not come -- at least so it seemed to the legislators at the state convention -- to risk educating ignorant white farmers who were practically serfs on their depleted farms. The convention, rewriting the Code of Virginia for the first time since it was adopted in 1830, felt that their effort should be centered on granting universal white manhood suffrage. (Virginia was the last state in the Union to do so.) A poll-tax was instituted at the same time in order effectively to bar many potential voters among "poor whites." To educate them, as well as to allow them to vote, would be but to add to the restlessness of this displaced portion of the population which could neither compete with slave labor nor move westward to new lands -- or so thought those convening in Richmond in 1851 to re-write the Virginia Constitution.

Having been the most thickly populated and the most prosperous of the colonies, Virginia, after the War of 1812, saw her prosperity steadily decline. Though the tariff on farm produce, including cotton, was often cited as the cause, it was probably more related to the fact that Virginia had fallen behind the times in methods of farming, depending on the use of labor rather than on improved machinery. Conway was, in a sense, correct in asserting that the beginning of the redemption of Virginia lay in educating the white population; he could hardly have realized, however, that to do so would have brought about a revolution in the class structure of the State that wealthy land owners were not willing to accept.

The power was, for the moment, held by a few established families on the eastern side of Virginia (the group into which

Conway himself was born), and this power was based both on slavery and on exploitation of the "poor whites." Though the Convention of 1850 corrected some of the re-apportionment inequalities between the western and the eastern sections of the state, the balance of power still leaned heavily toward the east. It was maintained only on the basis of keeping the Negroes enslaved and their rivals, the "poor whites," ignorant.

Not until a new constitution was necessary in 1869, after the Civil War, were the Negroes enfranchised and free education for all children established in Virginia. Horace Greeley was right in pointing out to Conway that free education for the white man could never be achieved in Virginia while Slavery persisted. Conway could not then have perceived this relationship between the Negroes' position and that of the "poor whites." He had yet to learn the truth of Greeley's editorial:

> Free Schools, or Common Schools of any kind, cannot flourish with Slavery. You may have them in cites and large villages, but not throughout a State like Virginia. The farms are too large, the wastes too extensive, the [white] children too widely scattered. Besides, the Poor lack the consideration and the spirit, the ambition and the energy, which is requisite to a general maintenance of, and attendance upon, Common Schools.[54]

Two experiences in the summer of 1850 affected Conway's "mere Virginianism," rendering him perhaps overly sensitive to Greeley's wise words. The first was the "mob murder" of a free Negro at Culpeper Courthouse in July 1850, and the second was a Methodist camp-meeting in Loudoun County in August of that same year. With both of these events Conway was involved, and both of them shook him profoundly. In December 1850 he wrote to his father that he had given up all idea of practicing law and would on his return home for Christmas apply for admission to the Baltimore Methodist Conference as a minister. The Conway parents, as well as his relatives and friends, were amazed by this resolution -- but no more so than Conway himself, who knew that he was renouncing an assured career in journalism and a distinguished future in the law by deciding to become, instead, a Methodist Circuit Rider. Why was he determined to follow this new course? The impact on Moncure of the lynching of a Negro at the very time when he was traveling around the neighborhood gathering evidence for his pamphlet on free education cannot be overlooked as an explanation of this seemingly sudden resolution.

Grayson was under sentence in the neighboring town of Culpeper Courthouse for murdering a white man named Miller. Since the evidence against the Negro was insufficient to convict him, the mob at Culpeper was furiously clamoring for his death. The Court of Appeals of Virginia ordered a new trial in Warrenton, but a mob of several hundred easily seized Grayson as he was about to be transferred and summarily hanged him. Grayson protested his innocence to the end; the fact that he had nothing to do with the murder of Miller was established after he had been lynched. This was the first case of mob violence that Conway had ever encountered; as usual, his indignation was expressed in print. Conway immediately wrote a letter to the Warrenton paper (July 20, 1850), in which he relieved his feelings with a fine flourish of rhetoric, reminding the citizens of Warrenton that, "the whole affair would read better among the records of the Spanish Inquisition, or of the feudal age of Britain, than by the light of the full moon of the nineteenth century."[55]

Conway's moral indignation was shared by people throughout the area who regarded the episode as tragic but of passing significance, and refused to consider it a real indictment of slavery. Now that Conway was involved with a serious study of so-called "universal education," the thought of slavery with its attendant cruelties cut across the line of his argument. Could the white men who lynched Grayson be educated to think of the Negro as a "man and brother"? Or was the Negro, an "inferior animal" to be controlled by the superior white race forever? His cousin, John Moncure Daniel, believed the Negro subhuman; moreover, his view was backed by the great scientist of Harvard University, Louis Agassiz. What was Conway to conclude?

In a lecture delivered in Cambridge, Massachusetts, in June 1850, Agassiz strongly suggested that the races of man were not derived from a single pair of ancestors but that groups of primates had evolved more or less simultaneously in various parts of the globe, some resulting in "inferior" and some in "superior" races. The Caucasian race was clearly at the top of the ladder and the Negroid at the bottom; nor was there any evidence that they would in time change places. Agassiz's lecture was enlarged and made into a long essay in the July 1850 *Christian Examiner*. Conway read the article and discussed the question with his former professor of biology at Dickinson College, Spencer F. Baird of the Smithsonian Institution of Washington. Since Baird supported Agassiz in his conclusions, Conway did not hesitate to present the theory of the permanent inferiority of the Negro race in the Franklin Lyceum of Warrenton, of which he was secretary, when asked to address an audience agitated by the lynching of Grayson.

No doubt Conway carried the argument further than Agassiz would have sanctioned when he insisted, since the Negro had been shown not to be descended from Adam, he could not have inherited Adam's depravity. Was not the Caucasian race then morally responsible for the non-Caucasians of the world? And did not the need for free education of the white man become even more imperative, since, as the superior race, it seemed to be ordained that he should have the same dominance over the Negro that he had over the lower animals? Some of Conway's companions, pro-slavery though they were, objected to the speaker's theory that a Negro was not, properly speaking, a man, and hence was not to be considered in relation to the Declaration of Independence. But none could answer Conway's question: If the Negroes are human, why should they not have the same rights as the white man? Conway's eccentric views created a small tempest in the lyceum of Warrenton.

Conway wisely gave up further public discussion of the Negro question, and devoted his time for the rest of the summer to his studies, surrounding himself with all available books on races, Biblical criticism, philosophy and biology. Besides writing *Free Schools in Virginia,* he wrote a fifteen-page essay defending the proposition that the Caucasian race is the highest human species.[56]

The essay, fortunately, was tossed into his drawer and never printed.[57] Fifty years later Conway drew it from its wrappings, having completely forgotten that he had ever written it. The inscription, "Warrenton, Va, Dec., 1850," brought back to him at once the ghost of his youthful self. He realized that the mere writing of those fifteen pages had made him aware of his own superficiality; it was then that he had experienced "conversion" to the cause of the Negro race more real than the so-called conversion to Methodism of his college days.

Methodism, as dogma, meant little to Moncure at any time of his life; the preachers' method of persuasion, however, suddenly seemed to him to offer the very way to reach the middle and lower classes of Virginia.[58] Looking back over his experiences as a child in a Methodist household, he realized that the preacher might succeed where the writer had failed. Accordingly, in August 1850, Conway took time out from his studies to attend a large Methodist camp-meeting in Loudoun County in order to observe both the speakers and the crowds. Having as a child always participated in such camp-meetings on the Rappahannock, Conway looked forward to the gathering, not far from Warrenton, of the "poor whites" he was interviewing and studying in the preparation of his pamphlet. He was surprised, however, to discover not only that the assembly of Methodists in Loudoun County was much larger than that he had known near Falmouth but also that it included the gentry of the region as well as humble folk with whom his father and mother had labored. Here was a tremendous force under the banner of Methodism; perhaps from a Methodist pulpit Conway might reach a wider circle than his pamphlet could ever touch.

These feelings were amply vindicated by the silence that greeted *Free Schools in Virginia* when it appeared the following October. Disappointed though Moncure was to realize that his pamphlet was largely disregarded, he still was not prepared to agree with Horace Greeley that slavery was the underlying cause of the plight of the "poor white." Conway had joined one of the pro-slavery Southern Rights clubs suggested by the Virginia senators, Hunter and Mason. The upshot of the conflicts in Moncure's mind was that he determined to read for the ministry with the hope of reaching the poor, deprived white population by traveling among them and bringing them at least a glimpse of a better life, which must include a sense of responsibility for Negroes.

Greeley was no doubt right in his insistence on the interrelation of the fate of the white man and that of the Negro. The last entry in Conway's Warrenton diary reads, "Had a violent fever that night," (Warrenton, Virginia, December 1850). The fever was more mental than physical, for Conway had at last to determined to devote his life to his fellow man, black as well as white -- though as yet he by no means felt that the first step must be the abolition of slavery.

Conway himself was unable adequately to explain his sudden determination to become a Methodist minister. It seemed to him, as he turned his back on Warrenton and his intention of becoming a lawyer, that his earlier reading on the essays of Emerson had a more profound influence on the decision than any of the events of the summer and fall of 1850. Though Conway at that time had been able to get hold of only the *Essays, First* and *Second Series*, of the writer who had opened new horizons to him, and had never seen Emerson's "Address to the Cambridge Divinity School," he nevertheless had grasped the fact that Emerson had brought into harmony the sacred and the secular, making both sacred.

To Conway it appeared that Emerson's transcendentalism differed only in stress from Methodist transcendentalism. Both were based on the individual effort to seek out the divine in solitude, though Emerson's presentation of the spiritual quest of every human being seemed to Conway to idealize all of life, whereas the "progressive sanctification" of the Methodist tended to separate him from the facts of daily experience. The study of Emerson's Essays made Conway aware of a new, untheological interpretation of his own sect and seemed to raise Methodism in his eyes.

Quite aware that his "mission" was always to be somehow related to rapidly unfolding political events, Conway stopped again in Washington on his way home to Falmouth to listen to the speeches in Congress. He was rewarded by hearing the debate then concerning the so-called "Boston riot" of February 15, 1851. Shadrach, a fugitive slave on trial in Boston, had been spirited out of the court by forty laughing, talking colored men who had simply entered the chamber, swarmed about him and sauntered out with him in their midst before anyone was aware of what had happened. Shadrach had escaped by the underground railway to Canada, thus flouting the new Fugitive Slave Act.

Only a month earlier, Conway had attended the dinner, honoring the author of the law; now he saw its true importance. He was astonished by the wrath and acrimony of Henry Clay, who leapt to his feet and cried out in a high, sharp voice, "This outrage is the greater because it was by people not of our race, by persons who possess no part in our political system, and the question arises whether we shall have a government of white men or of blacks." The debate, Conway remarked, "gave me much to think of."[59] A month later, on March 17, 1851 – Conway's nineteenth birthday – he received his appointment to the Rockville Circuit, Maryland, one of the most important of those included in the Methodist Baltimore Conference.

Great excitement prevailed among the "servants" in the elder Conway's house on the eve of the departure of his son. Eliza Gwinn, who had been in the Conway family since before Moncure was born, came to him late in the evening and asked him to follow her to the cabin where her husband, Dunmore, was awaiting them on the porch. Before the crowd of Negroes silently gathered among trees, Dunmore addressed "Mars Mone" somewhat as follows:

> *Mars Mone, I have had a vision. I saw you standing on a hill, and one came and blew a trumpet, and there came many people from the South; and another came and blew a trumpet, and a great number came from the North; and one sounded a third trumpet, and many came from the East; and a fourth trumpet, and a multitude from the West; and a host was around you, and to them all you spoke the word of the Lord.*[60]

Mistrustful of himself as a Methodist minister, Conway was deeply touched by this expression of love and confidence on the part of his father's old slave. After Dunmore's words, Conway found himself surrounded by his familiar colored friends, who silently pressed his hand and blessed him under the stars. The black man, whom he had recently decided was less than human, gave Moncure the only consecration into the ministry he was ever to receive.

Conway's return to Stafford County after his sojourn in the western part of the state; his renewed contact with family and friends; his affectionate interaction with his father's slaves - all made him aware of the complexities of his present feelings, not only in regard to his growing sense of the cruelty latent in race relations but also in his realization of hollowness of what he called

"F-F-V-ism" – First Family Virginia-ism. Was the concept of "the old Virginia gentleman" merely a myth? What had become of the utopia that Governor Spotswood had wished to build in Virginia for the working man? Were Captain John Smith, George Washington, Patrick Henry, mere names?

A decade later, Conway was still musing on these questions first stirred in him by his view of the contrast between western and eastern Virginia during his year and a half in Warrenton. Realizing that his New England friends, whom he had come to know when the Civil War estranged him from his Virginia home, had lost their sense of the noble past of his native state, Conway published an essay in *The Atlantic Monthly* of April 1862 entitled "Then and Now in the Old Dominion," in which he sought to explain to himself and to others how the entrance of slavery into Virginia in the seventeenth century had, in the nineteenth, turned the countryside he had known as a child into "a splendid ruin."

At the time when General Robert E. Lee was assembling his forces around Fredericksburg to meet Union Army General Ambrose Everett Burnside, Conway summoned in his imagination the historic land on which the Battle of Fredericksburg was soon to be fought. In somewhat rhetorical terms he remembered this earlier, happier time of his youth before the confusion of the Civil War:

> Through the fair slopes of Eastern Virginia we have wandered and counted the epitaphs as princely men and women as ever trod this continent. Yonder is the island, floating on the crystal Rappahannock, which, instead of, as now, masking the guns which aim at Freedom's heart, once bore witness to the noble Spotswood's effort to realize for the working-man a Utopia in the New World. Yonder is the house, on the same river, frowning now with the cannon which defend the slave-shamble, (for the Richmond railroad passes on its verge,) where Washington was reared to love justice and honor; and over to the right its porch commands a marble shaft on which is written, "Here lies Mary, the Mother of Washington." A little lower is the spot where John Smith gave the right hand to the ambassadors of King Powhatan. In that old court-house the voice of Patrick Henry

thundered for Liberty and Union. Time was when the brave men on whose hearts rested the destinies of the New World made this the centre of activity and rule upon the continent; they lived and acted here as Anglo-Saxon blood should live and act, wherever it bears its rightful sceptre; but now one walks here as through the splendid ruins of some buried Nineveh, and emerges to find the very sunlight sad, as it reveals those who garnish the sepulchres of their ancestors with one hand, whilst with the other they stone and destroy the freedom and institutions which their fathers lived to build and died to defend.

Well known to the readers of *The Atlantic* in 1862 as an abolitionist from Virginia allied with the enemies of his family, they were willing to follow him when he turned to the explanation of the Virginia they regarded merely as a slave state. "The true preface to the present edition of Virginia, which, unhappily, has been stereotyped," wrote Conway, "is to be found in a single entry of Captain John Smith's journal:

> "August, 1619. A Dutch man-of-war visited Jamestown and sold the settlers twenty negroes, the first that have ever touched the soil of Virginia."
>
> They have scarcely made it "sacred soil." A little entry it is, of what seemed then, perhaps, an unimportant event, - but how pregnant with evil!

In the same year, Conway pointed out, the Mayflower sailed to Plymouth with its shipload of men and women seeking freedom before all else. How hard and bleak was the soil of New England, compared to the fertile land of Virginia. Conway then quoted the description of Virginia left us by John Rolfe in his report to the King in 1616.

> "For the soil, most fertile to plant in; for ayre, fresh and temperate, somewhat hotter in summer, and not altogether so cold in winter as in England, yet so agreable is it to our constitutions that now 't is more rare to hear of a man's death than in England; for water, most

wholesome and verie plentiful; and for fayre navigable rivers and good harbors, no countrey in Christendom, in so small a circuite, is so well stored.

> "Virginia is the same as it was, I meane for the goodness of the seate, and the fertilenesse of the land, and will, no doubt, so continue to the worlds end, -- a countrey as worthy of good report as can be declared by the pen of the best writer; a countrey spacious and wide, capable of many hundred thousands of inhabitants."

Anyone who had traveled through the state, Conway commented, may go beyond the statement of Rolfe:

> Virginia is a State combining, as in some divinely planned garden, every variety of soil known on earth, resting under a sky that Italy alone can match, with a Valley anticipating in vigor the loam of the prairies: up to that Valley and Piedmont stretch throughout the State navigable rivers, like fingers of the Ocean-hand, ready to bear to all marts the produce of the soil, the superb vein of gold, and the iron which, unlocked from mountain-barriers, could defy competition.

The entrance of slavery into this garden spoiled the dream, wrote Conway. Virginia was now "a sleeping beauty awaiting the hero whose kiss shall recall her to life." Conway at eighteen poured all that he had learned, and all that Horace Greeley taught him in his review, into *Free Schools in Virginia*. He would understand for the remainder of his life the blight that slavery put upon the white as well as the colored race in the state that seemed to him to come as close to Paradise as any spot he had ever known. Summing it all up, Conway wrote:

> Comparing what free labor has done for the granite rock called Massachusetts, and what slave labor has done for the enchanted garden called Virginia, one would say, that, though the Dutch ship that brought to our shores the Norway rat was bad, and that which brought the Hessian fly was worse, the most fatal ship that ever cast anchor in

> American waters was that which brought the first twenty negroes to the settlers of Jamestown. Like the Indian in her own aboriginal legend, on whom a spell was cast which kept the rain from falling on him and the sun from shining on him, Virginia received from that Dutch ship a curse which chained back the blessings which her magnificent resources would have rained upon her, and the sun of knowledge shining everywhere has left her to-day more than eighty thousand white adults who cannot read or write.

Though *Free Schools in Virginia* failed to reach the legislators to whom it was addressed, the preparation and writing of this pamphlet so affected Conway that he left the study of law, and became a circuit-rider in the Methodist Church in order to reach the people for whom the Old Dominion was originally intended to be a utopia. Since the Negro slave had been introduced into the garden of Virginia by the Dutch in the seventeenth century, he, too, had to be assimilated through education. But these thoughts were only dimly understood by Conway when he set out from his home for Maryland and his first experiences as a preacher.

Chapter IV
Methodist Circuit-Rider

Early on the morning of Moncure's departure for Maryland, Walker Peyton Conway presented a beautiful chestnut horse to his son. The saddlebags on the shiny new saddle were stocked with all he thought Moncure might need for his two-day journey to Rockville. The final words of the elder Conway, as he said goodbye once more to his puzzling son, were, "Let the potsherd of the earth strive with the potsherds of the earth: seek higher things, my son!"[61] His father warned him, above all, not to relapse into politics! Whether Conway was setting forth, as one of his uncles teasingly suggested, as "a journeyman soul-saver," or as one intent on saving his own "enmeshed soul," he himself hardly knew. In any case, besides his Bible and the Methodist *Discipline*, Conway had packed into his saddlebags the *Essays* of Emerson, Richard Watson's *Theology*. Thomas Carlyle's *Latter-Day Pamphlets*, Jeremy Taylor's *Holy Living and Holy Dying,* and Coleridge's *Aids to Reflection.*[62]

Perhaps Moncure, as he turned his horse to the road, thought of the advice from his cousin John Moncure Daniel the year before urging him to go into journalism. "'Whatever you do,"' he had said, "'don't be a preacher. It is a wretched profession. Its dependence is on absurd dogmas. The Trinity is a theological invention, and hell-fire simply ridiculous.'"[63] Cousin John then wrote down a list of books that Moncure must read without fail, among which were the *Essays* of Emerson – the very essays that strengthened Conway's resolution to give up the law and become a minister. His older cousin no doubt would have been surprised had he known that Conway, on his way to Rockville, paused briefly at Aquia Church, "weird in its solitude and dilapidation," and tried to imagine his (and his cousin's) great-great-grandfather, the original John Moncure, in "the little black pulpit," high above the square pews the church had built a hundred years earlier. He remembered vaguely the legend that robbers had once used the Church for their lair.[64] Surrounding the old colonial structure, so soon to be used as a stable by Union troops, lay the graves of the young Methodist's ancestors – Moncures, Conways, Peytons and many more – all of them Episcopalians. No doubt Moncure paused to read a few of the inscriptions as he walked through the family graveyard to the quiet grove of ancient oaks beyond the white fence and untied the bridle of his horse.

As much interested in history as in religion, Conway stopped on the lonely road to Washington at "the dead town of Dumfries" to reflect on the fortunes of his grandfather, Dr. John Moncure Daniel, who had come to the neighborhood from Edinburgh, many years earlier, to set up a medical practice. Now only a few "tottering chimneys" remained to mark the spot where the doctor had lost his "girlish bride" and her stillborn child and moved away. A little further down the road, Conway visited Pohick Church, where Washington occasionally came to worship and where his biographer, the Rev. Mason Weems, sometimes preached. Conway was startled out of his reveries by encountering a solitary wayfarer between Pohick Church and Alexandria, an itinerant Corsican with a hand-organ, to whose tunes Conway paused to listen.

But Conway did not have time to indulge his wayward fancies after he reached his destination in Maryland. Fortunately, the Rockville Circuit proved to be flourishing with enough hard work to keep two preachers busy. Conway's senior was the Rev. William Prettyman, father of a Dickinson College friend, who had settled in Rockville with his pleasant family. These "excellent and educated people" welcomed the junior minister cordially; the younger circuit rider, however, was supposed to spend most of his days on horseback and his nights with the "brethren" near each meeting-house. Since Conway covered about ten appointments every week, in widely separated parts of the country, he seldom passed more than a day and night in Rockville, where he was guest in the cottage of "the widow Wilson." Conway was always glad to return to the "freedom and pretty walks" of "Sister Wilson's" garden, for he was often appalled by the upturned faces of the congregations in the remote, wooded areas of his circuit.

Were these people educated? Did they like plain speech as did the Quakers, or did they prefer flourishing rhetoric? He did not know. Not infrequently Conway experienced a kind of "pulpit-fright" under the fixed gaze of his strange brothers and sisters, who, though Methodists, were unlike those he had known in Virginia. Looking back over this period of his youth, Conway realized that he was then passing through a "morbid reaction" against the worldliness he had once admired and that he frightened his congregations as much as they frightened him. One Methodist family, after a stern sermon against dancing delivered by Conway, moved to another church.

Much of Conway's time, however, was necessarily passed in the quiet country lanes of Montgomery County. He soon discovered the solace of reading from one of the books in his saddle-bag while his horse nibbled the weeds by the side of the road. His habit was to toss the reins on his horse's neck when he started on his morning rounds, and then to lose himself in the pages of John Henry Newman, Thomas Carlyle, or Ralph Waldo Emerson, the new writer from Concord. Emerson especially enthralled him, for he seemed to make the everyday world fresh and beautiful. "The woods and flowers and birds amid which I passed made a continuous chorus for all this poetry and wit and wisdom."[65] When he reached the village or the camp-meeting where he was to preach a sermon, his thought was suffused with the idealism of the books over which he had been brooding. For the moment, Moncure forgot his resolution to use his power as a Methodist preacher in the interest of the poor of both races, for slavery existed here only in its milder forms.

Conway soon realized, however, that slavery in any form is a social evil. Riding the Rockville Circuit in Maryland, Conway for the first time came to know the Quaker community in Sandy Spring, where slavery did not exist at all, and he was astonished by the contrast between their neighborhood and those he had known in Virginia and in other parts of Maryland. Before joining the Baltimore Methodist Conference in 1850, Conway had never seen any "free society", and hardly knew that any such region existed. The Rockville Circuit, extending for about twenty-five miles on the Maryland side of the Potomac River, comprised twelve different congregations made up of people of all classes. "The land and society were generally about the same with that which I had always known in Virginia," Conway wrote,

> but there was one section, called Sandy Spring, which was quite different from any I had ever seen. It was a Quaker settlement; not, however, a village, but a succession of finely-cultivated farms, with pleasant residences, covering an area of eight or nine square miles. So beautiful and cheerful was this Quaker neighborhood, with its bright homes and fields filled with happy labourers -- the only happy Negro ever seen -- that I always experienced an exhilaration in riding there, and have often gone several miles out of my way to go through it to my appointments. I could tell the very line on the ground where the ordinary Maryland ended and the Quaker region began, and felt, when I touched that line, as a wayfarer might feel on leaving hot sands for a pleasant grove with singing-birds and butterflies.[66]

Riding past "the plain meeting-house situated in a beautiful grove" of the Hicksite Quakers of Sandy Spring one Sunday morning, Conway, "impelled by curiosity," entered and took his seat. After a half-hour silence, an elderly patriarch, tall and handsome, arose, laid aside his hat, and said, in a low, impressive voice, "Walk in the light while ye are children of the light, lest darkness come upon you," and resumed his seat. After a few minutes, each person present shook hands with his neighbor, and the meeting ended. Conway returned several times to the gatherings until one day he was invited by their leader, Roger Brooke, to accompany him to his comfortable old mansion, "Brooke Grove," for dinner. The ladies of the household, in their "mouse-colored gowns," were both pretty and witty, the dinner delicious, and the conversation interesting.

"Uncle Roger" and Conway repaired to the veranda later for a smoke, and, after a few pleasantries the older man asked the younger what he thought of the Quaker neighborhood. Conway remarked on the fact that the farms seemed more prosperous, the houses more substantial, the people happier and more cultivated than in any other section of the county. When Brooke asked him quietly how this could be explained, Conway was at a loss for an answer. "Has it ever occurred to thee," asked Brooke, between puffs on his long pipe, "that it may be because of our paying wages to all who work for us?"[67] For the first time in his life,

Conway found himself looking into the eyes of an acknowledged abolitionist. "No slave has touched any sod in any field of Sandy Spring," his host added. The implied arraignment of slavery came to Conway with a shock, for he still felt himself emphatically a southerner and as such a supporter of slavery.

Roger Brooke saw the effect of this remark on his young guest, and he politely turned the conversation to other matters. These few words, however, made Conway grasp at last the relationship of the institution of slavery to that of the general prosperity of a community. He thought, indeed, of becoming a Quaker, but Brooke gently reminded his impressionable guest, "Thee will find among us a good many prejudices, for instance, against music, of which thou art fond, and while thou art mentally growing would it be well to commit thyself to any organized society?"[68]

Conway realized that Uncle Roger's question admitted of only one answer, and he did not become a Quaker. Instead, he visited, with Brooke's daughter, Sarah, the nearby school for girls, "Fair Hill," where he listened to a lecture on "history" delivered by William Henry Farquhar and admired extravagantly "the lovely girls in their tidy Quaker dresses." For six months, Conway lamented, he had been riding by "this garden of beauty and culture," never imagining the scene within."[69]

On his subsequent visits to the neighborhood, theology was seldom discussed, for the Quakers were careful not to proselytize, their views expressed chiefly by their manner of living.[70] Many years later, after the death of Sarah, Conway wrote to her daughter: "Mrs. Sarah Farquhar was the very first lady of liberal religious opinions I ever met. She enabled me, while I was restless under orthodoxy but troubled with misgivings, to recognize that the sunnier faith might bring the sweeter character and lose none of the religious spirit.[71] Under the influence of these Quaker friends, Conway's "Methodism" fell away like an outworn coat, which had never, in fact, been a very good fit.

Moncure continued to make his rounds as a circuit-rider of the Baltimore Conference that year and the next until, at last, he was forced to admit to himself that the seed which had been dropped into his mind in Sandy Spring "had a vitality beyond all others that had been implanted." Conway did not accept Roger

Brooke's judgment of slavery, however, without making an effort to deny its truth:

> I confess that I struggled against it; for already I was committed to interests and relations in life which would be utterly revolutionized and overthrown by any confession of anti-Slavery opinions. But though pain and despair grew with it, the seed grew; in vain did I cease visiting Sandy Spring, where every garden and happy labourer reminded me of that Quaker habit of giving the labourer his wages; the rest of the land, with its waste places and its paupers and huts, groaned out their testimony to the old man's words.[72]

After his discovery of Sandy Spring, Conway could never again ride through the Rockville Circuit beyond the limits of "the neighborhood," without being aware of the daily abuse of Negroes by other Maryland landowners. Having often seen Negroes put up on the block for sale near his home in Falmouth, and having once as a child turned away from the sight of a cruel overseer with his lash, he now could no longer blink at "the clear perception that there was a great Wrong coiled about the land, and that it was Slavery."[73]

The idea of actually coping with the evil to which he had been accustomed all of his life entered Conway's mind only after he saw the effect of the enslavement of Negroes on the poor but respectable white families, very near Sandy Spring, whom he visited on his rounds. One of his favorite families among his Methodist flock, for example, was that of an elderly gentleman with three motherless daughters, all of them in frail health and unaccustomed to hard work. When the old man died, he thought he was leaving his daughters in comfort on a good farm worked by a number of slaves. Conway called again at the farmhouse several months later, and found it deserted, for the girls had liberated the slaves, sold the farm, and divided their money with the freed Negroes in order to give them some sort of a start in life. The sisters had gone to Philadelphia to earn their living as seamstresses since they were trained for nothing else. Conway never saw them again, but when he turned away from their door with their pathetic story in his heart, he knew that he must leave the Rockville Circuit and work against a social system that brought confusion to all who lived under it. The sight of the neighboring farms of Sandy Spring made it impossible for him to continue his mission among slave-owning Methodists.

As Conway wrote to an old friend in Sandy Spring in 1884:

> My first tottering steps toward the kingdom of heaven were taken at Sandy Spring. And now that old neighborhood, and they who dwell there, have receded into (or gone ahead into) a golden age. Often in the twilight I revisit the old scenes and faces; and sometimes have a vision of myself in old age returning to that spot where I buckled on my armor for a long and weary war.... Ah, how often have I longed for the old woodland walks, the dreams and glories of the days when every bush was a "burning Bush" there in Sandy Spring.[74]

Retracing the path of his "pilgrimage" for his London congregation, many years later Conway wrote,

> My orthodoxy caught fire: it was consumed by a great cause. The hope of seeing slavery lifted from the land, and the beauty of that oasis of free culture spread through my beloved South, rose within me, filled my horizon, until the old heaven of faith was forgotten, Jerusalem faded into antiquity, the dogmas became dry bones.[75]

As a Methodist circuit-rider, he wrote, for the benefit of his London friends:

> I preached to ten different congregations – preached every day, and twice or thrice on Sundays -- and some complained to the Presiding Elder that I mystified and alarmed them by bringing out everything in the Bible too plainly. I was advised to be more discreet. It dawned upon me that it was necessary to take God's word under wise supervision, to correct its tendency towards plain-spokeness.[76]

Conway's visits to the Quaker settlement in Maryland in 1850-1851 had made him at last admit to himself the truth of Horace Greeley's comment on *Free Schools in Virginia*, that there is no freedom for white men while slavery continues to exist.

Conway became more acutely aware of the distance he had traveled from the slave-owning Methodists he had always known when, in June 1851, he exchanged circuits, with a friend and preached in Fredericksburg, Stafford Courthouse, and Falmouth to congregations of old friends and neighbors. Among them he was conscious of the anxious, loving faces of his father and mother, his brothers, and his sister. Earnestly searching for the truth of his own heart, he was almost overcome with emotion as he attempted to preach to such an audience from the text, "Thou wilt show me the path of life."[77]

Ignoring the Methodist stress on heaven and hell, Conway presented religion as a possible guide for a useful life on earth, for he himself was seeking the "path of life" that would lead him into the fight against slavery. When after the service he joined his family in Conway House, his father -- on the whole pleased with his son's performance -- laughingly said, "one thing is certain, Mone: should the devil ever aim at a Methodist preacher, you'll be safe!" for he realized that Mane's sermon had not been that of an orthodox Methodist preacher, either in manner or in meaning. His manner, his father recognized, was that of a lawyer pleading his case in court. What his meaning was, his father hardly knew. The words with which the sermon had ended, "I must be about my father's business," meant to Moncure that he must be more concerned with the lives of the people around him, both black and white, than with the dogma of the Trinity or of Salvation. His father had approved in a general way his son's veiled words, without grasping their practical implication -- for Conway dared not discuss with his father his growing distrust of the Methodists' attitude toward slavery. As he later admitted,

> So accustomed had I been to regard Slavery as the very corner-stone of society; so bound hand and foot by my relations to it; so awed by that illusion of power with which a great Social Wrong can invest itself, that my new perception seemed to me to be a terrible secret, to be hushed and held down in my own breast.[78]

In his loneliness, Conway addressed himself directly to Emerson, for there was no one else to whom he could speak. November 4, 1851, Conway wrote ostensibly to ask him where he could find copies of *The Dial*, but really to put before him a "concern as deep as Eternity." How could a "minister of the Christian Religion," now in his twentieth year, assent to the "Laws" described by Emerson when he knew by doing so he would bring distress to his family and friends? Conway assured Emerson that he had read all his works since he first became aware of them a year earlier and had "shed many burning tears over them." Indeed, "I sometimes feel as if you made for me a second Fall from which there is no redemption by any atonement."[79] Years later, looking back over this period of adolescent anguish, Conway said that he was struggling with "a huge phantom" of dread as to how to explain his views to family and friends. Then "an angel came. It was Emerson."[80]

Emerson replied to Conway on November 13, 1851, with a long and thoughtful letter. He flattered the boy by observing, "I believe what interests both you and me most of all things, and whether we know it or not, is the morals of the intellect...A true soul will disdain to be moved except by what natively commands it, though it should go sad and solitary in search of its master a thousand years." Emerson ended his letter – "Yours, in all good hope, R. W. Emerson."[81]

"Here I had my marching orders, and gradually comprehended them," wrote Conway in retrospect.[82] "Struggles were necessary to cut myself loose from Southern politics and from orthodoxy, but they became light when I whispered to myself 'Yours, in all good hope.' My heart learned this note, and sang it to me in many a night of loneliness and poverty." Encouraged by Emerson's remark in the precious letter he had received, Conway was soon pouring out his heart again to his new confessor:

> "You have not let me sufficiently into your own habit of thought to enable me to speak to it with much precision."[83]

On December 12, 1851, after he had returned to Rockville, Maryland:

Dear friend:

With [your words]--"that contest to which every human soul must go alone"--still sounding in my ears, I will venture another word.

In his *Life* that has just been publ. I find that John Sterling says, in speaking of you, "I should find it more difficult than ever to write to him." I expect he did not find it hard after he rec. one from you; he did not, certainly, if it [was] so tender as yours to me. May I thank you for it. I have very many correspondents, but I might almost say yours is the only Letter that was ever written to me.

If I did not sufficiently disclose my habit of thought, as you say I'm afraid it's because I have none of my own. I have always thought it the meanest thing to have one's habit of thought molded by conventionalities: but that's just my fate. I feel as if I would come to a time soon when I shall be a slave, and unable to speak the Truth at all and so will have to be dumb. My Island is getting smaller every day. I am very wretched because I am not so in love with anything on heaven or earth sufficiently to give myself up soul and body. This is what I would know. Am I to be a Child of Reason -- go up on the hard bleak Rocks, cut myself off from all practical Effort for Good; or shall I not allow the Circumstances of Life, which God has placed me in, to speak for me? What is any man but a skeptic? Who shall forbid a wise skepticism, seeing that there is no practical question on which anything more than an approximate solution can be had?"

This is my grief for this Life. For God's sake, if you can, throw me some light on this. I could go through this Life dragging the dead corpse of the Community along, if I did not think I heard the Voice of God saying as it did to Cain for his sin -- I will set a mark on thee!

I am an ill-fated one who has everything that he doesn't want, nothing that he does. I think my eyes are inverted, for I see all things wrong and have to call them right. This world doesn't fit, and if I thought I'd get to a better house I'd give my room here out for rent and seek lodgings elsewhere. Just think now of one being made a

Natural Radical -- to whose soul Radicalism is an air to a bird -- and having his lot and earthly converse amongst talented Conservative -- Virginians, such as my Father's family and all my early friends are. The details would be worse, but I will not trouble you with them. I suppose you think it strange that I shd. trouble you at all. But I have no sympathy on Earth. If I were to tell the people to whom I minister, what my real troubles were -- there is not one in the Circuit who would not laugh at them.

I lately defended you from the charge of Atheism made by a young Quaker friend of mine[84] and if you could defend me from the reality of it, I would thank you. I think my ideas of Spiritual Life and Death, and of Good and Evil, are confused. If you think my other ideas are also infected with that disease, I pray you forgive it as also the freedom of my Writing to you at all.

I am a stranger to you personally, as far, that is, as our bodies are concerned. But in soul, as far as you live in your writings, I am sharer of your most private thoughts. When I look at a lovely Sunrise or Sunset or the moon or stars I say to myself, "I know what R. W. Emerson is now thinking of if he sees this."

Alas, I fear the time will come when the eternal divorce from all free spirits will come to me, and all things above and beneath drum me out from Nature "a Coward."

I have written in this free way to you because I know you to be conversant with the usual trials & temptations of the Young. I will not insist on your answering my Letter, amid your important duties, unless you think you could do me a benefit. I am looking out eagerly for yr. Life of Margaret Fuller, for I have not yet lost my love and praise for the Gifted & True. Yours sincerely

M. Conway[85]

Thus began a relationship between Conway and Emerson that lasted until Emerson's death in 1882.

Whether because of Emerson's influence or because of his own restless intelligence, Conway found that he had become gradually more concerned with "large human interests" than with theology. During his second year as a circuit rider, he not infrequently stole a few days from his familiar routine to visit relatives and friends in the nearby Capital and to listen to debates in Congress and in the Supreme Court. Here he heard Daniel Webster deliver an eloquent speech, which his great-uncle, Supreme Court Justice Peter V. Daniel, opposed with a minority report. Here, too, he sat through sermons of all denominations, visited book stores, called on the widow of President John Quincy Adams and attended the New Year "levee" at the White House.

All the sights and sounds of Washington were interesting to this boy from Virginia. When Lajos Kossuth, the Hungarian patriot, visited Washington to raise money for the cause of the independence of his country, Moncure listened to his speeches "with rapt heart," following him about Washington from the White House to the State Department and the Capital. Later he wrote in his journal: "Kossuth received to-day a large number of gentlemen and ladies, to whom he discoursed eloquently of the wrongs of Hungary. Many were moved to tears, and some ladies presented their rings and other trinkets for the cause of the oppressed. A large slave-auction took place at Alexandria just across the river on the same day."[86] (After the Compromise of 1850, slaves were not allowed to be sold in the District of Columbia). Abolitionists in the crowd, however, were unable to elicit from Kossuth, the defender of liberty, an expression of sympathy for the cause of the Negro; nor could Moncure discover any clergyman in Washington willing to preach against slavery.

The death of his older brother, Peyton, in March 1852, just before Conway began his second year as an itinerant preacher – this time on the Frederick Circuit of Maryland – drew Conway still further from the theological teaching of the Methodist creed. His brother, who had attended one of the camp-meetings conducted by Conway the previous summer, had expressed to him "the abhorrence of dogmas" and had shared "the ideal of a church of pure reason, absolutely creedless and unecclesiastical, uniting all mankind." Little did Peyton then know, wrote Moncure after Peyton's death, that he, Moncure, his younger brother, "was at that moment in mortal inward struggle with a creed!"

These views were still in his mind when Moncure entered into conversation with the Rev. William Smith, president of Randolph-Macon College, on the deck of the river-boat that carried him to his new post. "What is the principle of slavery?"

asked the Rev. Dr. Smith, sententiously, and received from the younger man a reply that no doubt surprised him. "It has no principle," said Conway. Dr. Smith promptly supplied this answer, "The principle of slavery clearly is the submission of one will to another, and government is inconceivable without it." "Then," said Conway, "government is inconceivably wrong." "The best government," explained the Rev. Doctor, as though speaking to one of his students, "is where the two elements of slavery and freedom balance. I only wish I had you in my senior class, to which I lecture on this subject every week."[87] Dr. Smith could hardly have known that this unorthodox colleague had already read the essays and lectures of Emerson, the great Unitarian abolitionist of Concord, which had altered his view of slavery, government, and religion. Nor did Conway himself quite realize how far his concern for slavery had carried him from the accepted views of his Methodist group.

Though Conway's new circuit was larger than that of Rockville, and more demanding, he nevertheless found time for reading. He lived in a cottage surrounded by a garden, "the haunt of humming birds," presided over by an ancient lady, "Mother Rice," and her servant, Becky. Conway's rooms opened into this small Paradise, and here he spent happy hours reading his "beautiful books," while Becky, a handsome "young African," sang hymns as she hung out the clothes or weeded the garden. After a morning spent poring over Thomas Carlyle's *French Revolution*, Conway wrote in his Journal, "How strangely, grandly, it reads out here amid sunshine, flowers, birds, simple-hearted countryfolk! Nothing so wonderful as War viewed from Peace."[88]

Carlyle's history inspired Conway to write his next sermon on the "Prince of Peace," which excited so much discussion in his congregation because of its anti-war sentiments that he was waited on by "several committees" who wished to understand more specifically the views of their unorthodox new preacher. Friendly as these men seemed to be, they – and Conway, too – realized that the junior circuit-rider spoke less and less in the style of the Methodist preachers they knew. Their worst suspicions of Conway's orthodoxy were confirmed when they listened to the funeral sermon preached by their minister on the occasion of Becky's untimely death. If they were surprised by his unconscious heresy, so also was Conway himself shocked to find that his views were not shared by the congregation. As he wrote in his diary: "My brethren, many of them, were astonished at my preaching at Becky's funeral that death was not the result of sin. I had not dreamed of the unusualness of the thought." Conway had, in fact, drunk deeper than he realized, not only of the transcendentalism of Emerson but also of the potion offered him by the New England magician, Nathaniel Hawthorne. Becky, with her intelligence, humor, unselfishness, and love of life, had come to symbolize for him the very spirit of the sunny garden. How and why did death enter?

In his garden, "where no fruits of knowledge were forbidden," Conway had read, for the first time, Hawthorne's *Scarlet Letter*, and had learned from the story of Hester Prynne, an entirely new way of regarding "sin," which, he discovered, "had a consecration of its own." Conway had already come upon Hawthorne's *Celestial Railroad* and his *Twice-Told Tales*; Hawthorne's romance, however, was a more important experience. "On the portal of the greater world I was entering, Emerson had long been set as Michael Angelo's 'Morning,' and now Hawthorne took the place of 'Night.' But it was night frescoed with galaxies and with wondrous dreams." Through the portal of this greater world, Conway saw new meanings that made his old beliefs seem outmoded and useless.[89]

Methodist dogmas became more and more unreal to Conway; he was, in fact, looking deeper into the human hearts of the men and women of his congregation as well as into his own. Then as always, his mission was personal; people sought him out for the very reason that they sensed that he was not orthodox and felt free to confide in him their sorrows and doubts. Nevertheless, Conway could not forget that his sermon preached at Becky's funeral had seemed to his congregation heretical.

Though all of his older advisors urged him to hold on to his Methodist religion, he nevertheless felt that he must give up his connection with the Methodist Church. He recorded in his journal: "I opened a correspondence with my parents on my scruples concerning the church and my remaining in it. It will every way be sad for them and me -- but 'what is that to thee – follow thou me!'"[90] By the middle of December 1852, Conway was, at his father's request, on his way back to Falmouth.

Troubled as the elder Conway undoubtedly was by the continued restlessness of his son, he could not have been altogether surprised by this latest resolution. Father and son had met at the Dickinson College Commencement of the previous June and had listened to the address on "Philosophical Tendencies of the American Mind," delivered by Dr. George Washington Burnap, Unitarian minister of Baltimore, before the college's Union Philosophical Society. Walker Peyton Conway, as a trustee of the college, was uncomfortably aware of the possibly heretical ideas latent in the speaker's words – though he was pleased to see his son, together with several other members of the class of 1849, receive an honorary master of arts degree after the address.

Perhaps the elder Conway was also pleased to listen to his son preach on July 4 in the same church in Carlisle where he had been received by the Methodist Church five years earlier. Conway's subject was "the cloud no larger than a man's hand," and it was directed not so much at the distinguished commencement guests (his father among them), as at President Emory's sister, Catherine, also in the congregation, who had just announced her engagement to a friend of Conway. The "understanding" the two had reached several years earlier had been broken; the "cloud" over Moncure's mind was his growing awareness that he could not remain in the Methodist Church and that Catherine could not forsake it. "There was a subtle lightening in that cloud," wrote Moncure, looking back years later at the "anguish" of that period in his life, which struck something in him even deeper than the dogmas he was about to give up. "From some such experience," he concluded, "came the motto of our family, *Fide et amore*. My old faith and first love crumbled together."[91]

Conway's father and his friends praised him for his impassioned sermon, not realizing that Conway was giving his first expression to a vision that was to carry him forever beyond the confines of Methodism. "Why should I not raise my little cloud, assert the claims of a pure spiritual religion above all dogmas, and trust to its welcome by other famished hearts like mine?" he asked. Conway returned to his circuit for a few more months after his trip to Carlisle, imbued with "new hope and strength." Having, he thought, come upon an idea, he reserved as much time from his duties as possible to write a series of articles on Jesuitism, which he felt "forbids free thought and free culture among the people" and was all too prone to survive in Protestantism as well as in Catholicism.[92]

Happily, Conway's sociable nature led him to spend a week in Baltimore with his Aunt Jean and his "many cousins," who were "musical, merry, cultured" and affectionate. To his delight, he discovered that the Unitarians were holding a conference in the city at that time, and Dr. Burnap was among them. Moreover, Dr. Burnap lost no time in introducing Conway to other members, and, finally, in inviting him to his home for dinner, where he toasted him with champagne.

The "Unitarian work of grace" over the summer with Mrs. Burnap and their circle of kind and cordial friends was so effective that Conway soon forgot the "work of grace" of both Methodism and Quakerism and resolved to follow the advice of his new friends and enter the Unitarian Divinity School at Harvard. His homeward journey led him through Sandy Spring, and Conway interrupted his travels to spend a day with Roger Brooke, who did not hesitate to say that he disapproved of his young friend's newest plan. Wasn't there the danger that a "school" would make up a creed for him, which he would finally be unwilling to follow? The very names of the men now captivating Moncure were "fiery," Uncle Roger pointed out with a smile – Henry Whitney Bellows, William Henry Furness, Jared Sparks and George Washington Burnap.

On his visit to Sandy Spring, Conway talked over his new decisions with William Henry Farquhar, his friend and contemporary. Like Roger Brooke, Farquhar was too advanced in his religious thinking for Moncure, who noted in his diary "A difference of opinion [with W. H. Farquhar] on the subject of Supernatural Christianity." However, he wrote, "I cannot give it up. It is too grave a thing to give up quickly and immodestly. I must study it." Breaking away from "Supernatural Christianity," like giving up his inherited belief in the rightness of slavery, required an exercise of reason for which Moncure was not yet ready.

Conway discussed the question of the relationship between reason and Christianity with Roger Brooke before he left the neighborhood, and his older friend, as usual, brought him solace by gently enlarging his range of knowledge. Brooke told Conway that a member of Congress once presented him a copy of Thomas Paine's *Age of Reason* with the challenge, "See if you can answer that!" He read the essay and then remarked to his friend that Paine was merely concerned with the abuses of Christianity and required no answer. Unfortunately, the errors were all too apparent; it was more difficult to employ one's reason on discovering the simple truth of Christianity beneath all creeds. In the course of their conversation, Brooke placed in Conway's hands his copy of *Age of Reason.* Conway had never before heard of the man or his book but was glad enough to tuck it in his saddlebag beside Hawthorne's *Scarlet Letter* and *The Blithedale Romance*, to be taken with him to Conway House for further consideration. Moncure's interest in Paine outlasted his commitment to creeds of any religious group and became, in a sense, a substitute for religion.

Conway reached his home ten days before Christmas 1852. Though welcomed with the usual warmth, it soon was all too apparent to him that he was breaking his parents' hearts because of what seemed to them abstract and metaphysical religious views of no importance. In reality, Conway knew, he was "aiming at a new world" based, to begin with, on the abolition of slavery, for as long as slavery existed there could be no true religion. Any hint of his strong anti-slavery tendencies only made the surface religious controversy with his family more acute. His father particularly was "stricke with grief" when he fully understood his son's determination "to avow and advocate the abolition of slavery."[93] Still hoping their son would change his course, the parents resolved to keep his views secret from the rest of the family and urged him not to associate in any way with the slaves, either in Falmouth or on his father's estate.

Once more Conway attended the Christmas eve service at St. George's Episcopal church, and once more he knelt with his family in the basement of Conway House singing with them, as usual, "Come let us anew our journey pursue." Once more he also observed "hiring-day" on New Year's in the market place of Falmouth. "As I saw the slave-hiring to-day," he wrote in his journal, "I found out how much hatred I had of the institution -- and how much contempt for the persons engaged in it." His expression was no doubt observed by those around him. "You look," said one, "as if you were not in the world."[94]

The contempt Moncure felt for this and other customs connected with slavery must have been apparent to the Conway household. His father, who disapproved of slavery in the abstract, was more embarrassed than angered by his son's abolitionism; for the elder Conway, as the leading layman of the Baltimore Conference in Virginia, was pitted against his brother, Judge Eustace Conway, the leader of the Southern Methodists.[95] Moreover, Walker Peyton Conway wished to stress the unity of the Methodist Church rather than the question of slavery, for slavery involved the idea of property. Judge Conway's pro-slavery Southern position was stronger than that of his brother; for the first time Judge Conway spoke to his eccentric nephew in anger.

As for the Negroes themselves, they understood that "Mars Mone" was now on their side and secretly approached him from time to time to tell him of their suffering. Moncure was astonished to learn that his old friends, whom he had thought reasonably happy in this obscure corner of Virginia, were deeply discontented. He knew then that the whole structure of slavery in the South was indeed undermined. Previously he had supposed the Negroes themselves were indifferent to freedom. Among the white people with whom he lived a concerted silence reigned on the whole subject of slavery.

Little that Moncure heard either in the homes of his friends and relatives or in the meetings of the Young Men's Society in Fredericksburg, which he attended during his two months at home, would lead him to believe that any of them shared his views. There was, for example, Judge Eustace Conway, who in the recent campaign had nominated Franklin Pierce, the Democratic candidate for president. Pierce, a New Englander dedicated to the support of the Fugitive Slave Act, had been overwhelmingly victorious over his anti-slavery opponent, General Winfield Scott. Still more disillusioning, Conway's latest literary god, Hawthorne, had written a campaign life of Pierce with only a passing remark to the effect that slavery was an evil that in time Providence would cause "to vanish like a dream."[96]

Conway wrote in his journal at this time, "I am often tempted to renounce all opinions but those of the company I am in," so laughed at and even persecuted was he for his beliefs. The sympathetic agreement of the young wife of a cousin with

Moncure's strange views on slavery so struck him that many years later he made her the heroine of a novel, *Pine and Palm*, on the growing conflict between North and South. The young lady, "distinguished for her wit and beauty."[97] had merely quietly observed that she never had been able to see that there was any justice in slavery.

Harassed by the feeling that in striving for a new America, "freed from chains, slavery, strife," he was bringing grief to his family and friends, Conway eagerly looked forward to his departure for Cambridge. Inasmuch as he seemed to be willing to sacrifice the human beings he loved for a utopia he dreamed of, was he not, like Hawthorne's Hollingsworth in *The Blithedale Romance*, a self-deluded reformer?

Small wonder that Moncure spoke of a visit to Conway House by William Henry Farquhar the weekend before he left for Cambridge as "one of those bright spots that are cast on my life's path so much oftener than I deserve, by Infinite Mercy." Conway needed the support of his Quaker friend to help him maintain his courage. He also wished his family to meet this remarkable man and to see for themselves how harmless he was. Conway regretted that Farquhar did not see his father who was, at the time, away on law business.

However, despite an exciting election then in progress in Falmouth, Moncure managed to bring together on Saturday evening an audience "composed of the most intelligent of the community, and persons of the most refined feeling," to hear his friend lecture. "I must say I think he had spiritual guidance in telling them just what they ought to have heard," Conway wrote Farquhar's sister-in-law. Unconsciously describing his own response to the religious ideas of "Mr. Wm. Henry," Conway wrote, "he was just enough radical to keep them from thinking themselves what they ought to be -- and just conservative enough to preserve his influence on their minds, and forbidding any reactionary emotions. If that Lecture has not done good, I am more mistaken than I ever was."[98]

The next day Conway was asked to take the place of the Methodist minister in Fredericksburg, who had been called away from his pulpit. He chose, as the subject for his last sermon as a Methodist preacher, "Charity," and attempted to conceal the heresy in his heart from the congregation, which did not include his father.[99]

Walker Peyton Conway indeed was increasingly aware of the dangerous ideas that had taken possession of his son's mind and did not doubt they were attributable not only to his new friends but also to the books he had noticed in Moncure's room. Pointing to their strange titles, he said, "These books that you read, and are now about to multiply, affect my feeling as if you were giving yourself up to excessive brandy. I have considered my duty and reached this conclusion: I cannot conscientiously support you at Cambridge. So long as you stay in this house you are welcome to all I have, but I cannot assist what appears to me grievous error."[100] These were the father's last words to his son before his departure. Conway accepted them as just.

How attractive these books seemed to Conway, once he had arranged them in his room in Divinity Hall! In a letter to Mrs. Charles Farquhar, he wrote, on March 2, 1853, "I wish you could give me a call just now and see how comfortably fixed lam. You wd. find me in a delightful room to myself; a carpet just made up and put down today, and which if you were to see I think you'd say was 'tasty'; a radiant Anthracite fire is in a cheerful glow in the grate; a well-shaded Lamp is shining on this paper; and my Library is all fixed up, and is as full of beauty as of heresy."[101]

Chapter V
Harvard Divinity School

Conway kept his promise to his father and did not speak to the "servants" concerning slavery. He had no reason to explain to them his views, for all the slaves in the neighborhood recognized Moncure as their friend. "Aunt Nancy" whispered to him, as he said goodbye to the slaves in their quarters the evening before his departure, that her husband, Benjamin Williams (his real name was Collin Williams), had run away to Boston, where she hoped "Marc Monc" would be able to trace him.[102] Conway assured her that he would attempt to get word to her through an intermediary.

On the morning of February 14, 1853, Moncure ordered his horse saddled and took a farewell canter through the familiar Virginia countryside. He then hitched his beautiful bay to a poplar tree by the white fence of Conway House and laid his leather bags on the new saddle -- gifts from his father which he must now return. Having said goodbye to his mother and the younger children, he was driven to the Fredericksburg station in the village hack. Here he found a circle of relatives waiting on the platform (all of them women) to shake his hands and wish him well on his new venture among the northerners.

Conway left for Baltimore, carrying with him "a good stock of clothing, 140 books, and about a hundred dollars."[103] He was also well supplied with a cheerful interest in every kind of new experience and a resilient self-confidence, for he was almost twenty-one and had already accomplished more than most men twice his age. Well known locally as a promising journalist and writer who had already published a book, he had also proved his ability as a lawyer and a Methodist preacher. Now he was about to begin a fourth career dedicated, in general, to the cause of mankind, but more specifically to a fight against slavery in the United States. This he proposed to prepare for by studying at the Harvard Unitarian Divinity School.

No doubt Conway, as he looked out of the train window, thought more of the cousins with whom he was to spend a week on his way to Cambridge than of the distant goals of his new life in the North. On his first evening in Baltimore his relatives took him to hear William Makepeace Thackeray lecture on the English humorists, an experience he never forgot. As Conway wrote many years later in his *Autobiography*: "He was the first great literary man to whom I had listened, and his noble presence, his simplicity, his felicities of thought and expression, so impressed me that in after years, when I occasionally saw him in London, he still appeared to me as if framed in that hall with all the beauty and intelligence of Baltimore before him."[104]

Though Conway had left the Methodist Church, he did not fail to attend the services on Sunday morning at the Charles Street Methodist Church of Baltimore, where he found a friendly welcome among his old associates. "I mixed with them much in Balt. -- & they recd. me as kindly as ever," he wrote to Mrs. Farquhar in Sandy Spring.[105] Though his "brother preachers" among the Methodists argued with him, they did so with less bitterness than he had feared. In the afternoon, Conway wrote, he went with "a young lady" to the Friends' Meeting in Lombard Street, and in the evening he listened to his Unitarian counselor, Dr. Burnap, lecture on the atonement. Conway found friends among the Methodists, the Quakers, and the Unitarians, but he subscribed to none of their creeds.

As Conway passed through Philadelphia, he called on his former Latin professor at Dickinson, Dr. George R. Crooks, now the Methodist preacher at Trinity Church. Dr. Crooks assured him, if he allowed no man to be his master in the Cambridge Divinity School, and if he diligently applied the ancient languages to the text of the bible, worked out his own creed, and brought him the results on his next visit to Philadelphia, he was sure to subscribe to Conway's personal creed. No "doctrinal differences" ever alienated Conway from his old teacher, whom he looked upon as his "patron."[106]

Conway spent an evening in the home of the well-known anti-slavery Unitarian minister, the Rev. Dr. William Henry Furness, with whom he had been in correspondence.[107] Here was an ideal home, it seemed to this Virginian who had just parted, rather unhappily, from his family; the Furness household, he wrote, is "consecrated to truth, humanity, literature, and art." A son of the family was then preparing to enter Harvard College. Thus, Moncure felt he would have at least one friend in Cambridge to turn to in his loneliness.

Conway's diary of his first few days in Boston indicates, however, that he allowed himself little time to feel lonely. On his arrival he went at once to the Marlboro Hotel, suggested to him by a fellow traveler, and here he found comfort in the familiar routine of a Methodist hostel. "It is a very orderly, pleasant, and orthodox place," he wrote, "They have prayers morning and night, at which a piano with aeolian is used. The first thing that strikes me hereabouts is the extreme culture of music. After prayers there is singing till bedtime." The next day Moncure carried a letter of introduction from Dr. Burnap to a fellow Unitarian minister in Boston, who guided his guest to "historic places" all afternoon and gave him "much needed instruction" as to their significance. Conway was at once "perfectly charmed with Boston."

On Sunday morning Conway went to hear the great Theodore Parker speak at the Music Hall, which had been engaged for him in 1852 by Congregationalists after Parker had been barred from all Unitarian pulpits of Boston.[108] That evening Conway wrote in his diary. "His sermon was on Good and Evil Temper. Text, Prov. xv, 17, 'Better is a dinner of herbs,' etc. I don't like him at all, and wish I had worshipped at King's Chapel with Mr. Peabody, whom with his whole family I Love."[109] In his letter to Mrs. Farquhar, Conway described Parker as bald, with stray locks of grayish hair; "He has not an open fair face or a transparent eye," he wrote. "Altogether I do not like Parker's appearance." But his manner was impressive, especially his voice. His sermon, which he read, was as fine as his books -- one might call it "a good practical Lecture."

On the whole, Conway was sorry that he had gone to hear this strange preacher who kept the congregation "in a constant titter of Laughter" by his "odd and comical words in anecdotes." The visitor from Virginia could not get over the impression that he was listening to a "Comedy" in a vast hall not at all like a church. Moreover, Parker boasted that he wished to address "the publicans, etc."; his audience was "composed of [the] roughest people I ever saw -- the mustachioed men and rouged females." There were "various opinions of him here," he wrote, but he had to report that “a nearer sight has not given me an exalted impression of Theodore Parker.” No doubt he had already heard discussion of this famous member of the class of 1836, who in 1843, had been asked by the Boston Association of Ministers to resign his membership – which Parker had refused to do. Conway, still sharing the ideas of the orthodox Methodists and Unitarians as to how a minister should conduct a church service, could not measure the courage behind Parker’s abrupt and humorous manner.

Almost ten years later, under very different circumstances, Conway recalled for English readers his early impressions of Parker, by that time well known in England for his anti-slavery views. Conway then referred to the first time he heard Parker preach as one of the important experiences of his “prickley-pear growth.”

> There was something triumphal in the scene of the four or five thousand well-dressed and cheerful people gathered in that beautiful hall, with its pure white wall and lofty blue ceiling, which almost cheated the eye into believing that it was looking through to the sky beyond. When the choir, which was behind the preacher, had sung an anthem from Mendelssohn, the grave and even sad-looking man arose for an utterance which could scarcely be called a prayer, but was more like a spoken hymn of thankfulness. He began, “Our heavenly Father and our Mother,” in a voice which can never be forgotten by any who have heard it, and was the only outward endowment of oratory which Parker possessed. No matter what he said, no one could even associate with it any idea of affectation or levity.[110]

The man who had impressed Conway at the beginning of his studies at the Harvard Divinity School as embarrassingly informal came to seem to him one of the nobler exponents of a religion that included social justice to all men. On his arrival in Boston, however, Parker’s independent and liberal form of Unitarianism did not at first bring solace to Conway. He was disturbed not so much by the possible heresy of Parker’s ideas as by "the lack of anything in the Music Hall or in the secular music sympathetic with his lonely and forlorn heart."[111]

The home of Dr. Ephraim Peabody, on the contrary, was overflowing with music and gaiety. Here Conway found it an easy matter to "slip out of Methodist Sabbatarianism" and into Unitarian sociability. After a merry supper Conway went to the Music Hall with the Peabody family and was lifted out of himself by the experience that awaited him there. "At night," he wrote in his diary, "I heard my first oratorio ('Messiah'). 0 the ineffable delight! Fifty sermons such I heard in the same place in the morning could not breathe as much piety and sublimity through my soul as that grand oratorio."[112]

Conway's hasty judgment of Theodore Parker underwent a complete change when, a few days after his arrival, he descended from the clouds and made up his mind to discover Benjamin Williams' whereabouts. Armed with a letter of introduction, he called upon Parker and found him in his book-lined study, his grandfather's musket on the wall behind him[113] Though Parker greeted his guest courteously, something in his hard, New England manner filled the young man from Virginia with misgivings. However, Parker took down the name of the fugitive slave, appointed a day for Conway to return to his office, and then spoke to him of Emerson with such warmth that Moncure began to suspect he had found a friend.[114]

Several days later, Parker led Conway into the Negro district of Boston and knocked on the door of a colored family with whom he seemed to be on cordial terms. "This is a Virginian," said Parker, introducing Conway to the gathering, "but an honourable Virginian, who wishes to find one Benjamin Williams, who some time ago escaped from his master in Stafford County, Virginia, and for whom he has a message from his wife, Nancy Williams. I hope you will be able to discover Mr. Williams."[115]

While one of their number left the house to consult with neighbors, Parker carried on a pleasant, low-toned conversation with those around him. Conway was amazed by his sweet and gracious humility and by the homage paid their visitor by the group. Word soon came back that Benjamin Williams was well-known in the neighborhood and that he had recently escaped to Canada. Moncure, through an agreed-upon intermediary, transmitted the message to his wife in Falmouth. Theodore Parker taught Conway by this experience that liberal religious leanings were often associated with anti-slavery ideas. However, Conway's year and a half at the Harvard Divinity School turned him into an ordained minister of the Unitarian Church despite his early contact with Parker, who, he soon learned, was ostracized by the faculty of the Divinity School.

Equally important to Conway at this time was his interest in all forms of music and literature. Fortunately, he was thrown at once into the midst of the writers whose poems, essays, and novels he had been reading with wonder and delight since he had first been roused from his "Virginia Sleep" by Emerson's essay in *Blackwood's Magazine*. Literature, like religion, was to open his mind slowly to an understanding of the true significance of the Negro problem.

Music, too, played an important part in the education of this many-sided and eager young freshman. By the second of March, Conway was settled in his room in Divinity Hall, which "is the pleasantest situation in the University," he wrote Mrs. Farquhar. "It is remote from the other buildings. It has lovely foliage and scenery. It has a Chapel for morning & evening Prayer: it is ornamented with green wreaths, with pictures – and with a Cross made of moss above the Pulpit. The Organ is beautifully decorated, & is a sweetly-tuned instrument: M.D.C. is to be the Organist for the next term by request & appointment." To be sure, "the hail and snow are pattering loudly at. the window," he wrote, "but all is cozy within." Conway "had contemplated spending the evening at Prof. Longfellow's" but had decided that, unlike the Alpine Youth in "Excelsior," he could not buffet the "snow and ice."

Conway's love of music provided him with a means of subsistence and consoled him in his loneliness. Since only seniors in the Divinity School were allowed to earn money by preaching in the neighboring churches, Conway augmented his dwindling funds by playing the organ in the school chapel six days a week, at morning and evening prayers, for fifty dollars a year. Fortunately, Dr. Burnap insisted on sending him a loan of $160 when he heard that Moncure's father would not support him in his new venture. These two windfalls, together with his own small remaining sum of money, seemed to Conway more than sufficient, especially when Dr. George. R. Noyes, a well-disposed professor at the Divinity School, offered to pay forty dollars a year for twice-weekly lessons in organ-playing.

Before many weeks had passed the young Virginian had become to a widening circle of friends such an interesting personality that he was frequently invited to dinner or tea. As he put the matter to himself, "I suppose my coming so far from my relatives, and my parting with Virginia for love of religious and political liberty, led some to invite me to their homes." Henry Wadsworth Longfellow, with whom Conway was studying Goethe's "Faust" at Harvard, frequently invited him for an evening at Craigie House. On March 13, 1853, Conway hastily jotted into his diary: "Spent the evening with Longfellow! O what an event! I found him every way worthy of his works, with a sweet and smiling family around him. A pleasant young English woman was there, -- Miss Davis. Topics: Modern Authors, Personalities of Boston." Longfellow's "personality was potent,"[116] wrote Conway, who elected as many "general college studies" as possible, by no means wishing to limit himself to theology.

Then there was James Russell Lowell, to whom Conway was soon introduced; he, though entertaining in conversation, seemed to Conway's "Southern provincialism" to reflect a certain New England provincialism. Lowell, on a swim in a pond on the outskirts of Cambridge, proved "an admirable swimmer," perhaps to the discomfiture of the southerner who had never loved the water. Conway felt the poet who had written the "Fable for Critics" and had so cleverly presented the "leaders of thought," such as Emerson and Parker, did not seem really to understand their thought nor to feel much interest "in the great problems that filled the air with discussion."[117]

A third well-known "personality" with whom Conway came in contact in the early months of his Cambridge days was Andrews Norton, retired professor in the Divinity School and the epitome of the conservative Unitarianism of his generation. Since so many of his professors idolized Daniel Webster and opposed abolitionists, Conway was pleasantly surprised to discover that this old scholar deplored the pro-slavery views of most of his colleagues.

What was Conway to make of the views of another professor, Louis Agassiz, under whom he studied, whose published works he had so eagerly read? "From Agassiz I derived great benefit," he admitted, for here was a great teacher. "When he rose before us in his class, a rosy flush on his face indicated his delight in communicating his knowledge. His shapley form, eager movements ('his body thoughts'), his large soft eyes, easy unconscious gestures, and sonorous English, with just enough foreign accent to add piquancy, together made Agassiz the perfect lecturer."[118] When the weather turned warm, Agassiz used to take his class into the nearby country; occasionally he invited the group to his home in Nahant. There, seated upon a rock, Agassiz showed his students "the autographs of the glaciers recording their ancient itinerary." A question period followed the last lecture of the week, and Conway, who had not missed the implications of Charles Darwin's epic research, was less convinced than he once was by Agassiz's assertion that there are "lower" and "higher" races in the human family. He threw himself into the "ernest discussions" of questions important to his understanding of slavery, which was slowly undergoing a change.

But the "personality" to mean most to Conway he did not meet until nearly the end of his first term at the Divinity School. Dr. John Gorham Palfrey,[119] one of the few professors at the school with genuine anti-slavery views, suggested, when he learned of Conway's admiration for Emerson, that he by all means make a trip to Concord. Dr. Palfrey found Conway's point of view especially interesting. Though now a professor at the Divinity School, he had once been elected to Congress as a spokesman for the cause of abolition. When Daniel Webster lent his support to the Fugitive Slave Act, however, Palfrey's radical views cost him his seat and stopped him from winning the governorship despite Emerson's famous anti-Webster speech in support of his candidacy. "Emerson stands very high in the esteem of the Unitarian hereabout," Conway noted in his letter to Mrs. Farquhar. He told her that Mr. Palfrey had proposed to take him to Concord himself to meet Emerson. "The invitation is pressing" wrote Conway, "but I think I will not go. I am afraid to see Emerson, lest I shd. not find him as majestic as his Essays." Several months later, however, Conway decided to risk a meeting -- but he would make the trip alone.

On the morning of May 3, 1853, Conway took the train for Concord to meet, at last, the man who had changed the course of his life. Several days later, May 5, before his impressions had dimmed, Conway wrote the following account of the experience to Mrs. Farquhar":[120]

> I cannot resist the temptation that I have this morning to take you on a Pilgrimage that I made on day before yesterday, (2d.)[121] Then whither do you think I ed. have flown on that sweet day? -- To see the Sage of Concord, R. W. Emerson! Yes, if Tuesday wasn't a dream, I spent the day at his house. Early in the morning before breakfast I ran down to the Depot without apprising any one. At near half-past six I took the cars; swiftly passed through Westham, Wallham &c.-- when lo! I found myself on the spot where the Revolutionary War which gave us all (negroes excepted) Freedom ...
>
> After wandering about over various scenes, I found my feet drawn as by a loadstone down on the Lexington road; and at abt. 10 o'clock, I stood at the front gate of a pleasant-looking white house, embosomed in green furs [sic], and with neat walks leading to the door. Altogether I don't think I cd. ever have passed this house without feeling that Emerson lived there. -- In one more moment I was in his presence! I didn't behave quite as extravagantly as Bettine von Arnim when she went to see Goethe, -- leaped into his arms, burst into tears, and sobbed herself into a profound slumber; but I felt very nervous when that tall thin figure crossed the room and shook my hands as an aspen might shake. I was very nervous and my hand trembled when I gave him a letter of Introduction from one of his valued friends. After reading it he got up and gave me a cordial greeting. He then sat down to arrange some papers &c. I had a moment to glance around this room which had been the birth place of so many fine thoughts. Over the mantle was a famous picture of the Parcae, wh. was copied from the original of Michael Angelo in Italy. It is a most exquisite work, -- the three Fates standing together & one abt. to clip the thread. A head of Dante on one hand and Petrarca on the other: a framed Portrait of Carlyle, and a daguerre of him taken in London; -- and with these

strangely enough a picture of the ascension of Christ, adorns the wall. There is also a picture of a villa near Rome wh. Emerson admired when there, and Margt. Fuller was bringing for him in the fated Elizabeth; it was found afterward.

The room looked plain, comfortable, somewhat quaint. I was sorry to find that it was warmed with a flue.

The first thing that I felt was a thrill that such deep-seeing eyes shd. be fixed on me. His glance was distressing enough: he was obviously measuring my poor little gill in his gallon measure. He straightway entered on an examination of my attainments. He knew in about a half hour everything I had ever read and what I was ignorant of. He then found out what kind of people I had met with, and was much delighted he sd. that my experience like his 'had found much wisdom under the broadbrim.' He told me of his asking a Quaker in Penn. whom he had asked why he thought they had so much crime in N. Eng.-- and he had replied 'Because you have so many steeple houses' where at E. laughed heartily .... He had the highest words always for Quakers, and feared the race of "Truthspeakers" had died with George Fox. About this time he let the full blaze of his volcanic light on me. Such electric words never touched me before. Eloquent, wonderful, grand and simple his speech flowed constantly, bearing the wealth of ages on it. As for telling you what I think of Emerson I wd. as soon seek to tell you of Niagara whilst I was looking at it, if I shd. ever have that fortune. For Emerson is our Niagara.

That day was an Era with me. I saw a great man. He treated me with much simple tenderness,-- a constant smile playing over his features, which are very classic and handsome. He is rather tall, thin, with a look however of health.

He looks like a boy; his hair is light, not the least gray. He dresses plainly. He read me some poetry he had privately translated from various Orientals:-- he reads Poetry just like Mr. Wm. H. does.--He gave me much interesting information abt. Margt. Fuller that couldn't be put in her public Memoirs: he showed me two daguerres of her, one taken in St. Peter's, Rome, which shows her to be emaciated. He also took me to Wm. E. Channing's (whose wife a sister of Margaret's) He has a sweet family: a little daughter named Margt. Fuller Channing. I had intended leaving about 12 o' clock,--but he sd 'he hadn't done with me'--so he showed me all the rare bks. in his marvelous Lib. Gave me a list of where I ed. get some of the most valuable of them, which nobody else ed. get. He made me a valuable present,--a London Ed. of Margt. Fuller's famous "Woman in the Nineteenth Century," which is now entirely out of print on both sides of the Water; --an edition rendered more valuable by her having sent it to him fr. London just before going to Rome, and it has in it written in her own hand "Presented to R.W. Emerson by S. M. F. Jan'y 6th 1846." Now isn't that a Treasure!

He took me in to introduce me to his family. His wife is pale – looks as if she might have been pretty: nothing extraordinary about her that I ed. discern. He calls her 'Queeny'-- For goodness sake tell me what that means? She seemed amiable and sensible. I was more taken with his eldest daughter who sat next to him, and with whom he carried on a sort of bantering conversation, turning once to me and saying "This daughter of mine, Mr. Conway, has the good sense to think that this life wd. be worth something if it were not for vile men and boys. Only last night she refused a May-party because the boys wd. dance there." Nelly (for so he calls her) seemed a picture of satisfaction when he was running on thus. She is evidently 'father's image'; though I thought that little Edith was 'mother's joy'-- a bright gossiping pretty little girl. He has one son, Edward Waldo, between the daughters and abt. fourteen I shd. say.

In the afternoon he took me on a walk of some four or five mils (sic) – showing me the favorite walks & haunts of the celebrated Concord circle Channing Hawthorne Thoreau &c. He took me to visit this last,--

who is a naturalist & can't live unless snakes are coiling around his leg or lizards perching on his shoulder. He once lived in a hut by a river 10 feet square wh. he built himself, and lived there 2 years! He is the author of a most interesting work on the scientific associations of that region of country. He asked me abt the Theological studies of this School. "What do you study mainly?" "The Scriptures." I answered. "The Hindoo Arabic or Jewish"? he asked with great naivete. I burst out into a loud laugh. Emerson sat across the room & also commenced laughing,--remarking that it was rather dangerous to bring me near such a scoffer as Thoreau.[122]

I took my leave for Cambridge about the 6 o'c. train. I shall never forget that day! --I have told you all abt. it which I don't know that I ought to have done as all don't admire him as I do.

Back in his room in Cambridge, Conway wrote in his journal:

> "May 3. The most memorable day in my life; spent with Ralph Waldo Emerson!"[123]

Conway lived through the experience again when several days later he described it all to Mrs. Farquhar. He closed his letter to his friend in Sandy Spring with the words,

> "I often wish to be in yr. quiet neighborhood," and added, perhaps not altogether sincerely:
>
> This sort of life is too exciting: to have ever constant company in Poets, Philosophers, Doctors of Divinity etc. etc. - is not the thing. It's as exciting as hard-drinking. I wd. not live in Mass. for the world, if I cd. help it. I shall be glad when the constant whirl of dinners, tea-parties, orations, Lectures, shall be over. Even now I must stop & get ready to go to the famous Hale dinner where all the freesoil celebrities are to be. Parker, Cassius Clay, Ivy of N.Y. and hundreds of others. I am going with Mr. Palfrey's family, So now goodbye.

Fortunately, the term was drawing to a close and Conway was able to exchange the whirl of Cambridge and Boston for the quiet village life of Concord. The Emersons found for him a room in the cottage of the Misses Hunt, just outside the town,[124] and the new arrival was soon a member of the life of the community. The sisters were cousins of an unfortunate girl who had drowned in the Concord River. Hawthorne, who had helped recover the body, later made use of this village tragedy in *The Blithedale Romance*. Hawthorne himself no longer lived at the Old Manse, but Conway had caught a glimpse of him on his earlier visit to Concord as Hawthorne walked slowly down the avenue of trees leading from the home he had made famous. Conway gazed at "Prospero" with his "soft-flashing unsearchable eyes" but did not speak to him.[125] When he returned to the town the following summer Hawthorne was in Liverpool, and the Old Manse had become the cheerful home of Mrs. Ripley and her family.

Thoreau honored Conway by inviting him to join him for a walk soon after his arrival in Concord. When Conway entered the Thoreau home, he found the household in a state of agitation because of the appearance at their door at daybreak of a fugitive slave from Virginia, whom Conway recognized as one from his neighborhood. The next day the fugitive was off for Canada, and Thoreau and Conway enjoyed the first of many walks they took together that summer.[126]

Though Thoreau was not talkative, his occasional monologues, delivered to his younger companion on their walks around the fields and woods, seemed to Conway as extraordinary as any university lecture he had ever heard. "I remember," he wrote, "being surprised at every step with revelations of laws and significant attributes in common things -- as a relation between different kinds of grass and the geological characters beneath them, the variety and grouping of pine-needles and the effect of these differences on the sounds they yield when struck by the wind, and the varieties of taste represented by grasses and common herbs when applied to the tongue….Deep in the woods his face shone with a new light." The "valuable hints about reading" passed on by Thoreau, between his comments on nature, were equally important to Conway. Old English Chronicles, Elizabethan plays, poetry from the Greeks to Goethe, Oriental philosophy, antique books of travel, all was of interest to this extraordinary poet-naturalist. "He had as a touchstone for authors," Conway reported, "their degree of ability to deal with super-sensual facts and feeling with scientific precision."[127]

During Conway's "halcyon summer" in Concord, Emerson not only guided his visitor in his reading but also insisted on his taking the precious volumes (most of them Oriental poetry and philosophy) to his hillside home. "'What are they for?"' asked Emerson, as Conway left with the *Bhagavat Geeta,* the *Gulistan* or the Persian *Desatir* under his arms.[128] Emerson also walked with his younger friend through the streets of Concord; on one occasion he pointed out to him the venerable figure of Samuel Hoar, telling him the story of his futile trip to Charleston (1844) to plead for the release of the colored seamen from Massachusetts ships, imprisoned there because they were Negroes.[129] Conway soon come to know old Mrs. Ripley, the widow of the Rev. Samuel Ripley, a relative of Emerson, and also her friend, Elizabeth Hoar, two Concord blue-stockings, unlike any women Conway had ever encountered in Virginia. Conway found in Mrs. Ripley a woman able to sympathize with what he considered his advanced religious ideas. Her remark, "I cannot believe in miracles, because I believe in God."[130] was cherished by Conway.

A notable feature of the Concord community was the series of lectures at the village lyceum. Agassiz, though a foe of Emerson on evolution, was one of the speakers during Conway's summer in Concord. Together with other literary people, he was invited to Emerson's home after the lecture to confer with the great scientist from Harvard, who refused to accept Darwin's views. Only Conway's own words can describe the conversation in Emerson's living room between Agassiz and Amos Bronson Alcott, "who lived and moved in a waking dream." According to Conway,

> After delighting Agassiz by repudiating the theory of the development of man from animals, [Alcott] filled the professor with dismay by equally decrying the notion that God could have created ferocious and poisonous beasts. When Agassiz asked who could have created them, Alcott said they were various forms of human sin. Man was the

> first being created. And the horrible creatures were originated by his lusts and animalisms. When Agassiz, bewildered, urged that geology proved that the animals had existed before man, Alcott suggested that man might have originated them before his appearance in his present form. Agassiz, having given a signal of distress, Emerson came to the rescue with some reconciling discourse on the development of life and thought, with which the professor had to be contented, although there was a soupcon of Evolution in every word our host uttered.[131]

Agassiz's refusal to accept Darwin's conclusions on evolution, it was rumored, was traceable to the religious leaders of Boston, one of whom was his father-in-law, Thomas Cary; in any case, his assertion of the diversity of the origin of races became, in Boston and elsewhere, an argument used to justify the continued suppression of the Negro by the white man. When Conway returned to the Divinity School in the fall of 1853, he became increasingly aware that the orthodox members of the faculty, those who were defending the supernatural against the more rational interpretations of the Bible by such men as Theodore Parker, were also men who were against the abolitionists. Parker once asked a student what was stirring at the Divinity School; the reply was, "One professor is milking the barren heifer and the other is holding the sieve."[132] Though Conway would by no means subscribe to this description of the school he enjoyed, he longed for the more invigorating thought of his Concord Lyceum.

Hearing that Emerson was to give a lecture in a series then being offered at Concord, Conway persuaded two of the students at the Divinity School and a young law student to hire a sleigh with him and drive the seventeen miles to Cambridge and back. The snow was deep and hard that night, and the temperature below zero; they discovered on their arrival, however, that the Concord Town Hall was closed. An announcement was nailed to the door, saying that the lecture was indefinitely postponed. The three young men then drove straight to Emerson's home, where they were received with warm hospitality, hearty refreshments, and an evening of delightful conversation.[133]

Several days later, Conway received a note from Emerson, still chagrined by the supposed disappointment of the young men, offering to talk to a group of Divinity School students in Conway's room if such a meeting could be arranged. The paper was entitled on "Poetry," and it was read on a Saturday afternoon, in the more comfortable room of one of Conway's friends to a group that included only two students from the school.[134] Mr. and Mrs. Longfellow; James Russell Lowell and his widowed sister; the English poet, Arthur Hugh Clough, visiting Cambridge; Charles Eliot Norton and his two sisters, Jane and Grace; Franklin B. Sanborn, and several other distinguished guests were present.

A silence followed the reading of the paper, and then a musician, Otto Dresel, moved quietly to the piano and played several selections from Mendelssohn's "Songs Without Words" as the only fitting comment on Emerson's talk. It soon became known to the authorities of the school that the students had organized a school-within-the-school for the "Emersonian cult." Conway and his friends were called upon the carpet by the dean and reprimanded for bringing Emerson back to the Divinity School, where, in 1838, he had caused such a stir by his unorthodox lecture.

The thought that Emerson expressed that afternoon was basically concerned with the unity of all life, in the physical and the spiritual world, "the lower pointing to the higher forms, the higher to the highest." "There is one animal, one plant, one matter, and one force."[135] Though the lecture was entitled "Poetry," it was clearly a reply to Agassiz's rejection of Darwin's theory of evolution. It was well understood in Cambridge and Boston that Darwin's perception of the common origin of man carried the belief in the equality of races. To the orthodox, Agassiz's assertion of the inequality of races, springing from unrelated ancestors, offered a scientific basis for slavery and the uninterrupted flow of cheap cotton to the factories of the North.

"When I was a member of Divinity College," Conway wrote many years later, "the theology taught was still a slightly rationalistic Unitarianism and the sciences qualified by it (though Agassiz would not admit miracles). Some of the students were finding their real professor in Concord."[136] Five years after his "Divinity School Address" (1838), Emerson was still unwelcomed as a speaker in the school; the students, however, were seeking him out in Concord, and, indeed, inviting him to address them in their rooms.

Emerson was the teacher who meant most to Conway during his months at the Harvard Divinity School. "You think my love for Emerson will not be enduring," he wrote on the last day of the term, January 17, 1854, to Mrs. Charles Farquhar, when all the students were leaving, and he had decided to remain in college to catch up with his unanswered letters:

> Your remarks and the reason for it remind me of a similar one reported in Miss Bremer's book. "How" she asked of a lady in Concord (I think), "how can you so revere and love Mr. Emerson, when he does not acknowledge the Highest whom we love?" "Oh,' was the reply 'he is so lovely and so faultless".' This is all any one can say who loves Emerson.-- I don't for an instant admit or dream that he has not the highest, most religious soul in the country, as well as the best culture and genius. I don't understand what persons mean when they think him irreverent.
>
> I remember when I introduced him at home,-- that on reading his writings Pa was severe on him because he had made me discontented (as he thought) with everything. One uncle, whom Mr. Farquhar knows, called him 'daredevil' because he expressed what had been my uncle's private convictions in his fresh years. Another uncle thought like Sir L. Dedlock, that it would "open the floodgates." Sister Mildred looked upon him as a Chinese puzzle.-- But my Mother, who has a most deeply religious soul, read him, and did not wonder that I love him. What I love him for is, not particularly, his philosophy or skepticism, but that he is heroic, truthful,-- and because I never read his words or hear him speak to me without feeling ennobled. He helps me to scorn dapperness and hypocrisy, and to live and be myself.[137]

If Emerson made Conway feel ennobled, Parker made him think. Emerson left the Unitarian Church and tended to avoid argument on religious and political questions; Parker remained in the church, though he lost his pulpit, and welcomed direct combat.

"He hit hard," wrote Conway, "and no blow was too hard for the Unitarians to deal to the man who justified all the taunting prophecies of the orthodox as to the inevitable results of their position." The result was that Parker, like Emerson, had a loyal following in the Divinity School where orthodox Unitarianism was still in control. As an independent Unitarian who addressed large congregations in Boston's Music Hall, Parker further disturbed his former colleagues by defending fugitive slaves -- with pistols if necessary -- while most of the professors at the Divinity were quietly pro-slavery in their views. [138]

When the class of 1854 was graduated, Conway and the majority of the students voted to ask Theodore Parker to deliver the address at their graduation. To their invitation, however, Parker replied, "I should rejoice to do it; but the faculty have already been embarrassed by the reputation of your class for religious radicalism, and it is not right to press them further: therefore I decline: get a liberal man less notorious than myself."[139] Parker suggested Dr. Furness of Philadelphia in his place, and he accepted the invitation.

Theodore Parker, while still an obscure Unitarian preacher, had listened in 1838 to Emerson's address to the Divinity School. That night he wrote in his journal: "My soul is roused, and this week I shall write the long-meditated sermons on the church and the duties of these times."[140] Thereafter, Parker was a frequent visitor to Concord, where he would repair to commune with Emerson, "the first of men to him," and then return, "serene and happy," [141] to continue his fight in Boston for a more rational and humane religion and a stronger stand against slavery. Association with these two unorthodox Unitarians, Parker and Emerson, neither of whom was welcome at the Divinity School, provided Conway with the best possible education for the "unfettered ministry" he had been seeking since his early experiences as a Methodist.

Having been through "manifold theological views," Conway wrote Mrs. Farquhar in January 1854, he had come out "burthened with the practical aspect of life. [142] What to do next? How to do good? -- here is the vast and absorbing question. How can I persuade my brothers to take better views of God and the world, to abolish Slavery, -- to educate all, -- to live peaceably: Of course I wd. not be burthened with such questions if I did not feel that I was called to try in this direction," Conway wrote in a moment of restlessness characteristic of his many-sided, inquiring mind.

Much as he appreciated his training, was it enough, he asked, "to animate homes and towns with sweetness and light, to see after charities, to encourage reading, culture, attention to health, elegance in social life, art, good taste, pretty amusements?" Did not these worthy concerns make "a sufficient task" for a Unitarian minister? Perhaps they did. Conway was glad to assume such duties and welcomed the invitation from Charles Norton to help him teach in a night school for the poor recently opened in Cambridge. Though Conway was "profoundly moved" to see a room crowded with adults eager to learn the rudiments of reading and writing, he noted that all who attended were white. He had at last come to agree with Horace Greeley's comment on his book on free education, that "the poor whites of Virginia could never be educated until the slaves were free,"[143] but wasn't that remark as applicable to Massachusetts as to Virginia?

The many "fine spirits" among his teachers had traveled far, he felt, from the superstitions and tyrannies of the old Calvinists. They had done admirably in encouraging "domestic virtues and individual culture." but they had "failed to heed the warning voice of their great leader, [W. E.] Channing, that slavery was an intolerable wrong which would imperil the nation." Thus, the Divinity School had lost not only such leaders as Emerson and Parker but also the full allegiance of many students, who, like Conway, considered themselves "rationalists" and "freethinkers." Not theological problems, but those having to do with war and slavery, non-resistance and the treatment of criminals -- questions related to "human life and society" -- were debated by the students in their weekly discussions in the chapel with a "moral earnestness almost too intense." Against a rather orthodox faculty, a new generation of students was slowly liberating the old stronghold by listening to voices more in tune with the issues of the day, scientific and social as well as political.

Anthony Burns

Chapter VI
The Anthony Burns Affair

Senior year at the Harvard Divinity School was a happy one for Conway despite the distracting question of what to do next. There were plenty of vacant pulpits to be filled in the small towns surrounding Cambridge, and he was always entertained by "the best families" in the neighborhood, for he never failed to find a friendly response to his warmed-over Methodist sermons. When not himself preaching, he took pleasure in listening to the sermons of the eminent Unitarian clergy of Boston, to Ephraim Peabody, Thomas Wentworth Higginson, William Henry Channing, Theodore Parker and others. Though many of these men were preaching a social and doctrinal theology at variance with that of his professors, Conway was not at this time prepared to argue the issues. For the moment, life was full, varied, and interesting. Decisions could wait.

Occasionally old friends from Virginia and Maryland appeared in Cambridge to see how the wanderer was prospering, and, incidentally, to give him a good meal at their hotel. William Henry Farquhar, for example, came up from Sandy Spring; he discovered that Moncure was eating at the vegetarians' table· in the dining hall of the Divinity School and wrote to Mildred that her brother was not sufficiently nourished. The elder Conway sent off a letter at once urging his erratic son to accept an allowance, but Moncure promptly refused, assuring his father that he lived on vegetables in order to save money for concerts and theaters. No matter how absorbed he was in the religious and social discussions around him, he never missed a chance to enjoy music and drama -- or, indeed, picnics, parties and dinners. Better to eat meatless dinners than to miss his share of Bostonian "culture."

More serious concerns over the questions of the extension of slavery in the West, however, were borne in upon Conway before the year was over. On March 3, 1854, he wrote anxiously to Emerson concerning "the big black Nebraska bill" that threatened to permit slavery in that new state. "I need another

Essay on Compensation," he wrote, "to enable me to see any other result from this Nebraska bill than the making of that beautiful Country a Slave-breeding sink and the perpetuation of the Institution for a hundred years by making it rich."[144] Conway's worst apprehensions were realized. On May 30, 1854, the Missouri Compromise of 1820 was repealed and the Kansas-Nebraska Act passed. The pro-slavery forces were gaining ground. Nor, as he had already learned, was Boston exempt from the battle.

Before Conway graduated from the Harvard Divinity School, in May 1854, Anthony Burns, a fugitive slave from the South, was arrested in Boston.[145] Burns was a tall, intelligent Negro, of twenty-three, from Stafford County. He had been known to Conway all of his life, for he belonged to Colonel Charles Francis Suttle, a neighbor of his father. Conway remembered with chagrin that Suttle was the very man who had run against his uncle, Richard Moncure, for a seat in the Virginia legislature in 1848. Not only had Suttle lost the election, but Conway had satirized him in a lampoon published anonymously in the Fredericksburg paper. William Brent, Suttle's agent who accompanied him to Boston, had a remote connection by marriage to the Conway family. Here was a real test of Conway's conflicting loyalties! Should he support the right of his Virginia neighbors to claim their runaway slave? Or should he stand behind his new friends, the abolitionists of Massachusetts, who had argued in vain against the Fugitive Slave Act?[146] A mere Divinity student of twenty-two whose loyalties were divided between the North and the South, Conway did neither; his connection with the Anthony Burns affair,[147] however, marked a turning point in his life.

On May 24, 1854, Burns was seized as he emerged from his place of work in Boston, falsely charged with robbery, and rushed summarily to the courthouse where he was suddenly brought face to face with his former owner and his agent. Before he had had any legal advice, Burns was questioned by the slaveholders and was immediately cornered into admitting his own identity and his relationship to the two men. "Why did you run away from me?" asked Suttle, to which Burns replied with a misstatement easily uncovered in his trial. "I fell asleep on board the vessel where I worked, and, before I woke up, she set sail and carried me off."

So far, the proceedings had been kept entirely from the press, as doubtless the United States commissioner, Edward G. Loring (who was also probate judge) intended until the recalcitrant slave was safely on the vessel bound for Virginia. However, at the hearing in his office on the following morning, Richard Henry Dana Jr. and Charles M. Ellis, both attorneys, unexpectedly appeared and offered their services as counsel for Burns. Dana, the author of *Two Years Before the Mast* and a lawyer dedicated to the protection of the abused, had been alerted by Wendell Phillips of something afoot at the courthouse. Theodore Parker, who always appeared when a fugitive slave was in danger, managed to confer with the prisoner and urged him to accept counsel. "It will be no use," Burns replied, "They have got me. I shall have to go back. Mr. Suttle knows me -- Brent knows me. If I must go back, I want to go back as easy as I can."[148] Judge Loring was about to render his verdict without further trial but was dissuaded by Dana.

The issue was soon taken out of the hands of Burns and his advisers, however, for the news filled the afternoon papers of May 25. A mass meeting was announced for that evening in Faneuil Hall. The people of Boston realized at once, if the right of Virginia slaveholders to force citizens of Massachusetts to seize and return fugitive slaves were upheld by the federal government, then the cause of slavery in the whole country would have scored a tremendous victory. Everyone knew that the passage of the Kansas-Nebraska Act, extending slavery still further, was just then in the balance.

An overflow meeting of abolitionists, concerned citizens, politicians and mere riffraff gathered in the historic hall that evening. When the commanding figure of Wendell Phillips, the eloquent lawyer who had joined the abolitionists, stepped out on the platform, the crowd, roused by rumors of violence to come, was suddenly silent.[149] "There is now no law in Massachusetts, and when law ceases, the people may act in their own sovereignty," he declared authoritatively. "I am against squatters' sovereignty in Nebraska, and against kidnappers' sovereignty in Boston." All in that vast hall, considered by the humblest man among them as "the Cradle of Liberty," responded to Phillips' stirring challenge: "See to it, that tomorrow, in the streets of Boston, you ratify the verdict of Faneuil Hall, that Anthony Burns has no master but his God."

Theodore Parker,[150] in a low-pitched voice that brought immediately silence, then addressed the milling throng as "fellow subjects of Virginia." They were forced, said he, by the federal government to obey laws at variance with those of Massachusetts. When, at the close of his speech, Parker suggested that the crowd gather the next morning at the courthouse at nine, a shout arose, "To-night! To-night!" "To the Court-house! To Revere House for the slave-catchers!" The combined efforts of both Phillips and Parker had hardly managed to quiet the tumult when a figure appeared on the balcony and shouted, "Mr. Chairman, I am just informed that a mob of Negroes is in Court Square attempting to rescue Burns. I move that we adjourn to Court Square." No motion was made; in an instant the crowd had rushed from the hall and was pouring through the streets, up the hill to the courthouse.

Spontaneous as the responses of the crowd might have seemed to an observer of these events, they were the result of a hastily conceived plot by the Boston Vigilance Committee. Higginson, a member of this Committee, organized in 1851 after the passage by Massachusetts of the Fugitive Slave Act, described the affair some years later:

> The man [Anthony Burns] must be taken from the Court-house. It could not be done in cold blood, but the effort must have behind it in the momentum of a public meeting, such as was to be held at Faneuil Hall that night. An attack at the end of the meeting would be hopeless, for the United States marshal would undoubtedly be looking for just that attempt, and would be reinforced accordingly; this being, as we afterwards found, precisely what that official was planning. Could there not be an attack at the very height of the meeting, brought about this way? Let all be in readiness; let a picked body be distributed near the Court House and Square; then send some loud-voiced speaker, who should appear in the gallery of Faneuil Hall and announce that there was a mob of negroes already attacking the Court-house; let a speaker, previously warned, Phillips, if possible, accept the opportunity

> promptly, and send the whole meeting pell-mell to Court Square, ready to fall in behind the leaders and bring out the slave. The project struck me as an inspiration. I accepted it heartily, and think now, as I thought then, that it was one of the very best plots that ever -- failed.[151]

The plot failed simply because the throng gathered in Faneuil Hall was so vast that the plotters were unable to communicate. The platform was crowded, the staircases, the hallways were packed; once the speeches began, it was no longer possible for members of the Vigilance Committee to hear the speakers. Phillips never received the message of the plans; Parker was completely nonplused. Higginson and other members of the committee, having collected clubs, sticks and firearms on the Square, had quietly stolen through the dark streets early in the evening to await the outcome. Higginson himself took up a position near a half-open door on the east side of the courthouse, ready for "the trap to be sprung." Nothing but silence and a few lights in the windows above, where the Supreme Court was holding an emergency meeting! Presently, around the corner of the square, the mob appeared; Higginson scanned their faces as they rushed by, hoping to see his friends. In an instant he realized that "the froth and scum of the meeting, the fringe of idlers at its edge" were there, wildly shouting and seizing the clubs and sabers provided. His friends on the platform, "the real nucleus of that great gathering," were not to be seen; in the wild rush for the doors of Faneuil Hall, they had been unable to leave the building.

The details of the ensuing events will never be known. According to Higginson, he and several others were soon hammering in the southwest door of the courthouse with a tremendous beam provided for the purpose. The door gave way, and a small group of men found themselves face to face with six or eight policemen inside the building, one of whom was killed in the melee. Higginson, beaten about the head and severely cut on the chin, retreated to the front steps, while the marshals, their pistols pointed, took up their position on the staircase within.

In the watchful silence that followed, out from the crowd below stepped the well-known figure of Amos Bronson Alcott. "Why are we not within," he asked poor bleeding Higginson, as he waved his stick at the empty hall of the courthouse. "Because," replied Higginson, "these people will not stand by us." Alcott calmly advanced up the steps, leaning on his cane. As he peered within, and all eyes of the crowd below were focused upon him, suddenly a shot rang out from the courthouse, hitting no one. Alcott, finding himself without supporters, turned around, and slowly retreated without a word of comment. Thus, the attempt to rescue Burns by force came to a close.

Two companies of artillery soon arrived, and a little later two of marines. Meanwhile, Colonel Suttle and Brent, who had been hiding in an upstairs room during the confusion, quietly slipped out by an unattended side door and returned through the dark and empty streets to Revere House. At least one result was achieved; Judge Loring postponed the hearing of the case from Friday to Monday, giving Burns' counsel, Richard Henry Dana Jr., time to prepare his brief.

Word of these events stirred the undergraduates of the Harvard Divinity School. A number of southern students living in Cambridge assembled over the weekend to offer their sympathy and aid to the slaveowners. When Conway was invited to join the group, he amazed his fellow southerners by replying that his sympathies were with Anthony Burns and not with his owners.

On Sunday, Conway joined the vast gathering assembled to listen to Theodore Parker. Instead of reading the prayer circulated to all the churches on behalf of Burns, Parker said quietly, "I have no intention of asking God to do our work" and prayed instead for moral courage to combat slavery legally.

On Monday morning, May 29, Conway tried to get into the courthouse where the trial of Burns opened. The whole square was guarded by soldiers, however, and Conway, after regarding the scene and exchanging a few words with Dr. Oliver Wendell Holmes, returned quietly to Cambridge. News of the able defense of Burns by Dana and Ellis gave rise to the hope that Burns would be freed. Further rumors that a certain Negro minister, the Rev. L.A. Grimes, was raising a fund for the purchase of the slave made public indignation subside somewhat.[152]

Conway, meanwhile, had called on Colonel Suttle and William Brent at Revere House and heard Suttle declare, if the decision went against him, he would attempt to seize Burns by force and return with him to Virginia. "This purpose," Charles Stevens recorded in his history of the case,[153] "was announced by

Suttle on the morning of June 1 to a circle of southern friends at the Revere House, and in the hearing of the Rev. M.D. Conway, of Washington, who subsequently stated the fact to Charles M. Ellis, Esq., of Boston, and the Rev. George E. Ellis, of Charlestown." Suttle had by then changed his comfortable quarters in the Revere House to the attic of the hotel, where he was guarded by four armed men. In order to keep Suttle in a state of terror, four or five Negroes kept a constant vigil on the streetcorner below his window.

Conway was fully aware of the personal danger to Suttle and Brent, who, though by no means his friends, were fellow Virginians and neighbors. Hastening with Wendell Phillips to a meeting in Tremont Temple, he saw Higginson holding his coat over his bleeding chin while Parker cautioned against violence. Parker regarded the slave's fate as already sealed and would not advise any risk that he himself would not share in an attempt to rescue him. As he left the meeting, Conway was approached by a group of men he had never seen before and quickly surrounded. Their spokesman said, abruptly, "I am told that you are acquainted with the two slaveholders." "Yes," replied Conway. "Can you not call on them and find out the number of their room in the Revere House?" "No," he answered, and walked rapidly away.[154]

When Judge Loring rendered his verdict against Burns on June 2, Suttle and Brent were nowhere to be found. The supposition is, told of the outcome in advance, they had slipped away to a United States revenue cutter waiting in the harbor. Between lines of troops ordered out by President Pierce, Burns was escorted to the ship, the last fugitive slave ever to be returned to his master by Massachusetts.

News of the passage of the Kansas-Nebraska Act on May 30 had made the situation still more tense; several regiments of state militia were added to the defense against the throngs of people from outlying towns who had moved into Boston to protest the return of Burns and the passage of the act permitting slavery in the new western territory. Windows between the courthouse and the harbor were draped in black and a coffin displayed on which were written the words, "The Funeral of Liberty." In the course of the short march, mounted soldiers with fixed bayonets charged the bystanders, leaving several men wounded on the street. Observing these stirring scenes from the edge of the crowd,

Conway fully realized that it had been within his power for a moment to have made matters more difficult for Colonel Suttle. He was, however, a Virginian as well as an abolitionist; though he would not defend the slaveholders, neither would he betray them.

In a sermon two years later, Conway described what the experience of seeing Anthony Bums returned to the revenue cutter had meant to him:

> I passed along the sidewalks of the city; not at all attracted by seeing the slave returning. Why should I be attending to Anthony Burns? Him I had seen when a child, for his master and I were born in the same county, and lived in the same village; slaves with handcuffs, I had seen passing our village streets in gangs all my life. But there was one sight which I had never seen, which absorbed me now.

The sight new to Conway was that of the New England men, women, and children, five thousand strong, from all parts of the State, who with tears streaming down their cheeks, had thronged to Boston to protest the return of one slave. Though the "slave power had always found its right hand in the North," the "terrific fact" of one chained slave among five million made these New Englanders realize for the first time the enormity of the Fugitive Slave Act, which they had blandly supported in Massachusetts.[155]

When Suttle, with his agent and his slave, returned to Falmouth, he let it be known that "the only fellow townsman he had in Boston [namely Conway] had been opposed to him." After four months in a Richmond prison, Burns was sold to a plantation-owner further south.[156] Conway, still in Cambridge, was the recipient of letters from family and friends upbraiding him for his abolitionist views. Perhaps for this reason he delayed his return home. On which side did he belong, on that of the North or on that of the South?

On July 4, 1854, the annual gathering of the abolitionists, over which William Lloyd Garrison presided, took place in a grove of trees near Framingham. Here Conway voiced a brief plea for the peaceful separation of North and South. His recent experiences made him aware of the angry passions about him, and these Conway dreaded even more than slavery. Stormy speakers, one after another, mounted the platform after Conway and spoke fiercely for and against slavery; Moncure remained somewhat aloof from either side.

In the course of the meeting, an aged Negro woman, known to the group as "Sojourner Truth," mounted the platform amid general applause as a young man from the South spoke vehemently in favor of slavery, calling on God as his witness. Sojourner Truth interrupted his speech by crying out in a shrill voice, "Young man, I don't believe God Almighty ever hearn tell of you!" Laughter greeted her remark, and the Carolinian was silenced.

Thoreau, observed in the grove, was asked by popular acclaim to speak. His speech, Conway remembered, was "brief and quaint"; he declared himself in sympathy with the "Disunionists," and remarked that the case of Anthony Burns had long ago been decided by God and not by "Edward G. God" (referring to Edward G. Loring).[157]

Garrison read aloud the Declaration of Independence, and then contrasted it with the Fugitive Slave Act -- and the verdict of Loring surrendering Anthony Burns. He lit a match to each document as he spoke, crying in a loud voice, "And let all the people say Amen!" As the answering "Amens" arose, Conway must have been reminded of the Methodist Camp meetings he had so often attended as a child in Falmouth. When, however, Garrison lifted the Constitution of the United States aloft, and held it burning before the crowd as the original "covenant with death and agreement with hell," hisses as well as "amens" were heard in the grove.

As for Conway, he realized then that Garrison was "a successor of the inspired axe-bearers, -- John the Baptist, Luther, Wesley, George Fox." He himself had found that he could not work with organized groups, Methodist, Quaker, or Unitarian, knew he could not join the American Anti-slavery Society under Garrison as president. To him there was a dangerously Calvinistic sound to the phrase "covenant with death and agreement with hell." To this young Virginian "Slavery was not death, nor the South hell." Like many abolitionists, he yearned for a peaceful separation of the sections of the country that hated each other, knowing, as he did, that good people were to be found in the North and in the South. He believed that "slavery was to be abolished by the union of all hearts and minds opposed to it, -- those who believed emancipation potential in the Constitution, as well as the Constitution burners."[158]

When the picnic baskets were spread out on the grass and these friendly New Englanders invited their guest from Virginia to share in the feast, Conway found himself almost as lonely as the Carolinian whom Sojourner Truth had shouted down. Would she indeed have shaken her fist at him too had she known his divided sympathies? An elderly clergyman, and well-known abolitionist, the Rev. Samuel Joseph May, seated near him at lunch, tried to explain to Conway that Garrison was inveighing not so much against southerners as against the northern supporters of slavery who put their business interests before their religious convictions.[159] The abolitionist movement was essentially religious, he said, and had to be fought in the North as well as in the South.

When Conway returned to his room in Cambridge, he found a letter from the First Unitarian Church in Washington inviting him to preach there during the month of September. Perhaps here he would discover how to make the future of the Negro the concern of Christians, who were not impelled to burn the Constitution in their zeal. He was soon on his way to Washington, determined to carry on the anti-slavery struggle from the pulpit after the example of Parker.

Conway found Washington in a turmoil of discussion of the very issues he had faced in Boston. Charles Sumner, senator from Massachusetts, had made a prophetic speech in Congress in May, opposing the passage of the Kansas-Nebraska Act. "In passing such a bill," he said, "you scatter from this dark midnight hour to seeds of harmony and good will, but broadcast through the land dragon's teeth which ... will fructify in civil strife and feud."[160]

The seeds took root at once. A futile struggle to repeal the Fugitive Slave Act resulted finally in the formation of a new party called "Republican." In September a state convention was held in Worcester, Massachusetts, and here Sumner made a fiery speech pointing out the imperative need for a party dedicated to opposing the pro-slavery forces. He reminded the convention that the "pride and glory" of the Commonwealth of Massachusetts had been "trampled in the dust" by the verdict against Anthony Burns. Massachusetts, he said, should have defied the federal law since the law itself was wicked. Governments as well as men must not hesitate to "obey God rather than man." Sumner's opinion was sustained, and Massachusetts at the next session in effect nullified the Fugitive Slave Act.[161]

Sumner's speech helped to disrupt the organization of the Whig party, leaving the way open for the new Republican Party. His question, "Are you for freedom, or are you for slavery?" which he put in his extensive speech-making travels in the West, helped to clarified the issues at this critical moment when many a Whig was neither for freedom nor for slavery but rather for his business interest. "Conscience Whigs" and "Cotton Whigs" did not belong in the same party, said Sumner.[162]

Fully aware of the fact that slavery, the burning question of the day, was permitted in the District of Columbia, Conway attempted to cast his opening sermons on September 10 and 17, 1854. in religious rather than political terms. At the same time, he made perfectly clear his attitude toward slavery. Conway's sermon of September 17 was a challenge: "When we are in the midst of our ease and free enjoyment, does not God's whisper sometimes strike the ear, as it came to Cain, 'The poor African, thy brother, where he is?' Alas! How often our reply is in the tone of the first murderer, 'I know not. Am I my brother's keeper? Shall I interfere with slavery?' This answer, this plea, hoary-headed as it is, I arraign before the bar of the soul today. You are your brother's keeper, and are bound by the conditions of your own nobility to stand by him, be he white or black. -- For man is one, and one member cannot suffer but all suffer; one cannot be a slave but all are to some extent slaves."[163] His words were so well received, in spite of their anti-slavery tone, that he ventured to write a note to his father, suggesting that he might soon risk a visit to the family in Falmouth. His father replied promptly and firmly on September 18, 1854:

> I cannot refrain from saying I was truly glad you did not find it convenient to come down to-day... I have reason to know that it was fortunate for you that such was the case, and it is my sincere advice to you not to come here until there is reason to believe your opinions have undergone

> material changes on the subject of slavery. If you are willing to expose your own person recklessly, I am not willing to subject myself and family to the hazards of such a visit. Those opinions give me more uneasiness just now than your horrible views on the subject of religion, bad as these last are.[164]

Conway was not so much grieved as he was puzzled by the letter he received from his father. Could rumors of his connection with the Anthony Burns affair have preceded him to Falmouth? In any case, Conway decided to leave his father's letter unanswered for the moment and to put his full attention on his sermons; they should be, from that time on, more explicit in their statements concerning slavery, for the congregation must know his views before they offered him a permanent position.

In his final sermon before the election of the new minister, on October 29, Conway chose as his text "Thy kingdom come," and declared: "The church must hold itself ready to pass free judgment on all customs, fashions, ideas, facts; on trade and politics -- and, in this country, more especially hold itself ready to give free utterance in relation to our special national sin -- the greatest of all sins -- human slavery."[165] Fifteen minutes after his sermon was ended, Conway was called to the ministry of the First Unitarian Church of Washington despite his announced views on slavery. Soon he was established in comfortable rooms. On November 6, he was happily writing to Emerson:

> I have been preaching at the Unitarian Church in this City since the first of Sept., and have just been invited to settle here. I don't know what villainy has brought me this fortune, -- but I shall accept it and allow it to work its own results. People, I think, are getting to be indifferent to ones views so long as they are sure he thinks and speaks from conviction.

Conway, now preaching to a crowded church, in which were many "eminent citizens" of Washington, felt confident that the honesty and candor of his views on slavery would make him acceptable to this predominantly Southern congregation. "Channing," who had desired the position, he wrote Emerson in this same letter, "was much admired here for his eloquence and would have been called had he "not been considered as connected with northern political parties." [166] Conway told them he "had conversed with Channing and agreed with him on the slavery question" but "being a Virginian made the difference." He hardly took into account that he was not only a Virginian but a very well-connected one, his great uncle, Peter V. Daniel, being an associate justice of the Supreme Court.

Conway was confident that, single-handed, he was going to be able to carry the message of Emerson, Parker, and the other enlightened abolitionists to his new congregation. However, he wrote, "I don't like to commence preaching here without first going to Concord, placing myself on the counter to hear if I 'ring clear." Unable to find time for the trip. Conway. had, at least, procured a copy of Thoreau's new book, *Walden.* "I read Thoreau's book with deep interest," he wrote, "I really did not think he was so much a Poet."

But Conway found three points on which to criticize his Concord friend.

> I object to his Philosophy, 1. That it hasn't optimism enough -- reverence for facts. 2. That one couldn't pursue his Art of Living & get married. 3. That one hasn't time to spend or strength to spare from what is his work to take care of such universal rebellion.[167]

Conway felt that he had at last found his work. He spent his first weeks in Washington writing a history of the church, collecting his material not only from old record books and the minutes of trustee meetings but also by visiting the older members of the congregation.[168] He discovered that early in the nineteenth century several families in Washington had the custom of meeting on Sunday afternoons to read aloud Unitarian literature, and on this foundation of progressive thought the First Unitarian Church had been built. John Quincy Adams during his presidency and William Cranch, chief judge of the circuit court of the District of Columbia, were both members of the congregation.[169] John C. Calhoun was also a regular supporter of the church and attended it when he was in Washington. Visitors of national reputation were frequently invited to occupy the pulpit, one of the most popular being Conway's predecessor, the well-known Unitarian minister, Dr. Orville Dewey.

Conway's sermons were well reported in the press as far away as Richmond. His father and mother, perceiving that he was not so dangerous after all, wrote cheerfully urging him to come home for a visit. Several Unitarian friends said that they would procure for him a hall in Fredericksburg if he would preach there; for the sake of his family, he refused.

Early in 1855 Conway delivered two discourses in a Universalist church of Richmond. While there, Conway stayed with his well-loved uncle and aunt, Mr. and Mrs. Travers Daniel. They listened to both of his sermons but offered no comment either on his religious views or his attitude toward slavery. Conway had been invited to Richmond to expound unorthodox views, and this he unquestionably did. Uncle Travers contented himself by observing that he feared Unitarians tended to cultivate the head rather than the heart, and this admonition Conway took in good spirit as perhaps containing a useful hint for the returned exile.

The visit to "the dear old home in Falmouth" began propitiously with affectionate welcome from family and servants alike. However, as he walked back to Conway House in the evening, after visits to the homes of nearby relatives, Conway was twice spoken to in the darkness by Negro voices he did not recognize. They whispered to him that his connection with Tony Burns was known among the colored people, and that they were expecting further "instructions" from Mone, whom they considered their friend and leader. Conway disclaimed any intention of organizing an insurrection among the Negroes and returned home shaken by the encounters; he realized that his Boston activities were now well known in Virginia and might lead to dangerous consequences.

The next morning, as Conway was walking down the main street of Falmouth, he was quickly surrounded by a group of young men -- several of them former classmates and friends -- who told him without mincing words that his presence in the town would not be tolerated. His suspicions of the night before were confirmed when one of them said, "Charles Frank Suttle says that when he was in Boston you did everything you could against him to prevent his getting back his servant Tony Burns, and that you are an abolitionist. There is danger to have that kind of man among our servants, and you must leave. We don't want to have any row."[170]

By that time several well-known ruffians had joined the group in the middle of the street. Conway was told as they slowly closed in on him, for the sake of his family, he would be spared tar and feathers if he would agree to leave Virginia forever. Conway assured the crowd, though he was certainly in sympathy with Tony Burns, he had done nothing to endanger Suttle or Brent. Realizing that false rumors were circulating that might endanger his family, Conway agreed to leave the next day and was permitted to return home unharmed.

Without a word of explanation, Conway cut short his visit by two days and was driven across the bridge to the railroad station of Fredericksburg by the old family coachman who hardly suspected that he was driving his young master into exile. By chance his uncle, Dr. Valentine Conway of Stafford, boarded the train at the next station; having heard of the scene in Falmouth, he upbraided his nephew bitterly for having become an abolitionist. He, too, had heard the rumors of the Anthony Burns episode in Boston. Fortunately, the melancholy of age twenty-three is often exaggerated. As Conway wrote. in his *Autobiography*:

> When I visited Fredericksburg twenty years later, to be welcomed and feted by those who once drove me away, uncle Valentine again accompanied me on the cars in Stafford, and said: 'When we last rode together here, I reproached you for your abolitionism, you made a reply I never forgot. You expressed wonder that we Virginians did not see that the agitation against slavery was a part of a world wide movement for human liberty, -- a movement whose force was immeasurable and inevitable and would ultimately overwhelm our Southern institution. Your prediction has been fulfilled.' We looked out on the dear old fields of Stafford which the tramp of armies had desolated.[171]

Between these two conversations with his uncle Valentine, the Civil War had been fought and lost.

In the winter of 1854, Conway, after the departure of his uncle, was left with the terrible realization that slavery not only crushed the Negro but also destroyed familiar and loving relationships among the whites. The searing experience of being denounced by the townspeople of Falmouth and by his relatives as well made Moncure more willing to believe that the scenes described in Harriet Beecher Stowe's *Uncle Tom's Cabin* might have more truth in them than he thought when he had glanced through a few chapters as they appeared in the *National Era* in 1852. When he reread the book, he did so with clearer eyes, recalling half-forgotten scenes he had witnessed as a child in Stafford County and as a young law student in Warrenton. At least such things might have happened in states further South. Conway still loved Virginia and had no intention of considering himself an exile from the State, though he might for the moment find it expedient to stay away from Falmouth. Late in February 1855 the question was put out of his mind by his ordination by Dr. Burnap as the minister of the First Unitarian Church in Washington.

In a few months the impulse to be on the road once more overcame Moncure. In April 1855, having found another Unitarian minister to fill his pulpit, Conway seized the chance to travel with his organist to parts of Virginia he had never seen. After visiting Harper's Ferry, Weir's Cave, and the Natural Bridge, the two young men found themselves in Charlottesville strolling across the beautiful campus of the University of Virginia. The very sight of bands of students and faculty on the grounds of Thomas Jefferson's own university stirred the missionary zeal of this traveling minister; he lost no time in securing a hall and posting announcements of "an unorthodox sermon" to be preached by himself the next day, which happened to be a Sunday.

The citizens of Charlottesville were as eager as the Athenians of old to hear "some new thing," and the hall was crowded, mainly by university people. Conway was prudent enough to limit his thoughts to the rationalism of the great founder of the University of Virginia, Thomas Jefferson, and made no reference to slavery. The discussion that followed the sermon of this interesting visitor, whose reputation was well known through the *Richmond Examiner*, the *National Intelligencer* and other papers, was altogether friendly and scholarly. At one point Conway amazed his audience by bringing forth a little Greek New

Testament he habitually carried in his pocket and proving to them that his text (II Tim. iii, 16), "All Scripture is given by inspiration of God," should, in fact, have been translated, "Every Scripture inspired by God is profitable."[172] The text thus translated, he pointed out, lends itself to a more rational interpretation. The day's experience was so successful that Conway half-dreamed of the possibility of grappling with the "dark and evil powers" of slavery in his own Commonwealth of Virginia despite the memory of his visit to Falmouth. The dream did not last long.

In the evening, while walking about the campus with his friend from Washington, he observed a huge bonfire around which the students with blackened or masked faces were making a wild "hullabaloo." He soon learned the cause. A near relative of Harriet Beecher Stowe had just arrived in Charlottesville to visit Mrs. McGuffey, the wife of Professor William Holmes McGuffey, famous for his *Readers*. The students had seized the occasion for burning in effigy the author of *Uncle Tom's Cabin*. People in the hotel where the young men were staying assured Conway that "Mrs. Stowe was only the pretext for a frolic" and that he should not take seriously the antics of students who hoped that "the Faculty might be timid about repressing an orgie disguised as an expression of Southern sentiment." They too, of course, shared the same sentiment against Mrs. Stowe. Conway left Charlottesville feeling "an impassable barrier" to entering any ministry in Virginia.[173] He was in a sense self-banished from the state he never ceased to love.

Soon after Conway's "exile" from Virginia, he consulted with Samuel McPherson Jahney, the Quaker preacher of Loudoun County Virginia.[174] Conway remembered that he had sympathized with him when the Virginia legislature had turned a deaf ear to his youthful pamphlet, "Free Education for Virginia," and he hoped to enlist his help in further work for Negroes. The two men framed a petition asking the legislature to repeal the law forbidding the teaching of slaves to read and enact a law forbidding the separation of families sold into slavery. The petition was sent but was never read in the legislature; nor was there any explanation for neglecting it. Conway did receive a private letter from a member saying that, of course, no such petition could possibly be read in the Virginia legislature; that all social systems have evils and that those of the southern way of life were no greater than any others. Conway at last understood; not only could he not preach in Virginia but also he could not make his voice heard in the legislature, where his father and uncles were respected figures. He resolved to put his whole heart into his sermons. From the time he first became a Methodist circuit rider, he had believed the anti-slavery movement in America was essentially religious in nature, and not, as many assumed, political.

Conway's first-hand experience with the Anthony Bums affair made him comprehend the full strength of the pro-slavery forces both in the North and in the South. In the North it had become apparent to him that his abolitionist friends of Concord formed, in fact, but a spearhead movement. They were unable to withstand the Fugitive Slave Act which had been supported in Congress by Daniel Webster and Edward Everett, senators from Massachusetts, and put into action against Tony Burns by Judge Loring. Theodore Parker, William Lloyd Garrison, Wendell Phillips were noble crusaders against an overwhelming majority. The capture and trial of Anthony Burns and his return to Virginia illustrated the untenable position in which that infamous act had placed the country. "So long as there was Slavery in America," Conway concluded, "there was no region where that remorseless spirit was not felt."[175]

Aware of these conflicting thoughts and feelings, Conway resolved, as he took up his duties as minister to the First Unitarian Church in Washington, "to pursue a quiet though not silent course concerning slavery, and not to break completely with my beloved Virginia."[176]

Chapter VII
Unitarian Minister in Washington

Conway had written to Emerson in November that he had not liked the idea of beginning his preaching in Washington without first going to Concord to visit his old friends in order to be sure that he still "rang true." This he did late in the summer of 1855, taking with him his eighteen-year-old sister, Mildred. On the last evening of his stay in Concord, Emerson showed him a new book, *Leaves of Grass*, by an unknown poet, Walt Whitman, and suggested to Conway that he might call on the poet on his way back to Washington.[177] Conway procured the slim volume at once and read it "with joy" on the steamer coming down from Boston to New York. "Democracy had at length its epic," he said to himself, studying the frontispiece-sketch of Walt dressed as a laborer. Conway at once decided that the poem was "prophetic of the good time coming when the vulgar herd should be transformed into noblemen.[178] Here was a poet with whom he must confer.

Leaving his sister with a friend in a New York hotel, Conway took the ferry to Brooklyn, and, after walking "fearfully far" between rows and rows of "small wooded houses with porches," discovered Whitman revising some proof in his printing office several blocks away. In a blunt but not unpleasant manner, Whitman offered Conway his one chair (without a back), and took his seat at the cluttered desk. Emerson was the first subject of the conversation, which continued for many hours. Whitman told Conway that Emerson was the only person who had ever visited him because of his book. So pleased was he with his guest that he insisted on crossing the ferry and walking with him through the streets of New York. "He seemed 'hail fellow' with every man he met, -- all apparently in the labouring class," Conway wrote to Emerson on his return to Washington on September 17, 1855.

To this young aristocrat of Virginia, who nevertheless had been brought up by his Methodist parents with a deep concern for the poor and afflicted, Whitman's manner was in itself a study in democracy – or was it? "He says he is one of that class by choice, that he is personally dear to some thousands of such in New York, who 'love him but cannot make head or tail of his book,'" wrote Conway. "He rides on the stage with the driver. Stops to talk with the old man or woman selling fruit at the street corner. And his dress, etc, is consistent with that. I am quite sure after talking with him that there is much in all this of what you might call 'playing Providence a little with the baser sort.'"[179]

Conway reread *Leaves of Grass*, on his return to his hotel, this time aloud to his sister and her friend. He concluded that Emerson's pantheism was the main source of Whitman's inspiration, which was also affected by his Quaker upbringing and his reading of the Bible. He decided, too, that his informal manner of address was carefully studied. Conway invited Whitman to "an early dinner" the next day with "the girls" at the hotel. Whitman appeared "in baize coat and chequered shirt, in fact, just like the portrait in his book. The ladies were pleased with him; his manners were good, and his talk entertaining."[180]

In the course of these two days Whitman and Conway discussed Shakespeare, Homer, the Democratic Party, *Leaves of Grass*, the Fugitive Slave Act, and many other subjects. Whitman said to Conway when they parted, "I have not met any one so charged with my ideas as you." To Conway, Whitman was "a revelation of human realms" which, till then, he had known only through books. The humble Methodists, among whom he had grown up, were, in a sense, "apart from the world;" for the rest, he had "scholars or persons of marked individuality." Except for the Negroes, he "had known nothing of the working masses," among whom Whitman had moved in "the disguise of their own dress."[181] In his enthusiasm for *Leaves of Grass* (the only book by Whitman that Conway ever liked), Conway felt that he had discovered a new religion, that of humanity.[182]

"A bundle of dogmas" inherited from the Methodists seemed to roll from his shoulders as he saw more imaginatively the actual men and women around him through the eyes of the poet. Similarly, the dogmas of Unitarianism simply faded away in the company of Whitman. "How small a part of my new religion did I learn from those entertaining studies at Divinity Hall!" he wrote. Orthodox Unitarianism, like orthodox Methodism, had provided no answers to such complex and tragic problems as those brought into focus by the capture and return to Virginia of

Anthony Burns. Association with Emerson, Thoreau, and finally with Whitman, suggested a freer, more generous, and, at the same time, more difficult role to be played in Washington by the Unitarian minister in the years ahead. "In fact," wrote Conway, looking back on this period of his life, "I was not equal to all this. I was too young; half of me was a boy and wanted to play. I needed a master! But in my own profession who was there in Washington to look up to?...the sweet friends to whom I looked up in many things looked up to me for guidance in the great issues of the time. And what guidance could I give in my twenty-fourth year?"[183]

On his return to Washington, at the end of his holiday, Conway found the great issue was not slavery but yellow fever, which had been raging during the summer months in Norfolk and Portsmouth. Sermons were being preached in churches throughout the city proving that this "terrible plague" was a judgment sent from heaven to punish the sinners of Virginia. Conway helped his congregation to raise a large sum of money for the sufferers, but he preached, on September 17, a sermon asserting that he saw the Devil in the pestilence rather than God. The Devil, he said, was the slum conditions under which the poor were permitted to live in every large city. The congregation was so pleased with his sermon that they had it printed and distributed among the churches of the city, agreeing with their minister that a "Day of Prayer," ordered by the Common Council, should not be observed because of the financial loss to working people and because such gatherings disseminated germs.[184]

The fame of Conway's rational approach to the problem of the relationship of sin and disease caused his church to be crowded several weeks later when, the yellow fever having abated, the services were resumed. This time Conway preached on "Pharisaism and Feasting." Again, he pointed out that knowledge rather than superstition would ease our human lot. This sermon, too, was printed as a pamphlet by his congregation, and Conway was rewarded by a note from Longfellow: "Thanks for your brave and manly discourse on the 'Fast.' It is a true and valiant word."[185]

The success of these sermons gave Conway a false sense of the liberal views of his congregation. Despite the warning of his predecessor, Dr. Orville Dewey, Conway freely stated his views on slavery in his sermons. Dewey, a friend and follower of

Daniel. Webster, as Conway knew, believed neither in slavery nor in abolition but in discretion. But Webster was now dead, and Charles Sumner, who had opposed the Fugitive Slave Act, had been elected senator from Massachusetts in his place. Conway, therefore, was unimpressed when Dewey told him he had once aroused the wrath of the congregation by referring to the question of slavery and warned his young friend, if he expressed anti-slavery views in Washington, he would certainly not be able to hold his position in the Church.

Feeling only the generous and sympathetic support of his distinguished congregation, and encouraged by the presence of the new senator from Massachusetts, Conway was able for over a year to ignore "the small cloud", slavery, in the fair sky above him. "This cloud might by symbolized by one pew, more finely cushioned than the rest," Conway wrote years later. "It was that in which President Fillmore had sat -- undisturbed by any allusion from the pulpit to his having signed the Fugitive Slave Act."[186] Conway's religious heresies were in fact less disturbing to his congregation than his views on slavery. This, however, he had yet to learn. A conversation with his great-uncle, Justice Daniel, might have given him a hint as to what to expect from his congregation. On a visit to his uncle, Moncure had ventured to bring up the ideas of the abolitionists, and his uncle had promptly closed the discussion with the comment, "I fear those people are very wicked."[187]

Despite his uncle's remark the issue of slavery was no longer avoided by Conway in his sermons. When the Thirty-fourth Congress opened on December 3, 1855, Conway saw that the Kansas-Nebraska Act had made it impossible for the country -- or his church -- to ignore the challenge before Congress. Would Kansas be admitted as a state into the Union according to the constitution proposed by the convention of anti-slavery Kansans meeting in Topeka, or would Congress recognize that legislature chosen by the pro-slavery "Missouri ruffians"? Before an answer could be given, something very like civil war had broken out in Kansas. On December 14, after a heated discussion of the question in the Senate, Senator Summer wrote to Theodore Parker, "All things here indicate bad feelings. I have never seen so little intercourse and commingling among the senators of opposite opinions." Both Sumner and Parker were members of the

Massachusetts-Kansas Committee that had helped finance emigrants from the Northeast to Kansas to contend against the pro-slavery invaders from across the border.

"It is not possible," Emerson had said, "to extricate one's self from the questions in which our age is involved."[188] He had on February 6, 1855, spoken before the American Anti-Slavery Society of New York, proposing that the southern slave-holders be compensated for the loss of their slaves. Conway agreed with Emerson that one could not avoid the issues of the day but knew that Emerson's proposal would never be accepted by either the North or the South. To him it seemed that the forces of the "new South" and the "new North" were evenly balanced and that the hostility rapidly mounting between them was more religious than political – though concealed under the language of the Constitution and the Compromise Act of 1850.

An older generation had with difficulty maintained the status quo, but the new generation in both the North and the South had become more outspoken and more fanatical in tone after the fighting had broken out in Kansas. Abolitionists in the North, referring to the slave, asserted that "God by our conscience and the Declaration of Independence demands his freedom;" firebrands in the South declared that "God by his providence and by his word has decreed the Negro's slavery." Conway understood the religious undertone of the political debates all too well -- and foresaw that the outcome would be war. Having been nurtured in the South and educated in the North, Conway felt that he was peculiarly fitted to voice a view that he realized would not find many sympathetic ears in his congregation. Separation of North and South seemed to him the only means by which war -- which he hated worse than slavery -- could be avoided.[189]

On January 24, 1856, President Pierce in effect instructed Congress to recognize the government set up in Kansas by the pro-slavery emigrants from Missouri, with which, he stated, the federal government was powerless to interfere. On January 26, Conway preached on a previously announced subject, "The One Path; of the Duties of North and South," before a large congregation that included many congressmen attracted by the subject.[190] Before delivering his sermon, Conway submitted it to one member of his congregation, Daniel Reaves Goodloe, who was himself an anti-slavery exile from North Carolina. Goodloe's approval encouraged Conway to deliver the sermon, which was at once printed as a pamphlet and widely circulated in Washington.

Conway, in his sermon, urged that the question of slavery be looked upon as a moral and not a political one. "It was the saddest day that ever dawned upon the country, when this was made any other than a moral question." He further pointed out that both the North and the South were responsible for slavery, since both were members of the federal government. Possibly, he suggested, an impasse had now been reached which could only be resolved by dissolving the Union:

> If the two portions of the country cannot unite, and feel at the same moment ready to face the Eternal Judge, with the full conviction that they are each completely true to God, and to every man, white and black, bond and free, let them sink together beneath the waters under the earth but never, never unite or remain united.[191]

Remembering his own recent experience in Falmouth, Conway pointed out that the South had erred in suppressing free speech. But the North, he said, was guilty of supporting the Fugitive Slave Act. "What abject cant is it to say the North has nothing to do with Slavery!" shouted this young Virginian from the pulpit to his confused congregation. He himself was opposed to slavery, but Conway knew from experience that many honest people in the South believed slavery to be morally right. Though the men and women he most admired in the North were abolitionists, Conway had learned also from experience that many in the North cynically supported slavery for their own commercial or political advantage.[192] What then was "The One Path" for honest men on both sides to follow?

> We can all imagine two men of entire candour and courtesy -- the one Southern, and believing slavery right in itself, the other Northern, and believing it wrong -- coming to an understanding on the subject; the common postulates being that neither must himself do what he believes essentially wrong.[193]

The only "right thing" for those who were unable to establish a common ground was to separate, for no society could be built on what half the population considered morally wrong. "First pure, then peaceable," was the text of his sermon. Both the North and the South were "impure" in their attitude toward slavery.

Horace Greeley, with his eyes-half closed, listened to the sermon and at once telegraphed a summary to the *Tribune*, ending with the remark;

> As Mr. Conway is a native of Virginia, and has spent nearly all his days in slaveholding communities, it will hardly be pretended that he does not know what slavery is. His discourse was very able as well as fearless, and was heard with profound interest by a most intelligent congregation. Mr. Conway expects to lose his pastorship because of it. I have heard him before speak incidentally in the same vein, but never before so clearly and fully."[194]

Whether because of this news story in the *Tribune* or merely because of the known anti-slavery position of his paper, Greeley, two days afterwards, was assaulted on the steps of the Capitol by Congressman Albert Rust of Arkansas. The outcome for Greeley might have been worse had Rust not been somewhat inebriated. Greeley's wounds were sufficiently severe, however, to keep him confined for a few days, enabling Conway to call on him several times and to talk over with him his views on the political situation, as well as his own relation to his Church. As a result, Greeley telegraphed the *Tribune* on February 9: "I was mistaken in stating that the Rev. Mr. Conway expected to lose the pastorship of the Unitarian Society here. That was the inference of a mutual friend, not Mr. Conway's own apprehension. He preached as he thought just, and has no belief that his society will dismiss him for so doing."[195]

Greeley's correction in the *Tribune* might have inspired the church committee to insert a reproof of their minister in the annual report of February 1856 rather than ask for his resignation. The committee stated that it "deeply deplored" the fact that Conway had discussed "in the pulpit a much vexed and angrily contested political question, and this too at a season of great political excitement." Conway replied to the committee at once by preaching a sermon on February 17 from the text, "Stand fast therefore in the liberty wherewith Christ hath made us free," and reminded his congregation of the historic tradition of liberal thought on which the Unitarian Society was based. The pamphlet was published with the title, "Spiritual Liberty." He learned from the events that followed that "Slavery was still too potent at the Capital to tolerate my antislavery discourses."[196]

A certain ominous peace followed this sermon, at least as far as the minister himself knew.[197] In April, however, Conway received from the committee a letter stating that many friends of the Church were apprehensive of future disharmony in the congregation if their minister should persist in his references to slavery in his sermons. The letter ended with a carefully worded suggestion:

> Should you determine otherwise, however, it is respectfully submitted whether it would not be better that our connection should cease at once, than that our hitherto united and harmonious congregation should be broken up; that the small band who so long struggled to maintain and sustain a pulpit devoted to the cause of Unitarian Christianity should be scattered, and the high purposes of their organization sacrificed to advance the purposes of this or that political faction.[198]

To this letter Conway made no reply. However, the Church building itself made its own answer -- its southern wall began to bulge ominously and then to crack so extensively that it was no longer safe for services. Nor could a divided congregation possibly raise money to rebuild the church. Conway proposed at once that he go on a money-raising journey to the Northern Churches; the committee that had recently hoped to dismiss him now gladly granted him permission to do what he could to rebuild the crumbling church. Many saw these events as a clear omen from above. Conway saw in them a chance to sway the pro-slavery members of his congregation by timely aid from his anti-slavery friends in the North.

Conway's first stop was at a gathering of liberal Quakers and Unitarians on May 22, 1856, in a "beautiful grove" in

Longwood, Chester County, Pennsylvania, where he made a plea for his church. Lucretia Mott, who attended the meeting, responded to the speech with eloquent approval and lent her aid in collecting a substantial sum for the repair of the church in Washington. Conway's address was sufficiently distinguished to inspire a member of the group to write a letter to the *Tribune* (May 29, 1856) ending with the remark, "Lastly, I may mention a brave and manly speech upon Slavery, by the Rev. Moncure D. Conway of Washington manifesting all possible charity toward the slaveholders, he nevertheless denounced the system, and pledged his endeavor against it in bold and refreshing terms."[199] The next day, Conway read in the papers that, at the very moment when he was delivering his address, Charles Sumner, senator from Massachusetts, was being beaten over the head by Representative Preston Smith. Brooks of South Carolina for his speech on May 19, 1856, "The Crime Against Kansas."

Conway continued on his way to Concord where he arrived early in June and spent several nights in the Emerson home. Emerson appeared to Conway depressed by the latest news of the attack on Senator Sumner; he observed, "It looks as if in this matter of slavery the nation had gone a turn too far for recovery." Emerson called a meeting at the town hall of Concord where a "substantial sum" was raised for Conway's church.

Full of the news of Sumner's injuries, details of which were appearing in the papers, Conway stopped off in Philadelphia on his return trip to call on his old Unitarian friend, Dr. W. H. Furness, and discuss with him Sumner's speeches in Congress and the reasons for Brooks' fury.[200] The facts, as given in the newspaper reports, could now be pieced together. Brooks, a complete stranger to Sumner, had suddenly appeared at his desk on the floor of Congress, after the session was over, and, with a brief statement that South Carolina and Senator Andrew Butler (Brooks' uncle) had been insulted by Sumner's speech, lifted his cane and rained blows on Sumner's head, leaving the senator unconscious.

Furness and Conway agreed there were several regrettable terms in the speech -- mainly against Senators John Murray Mason and Stephen A. Douglas -- but the real cause of Brooks' anger was that he did not understand Sumner's literary allusions to Don Quixote and Sancho Panza, which he took to be insults directed at his uncle. [201] Sumner had likened Butler to Don Quixote, paying his respects to "the harlot, Slavery," and Douglas to "the squire of Slavery, its very Sancho Panza, ready to do its humiliating office." The underlying cause of the attack, they agreed, was the mounting tension between the North and the South -- neither of them admitting that their friend had spoken immoderately and personally.

While Conway was still in Philadelphia, the first convention of the newly organized Republican Party convened in Morristown, New Jersey, and nominated John Charles. Frémont for the presidency. "Hopefully" working for "the dissolution of the Union," the American Anti-Slavery Society, of which Garrison was president, gave its full support to the new Republican Party. Though Conway never joined the society, he attended the meeting and decided that henceforth this was to be his party, non-partisan though he had declared himself. The sole aim of the Republicans was to free the federal government from all connections with slavery, and the title of the candidate was the "Pathfinder."[202] Conway felt a certain poetic appropriateness in the very title of the candidate since he was to stand for the idea that Conway himself had espoused in his sermon, "The One Path."

On his return to Washington, Conway found the atmosphere – and especially that of his own congregation – charged with excitement over the recent quarrel in Congress. Brooks was their hero, Conway soon discovered, while Sumner – whom they considered properly chastised – was still confined to his bed. Conway often visited the senator and read aloud to him the daily newspaper reports of the course of the investigation and trial of Brooks. As the summer advanced, Conway's indignation mounted, especially when it became known that Brooks was to receive only a reprimand for the assault, that his friends proposed to honor him with a dinner, and that the students of the University of Virginia had sent Brooks a gold-headed cane as a memento of the attack in defense of the "honor" of his uncle. The *Richmond Enquirer* of June 12 summed up the view of the papers of the South when it said, "In the main, the press of the South applauds the conduct of Mr. Brooks without condition or limitation."[203]

The realization that the North and the South were so drastically opposed to one another in their comment on Brooks' assault, together with the daily news of the fighting in Kansas, convinced Conway that, without a strenuous effort on the part of all concerned citizens, war could not be avoided. Looking back on this period many years later, Conway wrote, "We were all caught in the whirlwind. This struggle in our church represented nobody's calm sentiment or purpose. Washington was under menace; congressmen went armed to their seats; we were warned that our church would be mobbed."[204] The excitement soon spread to Falmouth: "I think you had better not come here under the circumstances,"[205] his mother wrote on July 5, 1856, in reply to Conway's suggestion that he might slip away to Virginia for a family visit.

Believing that war itself was now the great danger to the country, Conway took as the subject of his sermon of July 6, 1856, "War, and its Present Threatenings." His text was, "He who takes to the sword shall perish by the sword," and his example was the Crimean War, just than drawing to its bloody close. Conway must have astounded his congregation as he lashed himself into a rhetorical fury against slavery and its accompanying war. He spoke, he said, in the presence of "the fearful vision" of war, knowing that this would be his last sermon "in the dear old church." At times he became so moved by his own words that he could continue only with the greatest difficulty. "Slavery takes naturally to bludgeons or pistols," said this youthful preacher with Sumner in mind. "Freedom should as naturally take to reason, truth of thought, speech, and act." Looking down at the faces before him, Conway practically challenged them to dismiss him. Throwing caution to the wind, he declared:

> For every man in this country Slavery has a bribe ... [Slavery holds] a lash over all who will not obey its behest...I feel the presence of its great infernal power in this house to-day, -- there lurking among you, whispering, 'Don't stand such preaching as this; if you do your friends will turn away from you, and you will be called an abolitionist.' It is up here whispering to me. 'If you do not stop this preaching against slavery, it will have cudgel over your head, -- your friends will be fewer than they are now.' ... One thing is now forever settled, that the subject is to be definitely dealt with. It is up now, and cannot he

put down by any power, nor postponed. Henceforth no freeman is ever going to be quiet.[206]

When Conway ended his sermon that morning, he announced the hymn as usual, and the organist played the tune. The choir, however, remained silent, not so much from disapproval of their minister's words as from sheer stupefaction at his boldness. Many pro-slavery members of the church had already ceased to attend, but the pews were filled with anti-slavery supporters who pressed forward after the service to shake the hand of the preacher. Conway's sermon, since it bore on the crucial question of slavery, was headline news throughout the country. He received support for his views, he says, from "eminent men in all parts of the country." A typical letter of approval came from a group of leading citizens in Jefferson, Ohio, among whom were the father and brother of William Dean Howells.[207] However, Conway knew then and later that he should not have spoken as he did, for "harmony had left that old church forever."[208]

A week later, July 13, 1856, the church committee called the congregation together and put before the members the question as to whether a minister who "persists in this desecration of his pulpit shall continue in the exercise of his function as a pastor."[209] Since the meeting was packed with Conway's supporters, the question was not voted on that night but was referred to a special committee. Services in the church were suspended until the first Sunday in October when the resolution to request Conway's resignation was to be voted upon. Conway continued to preach in a hall engaged by his friends, and this was filled every Sunday.

Conway decided to put the whole case before his friend, the Rev. William Henry Channing, then in London. Channing had occupied the pulpit of Conway's church for several months and had wished to be appointed minister. Channing was the nephew of the great Unitarian preacher of Boston who, for many years, had been known for his stand against slavery. He was a friend of Emerson's and shared with him the hope that emancipation might be effected by purchase of the slaves -- a view that Conway too had looked upon with favor while in Massachusetts. Channing's wise and tactful reply to Conway's letter of August 13, 1856, opened with the remark that he had envied Conway's opportunity of preaching at the First Unitarian Church of Washington, for it had seemed to him good way to further the fight against slavery. He, became reconciled to his disappointment, wrote Channing, because he believed that a young Virginian acquainted with the evils of slavery at first hand could speak more persuasively than he with his northern prejudices.

Channing had followed Conway's career with sympathy and approval. "You have done well," he wrote, but now he was no longer in sympathy with his friend's position. "I must go on to say, if I understand your views of the policy fitted for the crisis, I disagree with you," he wrote. "And pray set me right if I am wrong. Ever since, at the time of Texas annexation, it became clear that it is the fixed will of the people of the United States of America not to break up the Union, I have said, 'There is but one work to be done there, and that is to make the Union free.' The wise, just, honourable, and humane way of doing this – as for five years and more I have taken every fit occasion to argue – is by a common cooperative movement for emancipation, at the common cost."

Channing here voiced Emerson's proposal for reimbursing the slaveholders. Like Conway, however, he had little hope for a solution. Nor as a New Englander could he agree with Conway as to the hope of a peaceful disunion of North and South. According to Channing:

> The slave oligarchy has mistaken Northern magnanimity for meanness and madly resolved to keep their pecuniary and political advantages, they now trust the reactionary spirit of the age and stake their all for a universal slave empire. The real question at issue then – forced upon the freemen of the United States of America – is, "slavery extension or slavery abolition throughout the length and breadth of the land." All concealment is thrown away. All compromises are gone forever. We must come to a settlement of the question once for all. Are we to yield to the slave oligarchy? Are we to leave the Union or are we to subdue the "faction"? We are not to yield one hair's breadth to their preposterous claim of "balance of power," – meaning, thereby, submission to their usurped rule. If

> anybody leaves the Union, it must be the slaveholders. And if they remain they must agree to change their institutions, necessary time and aid for so doing being ensured. That is the "ultimatum" at which I arrive, after maturest consideration. Dissolution of the Union involves war inevitably without thereby necessarily destroying slavery. If there must be war then, let it be for the abolition of slavery within the Union. Henceforth this should be our watchword: "The Union shall be kept, and that Union shall be free. The Union of Freemen forever!"[210]

Conway did not think emancipation could be achieved within the Union, nor did he consider the suggestion that disunion might cause war and in no way help the slaves. From the tone of the letter, rather than from the thought expressed, Conway believed he saw a way of reuniting his own congregation. Why should not the committee offer the position to Channing? This possibility Conway decided to keep in mind until he had heard the final decision as to his own future from the church committee.

After a stormy argument at a meeting of the congregation on October 5, the resolution to drop the minister was passed by a majority of five, for many of Conway's friends had not returned to the Capitol from their summer vacations. A practical problem immediately arose. Those who supported Conway pointed out the money he had raised for the repair of the church had been donated in good faith by friends in the North who believed they were aiding the anti-slavery forces. They proposed, therefore, that the congregation split and that the anti-slavery members use the money to build a new church of their own.

Conway, in his perplexity, wrote at once to Emerson telling him that he had been dismissed from his position in the Unitarian Church, and asking him to write a letter stating that the money raised in Concord was to be used for the church building only if the Church maintained its anti-slavery position.[211] This Emerson did as soon as he heard from Conway. Emerson's letter began, "My dear Sir, -- I remember well your pleas for the 'Church of Freedom' in Washington, made in our town hall last June," and, after a full review of the agreement, ended, "I entreat you and them not to make us ashamed of our spending, by perverting the church to the support of slavery."

All the money Conway had received from the group in Concord, and from other sources, he deposited with the treasurer of the church to be held subject to his order. Many of his friends and supporters were still urging him to establish a new church with a more liberal attitude toward slavery. Instead, Conway suggested the appointment of Channing for a reunited church and accepted an invitation he had received from the First Congregational Church of Cincinnati, for his fame had traveled westward.[212] Conway's congregation -- which never ceased to love their young minister -- accepted his suggestion and his resignation in good spirit and listened with mixed feelings to his farewell sermon late in October.[213] Conway said goodbye to his congregation with tears. In his heart, he felt that he had destroyed "a beautiful world," for he had many devoted friends and relatives in Washington. But for the tension caused by the political situation, he might well have spent the rest of his life preaching to "an educated and refined congregation." Most of his sermons, indeed, had had nothing to do with slavery; they were literary in tone and often made use of little-known stories from mythology as well as the Bible. Conway had "formed many intimate friendships with thoughtful individuals"; he had no political or social ambitions; he was happy in his "dear little study on Sixth Street." He was even slowly mending his ties with his family in Falmouth as a long letter from his mother indicates:

> Your father was much gratified as your affectionate remembrance of him in your letter. For me, I rather think that the trials and sorrows of my children, if endured for conscience sake, are the most nourishing aliment for my parental love, even when I cannot myself see the necessity of the ultra position you have assumed. But "let every man be fully persuaded in his own mind, to his own master he standeth or falleth," is my doctrine, and I cannot presume to encroach on the rule which God has prescribed.

Conway received his mother's letter in November 1856, soon after his arrival in Cincinnati as minister of the First Congregational Church of that city. Having rebelled against the church of her youth, Mrs. Conway was better prepared to hear her son had modified his Unitarianism and become a

Congregationalist![214] Conway was already homesick and was planning to return to Washington for Christmas. He invited his mother to join him in Baltimore since both his parents thought it undesirable for their son to visit the family in Falmouth. His mother pointed out to him in her refusal,

> I cannot leave home at Christmas: I am the greatest slave here at any season to the servants of our household, who are raised in such a state of dependence of thought and action that they will not even make an effort to make their own clothing, -- indeed are too stupid to know how unless I direct him. Oh, what a thralldom to me -- the white slave -- mentally and bodily! I often think that if some one were to arouse me some morning from my sleep with the intelligence that every one had left the premises, I should feel such a sense of freedom and relief from responsibility (more oppressive as I grow older) that I should be heard singing Te Deum laudamus, -- could I but banish the knowledge that they would be in a state of extreme suffering and that their numerous babies would perish. If any abolitionist could know exactly what I have endured from over-pressure of work for thirty negroes for the last month, and the worry I have had to get them to do any work for themselves, they would look upon me with greater pity than on them.

Conway read his mother's letter soon after James Buchanan was elected as president in November 1856. Mrs. Conway's weary comment reminded her son of their political differences about which he had said nothing to his family. Nor did he recognize the wisdom of his mother's words:

> So Buchanan is elected according to report. I feel little interest in politics, it is so low in its grade here, where every principle is involved in the narrow limits of party, till I feel ready to exclaim with a Scotchman, on one occasion, "Knaves all." I care nothing about it, except I believe that Fremont's election would put links in the chain of slavery a hundred years long; for disunion would ensue, and then the South would have proslaveryism

> carried to a revengeful extent, and so end all our efforts to keep their condition among us who wish to do what we can for them as comfortable as may be under existing circumstances. I think both ultra proslavery men and abolitionists of the rabid fire-and-fagot sort say in their hearts there is no God to "hear the groaning of the prisoner." God's mills grind slow, yet they grind exceeding small, and he will right what abuses he sees on the earth by his own means in this or any other matter. And his greatest reformations have ever been commenced through all time by the small human means, without knowledge of what their efforts were to lead to, -- they only doing what duly personally required of them.[215]

The election of Buchanan was a bitter disappointment to Conway. He had hoped that John C. Frémont might hasten the grinding of "God's mills," for Frémont would have put an end to the war in Kansas -- or so Moncure thought. No doubt the slave states would then have seceded, but their loss would only have defined more clearly the limits of the land of freedom. "Disunion means a truer Union," he felt; slavery would eventually come to an end without war. Such were the illusions of Conway and many others at that time of mounting tension.

Conway could not hope to explain his strange career to his family in Falmouth with whom he disagreed in politics as well as religion. "In my Virginia home," he wrote, "Love remained, though for a time draped as for one dead; and one heart even believed in me, I suspect, at the cost of her strict orthodoxy."[216] But family ties, though strained, were never broken. "I shall see little of you henceforth myself," his mother had written in the same letter of November 1856, "but I hope that you will one day have a home where your sister and brother can visit you, -- if you get a sensible, good, lady-like wife." In spite of the stresses and strains of the times, Conway managed to keep in touch with his family in Virginia. He soon found just such a wife as his mother described, seated before him in his new congregation, and was married before his first year in Cincinnati was over.

In 1858, not many months after Moncure took up his new duties, he gathered together his sermons of the last two years, called them *Tracts for To-day* and dedicated them to his father and mother as follows:

To My Parents

> I dedicate this book, knowing that, whatever they shall find here which shall recall painful differences of belief, it would grieve them far more to think that I had swerved from the lessons of directness and sincerity which, by word and life, they have ever taught as before all, and which they have a right to claim from me always and everywhere.[217]

It is to be hoped that this little volume of fourteen sermons -- vague in theology, rhetorical in tone, but undoubtedly inspiring to the congregations who heard them – brought some comfort to the long-suffering couple in Conway House. The events of the day, however, soon caught up both Conway and his parents. On March 6, 1857, two days after President Buchanan took office, Chief Justice Roger Brooke Taney handed down the decision of the Supreme Court in the Dred Scott case. The whole country moved closer to war.

Chapter VIII
Cincinnati and *The Dial*

On the day in November 1856 that Conway took over the ministry of the First Congregational Church in Cincinnati, a friend observed to him, "There are about ten millions of dollars in that congregation."[218]

After several weeks, the young minister concluded that the real reason the rich man in the Bible story found it difficult to enter the kingdom of heaven was that he was loath to spend his money on humanitarian reforms while here on earth. Conway decided to urge on the members of his wealthy and fashionable congregation a fresh interpretation of their Christian duty and began his first sermon with the words, "I determined not to know anything among you save Jesus Christ and him crucified." The figure nailed to the cross, said he, was that of the fugitive slave; it was also that of the drunkard, the prostitute, the insane, the diseased, and the neglected. In a sense, the new minister argued. reason itself was perpetually crucified by superstition, fear and selfishness. Cincinnati lacked hospitals, schools, housing. He pointed out that the means were obviously available among the rich of the city; all that was needed was an open heart and the courage to act in the tradition of the Reformation.

"Good sentiments" were not enough to redeem the world from "the evils which afflict and degrade mankind," Conway declared. If all men claim they favor freedom and condemn slavery, why then is slavery practiced in some form in every part of the world? Remembering his recent experiences with the Unitarian Church in Washington, Conway said to his new congregation, "There are those who would suppress a free discussion of the slavery question in the country, and especially in the pulpit." These same people are indignant when told that they are supporting the attacker of Senator Sumner. Though men know that slavery is an evil, they are willing to "go on in their serene way, condemning all who lift a finger" for the destruction of this evil.

The men of Boston, who had taken no stand against the Fugitive Slave Act, were suddenly overcome with anger and emotion when they saw Anthony Burns carried manacled through the streets back to the ship that returned him to his master in Virginia. The triumph of "the cause of African Freedom," Conway told his congregation, is more important than any of the other reforms with which the church was concerned. "We devote ourselves to what is easy to devote ourselves to," rather than to a cause such as the abolition of slavery, which is entrenched with interests, laws, powers, talent, and wealth on its side."

"I stand before you a stranger," said Conway in closing his first sermon in Cincinnati, "an exile from my church, robbed by Slavery of that first and dearest association; robbed by Slavery of my own home; my parents forced to go to a distant city to see me, -- you will allow me some reason for hating slavery."

Conway soon discovered that his conservative congregation loved him the more for his impassioned words against slavery. Cincinnati was at that time the first stop of the Underground Railroad between Kentucky and Canada, and the daily sight of groups of escaping slaves was a familiar one. Perhaps also, in this initial sermon, his listeners recognized the voice of Emerson, whom they had frequently heard on the lecture platform of the Cincinnati Lyceum, who a decade earlier had publicly allied himself with the abolitionists.

In January 1857, Conway, learning that Emerson was on a western lecture tour, urged him to include Cincinnati in his circuit. On January 29, Emerson wrote to his wife from Cleveland: "I very reluctantly decided to stay at Cincinnati, having many times in heart turned my face homeward not wishing to trust the prairie any more." But Conway had "worked so hard, and filled the papers with paragraphs and persuaded so many people that they ought to be glad to listen that it seemed perverse, when the days were really at my disposal, not to stay." Emerson came and stayed a week, addressing large audiences on beauty and poetry, the subjects of two unfinished essays he had with him. "Mr. Conway has taken a deal of pains for my Benefit," wrote Emerson to his wife a few days after his arrival.[219]

Emerson would no doubt have been surprised had he ever learned how his presence affected the impressionable young minister who was his host. Without warning Conway in advance,

Emerson quietly took his place in one of the front pews of the First Congregational Church on the Sunday morning of his visit. While Conway was administering the sacrament to members of his congregation, he happened to glance up over the bowed heads before him and catch the eye of Emerson. He remembered at once that Emerson had left the ministry because of his disbelief in this ceremony, and Conway never again conducted a communion service; the new minister's unorthodox interpretation of ritual proved in time less acceptable to his congregation than his stand on slavery.

Though Conway was soon dubbed "heretic" by some members of his flock, his sermons, fully discussed in the newspapers, brought renown to the church as well as to the minister. Conway could hardly meet the demands for lectures and sermons that poured in on him from neighboring congregations, Methodist, Presbyterian, Catholic, also Jewish. Curiosity concerning this eloquent and lively young Virginian, both the son of a slaveholder and a disciple of Emerson, made Conway a well-known personality on the streets of Cincinnati.

A test of Conway's attitude towards slavery came during his first spring in his adopted city. Citizens of Cincinnati interpreted Chief Justice Taney's decision in the Dred Scott case as meaning that "black men have no rights which white men are bound to respect."[220] Scott, a Missouri slave, had sued for his right to freedom when his master had taken him first to the free state of Illinois and then to the northern part of the Louisiana Purchase, where, according to the Missouri Compromise, slavery was forbidden. The Supreme Court declared, however, that no Negro or descendant of a slave could be considered a citizen of the United States and therefore could not bring his case to a federal court. Moreover, said the court, Congress had no right to forbid slavery in the territories and the Missouri Compromise, hitherto untested, was never valid.

The decision, which delighted the pro-slavery Democrats in the South, was a challenge to the new Republican Party of the North. As usual, Conway was torn between his sense of loyalty to the South and his allegiance to the anti-slavery ideas of his friends in the North. It seemed to him that Taney, in the Dred Scott decision, had interpreted the question in the light of the constitution, expressing no view at all concerning the right or wrong of slavery itself. Taney and his supporters were misguided, he thought, in that they failed to take into account the fact that the framers of the constitution were for the most part anti-slavery men, forced to yield to South Carolina and Georgia in order to gain support for the new government.

George Hoadly, Cincinnati Superior Court judge, later governor of Ohio, and Alphonso Taft, who became United States attorney-general, were members of Conway's congregation and his personal friends.[221] Neither of these men regarded the Dred Scott decision as legally sound. [222] Nor were they under any illusion as to the effect of the verdict on Cincinnati, the southernmost station of the "Underground Railway."[223] Just as Hoadly and Taft had predicted, thousands of Negroes broke up their homes in Cincinnati after the Dred Scott decision and fled to Canada. Thousands more streamed over the Ohio border from Kentucky, unless waylaid by their owners, and moved across the city on their way North. "The decision, which made slavery virtually the law of the land, was as the trump of Judgment Day," wrote Conway in his *Autobiography*.[224] Finding himself associated at last with an anti-slavery congregation, he saw no "cloud on the horizon" caused by his political views on the Dred Scott verdict.

Conway was soon to learn, however, that unanimity of opinion on slavery did not prevail in the West any more than in the East. Sent by his board to a Conference of Western Unitarian Churches, in Alton, Illinois, Conway was soon involved in controversy. When delegations from Kentucky and Missouri objected to the proposal that the churches adopt a stronger anti-slavery platform than the weak stand they had taken three years earlier, Conway was asked to prepare a new resolution. Though he consulted with moderate members of the conference before submitting his suggestion, the final wording of the manifesto failed to resolve the conflict that threatened to end the conference. When news of the controversy reached Cincinnati, Conway was described in the *Enquirer* as "an ambitious agitator."[225] From now on, he knew that there was, indeed, a "cloud on the horizon." The *Christian Inquirer*, the New York Unitarian organ, wrote of the meeting.

"In short, it was the old, oily, lukewarm, doughy, cottony talk, heard any time in the last ten years in conferences, caucuses, pulpits, and the corners of the streets; a part of the great, weak policy of do-nothing, say-nothing, stand-aside-and-let-alone acquiescence and compromise, under which Slavery has grown so strong, rampant and aggressive, and Liberty so emasculated and paralyzed."[226] However, since the stronger resolution was finally passed, Conway felt that he no longer was under an obligation to preach anti-slavery sermons. What a chance for him to follow his own growing interest in literature, science, philosophy, music, and art!

Conway was by then thoroughly enjoying the gay and cultivated life of Cincinnati into which he threw himself with his customary ardor. With the exception of Boston, Cincinnati was the most musically inclined American city. Since a third of the population was German, the city could support a fine orchestra, many choral societies, and an operatic season in Pike's Opera House, where Conway heard the famous French-Italian Adelina Patti sing as a girl. There was, moreover, a public library where Conway read widely in all directions.

Best of all, there were in the town two flourishing theaters. Conway found himself able for the first time to "indulge [his] passion for the drama," for which he had acquired a taste in Boston. These theaters were sustained throughout the year by stock companies, but occasionally they welcomed traveling actors such as Edwin A. Sothern, whom Conway came to know personally, Charlotte Cushman and Fanny Kemble, whom he had met at the home of the Longfellows. Conway was soon invited to join the literary club that met every week to enjoy cigars, Catawba wine, recitations, and satiric squibs on the personalities of the town. Besides the usual round of dances, picnics, and masquerade balls, there was a lecture hall, for the lyceum had not yet given way to vaudeville later seen in many cities and towns. Here Conway heard old friends such as Edward Everett, Oliver Wendell Holmes, Louis Agassiz, Wendell Phillips, and Henry Ward Beecher with whom he had the opportunity to discuss the issues of the day. Lectures, social clubs, theater, church, concerts, and school seemed to the young minister natural partners in the never ending struggle to soften, elevate, and enlighten the hard hearts and superstitious minds of men and women.

Conway missed no opportunity to widen his own horizon and was soon writing reviews of "the classical concerts, the picture exhibitions, the operas, and plays." Learning that Horace Mann, whose "Report From Massachusetts" had challenged him to write his pamphlet on education, was the newly-appointed head of Antioch College in Yellow Springs, Ohio, Conway visited that institution early in 1857, hoping to interview Mann for the *Cincinnati Gazette.* When he arrived, Conway made his way to the only inn of Yellow Springs and was soon conversing with the solitary guest, a beautiful woman who told him that the inn had been built by a now-defunct community called "Memnona." The community (suspected of free-love tendencies) had been denounced by Horace Mann and his wife. When Conway called on Mann the next morning, he found him still outraged by the very thought of Memnona, which he called "the superfetation of diabolism upon polygamy."

After listening to him address the students in the college chapel, Conway concluded, though Mann was "radical in politics and a rationalist in religion, the puritan survived in his ethics." But he admired the "tall slender Horace Mann, with his pure, intellectual face beneath its crown of white hair."[227] He returned to Cincinnati convinced that coeducation had "a refining" influence on the boys and girls of Antioch College, who thoroughly enjoyed "their weekly receptions, concerts and theatricals." Conway's visit to Yellow Springs and his interview with Horace Mann were duly written up for the *Cincinnati Gazette* under the pseudonym "Optimist" -- a signature soon recognized in the town as that of the new minister of the First Congregational Church.[228] A journalist as well as a preacher, Conway saw no reason why the two roles should not strengthen one another. His congregation, however, soon grew uneasy.

Conway's religious heresies and his anti-slavery views seemed less alarming to members of his church than his interest in the theater, on which a minister in the Midwest in the 1850s was expected to frown. Years later, Conway wrote, concerning his "happy years" in Cincinnati, that his "disbelief in miracles brought on a struggle" among the members of his congregation, who also "expected me to be more puritanical..."[229] Conway, however, responded to the whispered criticism of his flock by preaching a sermon on theater-going. As usual, the subject of his sermon was announced in the newspapers, and consequently the First Congregational Church, on the morning of June 7, 1857, was filled with all the actors, actresses, and theater managers of the town. To their delight Conway pointed out from his pulpit that the theater was one of the most important cultural assets of any community and should be considered a natural ally of the church. In an informal way, the theater people of Cincinnati adopted Conway as their chaplain, never failing to send him free tickets to their performances. Conway's sermon on the theater was printed and widely circulated. In a moment of bravado, he sent a copy to his family in Falmouth and was astonished to learn in a letter from his mother that his father had read it aloud to the family, remarking, 'I am not prepared to object to one word in it.'"[230] A Methodist in Falmouth was, after all, still a Virginian!

Sometime during his first year in Cincinnati, Conway met and fell in love with a member of his congregation, Ellen Davis Dana, whom he married on June 1, 1858. Ellen, a beautiful, brown-eyed woman of eighteen, came from an old and distinguished New England family and was as "sensible, good and lady-like" as Conway's mother could wish. At the time, Ellen was also as friendly and as interested in new ideas and in people as Conway could desire of a wife, who must also have enough commonsense for two.

The Rev. Dr. William Henry Furness came from Philadelphia to marry the couple under a bower of white roses which fond members of the congregation had constructed for their minister and his bride. A musical society of Cincinnati serenaded the pair, and the entire bridal party, including Dr. Furness, boarded a steamboat and set off on an excursion down the Ohio River to Mammoth Caves, Kentucky. Moncure and Ellen were provided with a bridal stateroom, appropriately decorated with Venuses, Cupids and garlanded Graces, while their cheerful companions stowed themselves away in the narrow quarters of the cabins. When the boat put in to shore, the bride and bridesmaids donned "indescribable bloomers" and spent a happy day groping about the "weird underworld" of the cave. It was a perfect honeymoon for a sociable couple, especially when the groom was interested in geology as well as theology and both the bride and groom were poor.

Though Conway had lost all of his savings ($2,000) in the crash of 1857 and was constrained to ask for an advance of his salary in order to set up housekeeping, the year 1858 was a happy one in every way. Conway was earning a handsome salary of two thousand dollars, he was writing for magazines and papers, and he was in great demand as a preacher to Catholic, Methodist, and Jewish congregations. In the evenings, the small house at 114 Hopkins Street was always full of guests, many of them actors, writers, or visiting lecturers, and conversation was marked by lively discussion of such subjects as "Women's Rights," Darwin's new book *On the Origin of Species* (1859), politics, or the latest opera. Conway and his wife were inclined to look upon their poverty as "a sort of joke," even after the arrival of their first child, for what could life hold that they did not possess?

One suspects that the joke was more apparent to Moncure than to Ellen, and it was she who consulted two tried and trusted members of the congregation as to how best to invest their small savings. Serious young minister though he was, Conway was a member of a flourishing chess club in Cincinnati and, for a while, edited a weekly column on the game for the *Cincinnati Commercial.* Having been brought up in a Methodist household where card-playing was frowned upon, chess was the only indoor game he had mastered.

So fascinated was Conway by the game, when he found himself in New York in the summer of 1858, he hastened to the Chess Club to watch the experts. A world champion, Paul Morphy, happened to be present. and soon Conway was drawn into the magic circle. Morphy, a small, low-voiced, gentlemanly fellow, with melancholy eyes, agreed to play with him, giving him the handicap of a rook. Conway was beaten five games out of six; Morphy permitted the sixth game to end in a draw, hoping that Conway would play again. The delightful sensation of being beaten by Morphy seemed to Conway to counterbalance the material loss. As he wrote in a letter to a friend, "When one plays with Morphy the sensation is as queer as the first electric shock, or first love, or chloroform, or any entirely novel experience. As you sit down at the board opposite him, a certain sheepishness steals over you, and you cannot rid yourself of an old fable in which a lion's skin plays a part." As Conway admitted, "I had already received a domestic suggestion that it was possible to give too much time to an innocent game, and the hint was reinforced by my experience with Morphy."[231]

The letter was the basis of an essay entitled "Chess" that Lowell accepted for publication in *The Atlantic Monthly* (June 1860), and thus his losses were recouped. Conway resolved henceforth to confine his chess-playing to vacations or to sea-voyages and never again to play for money!

The real object of Conway's trip East was to visit Emerson in Concord and to converse with him on a subject that interested them both, the parallel evolution of the physical and the spiritual man. Conway was then at work on a book on demonology in which he sought to explain the growth and development of the concept of the devil. Emerson suggested to him that he sum up their conversation of several days on evil or the devil in terms of "the electric word pronounced by John Hunter a hundred years ago -- 'arrested and progressive development'" -- and that he insert a paragraph into his essay on the devil (without naming Emerson). This Conway did:

> Every animal is a man in this arrested development. The quadruped develops more and becomes an ape; arrested there for an aeon, the development rises to the savage; the next wave of the on-flowing tide of life rises to man, -- no longer arrested and bound to the earth by his forefeet, as in the wolf, nor only partially released as in the orang-outang, nor held by passion and ignorance as in the savage.[232]

Conway's tract, *The Natural History of the Devil*, appeared early in 1859 and soon became the theme of a number of his sermons against supernaturalism, in which he sought to explain the problem of evil in anthropological terms. His congregation, preferring the old miracles, realized with disquietude that their minister's interest had strayed from theology, at least of an orthodox variety. Not only science but also literature fascinated him; quotations from Robert and Elizabeth Barrett Browning, Matthew Arnold, Arthur Hugh Clough, William Wordsworth and Alfred Lord Tennyson frequently adorned his sermons. More alarming still, Conway quoted freely from Michel de Montaigne, Voltaire and even Thomas Paine!

The Congregational religion, Conway assumed, should encompass all aspects of life; he soon discovered the limitations of Congregationalism as he had those of Methodism and Unitarianism. The Congregationalists of Cincinnati bore with their minister, be it said, more patiently than had either of the other sects even when he remarked, "I feel, my brethren, a deep conviction that our mission as a Free Church is not so much to rationalize popular Christianity as to humanize it...Theology must pass in giving birth to Humanity, taking its place with Alchemy and Astrology."[233]

Conway's interest in literary and legendary material had long been familiar to his congregation, for he frequently enriched his sermons by the use of non-biblical sources. The thought that "inhumanity in man or nation must always prove a demon of unrest," on which he had preached soon after his arrival, had illustrated, for example, the fable of the wandering Jew. In this sermon he had declared, "That fable of the Wandering Jew shall be a dread reality to the heart which knowingly drives from its threshold the Christ who falls there in the form of those who now bear the cross of wrong and oppression, and toil up the weary hills of life to their continual crucification."[234]

Though Conway's sermon was against slavery, it was equally applicable to the Jews of Cincinnati, who at that time were being persecuted in many small ways. His sermon resulted in many friendships among Jews, notably that of Dr. Isaac Wise of the Hebrew Union College, who invited him to speak to his congregation in the Jewish synagogue. Conway found himself in the company of highly cultivated men and women. They seemed to him to be simple deists, untouched by any superstitions, and in many ways more enlightened than Protestants. Clearly, Conway was moving further and further away from the beliefs and attitudes of his own congregation.

In the spring of 1859 about a third of the church membership decided to form a new congregation, to build The Church of the Redeemer where they would no longer have to listen to sermons against the "miracles" they loved and where they could receive communion in the manner familiar to them. In his "Inaugural Address," preached on May 1, 1859, Conway spoke in a personal manner to those who remained in the old church with words somewhat suggestive of Walt Whitman. "Welcome to a Church where you need not lay down your manliness and your honest faith at the threshold when you enter! Your minister is not clerical; he does not consider himself above going to the theater, nor does he hesitate to come in contact with the flatboatmen, for he has no "purple and fine linen" to be soiled. Rather, said Conway, he comes before his congregation as "a plain man among men, trying according to the gift that is in him to instruct his fellows, liberate them from what he conceives to be error, and point them to the path of a manly, virtuous and blessed life." After the separation, both churches grew and flourished.[235]

In July 1859 Conway went to Boston to attend the annual meeting of alumni of the Harvard Divinity School; the visit proved more significant than anticipated. Remarking on the absence of Theodore Parker, then learning of his serious illness in Rome, Conway proposed that the alumni send Parker a note of sympathy and a prayer for his recovery. Conway was promptly asked to draw up the resolution, since the Unitarians had recently denounced Parker for his outspoken anti-slavery views. The Rev. James Freeman Clarke, an abolitionist known for his orthodox theological views, presented the resolution to the meeting, but the motion was greeted with such an angry outburst against "Parkerism" that Conway offered to rewrite it in milder form. "We don't want it in any shape!" one member shouted.[236] There the matter rested, for neither Conway nor Clarke would withdraw the original motion. A direct vote on the question was avoided, but word of the meeting appeared in the Boston papers and brought discredit on the orthodox Unitarian Church.

Conway breakfasted the morning after this meeting at the home of Lowell, where, among others, was Edmund Quincy. Having read the morning paper, Quincy jokingly said, "So you couldn't get the Unitarians to pray for Parker," and all joined in the laughter at Conway's expense. Since Conway had learned from Parker not to believe in miracles, why should he have attempted such a miracle as softening the hearts of Unitarians of the militant variety? Only the slow evolution of the savage could change the vindictive nature of men hardened into creedal grooves.

A few months later Parker lay dead in Italy, and the intolerance lingering in Unitarianism soon faded away; for all at last recognized his greatness: "a heavy burden rolled from the shoulders of the young generation at the foot of Parker's cross."[237] Had Parker been well enough to join his fellow abolitionists in defense of John Brown in October 1859, the extravagant words of this courageous man would no doubt have amazed Conway as did those of his other New England friends.[238] Having been more involved in church matters since graduation from the Divinity School in 1854, Conway did not realize that the Boston Vigilance Committee that had defended Anthony Burns had continued to work, under various names, in defense of Negroes. The same men now formed the nucleus of the supporters of John Brown; Parker's relationship to this group was better known to the Harvard Divinity School than to Conway.

On October 23, 1959, a few days after Brown's frustrated attempt (October 16-17) to stage an insurrection of slaves in western Virginia, Conway delivered a discourse, later published in a Cincinnati paper, in which he described Brown's seizure of the United States arsenal at Harper's Ferry as "worse than a crime, -- a blunder." His action, said Conway, was that of a deluded madman. In this same discourse Conway declared that his fellow abolitionists would certainly denounce Brown's bloody methods. Conway spoke too soon; even Emerson, in an address at Concord, scornfully referred to those "who can only cry Madman! when a hero passes!" While the verdict was pending, Emerson said "if John Brown died on the gallows he would make it glorious like a cross."[239] On October 30, Henry Thoreau announced that he was going to speak in the Concord Lyceum with or without the approval of the Republican Party, and there he praised the Christ-like heroism of Brown in boldly taking a stand against the United States.[240] In a speech on November 1, 1859, Wendell Phillips said "The Lesson of the Hour" was "insurrection" – "In God's world there are no majorities, no minorities; one, on God's side, is a Majority." [241] The "one" Phillips referred to was Brown. Soon Conway's friend, Garrison, pointed out that "spiritual weapons" are sometimes insufficient and applauded Brown and his small band of followers.[242]

John Brown, who had lectured and visited in Concord in 1857 and 1859, was personally known to these men and become for them the symbol of a noble cause. On March 4, 1858, he had met with them at the invitation of Parker and had partially disclosed his plans for leading an insurrection among the Negroes of Virginia. From the secret "Massachusetts- Kansas Committee," Brown had received not only encouragement but also money.

Conway knew nothing of these plans at the time though he was on friendly terms with all those involved.[243] He was amazed by the response to Brown's attack at Harper's Ferry of men whom he had accepted as guides and leaders.

Conway was swept off his feet by "the enthusiasm and tears of (his) anti-slavery comrades." Two days after the execution of Brown on December 2, 1859, he preached a sermon exalting "to the right hand of God" that "God-maddened old man," Brown. "Is John Brown a hero?" he asked "It will one day be told, to prove his stupidity of this age, that such a question was asked by sane men; that there were eyes so dull that they could not see, in a man dying for religious principles, anything more than 'fanatic', 'mad man' 'traitor'."[244] Conway soon recovered his equilibrium. In a review of *The Public Life of Captain John Brown* by James Redpath (1860), Conway warned his readers not to equate Brown with the great biblical heroes. "John Brown's method of dealing with slavery," he wrote, "was apiece with his false theology and his uncultured mind; his virtue, his fidelity are what makes the world fit to live in."[245]

Conway lived to regret his December 2 sermon on John Brown. He realized too late, in a moment of national tension such as that caused by Brown's six-weeks' trial, how all were victims, including Theodore Parker and Emerson. As he wrote many years later of John Brown, "I am convinced that few men ever wrought so much evil."

> On either side of the grave of a largely imaginary Brown wrathful Northerners and panic-stricken Southerners were speedily drawn up into hostile camps, and the only force was disarmed that might have prevented the catastrophe that followed. Up to that time the antislavery agitation had marched on the path of peace, and every year had brought further assurance of a high human victory in which South and North would equally triumph. But how we were all Brown's victims -- even we antislavery men, pledged to the methods of peace.

For his anti-slavery friends in New England, Conway could find a sort of excuse, or at least an explanation, of their lauding of Brown and their attempt to present him as a national hero and, indeed, saint -- no matter how violent or devious his methods. They had inherited, thought Conway, "from the old Puritan spirit and faith in the God of War," a natural response to a wild fanatic such as this old man from Kansas, who was himself a displaced New Englander. Conway, on the other hand, "had been brought up in no such faith" but rather "in the belief that evil could be conquered only by regeneration of the evil-doer."[246]

Conway's study of old myth and legend made him quite aware of the guns of the hoary old God of War that now began to show himself in every part of the land; the problem was to make the voice of reason heard when the War-God had been roused. A correspondent in the *Cincinnati Enquirer*, thinking Conway had been all too clear in his anti-war attitude, wrote: "Any man professing to be a Christian minister, who classes Jehovah, the Christian's God, in the same category with Mars and Jupiter and Odin, the barbarous and licentious creations of a heathen imagination, and says, as did Mr. Conway, that our God of Battles is no better than those pagan deities, should be indicted under the statute against blasphemy, if there be one in your state laws"[247]

Far from discouraging Conway's scientific and anthropological approach to man's illusions, such attacks made the minister more determined than ever to enlighten his congregation.

After Darwin's *On the Origin of Species* came out in December 1859, Conway felt that his views on miracles and on the evolution of man through struggle, rather than by divine action, had been vindicated. He was not long in hailing Darwin's achievement in a sermon: "Now comes Darwin and establishes the fact the Nature is all miracle, but without the special ones desired: that by perfect laws the lower species Gere trained to the next higher and that to the next - until

Striving to be man the worm
Mounts through all the spires of form."

Without any intention beyond uttering a "simple theory of nature," said Conway, dogmatic Christianity had been dealt a death blow. "Henceforth all temples not founded on the rock of natural science are on the sands where the angry tides are setting in."[248]

Fortunately for Conway, not long after the appearance of Darwin's work Emerson came to Cincinnati to deliver another lecture in the regular winter series of the Mercantile Library Association.

Conway again had the pleasure of exciting talks with Emerson on the subject of evolution. Neither he nor Emerson, he thought later, took into account "the boundlessness of the time in which nature had wrought." Nor did Conway realize until after many years that it was possible for man to develop downwards as well as upwards and to drag his world with him. He was interested in substituting rational thought for superstition and prejudice, and Darwin, even partially understood, was a suggestive teacher.

Conway and several members of his Church persuaded Emerson to deliver more lectures for which they paid Emerson very generously by selling tickets in advance. "Leading citizens" invited Emerson to luncheons and dinners so that every moment of his time was filled. "We had," wrote Emerson, "a festival week never forgotten." Conversations after the lectures in the drawing room of Judge Hoadly and his wife must have seemed to Conway like a renewal of the old Concord days.

Conway's interest in all variety of thought, as nurtured by Emerson and many other eastern friends, led him in Cincinnati to a room on Fourth Street where a small society, "The Infidels," held meetings every Sunday afternoon. The minister enjoyed an "obscure corner place" in these gatherings attended by men whose grammar was faulty but whose thought was marked by good sense and a certain eloquence. Thomas Paine seemed to them the apostle of religious freedom; Conway was struck by the fact that hitherto he had only heard Paine's name mentioned with abhorrence by preachers.[249] He became increasingly interested in the legends that had grown around Paine to which both his admirers and detractors had added their portion. Traces of the old legends about the wandering Jew and Faust had spread around his name.

Conway resolved to go to the library and find out the facts concerning this misunderstood theist. His "unprejudiced investigation" brought him to the conclusion that Paine was, in fact, an unsung hero of the American Revolution and so considered by Washington, Benjamin Franklin, John Adams, Jefferson, and other leading statesmen. What a subject for a sermon, especially at this moment of national confusion! Conway announced that Paine's birthday, January 29, 1860, would be observed by a sermon on Thomas Paine,[250] and as usual the church was crowded by townsmen as well as church members. Far from criticizing Conway for his choice of a subject, the congregation was delighted. The next day he received a written request, signed by many citizens of Cincinnati, that his sermon be published.

Conway became the rallying point of the freethinkers of the city, and his task now seemed to him to grapple with what he considered their errors. Though a theist, he was not an atheist -- as were many of his new followers. No doubt his discussions with these "Infidels" influenced his sermon on "God" that disturbed his congregation even more than his discourse on Paine. This sermon, questioning the concept of free will, stirred up a newspaper controversy in and around Cincinnati of such widespread interest that the idea of starting a magazine where he could speak more freely, and at length, absorbed his imagination. Almost unconsciously Conway's thoughts had been turning more and more from any established church, though he preached to his group for several more years. Toward the end of 1859, the possibility of editing a magazine of his own now took practical shape. He chose the name made famous by his Concord friends, to whom he wrote at once for poems, essays or stories. Emerson promised to send him contributions.

In January, 1860, the first number of *The Dial* appeared, with "M. D. Conway" as editor. The preface ended with a grandiose paragraph:

> 'The Dial' stands before you, the reader, a legitimation of the Spirit of the Age, which ASPIRES TO BE FREE: free in thought, doubt, utterance, love and knowledge. It is, in our minds, symbolized not so much by the sun-clock in the yard as by the floral dial of Linnaeus, which recorded in the unfolding of higher life and thought, and the closing up of old superstitions and evils: it would be a Dial measuring time by growth.

In actual time -- not in the mystical time recorded on Conway's sundial -- the magazine lasted exactly one year. *The Dial* of December 1860 opened with "A Parting Word" to the readers: "With this number the publication of the 'Dial' ceases.

The simple reason for this is that the editor is unable to bear the labor it adds to his usual and necessary duties." The epitaph of the magazine was expressed in one word, "Resurgam," "I shall Rise Again.."[251]

In its brief year, however, the magazine published 200 articles (30 of which were written by Conway himself) and 70 reviews, all written by the editor. The books that Conway choose for review reflected his own liberal views and the breadth of his interests, from Darwin's *Origin of Species*, to the 1860 edition of Whitman's *Leaves of Grass*. Like *The Dial* of Concord, many pages of the magazine were filled with quotations from the writers of the East -- doubtless borrowed from Emerson during his summer in Concord -- and from Goethe, François Fénelon, Shakespeare, Alcott, John Henry Newman, Hegel and James Martineau. Besides contributions from Emerson, Conway printed four poems by William Dean Howells, verses by Clough, Sanborn and other now forgotten poets. Conway was properly proud of the fact that *The Dial* reflected the intellectual tone of the West, particularly the religious thought, which according to him, was basic to an understanding of the Negro problem. Nearly all of the contributors were, in fact, abolitionists, though controversial political questions were seldom presented in *The Dial*. "The Story of the West-Indian Emancipation" by Emerson, however, was the clearest, most downright statement he was ever to make on the subject of slavery.[252] In the July issue Conway himself wrote an essay on 'Theodore Parker," and in October reviewed seven books on the great abolitionist-preacher.[253]

Octavius B. Frothingham, well-known for his anti-slavery views, contributed a series of articles on "The Christianity of Christ,"[254] and a certain Orson Murray brought him an unorthodox essay "On Prayer" that he supposed Conway would be unwilling to print. "It made an explosion like a bomb," Conway wrote, because of Murray's praise of John Brown, not because of the defense of prayer. The editor appended soothing words to the article; prayer, he said, was "a part of nature like the songs of birds, and to be improved by culture."[255]

The first issue of *The Dial* carried a tale by Conway, "Excalibur: A Story for *Anglo*-American Boys."[256] Written in December 1859, it was an attempt to put into mythical terms the tale of John Brown and his effort to get hold of the sword supposed to have been sent to George Washington by Frederick the Great. Years later Conway told Carlyle that the whole story of the sword was a fabrication; Brown, however, did try to possess the sword used by Washington, causing the delay that was partly responsible for the failure of his plans. The story concluded that nobility and madness both marked John Brown's character.

The Dial was cordially received in the East and in the West. Letters of congratulations arrived from old friends such as Longfellow, Charles Eliot Norton, and Dr. Frothingham. The notices in the press throughout the state were favorable, but the one that particularly moved the editor came out in the *Ohio State Journal* of Columbus. By a young writer hardly known to Conway, William Dean Howells, the review reflects a Midwesterner's joy that something good could come out of Cincinnati, so far from Boston. [257] With something like an old Methodist "hallelujah," Conway ran to show the paper to his wife:

> That men should say what they think, outside of Boston, is of course astonishing. That they should say what they think, inside of Cincinnati rather relieves that marvellousness of the first astonisher. It is not true that men's minds are expanded in proportion as there is a good deal of land to the acre; or that a generous climate and fertile soil grow warm, rich hearts. After half a century stultification (we like that newspaper word) the nation is beginning to discover that true hospitality, courage, and generosity have their home in the North and not in the South. And we all know that the frozen hills of New England have sheltered in their bleakest ravines the spirit of free thought and open speech, after it had been banished from the South, the West, and the mercenary cities of the Middle States. Until now Boston has been the only place in the land where the inalienable right to think what you please has been practised and upheld. If Cincinnati can place herself beside Boston on this serene eminence, she will accomplish a thing nobler than pork, sublimer than Catawba, more magnificent than Pike's Opera House. "The Dial" is an attempt on the part of intellectual Cincinnati to do this, and the attempt is a noble one. We do not ask anybody to endorse the views

of M. D. Conway; but we hold up his course as one of brilliant success, in everything that makes success honourable, -- as that of a man singularly unselfish and devoted to what he believes the truth. He is the editor of "The Dial," but "The Dial," while it represents his views, shows the time of day by every intellectual light that shines upon it. It numbers among its contributors some of the most distinguished thinkers of New England, and it seeks to bring out all the thinkers of the West.[258]

Conway, for his part, reviewed Howells' first book, *Poems of Two Friends* (written with J. J. Piatt) in the March 1860 issue of *The Dial*, and soon the editor and Howells were meeting in Cincinnati. They shared not only many literary tastes but also felt very strongly about the political questions of the day. Both were anti-slavery, and both had been deeply moved by the John Brown verdict. Conway's sermon of December 2, 1859, and Howells' poem, "Old Brown," were included in *Echoes of Harper's Ferry* (1860), edited by James Redpath. [259] Moreover, both men were writing books bearing on the national crisis, influencing their own personal careers. Howells was writing a campaign *Life of Lincoln*, which earned him a four-year consulate in Venice; Conway published in *The Dial* his article on the Lincoln-Douglas debates and was writing *The Rejected Stone*: "or Insurrection vs. Resurrection in America. By a Native of Virginia," which earned him an interview with Lincoln.

The birth of a son in June 1859, the difficulty of extracting material from reluctant authors, as well as the expense, borne by Conway alone, of printing the magazine, all contributed to his decision to bring *The Dial* to a conclusion with the December issue.[260] Conway was in a sense correct in saying that *The Dial* was killed by the approaching Civil War. The magazine was never resurrected. The editor, like everyone else in the country, was seized by the political excitement of the moment, a prelude to a new chapter in his life and the life of the country.

The election of Lincoln in November – the first national victory for the Republican Party – split the Democratic party and changed the issue before the country from anti-slavery versus pro-slavery, to anti-slavery versus Union. Many believed that the secession of South Carolina in December, soon followed by that of six more states of the deep South, could be stopped by overlooking the question of slavery and maintaining the Union. To Conway the Unionists were surrendering to the pro-slavery factions of the North and the South. To Emerson, Garrison, Wendell Phillips, and other abolitionists, disunion seemed more desirable than a false union where the "nefarious institution" was permitted. "We at Cincinnati," wrote Conway, "were in the very thick of this conflict of pens and words."[261] He had no time for philosophical and discursive articles for *The Dial*; "the golden hour" for writing and speaking in favor of immediate emancipation was at hand.

Chapter IX
The Golden Hour

One summer evening in 1859, Conway walked home across the market-place in Cincinnati and found a crowd listening to a political speaker, addressing them from the balcony of a brick house.[262] Conway soon discovered that the speaker was Abraham Lincoln, and he looked up with curiosity at the tall figure above him, illuminated by the moonlight and highlighted by the lamps attached to the balcony. "His face," wrote Conway, "had a battered and bronzed look, without being hard. His nose was prominent and buttressed a strong and high forehead; his eyes were high-vaulted and had an expression of sadness; his mouth and chin were too close together, the cheeks hollow."

On the whole, Conway did not find Lincoln's appearance prepossessing. Then he heard his voice. His tone was full of variety, now earnest and shrewd, then humorous and direct -- "The charm of his manner was that he had no manner." Conway had thought he would pause for only a moment, but he stayed until the speech had ended. The words that Conway heard and remembered that evening were, "Slavery is wrong." To the Congregational minister, who had often stood on the bluffs overlooking the Ohio River and seen the slaves at work in Kentucky, these words were serious indeed.

The Kentuckians who had swarmed over the river to hear Lincoln speak made themselves known by their hisses and shouts after his declaration, "Slavery is wicked." Lincoln waited quietly and then said:

> *I find that every man comes into the world with a mouth to be fed and a back to be clothed; that each has also two hands; and I infer that those hands are meant to feed that mouth and to clothe that back. And I warn you that any institution that deprives them of that right, and the rights deducible from it, strikes at the very roots of natural justice, which is also political wisdom.*

Lincoln then repeated, "Slavery is wrong; and no compromise, no political arrangement with slavery, will ever last which does not deal with it as wrong." Even more binding words appeared the following year in the campaign *Life of Lincoln* by Conway's friend, William Dean Howells: "The government is expressly charged with the duty of providing 'for the general welfare.' We believe that the spreading out and perpetuity of the institution of slavery impairs the general welfare." Conway thought the words, "and perpetuity," meant that Lincoln had in mind the extinction of slavery -- not merely the restriction of it -- and he printed them in *The Dial* in bold type.[263] In the fall Conway cast his vote for Lincoln, believing that "the duty of providing 'for the general welfare'" meant that Lincoln would immediately take a stand against slavery throughout the country, not in the new lands only. The "Golden Hour" of emancipation had arrived. He soon found he was mistaken; this was the first and last time that Conway ever voted for a presidential candidate.

William Lloyd Garrison, editor of *The Liberator*, had long advocated immediate emancipation of the Negro in the name of Christian justice and in the face of the business interests opposed to him in the North as well as in the South. The idea of the "sacredness" of the Union appeared to Garrison and his followers as simply an illusion fostered by wealthy capitalists as a means of continuing an institution found profitable to northern cotton manufacturers. To Conway, as to Garrison, the anti-slavery movement was "a purely religious one"[264] and the Union "an altar on which human sacrifices were offered."[265]

With such thoughts and emotions in his heart, Conway watched Lincoln in the winter of 1861, on his way to his Inauguration, pass down the main street of Cincinnati under arches of evergreen, between waving banners of German, Italian, Irish, and Polish societies. He was to learn later that Cincinnati was the only city that cheered Lincoln as he traveled to Washington. He had to cross Baltimore in disguise to avoid the danger of assassination.

Conway felt a special empathy with the president, for he himself had been the recipient of threatening notes for his anti-slavery position. On one occasion, he announced "War" as the subject of his sermon, and a dozen "roughs," presumably from

Kentucky, armed with stout canes, quietly took their seats in the front pew awaiting the words of the preacher. When it became clear that Conway was not advocating the invasion of Kentucky by Union troops, but rather peaceful disunion, the men filed out of the church.[266]

Conway's hope was that the new president would, after emancipating the slaves, slowly restore the Union. But Lincoln had not been elected by popular majority, Conway realized. Already seven southern states, led by South Carolina, had seceded. So be it; let the president declare the slaves free in the rest of the nation. "In the face of every threat of disunion, "Conway wrote, "and avowedly because he promised to deal with Slavery as WRONG," Lincoln was elected, carrying with him the confident expectation of Conway and his abolitionist friends that now at last slavery would end. They did not forget that before his nomination, Lincoln had declared, "There is no reason in the world why the negro is not entitled to all the natural rights enumerated in the Declaration of Independence, -- the right to life, liberty, and the pursuit of happiness. I hold that he is as much entitled to them as the white man."

In his inaugural address, however, Lincoln amazed Conway and his group by approving an amendment to the constitution that seemed to take the abolition of slavery out of the hands of the federal government. Lincoln declared that "no amendment shall be made to the Constitution which will authorize or give to Congress the power to abolish or interfere within any State with the domestic institutions thereof, including that of persons held to labour or service by the laws of said States."[267]

To Conway as to most of the abolitionists, Lincoln's inaugural speech seemed tragically at variance with his campaign promises; they had hoped that he would immediately free the slaves when he came into office, but apparently he did not feel that he yet had sufficient popular support.

When Fort Sumter was fired upon on April 15, 1861, and Lincoln, without consulting Congress, demanded 75,000 militia to be supplied by the governors of the loyal states, the issue was clarified. The country was plunged into war. Virginia, until then undecided, at once seceded, as did Arkansas, North Carolina, and Tennessee; out of thirty-four states, eleven had seceded and joined the Confederate States of America. Torn between loyalty to

Virginia and loyalty to the Republican Party, Conway supported Lincoln. He thought that the president would now proclaim the emancipation of the slaves. For the same reason, many of Conway's peace-loving friends rejoiced when the shooting began. "Sometimes the smell of gunpowder is good," said Emerson. According to Conway, Wendell Phillips on January 20, 1861, shouted "All hail, Disunion!" to a large audience in the Boston Music Hall, for "beautiful on the mountains are the feet of him that bringeth good tidings, that publisheth peace." Phillips' address, on April 21, 1861, the Sunday after the surrender of Fort Sumter, illustrates the extraordinary change of attitude brought about by Lincoln's call for troops. Conway reported Phillips as saying:

> Many times this winter, here and elsewhere, I have counselled peace, -- urged, as well as I knew how, expediency of acknowledging a Southern Confederacy, and the peaceful separation of these thirty-four States. One of the journals announces to you that I come here this morning to retract those opinions. No, not one word of them! I need them all. -- every word I have spoken this winter, -- every act of twenty-five years of my life, -- to make the welcome I give this war hearty and hot. Civil war is a momentous evil. It needs the soundest, most solemn justification. I rejoice before God to-day for every word that I have spoken counselling peace; but I rejoice also with an especially profound gratitude, that now, the first time in my anti-Slavery life, I speak under the stars and stripes, and welcome the tread of Massachusetts men marshalled for war. The only mistake that I have made was in supposing Massachusetts wholly choked with cotton-dust and cankered with gold.[268]

As soon as Lincoln was elected, the vast and complex business interests supporting Union as the paramount issue began to be heard more clearly. It was against the abolitionists, rather than against the South, that they directed their fury. These forces, the abolitionists believed, "having by the compromise of the fathers an overbalance of representation, and by the invention of the cotton-gin a vast accession of wealth, had been able to buy up the leading pulpits and presses of the North, and to subsidize her leading statesmen, and thus to wield over the whole country the tyranny of an autocracy." Wendell Phillips did not hesitate to assert that Daniel Webster, senator from Massachusetts, had been one of the statesmen bought by the pro-slavery interests.

On the same Sunday, Conway preached a sermon in Cincinnati as rhetorical as that of Phillips; it was, in effect, a defense of the president's call to arms. The church was draped in flags of the United States for the occasion, and the whole congregation arose and sang the "Star-Spangled Banner" as the minister ascended the pulpit. The president, said Conway, was compelled by his oath of office to defend Fort Sumter as United States property; it was necessary for him to call for troops since Washington itself was in danger from the rebels who might thus be in a position to dictate the terms of the division that everyone knew must come eventually. Conway assumed, as did his congregation, that the militia were merely for the defense of the capital during the possibly dangerous period of emancipation.

Conway was soon astonished to learn that Lincoln had not summoned Congress at once but had ordered the troops to invade Virginia. Before many days had passed, he concluded that Lincoln's defense of a worthless fort (against the advice of General Winfield Scott and most of the members of the cabinet) was merely the act of "a politician who had proposed to render slavery eternal by a constitutional amendment, and was willing to barter for the Union all the anti-slavery enthusiasm that had responded to his summons."[269] Lincoln had announced that he would not compromise on the extension of slavery into the territories, and therefore on this issue the North would not have taken up arms. The actual invasion of a slave state put an end to further discussion by arousing sectional "loyalty" in the South, and anti-slavery fanaticism in the North. There was then "no halo of martyrdom around the head of Abraham Lincoln to shed glamour on his actions." To many it seemed that war might have been avoided had Congress been convened before July 4, 1861; to others it seemed that the war was not for the emancipation of the Negroes after all but merely a political move to insure continuance of the Union -- and power to King Cotton.

Such abolitionists as Emerson and Phillips, who had welcomed the first news of the war, became disenchanted as they more clearly perceived that Union, not emancipation, was to Lincoln the issue. William H. Seward, old-fashioned anti-slavery Whig and secretary of state, who subscribed to gradualism, was soon cynically warning the border states that they would be well-advised to support the government for tactical reasons -- since only by so doing could they preserve slavery in their states.[270] Pro-slavery clergymen in Boston, Philadelphia, New York and Washington were preaching sermons to the same effect. Union soldiers were instructed by the government to support the Fugitive Slave Act by returning to their southern masters any unidentified Negroes encountered above the Mason-Dixon line.

Lincoln, then, had led the country into a war for "a Union whose rivets were one with rivets of the slave's manacle."[271] When Conway was asked to become chaplain to Brigadier General Schenck's brigade in Virginia, he felt he must refuse.[272] Since Conway's church was closed for the summer after the last Sunday in June, he determined to spend the next months in the East, listening to speeches in Congress, visiting friends, attending conferences in an effort to make up his mind as to the position he should assume toward the war. When he reached Washington, he found that the city was an armed camp and that his former church was merely a storage house for war materials. Conway, from the visitors' gallery of Congress, listened with dismay to Lincoln's opening address on July 4 in which he made no reference to slavery.

Traveling North, Conway called on his old friends, Dr. Furness and his house-guest Charles Sumner, both of whom seemed to have more faith in Lincoln than he himself could summon. Conway knew slaves and their masters better than any northerner and was certain, if Lincoln would only declare for immediate emancipation, the slaves would leave the farms, their owners would return from the battlefields either to guard their slaves or to work their own fields. Thus, there could be no war. The slave-owners could then be paid by the government for their slaves, and the cost would be less than the expense of the army for a month. Sumner and Furness listened to Conway's views and urged him to devote himself to spreading his ideas through the North and the West.[273]

In New York, Conway attended a lecture by Henry Ward Beecher; in Boston he heard Edward Everett Hale Jr. He traveled to Newport with Horace Greeley, but he could not sympathize with Greeley's cry in the *Tribune*, "Forward to Richmond," where the Confederacy on July 20 had moved its capital. Conway still hoped that the Union army would merely establish border camps for slaves and force their owners back to the farms. Conway was frequently invited to preach in the towns through which he passed during the summer. He at last reached Easton, Pennsylvania, where his mother was staying with his sister, having found it "imprudent" to remain in Fredericksburg because of Mrs. Conway's strong views against the secession of Virginia. Her brother, Travers Daniel, attorney-general of Virginia before and after the war, had pleaded passionately in the Virginia Convention against secession, but after Lincoln's demand for troops from Virginia to fight southerners, the cause was lost. The minority prevailed, and the anti-secessionists left the convention without voting.[274]

Before returning to Cincinnati, Conway talked with Wendell Phillips, Octavius B. Frothingham, W. L. Garrison, William Henry Channing, James Freeman Clarke, George Luther Stearns, Horace Greeley, and all of his other old friends and associates in the abolitionist group.[275] On Sunday, July 21, he preached in a Unitarian Church in New Bedford, Massachusetts, to a large congregation, many of them Quakers. At the very moment whom Conway was upholding the banner of peace, insisting that no blood need be shed if the President would only come out at once for freedom for the slaves, United States soldiers were straggling back to Washington after the defeat at Bull Run. The retreat, thought Conway, was the inevitable result of the President's order to the Union troops to return all runaway slaves to their masters. Had they welcomed the fugitives, they in turn might have aided the soldiers.

Everyone Conway encountered in New England seemed to agree with him as to the importance of immediate emancipation. Emerson, with whom Conway talked over the news in Concord, observed, "If the Union is incapable of securing universal freedom, its disruption were as the breaking up of a frog pond. Until justice is the aim of war one may naturally rather be shot than shoot." On Saturday, July 27, Emerson took Conway with him to the Saturday Club in Boston, where Motley and Channing were the honored guests. The humiliation of defeat hung over the gathering, and it was painful to Conway to glance around the Parker House dining room at the sad countenances of the men who represented to him the great literary age of America. "The morning stars that had sung together for joy in the advance of every noble cause were now silent."[276] Perhaps, it was suggested, the president was really in favor of emancipation but felt he must have a decisive military victory before he could deal directly with slavery. Meanwhile, it seemed that the men sent from New England in response to Lincoln's call to arms were being used not so much to fight slaveholders as to catch their runaway slaves. In spite of the depressing atmosphere of the evening, Conway wrote home to his wife that he had had "a celestial evening with Emerson." He "thinks the reverse at Bull Run will do us good."

Conway returned sadly disheartened to Cincinnati at the end of the summer of 1861. "Alas, the antislavery fraternity was shattered," he wrote; "The President's determination to settle the issue by a duel had flushed our band like a flock of wild turkeys, and we could not get together again."[277] He decided to press for immediate emancipation with what means he commanded and began by convincing his own congregation -- among them Judge Hoadly, Alphonso Taft, William Greene and many other leading citizens -- of the importance and practicality of his proposal.

After consulting Senator Sumner and Secretary Salmon P. Chase -- both of them outspoken abolitionists -- Conway resolved to travel throughout Ohio addressing the people on the subject of emancipation. Sumner and Chase felt sure they could raise a fund in Washington to pay for the lectures and urged Conway to accept their support, but he knew that his position would be stronger if he could go before the people as "a man reared in Virginia, son of a slave-holder and entirely unpaid."[278] He allowed his friends in Washington, however, to engage the halls in which he spoke in every large city and in many villages of the state. His subject was "The Rejected Stone," the stone of justice for Negroes, the rejection of which had caused the Civil War.

Occasionally Conway met opposition to his idea of "immediate and universal emancipation," but, for the most part, the crowds that hear him seemed to be in such sympathy that he was encouraged to report to his Washington supporters that Ohio at least agreed with his proposition. A few voices were lifted against him; as Conway walked out of the lecture hall in Xenia, for example, he found a man haranguing a hundred or more people whom he had just addressed telling them, "Every word [of Conway's speech] was false as hell!" In Dayton, Clement L. Vallandigham, the leader of the Democrats and owner of a newspaper, warned his readers that Conway was one of the abolitionists who had helped bring on the war in the first place and now was planning to introduce into Ohio a horde of Negroes to take the work away from the white laborers. He advised that the speaker be put into a strait-jacket and held under the town pump in order to rid the neighborhood of a nuisance.

Whatever time Conway could steal from his speech-making and his Sunday sermons in Cincinnati, he devoted to the preparation of a small book that grew from these lectures on the same absorbing subject, the avoidance of a war and the immediate emancipation of the Negroes. The refusal of Washington to receive an ambassador from the Republic of Haiti, and Seward's evasive words, "The fact is, Washington cannot receive a black minister," focused Conway's thought on the book he was contemplating, "The Rejected Stone: or Insurrection vs. Resurrection in America. By a Native of Virginia."[279] The text was biblical: "The Stone which the builders rejected is become the head of the corner. And whosoever shall fall on this stone shall be broken: but on whomsoever it shall fall it will grind him to powder."

The stone, Conway pointed out, was Justice, and the figure for whom he was asking justice was the African Slave. Though the president did not seem to recognize it, the cause of the Negro was that of mankind. Were the rebels to lay down their arms at once, the government would be willing, he feared, to consolidate the Union "over the prostrate form of the Negro." The rebels, of course, had no thought of peace even if slavery were permitted, said Conway, and would continue to fight until the very idea of slavery was accepted in the country unless the government made it clear that justice to all races was their aim and not a compromised and false Union. "For to do justice to the Negro, is to lay the cornerstone of the Republic of Man. It is nothing else ... The Union is under compulsion to find its life by losing it."[280]

Conway, with the rhetoric of the preacher, traced the effort of oppressed people from the days of the Pharaohs to the American Revolution, and showed the pain and loss -- and the inevitability -- of every advance ever made. "Ages of Wrong have, like cold, hard glaciers, graven on this lowly stone the sacred signs of the Laws that cannot be broken." The male Negro, indeed, has become "the touchstone of our virtue."

> Our relations to the Negro make him for us the sign of eternal justice and inviolable honor. The gift derives its sacredness from the altar. The more lowly and incompetent that race, the more sacred its cause to all loyal men. His plea the Negro can only utter by the tongue or pen of other races; but his silence is more eloquent than any tongue or pen. He is absent from our pews, he is unfit for our parlors; but his absence bears a more withering rebuke to the wrong that has held him down in the ascending world, than his presence. He can only sign his plea with his cross-mark; but it is the indictment of humanity itself against us, and that sign of the cross affixed is the double seal of his ignorance and of the inhumanity which has caused it. Thus the black man withdraws before the universality of his issue, which becomes that between Absolute Right and Wrong.[281]

The "warning of the African" was as imperative to the North as to the South: "The Devil's Year draws to a close; bring out the ledgers! See, for every man bought and sold in the South, one was bought and sold in the North![282] The year has been given over to the Devil because men on both sides have truckled to Slavery for mean motives. Against this tyranny America has at last inaugurated a revolution, and has placed Abraham Lincoln in the White House. He, with the weapon of Truth, should be encouraged to lead the Resurrection against the Insurrection of the Confederacy. Everyone knows that slavery is the real cause for the rebellion; why, then does the Administration not declare Emancipation at once? Why this timidity?" The answer was simple; "The Administration fears to alienate certain persons in the North and (supposed) in the South from the cause of the Union itself, as separate from the Slavery question."[283]

It was for the American people, now that they had at last a president eager to represent them, to hand to the "Master-builder" the Rejected Stone, Justice to Man.

The book appeared early in October 1861 and was reviewed on all sides, usually with approbation. The "Virginian" named as the author on the title page was immediately recognized as Moncure Daniel Conway. Senator Sumner wrote that he had sent a copy to the president who was reading the book with interest. A group of Bostonians proposed to distribute it among the soldiers. Conway gladly gave up his claim to royalties for this large edition. Conway believed that the popularity of *The Rejected Stone* was due in part to the fact that it appeared just at the time when Major General John C. Frémont, in charge of military affairs in Missouri, issued a proclamation in that state declaring all slaves free. Lincoln considered the order unconstitutional, had it rescinded, and removed Frémont from his position. But the incident was discussed on every plantation in the South, and Conway's book became a part of the discussion.[284]

Encouraged by the reception of *The Rejected Stone*, Conway made plans at once to further its distribution among the soldiers. On December 1, 1861, he wrote to Emerson from Cincinnati: "I go next week, -- rather this week, -- on a hasty visit to Boston, I wish to try to get help in an effort to distribute 'The Rejected Stone' amongst the forty or fifty thousand soldiers who will winter in our camps in the West. I shall hope to get some subscriptions in Concord to that end." Conway then suggested that he should add to the fund needed by lecturing at Concord: "I have prepared and shall deliver tomorrow evening,--2nd Anniv. of John Brown's Execution,--a Lecture entitled 'The Death and Resurrection of Captain John Brown.' This I shd like to deliver at Concord, charging admission for the purpose above indicated."[285] Emerson accepted the suggestion, and Conway spoke at the Concord Lyceum early in December.

In January 1862 Conway was invited to lecture at the Smithsonian Institution in Washington. Though loath to leave his wife and two small boys in Cincinnati, he felt the opportunity too important to refuse.[286] He chose as the subject of his talk the title, "The Golden Hour," by which he meant to suggest that "the Golden Hour of the nation was that in which for the first time in its history the murderous madness of slavery had unsealed the constitutional war power to eradicate forever that root of all our evils."[287]

An interview with Sumner and several hours with Channing soon after his arrival in Washington made it clear to Conway that there were those in Washington who objected to his speech, a copy of which had been sent in advance. "As usual my doom has followed me," Conway wrote home to his wife on January 15. "There is at this moment a War going on about my speaking in the Hall of the Smithsonian." Thanks to the good offices of his friends and supporters, however, Conway could write to Ellen the next day that Joseph Henry, the director, "yielded the point about the Smithsonian after recording a long protest against the sentiments advanced."[288]

The lecture, on January 17, 1862, was attended by Chase, now secretary of the Treasury, and others prominent in the government; they heard an outspoken attack on the policies of the president in regard to emancipation. Senator Sumner suggested that Conway should call on Lincoln, together with W. H. Channing, to soften the impression made by the address. The president received them graciously the next day at 8 a.m. in the White House. Channing opened the conversation by saying that both he and Conway felt that the great opportunity to get rid of slavery throughout the nation had come. When the president asked Channing how he thought this might be done, Channing replied that he believed that the slave-owners should be compensated for their loss of slaves; Lincoln quietly remarked that he had been in favor of that plan for many years. Conway recorded his part of the interview as follows:

> When the President turned to me, I asked whether we might not look to him as the coming Deliverer of the Nation from its one great evil. What would not that man achieve for mankind who should free America from Slavery? He said, "Perhaps we may be better able to do something in that direction after a while than we are now." I said, "Mr. President, do you believe the masses of the American people would hail you as their deliverer if, at the end of this war, the Union should be surviving and slavery still in it?" "Yet, if they were to see that slavery was on the downhill." I ventured to say, "Our

> fathers compromised with slavery because they thought it on the downhill; hence war to-day." The President said, "I think the country grows in this direction daily, and I am not without hope that something of the desire of you and your friends may be accomplished.[289]

The issue between the president and his critic was thus clearly defined and never altered -- nor, indeed, did either allow an argument ever to intrude upon their polite, even cordial, deference for each other. As Conway described the meeting:

> Turning to me the President said, 'In working in the antislavery movement you may naturally come in contact with a good many people who agree with you, and possibly may overestimate the number in the country who hold such views.
>
> But the position in which I am placed brings me into some knowledge of opinions in all parts of the country and of many different kinds of people; and it appears to me that the great masses of this country care comparatively little about the negro, and are anxious only for military successes." We had, I think, risen to leave and had thanked him for his friendly reception when he said. "We shall need all the anti-slavery feeling in the country, and more; you can go home and try to bring the people to your views; and you may say anything you like about me, if that will help. Don't spare me!" This was said with a laugh. Then he said very gravely, "When the hour comes for dealing with slavery I trust I will be willing to do my duty though it cost my life. And, gentlemen, lives will be lost."

Conway left the interview with a feeling of depression. Although the president expressed profound sympathy for the southerners who had long ago become socially and commercially bound up with slavery, he did not seem to Conway to grasp the fact that he and Channing were really concerned with the effect of war on the whole country and not primarily interested in the fate of the Negro. It was clear that the president wished to preserve the

Union, at no matter what cost, and that he had no idea of any method, other than military, for holding the states together. Conway's idea that peace could be gained by immediate emancipation seemed to him merely a religious concept, not worth serious consideration. Conway determined then to recast his lecture, "The Golden Hour," with special reference to his conversation with the president and publish it as a book.[290]

Conway's resolution was strengthened by a visit with Dr. Furness on his way through Philadelphia following his conference with Lincoln. After "a musical evening" with the family, Conway wrote his wife, the conversation turned to Conway's recent book, *The Rejected Stone*, which, he learned, was beginning to make "a huge noise" among the Quakers in Philadelphia. [291] The edition, in fact, sold out; Dr. Furness promised that money would be forthcoming to distribute *The Rejected Stone* among the soldiers, and Conway promptly renounced any royalties that might accrue. Lucretia Mott, who was present, gave him her blessing and told him with satisfaction that he had quoted from the Bible seventy-one times in *The Rejected Stone*.

Invited to lecture before the Emancipation League in Boston on "The Golden Hour," Conway did not linger long in Philadelphia. Before leaving, however, he read his lecture aloud to his friends and wrote ahead to Emerson suggesting that he should deliver it in Concord while he was in the neighborhood. "Dear Sir," he began, "On Wednesday next (Jan 29) I shall deliver one of the Lectures before the Emancipation League on "The Golden Hour." – Of course I shall try and not return without my usual pilgrimage to my Mecca -- Concord. Tuesday I wd like to come; and I wd like to give my Lecture there. Having just been to Washington in company with W. H. Channing I had an extended interview with the President -- It is possible I might bring some tidings worth having.

"I also have a new view of this War & how to end it at once, which Channing & Furness & Lucretia Mott declare is absolutely necessary every one with any influence on public opinion shd hear at once. I am in dreadful pain with it because it is now not publicly recognized, -- & I know it is true." Conway added in a postscript, "The Lecture may either be paid of free; -- any money will go immediately toward the object I have before intimated to you and to myself."[292]

On January 27, Conway wrote to his wife from the Parker House in Boston, saying that Emerson had replied to his letter, had arranged a lecture for him in Concord. Conway had ridden up to Boston with Horace Greeley ("I never knew him so bright"), that he had had a long talk with Wendell Phillips, who told him that he quoted from *The Rejected Stone* repeatedly and was sure that "one of the Funds" would contribute to its distribution. [293] Phillips also told Conway that Charles Sumner had evidence of Conway's success in the West and that he and Sumner would contribute to the expenses of further lectures if Conway were ready.[294] Conway's "new view on this war and how to end it at once seemed to him to meet with hearty approval from his friends among the abolitionists.

Before his lecture in Boston, Conway was the guest of honor and only speaker at a dinner in the Parker House attended by about thirty of his old associates, among them Emerson, Holmes, Lowell, James T. Fields, and a number of Harvard professors. Conway made his interview with Lincoln and other leading men in Washington, rather than his scheme for peace, the subject of his talk. He had much interesting news to present and held the group spell-bound. Senator Sumner had told Conway of his encounters with Secretary of State Seward, which had convinced Sumner that the wily Seward was making an effort to persuade the president of a real danger of conflict with Great Britain. Seward could produce no evidence for his warning, but Sumner suspected that he had spread the alarm in order to make the border states forget the question of slavery and support the government against England.

Shortly before the firing on Sumter, Seward had put his "Thoughts" before Lincoln. He advised, "Change the question before the public from one upon Slavery, or about Slavery, for a question upon Union or Disunion. In other words, from what would be regarded as a party question, to one of Patriotism or Union."[295] Emerson listened with interest, for he too had been invited to lecture before the Smithsonian Institution. He came to Conway's room in the Parker House after the dinner to discuss Conway's proposal for peace. The next morning Conway was on his way to New York to deliver his lecture once more to enthusiastic gatherings.

As a result of Conway's brief pause in the metropolis on his way up to Boston, he was urged by Horace Greeley and a group of eminent citizens to return to New York as soon as possible after his engagements in New England and to repeat his lectures on "The Golden Hour" at the Church of the Puritans. On January 30, Conway addressed an audience of at least 1,200 people who gathered "in spite of the unpropitious condition of the streets." According to the report of the *National Anti-Slavery Standard* of February 8, the lecture gave "unalloyed satisfaction to the whole auditory." The reporter went on to say, "Mr. Conway's central idea, of course, was -- Emancipation indispensable to the salvation of the country." This familiar message the speaker enforced "by arguments and illustrations, some of which were quite original, and, in the mouth of a native of Virginia, very forcible and convincing."

When Conway returned briefly to Cincinnati in February 1862, he found the city in the ferment of war. The hospitals were filled with wounded men, and "refined and cultured" ladies, including his wife, were learning to be nurses. All the more reason to return to Boston and see to the publication of *The Golden Hour* and the reprinting of *The Rejected Stone* by Tichnor and Fields. Soon Conway was writing happily to his wife (March 13, 1862), "I have just been to take breakfast with the Fields; had a delightful time: -- They had for breakfast bread, butter, fishballs, coffee, tea, fruit, a poem by Emerson and an article on Thoreau." On March 17, Conway reported that the printing of *The Rejected Stone* had begun and he had heard a lecture by Emerson at the Music Hall where he himself was engaged to talk the following Sunday.

"By the way," Conway threw in casually, "Mr. Lincoln said the other day that he had got the 'R.S.' by heart. He says he was astonished to learn that its author was really a native of Virginia. He also said to Chas Sumner that he was now convinced that this was a great movement of God to end Slavery & that the man wd be a fool who should stand in the way. Our cause never looked so bright to me as now." No doubt the news from Washington had been passed on to Conway by Wendell Phillips, with whom, Conway reported to his wife on March 8 he had just had a thirty-minute talk, ending with Phillip's exclamation "Thank God for Old Abe!" Quite as important as Conway's report of Lincoln's approbation was his remark in the letter of March 17 that he was sending his wife "an amusing and sensible pamphlet written by a first rate man here whom I've known a long time - Mr. Bird."[296]

Letters awaited Conway on his return to his home late in March from several "prominent men in Boston," Samuel Gridley Howe, George Luther Sterns, Frank W. Bird and others, proposing that Conway should become editor of a new journal, to be published in Boston, in support of immediate emancipation.[297] The invitation came to Conway just at the time when Wendell Phillips, in attempting to deliver a lecture in the Cincinnati Opera House, had been jeered by an angry mob of Kentuckians and Ohioans.[298] When stones and eggs came whirling toward the speaker, all the lighting was turned off and Phillips was conducted out of the building by a back door.

Phillips insisted, in spite of this experience, on speaking from Conway's pulpit the following Sunday. The opportunity to take a more aggressive part in the struggle, suggested by the invitation from the "prominent men in Boston," was just what Conway needed. He accepted at once, not knowing that the men who were urging him to edit the new journal, *The Commonwealth*, were members of the secret committee that had financed John Brown in Kansas and at Harper's Ferry. Nor did he know, after the execution of Brown, they had been summoned to Washington by the Senate Investigating Committee led by John Murray Mason. These facts Conway learned long afterwards.[299]

In May 1862 Conway attended the Conference of Western Unitarian Churches in Detroit, and proposed a resolution that was unanimously accepted: "That in this conflict the watchword of our nation and our church and our government should be, *Mercy to the South*; death to slavery!"[300] In June, Conway asked his church to grant him a six-month leave of absence. On June 29 he preached his last sermon to his congregation.

Conway was engaged to edit *The Commonwealth* not only because he was well-known for his abolitionist stand but also because he had not been implicated in any secret plots to aid John Brown. It was hoped, too, that he would add a literary tone to this small propaganda publication. The success of Conway's *Dial*, to which Emerson had generously contributed, was as much due to its literary quality as to the political views occasionally expressed.

The April 1862 issue of *The Atlantic Monthly* further enhanced Conway's literary claims and linked his name more closely with the New England writers. Emerson's Smithsonian essay, entitled "American Civilization," appeared in this number. In a footnote Emerson acknowledged his indebtedness to Conway, whose essay, "Then and Now in the Old Dominion," was also in this number of *The Atlantic.*

These two essays were followed by one of Lowell's long dialect poems in which, in the half-humorous style of Lowell's "Biglow Papers," he advised "moderate measures until we are sure that all other means are hopeless" in the matter of freeing the slaves. Lowell merely straddled the question before the country in his essay, "A message to Jeff Davis in Secret Session. Conjecturally Reported by H. Biglow."[301] These three documents, each characteristic of its author, reflect three attitudes toward the confused issue of the day -- that of the Virginian, homesick for the countryside of his own people, but tragically aware of the stubborn pride of the South in regard to slavery; that of the high-minded New Englander who spoke for the abolitionists of the country with little first-hand knowledge of the South; and that of the compromiser, found in the North and in the South, who chose to evade the issue, hoping that things would somehow right themselves.

Conway's charming essay draws a contrast between the Old Dominion of the eighteenth century, which produced the men who wrote the Declaration of Indcpendence and the Constitution, and that of the nineteenth century, which destroyed the freedoms their ancestors had died to defend. Emerson was troubled by no such double vision. After his long talk with Conway in the Parker House, Emerson was convinced of the soundness of Conway's proposal for immediate emancipation. In his essay on "American Civilization" he agreed that enough had been written to prove the wrongness of slavery. But, he asked, "can you convince ... the iron interest, or the cotton interest by reading passages from Milton or Montesqieu?"

> The power that has legs long enough and strong enough to cross the Potomac offers itself at this hour; the one strong enough to bring all the civility up to the height of that which is best prays now at the door of Congress

> for leave to move. Emancipation is the demand of civilization. That is a principle; everything else is an intrigue. This is a progressive policy, -- puts the whole people in healthy, productive, amiable position, -- puts every man in the South in just and natural relations with every man in the North, laborer with laborer.
>
> We shall not attempt to unfold the details of the project of emancipation. It has been stated with great ability by several of its leading advocates. I will only advert to some leading points of the argument, at the risk of repeating the reasons of others*
>
> (Note: * I refer mainly to a Discourse by the Rev. M. D. Conway, delivered before the "Emancipation League," in Boston, in January last.)[302]

"America," wrote Emerson, "is another word for Opportunity. Our whole history appears like a last effort of the Divine Providence on behalf of the human race." The southerner seemed to Emerson merely a semi-civilized individual with whom the northerner must deal. He accepted, however, Conway's formula for ending the war:

> But one weapon we hold which is sure. Congress can, by edict, as a part of the military defence which it is the duty of Congress to provide, abolish slavery, and pay for such slaves as we ought to pay for. Then the slaves near our armies will come to us: those in the interior will know in a week what their rights are, and will, where opportunity offers, prepare to take them, Instantly, the armies that now confront you must run home to protect their estates, and must stay there, and your enemies will disappear. There can be no safety until this step is taken.

Emerson ended his essay by asking, "Now in the name of all that is simple and generous, why should not this great right be done? Why should not America be capable of a second stroke for the well-being of the human race, as eighty or ninety years ago she was for the first?"[303]

To Conway, Lowell's contribution to *The Atlantic* in which his and Emerson's essays appeared, was a clear indication of "the almost hopeless condition of the public mind."[304] Conway was already engaged in writing his second book, *The Golden Hour,* and added several pages on Lowell entitled "Homer Nodding.[305] "I allude," he wrote, to the Rev. Homer Wilbur of *The Atlantic Monthly* for implying that "to release millions from dungeons, fetters, auction blocks, and raise them to life" is a "desperate measure" not to be undertaken. "Is it possible that any cataract should have been so formed over this once clear eye, that it now sees a state of Slavery to be a normal phase in the condition of human beings?" In celebration of Emerson's splendid leadership, on the contrary, Conway renamed Chapter X of his book, "How to Hitch Our Wagon To a Star." It opened thus:

> It is one of the signs of the times, that the revolution was strong enough to take up bodily the Sage of Concord, and set him in the capital of this nation to instruct our rulers.

Conway is here referring to the fact that Emerson, soon after his talk with him, went to Washington to confer with both Lincoln and Seward. Lincoln received Emerson with his usual courtesy and good humor, but Emerson, like Conway, came away feeling that he had not been fully able to express his ideas to the president. Emerson found Seward definitely unpleasant. According to Conway, the advice [Emerson] gave them may be summed up in one sentence, "Hitch your wagon to a star!"[306] Lincoln had no intention of accepting any such advice; Conway, on the other hand, was all too susceptible to the idealism of the Sage of Concord.

Conway's vehement feeling that the hour had come for immediately freeing the slaves was strengthened by his conversations with Sumner, Phillips, Garrison, Emerson and others; by the enthusiastic audiences he had addressed; by his interview with Lincoln; and by the scenes he had witnessed in the streets, the trains, the hospitals, and the churches as he moved about the country. A few weeks before the appearance of *The Golden Hour*, he was called upon to take immediate action on behalf of the Conway slaves who had been "freed" by the Union forces moving down the very roads between Antietam and Falmouth that he had known as a child.

Dunmore and Eliza Gwynn, former slaves whom Conway led along with others to Yellow Springs, Ohio, after emancipation.

Chapter X
"My Father's Slaves"

Before leaving for Concord, in the summer of 1862, Conway and his wife visited friends in Yellow Springs, Ohio, for a few weeks' vacation. One evening, in the midst of a chess game with the president of a local chess club, Conway was called away from the table by his wife, who handed him a letter from his mother.[307] Conway's opponent made a careful notation of the board, and the interrupted game was finished fourteen years later.[308]

The letter from the elder Mrs. Conway -- postmarked Washington, D.C., rather than Easton, Pennsylvania -- concerned his family slaves, now "freed" by the Union soldiers, and wandering helplessly in the woods and fields of Stafford County. All mails were disrupted by the war, and Conway had had no communication with any member of his family for many weeks. This letter reached him through the zeal of the Negro, Collin Williams, whom Conway had located in Boston nine years earlier. He had settled in Georgetown, D.C., with his wife, and had assumed the responsibility of keeping channels of communication open in every way he could. Conway knew only that Collin had somehow been entrusted with the letter which he now held in his hand. That same evening, Moncure started on a weary, three-day journey to Washington, determined, if possible, to rescue his father's slaves.

Mrs. Conway's letter told her son that two of the family slaves had been seen in Washington. The rest were still in Falmouth, behind Union lines without any means of earning a living. The two his mother referred to were, Conway assumed, Dunmore and Eliza Gwinn, who had opened a cake-and-candy store in Georgetown and were using their house as a refuge for Negroes moving North. Conway House, he had heard, had been turned into a hospital for wounded northern soldiers. His father had gone to Fredericksburg to stay with relatives during the occupation, and his younger brothers had joined the Confederate ranks. Conway had time to ponder these meager facts as he sat in the crowded train among the Union troops speeding eastward to fight his own people. General George B. McClellan, he knew, commanded the Army of the Potomac and was attempting to reach Richmond by way of the peninsula between the York and James rivers. General Irvin McDowell, after the defeat of his army at Bull Run in July 1861, was ordered to support McClellan and had moved the Union army through Falmouth, leaving confusion in his wake. Conway did not know whether his father's slaves were still wandering in the Stafford countryside or had escaped to join the Gwinns in Georgetown.

Curiously, Conway had recently received a small parcel from a Union soldier whom he had known slightly in Washington. In it he had found a cup and saucer and a silver spoon from his old home, which the soldier had rescued for his friend while his regiment was furiously destroying the furniture, the portraits, the china and the rugs of Conway House.

On reaching Washington on July 15, 1862, and settling into the home of his Unitarian friends, Mrs. Walter Johnson and her sister, where William Henry Channing was also living, Conway at once sought out Salmon P. Chase, who, he knew, would be glad to help in his search for the slaves. Secretary Chase took Conway to the office of Secretary of War Edwin M. Stanton, from whom he wished to secure a permit to search for the Conway slaves behind the Union lines and to escort them across the District and on to Ohio. Secretary Stanton refused the request, saying that he did not want more Negroes in Washington and the war situation in Stafford County was too critical for such an undertaking.

Conway accepted Stanton's rebuff and then went directly to Lincoln and stated his case to him. The president listened to his plans with sympathy -- knowing very well that he was talking with one of his own outspoken critics -- and agreed with Conway that it was his duty to protect his father's slaves, whom he did not consider "fugitive" since they would be in Conway's care. After warning Conway of the dangers, Lincoln directed him to the military headquarters of the District of Columbia, where Brigadier General W.J. Wadsworth immediately issued the necessary order: "The Rev'd Mr. Conway will be allowed to go to Falmouth and return on Government Boat and R. R. train."

Armed with his pass, which made no reference to Negroes, Conway set out for Georgetown to find his old friends, Dunmore and Eliza Gwinn. By winning the confidence of a group of Negroes standing on a street corner, Conway was led to the home of the Gwinns. Dunmore, Eliza and their infant daughter were living in the rear of their cake-and-candy store. They had managed, in the month they had been established there to save $60, which they were eager to use to help their friends make the journey to the District. Dunmore told Conway, to the surprise of his father, that all the Conway slaves had asked their master for their freedom and had obtained it soon after General McDowell's troops had entered the town and had declared the Negroes free. Though they wept when they said goodbye to their kind masters, none of them, not even the old and infirm, hesitated in their resolution to die as free men and women. Some had been able to earn a meager living by blackening the boots of the soldiers or washing their clothes; many were destitute and desperately in need of direction. The Emancipation Proclamation had not yet been issued; hence, no provision had been made for the confused Negroes, who were still officially considered "fugitive slaves" by the government in Washington.

Fearing that Falmouth might soon be taken again by southern troops, who would seize the "freed" Negroes and reduce them to a crueler servitude, Conway made up his mind to go to Falmouth as soon as possible and lead his little band of about thirty men, women, and children before it was too late. Meanwhile, in the Gwinns' small kitchen, he heard with fascination of the final release of the slaves attached to the Chatham estate whom Uncle Richard Moncure had tried in vain to help. Lacy, the heir to the estate. had broken Mrs. Coalter's will and sold most of the seventy slaves he had falsely won. General McDowell had commandeered the Chatham mansion for his headquarters and "freed" the twenty slaves remaining on the farm. Then he had led Lacy, the Confederate major, with his hands tied behind his back and his head hung low, through the crowd of Negroes whom he had wronged. They watched their hated master, said Dunmore, in complete silence, uttering no jarring word or imprecation as he passed.[309]

The story of the looting of Conway House, probably told to Moncure by Eliza and Dunmore that night, helped explain the parcel of souvenirs Moncure had received from the Union soldier.[310] General McDowell soon after the defeat at Bull Run had led the "victorious" Union troops down the deserted street by the Rappahannock River A shot from a window of the supposedly empty Conway Mansion had torn into the ranks of his soldiers, seriously wounding one of them. At once the men were ordered to batter down the front door and search the house, spreading destruction as they went. Rushing into Mrs. Conway's bedroom, the soldier who had known Conway in Washington recognized the portrait of his friend hanging over his mother's bed and cried out to his companions to stop their wild looting long enough to call in the slaves who were still occupying their quarters in the garden. Eliza Gwinn, hearing the news, entered the room before the other servants, shouting "It's mars' Monc, the preacher, as good Abolitionist as any of you!" Thus, the portrait of the "black sheep" of the family had saved Conway House. It was turned into a hospital, the wounded soldier being the first man to be cared for. Here Walt Whitman, a few months later began his nursing, not suspecting that he was in the abandoned home of his friend.[311]

Encouraged by his visit with the Gwinns, Conway spent the rest of the afternoon vainly searching for other Negroes from his father's home who might have escaped to Falmouth. Undaunted by a severe storm, he returned to the home of his friends in Washington determined to leave for Falmouth at daybreak the following morning.[312]

Conway said his goodbyes to the family early in the evening and mounted to his room. Instead of going to sleep, however, he lay awake, filled with misgivings concerning his adventure. How was he to find his Negro friends once he reached Falmouth? Would they know him after the intervening years? Would they trust a white man? Why was no mention made of Negroes on his military pass? Should he return to Georgetown and try to find Collin Williams?

The terrific storm that had broken over Washington during the afternoon grew more intense. Accompanied by thunder and lightning, the torrents of rain seemed to blot out the very street beneath his window. No cab would possibly undertake the five-mile trip to Georgetown. Conway was suddenly seized with the impulse to attempt the journey though he would have to go on foot and alone, without any knowledge of where Collin Williams lived. He pulled on his clothes and crept out of the house at about eleven o'clock.

Struggling through mud and rain for over an hour, Conway found himself among the absolutely dark shanties of Georgetown not knowing which way to turn. Then he noticed a flicker of light behind the black curtain of one small house and heard the voices of Negroes singing familiar hymns. Conway knocked at the door and was greeted by a dead silence; another knock, and then, "Who is that?" "A friend!" he replied, "Moncure Conway!" With a shout the Negroes within flung open the door; suddenly he was surrounded by all of his father's servants, who had arrived only a few minutes before and were dripping wet after their long journey through the drenching rain. "They were a sad-looking set." Conway wrote several years later:

> They looked as if they thought that Nature had taken sides against them, and the elements turned blood-hounds to pursue and yelp after them. Through a long and weary way of about sixty miles they had dragged themselves and their little ones, their beds and chests. Each family had three or four young children, and nearly every mother a babe at her breast. To me they seemed a first arrival of Israelites, who had come through the sea parted by the wand of God, their garments wet with its spray. Silent and gloomy they sat, trying to hush their children to sleep or quiet. They were all packed in one small cellar, over which the thunder crashed with alarming proximity.[313]

Maria Humstead, who had nursed Conway as an infant, sprang from the group and folded him in her arms as though he was still a child. While the thunder roared without, they sat far into the night and listened with shining eyes to Conway's description of the far-away land where he intended to take them. Conway did not speak of the troubles he knew lay ahead of them all, for Negroes were still considered contraband; the railroads demanded a $3,000 bond for everyone who dared to travel North. Angry pro-slavery mobs were apt to surround Negroes as they crossed both Washington and Baltimore, thinking them "fugitives." Anti-slavery mobs were also potential dangers since they might suspect Conway of kidnapping his father's slaves intending to sell them. Conway did not express these concerns to the circle of crouching Negroes. None of them had ever before been out of the small Virginia neighborhood in which they were born, much less seen a large city, a railroad, or a steamer.

After the children were hushed to sleep, their elders sat silent and gloomy – some in tears – listening to the storm without and thinking of their unknown destiny. Agreeing on the time and place of their meeting the next day, Conway returned to Washington, determined to make good his promise to lead his father's slaves to a new land "where never should they feel oppression, never hear of war again."

Though General Wadsworth, the military governor of the District, was willing to ensure Conway and his Negroes safe transit across Washington, he could not help them through Baltimore. This city was under the jurisdiction of Major General John Ellis Wool, an elderly officer terrified by the pro-slavery mobs that roamed the streets. After anxious consultation with Senator Sumner, Secretary Chase, and several other members of the cabinet, Conway procured a letter to General Wool authorizing him to grant protection to the group if the need should arise.

At last Conway, with his thirty or more colored people, and their "small world of baggage" was ready to cross Washington. A throng of contraband Negroes soon joined them, in part to cheer their pilgrimage and in part as escort. In Baltimore, trouble began at once, for only white people were permitted to travel on the cross-town stage coaches for the journey of several miles from one station to another. Hundreds of Baltimore Negroes, children as well as adults, immediately surrounded the group from Virginia, unable at first to decide whether the Virginian leading them was a slave-holder kidnapping southern Negroes with the idea of selling them or an abolitionist leading the group to freedom. Conway's followers must have made signs to the jeering, hissing crowd, for it was transformed in a moment to a group of helpful friends. Baggage was miraculously piled on wagons, children were lifted on boxes, and a triumphal procession formed to cross the city.

The procession was almost too triumphal. The excitement grew as the Negroes with their white leader passed through the streets until they reached the station on the other side of Baltimore where an angry crowd of whites was awaiting their arrival. Leaving the group to their fate, Conway hurried into the station to purchase the tickets for the trip, but he was greeted with the news there was no train to the West for three hours and "no room for niggers" in the waiting room. Conway approached the ticket agent, who just then arrived, and asked the price of the fare to Ohio; he was told, "I can't let those negroes on this road at any price." Without a word Conway presented his military order to the agent. When he had read the slip of paper, he looked up in amazement. "The paper says these are your father's slaves," he said. "Why, sir, you could sell them in Baltimore for fifty thousand dollars." "Possibly," replied Conway.

The agent was struck by the casual air of the Virginia slaveowner, who was not interested in selling his slaves. His attitude changed at once, "By God," he exclaimed," "you shall have every car on this road, if you want it, and take the Negroes where you please!" All obstacles vanished, and Conway was able to rescue his crowd, still on the curbstone outside, from the increasingly menacing throng of whites. With his tickets to Ohio in his pocket, Conway hardly noticed the curses and the jeers even when a voice called him "a damned Abolitionist, who had brought on the war."

At about eight o'clock in the evening the train pulled out of Baltimore. Conway observed, after putting the children to sleep on the benches of the car, their elders held a silent watch, making no preparations for the night. But when the train passed a small "wooding-station" in the middle of the night, the silence was broken and the singing and talking began. Conway learned later that this was the station that marked the dividing line between Slave State and Free State -- though how the Negroes knew this fact, since all were illiterate, he never understood. He surmised that probably Dunmore Gwinn, the leader of the group, had discussed the trip with Collin Williams in Georgetown and learned where to expect to pass over the frontier.

Once in Ohio, the Negroes talked with complete confidence to Conway throughout the remainder of the night, for these were the people whom he had known from his infancy and whom his father thought would never willingly leave the Conway family. He had written to his son concerning his Negroes, "The Northerners will see that these Negroes, instead of going to them, will remain loyally at our side through this ordeal." Now they spoke to Conway of their real feelings.

One and all knew that their freedom was the issue of the war; when news of the first battle of Bull Run and the rout of the Union forces had reached them in August 1861, their impulse was to go at once to join the Union forces, but they soon found the vigilance of their masters made this impossible. They again had assumed their quiet and obedient behavior while secretly exchanging information that had come to them by word of mouth -- who were the friendly generals and who the unfriendly (John C. Frémont was the most honored), where the battles were being waged, how the law stood in regard to the freeing of the Negroes. At the same time, many of their masters were spreading tales of the cruelty of the northerners and their plans to deport them. When the Confederacy was victorious at Bull Run, some "gentlemen" told their slaves that the war was over and the South had won. Such a state of despair spread among the slaves at this news that a number were actually ill.

Finally, the United States troops marched into Falmouth, in the summer of 1862, under General McDowell, who had spent the months after his defeat at Bull Run training his men for a longer and harder campaign. The colored population believed that Judgment Day had come and they were free at last. The burning bridges, the shells bursting over the river, the "poor whites" fleeing into the woods -- not their masters, for they had already left -- all made a vision like the end of the world as evoked by their preachers and announced by many a hymn. The Union soldiers found the houses of the town deserted, but the Negro cabins, they discovered, were filled with families on their knees praying for deliverance from the conflict they did not understand. Conway told his friends that they were not so wrong after all, for the Day of Judgment for the whole guilty land, North and South alike, had at last come.

Throughout these difficult days, Conway had kept in touch with his wife and their friends at Yellow Springs. When the train arrived in the morning the travelers found that a large old barn had been fitted out for their reception and food provided for their immediate needs. The Gwinns had been able to save a little money and with the assistance of the people of Yellow Springs moved into a small house at once. Before many days, all those able to work, either as farm hands, mechanics, or house servants, were fully engaged. Nor did the laborers of the neighborhood object as it became evident that there was enough work for all.

Having settled his father's slaves near Yellow Springs, Conway returned to Boston to consult about the first issue of *The Commonwealth* and to fulfill several speaking engagements. He took with him to Easton, Pennsylvania, a young colored girl, once his sister's slave, who wished now to be his sister's servant. Conway stayed with Julia Ward Howe and her husband while he was in Boston. He told these two ardent abolitionists something of his recent experiences, including an anecdote of a Negro who had approached the Union commander of Port Royal, Virginia, Colonel Lee, with the question, "Will you please, sir, tell me if I am a free man?" The commander did not know how to answer the Negro, for Lincoln had not yet proclaimed emancipation. The next morning Mrs. Howe gave Conway her well-known poem beginning, "Tell me, master, am I free?" as her comment on the cruel situation in which escaping Negroes found themselves.[314]

Conway repeated the story of his father's slaves in many speeches, both in this country and in England. One such speaking engagement was reported in the *National Anti-Slavery Standard* of August 4, 1862, then edited by Oliver Johnson.[315] The occasion was the celebration on the first of August, at ten-thirty in the morning, of the thirtieth anniversary of the emancipation of 800,000 slaves in the British West Indies. Samuel Joseph May opened the meeting in the Town Hall of Abington, Massachusetts, and introduced Garrison as the first speaker. Though the day was overcast, Garrison spoke to "troops of holiday-dressed people," including "a large number of our colored friends," who had come by train, by carriage, and on foot to commemorate the day.

Garrison told the audience, when the British Parliament passed the Emancipation Act in 1833 there was no rejoicing in this country "in view of that grand and glorious event -- none whatever," for "terrible consequences" were expected in this "slave-holding, slave-breeding, slave-driving, slave-trading nation." Garrison spoke briefly since, as he pointed out, "they were favored with the presence of quite a large number of speakers," who, he hoped, would follow his example and curtail their words.

The speech of the Rev. John Sella Martin of Boston (sandwiched in between two "appropriate" hymns) was not reported in *The Standard*. Nor were those of Wendell Phillips and half a dozen other speakers, for the "Speech of Rev. M.D. Conway" filled the remaining two and a half columns of the front-page article in *The Standard.* [316] Frequently interrupted by "applause" and "laughter," Conway's lively account of his recent experience in conducting his father's slaves to Yellow Springs occupied the morning hours and left no time for Phillips, who was to have been the next speaker.

Conway opened his address by a forthright attack on Lincoln's concept of his power as president. He is, Conway declared, "a tool which the masses are to move." Soon some smart Yankee would surely invent "an automation President," Conway suggested. Meanwhile, Lincoln "is simply staying there and receiving $25,000 a year until he can get a machine that will sign measures." The Proclamation of Emancipation will come, Conway assured the crowd, but "just too late to be of any practical benefit to the country." Having recently spent two weeks in Washington, "trying to cut some red tape," Conway said that he could vouch for the fact that "it is impossible for Abraham Lincoln to move faster than a tortoise; he had tied it and it is 'no go'" (laughter and applause). Meanwhile, McClellan and his army had bogged down in a swamp on the shores of the James River in a vain attempt to reach Richmond.

He cannot retreat, said the speaker jubilantly, for the peninsula is held by the Confederate forces, nor can he advance, for Richmond is too well guarded by Generals Robert E. Lee and Stonewall Jackson. Were Lincoln to issue a Proclamation of Emancipation immediately, McClellan would be able to summon to his aid Negroes now powerless to help. They would gladly act as guides, soldiers, or diggers of ditches. "But the President is a tortoise, and the army an elephant resting upon him; he cannot bring himself to declare the Negroes free," said Conway. He told a story to show that people in the West were already more willing than those in the East to accept emancipation:

> A negro man, on a Western car, lay, in the middle of the night, coiled up on a seat in the cars, fast asleep. A nicely dressed white man came in, and looked round, trying to

> find a seat. He went to this negro, and shoved him, and said, "Wake up, here!" "What's the matter?" "I want a seat." "I am a nigger; you don't want to sit by me, do you?" "I don't care whether you are a nigger or not; I want a seat." That is a sign. When a man is willing to sit down with a negro rather than stand up all night in a railroad car, it indicates a great change (laughter.)

No doubt Conway was describing a scene he had witnessed on the crowded train that had recently brought him from Ohio to Washington.

"Progressing at this astonishing rate in our willingness to accept the Negroes as fellow human beings," Conway continued, the government could permit them to "ditch and spade" for the Union army rather than die from neglect, as they were now doing. By assuring them a modicum of justice through emancipation, they would ally with Union forces rather than burden them with problems. "You have no idea," said Conway, "how much is to be done in Washington, Baltimore, and in all the Border States." To win the Negro and to push the line that divides the country further and further south, "Negro Reception Camps" should be set up for "fugitive slaves." Here they should be welcomed and their masters recompensed for their loss. But few in the North or South had thought of treating the Negro with consideration and thus enlisting the support of three million potential citizens. "The other day," Conway told his audiencc,

> William Henry Channing, the faithful minister of Washington, was walking in the street, and he saw a man with brass buttons on his coat -- and I suppose he was a soldier -- who was about to knock a negro down with a paving-stone. "What are you going to do?" says Channing, seizing him by the arm. "That nigger struck a white man; I am not going to stand by and see a white man struck by a d-d nigger." "Didn't the white man strike him first?" "Yes, he did; but isn't he a nigger?" Channing said -- "This is a land of equal rights." The man looked at him utterly paralyzed. The stone fell from his hand, and with a gasp for breath he walked away (laughter and applause). Now, two thirds of the people of the United States are just in that

> state of mind; and as soon as we seize them by the arm, rather roughly, and tell them, "Equal rights with this d-d nigger?" I am sure we shall paralyze them with astonishment, at least.

Neither Garrison nor Phillips had ever traveled in the South. They could hardly have understood, as they listened to the speaker, that Conway was here describing the behavior of a Union soldier. The relationship between master and slave that had always pertained in the Conway household was unknown to these men who had worked so long and so valiantly in the Anti-Slavery movement that they had both come to believe slaveholders were monsters with whom there could be no dealing. Garrison's pamphlet, "The New Reign of Terror" (1857) and Phillips' essay, "The Philosophy of the Abolitionist Movement," (1860) were the expressions of men who did not intend to state their case for abolition in fair or moderate terms.

"No Union with Slaveholders" was on the masthead of Garrison's *Liberator*: "the sooner the Union goes to pieces the better," wrote Phillips, for he considered the constitution itself a pro-slavery document. "Our aim is to alter public opinion," said Phillips. He and Garrison attempted to do just that by extensive lecture tours in the summer of 1862 and by conferences with the president. Neither Garrison nor Phillips had voted for Lincoln in 1861, for both feared he would compromise with the southern states on slavery. They were now as impatient as Conway for Lincoln to issue the Emancipation Proclamation. Conway, however, loved the "Old Dominion" whereas his older friends had grown to hate everything that had to do with the South.[317]

To Conway, who had no wish to put the blame entirely on the South, Washington itself seemed corrupted by pro-slavery sentiments, the virus that affected the North as well as the South. Conway told his audience:

> Washington, as I came out of it, seemed to me a mad and doomed city; and I felt as though I could take off my shoes, and shake from them every particle of dust that belonged to it. It seemed to me to be the representative, the symbol, of a state of things that must pass away, and is passing away. It seemed to me to be the representative

> of a past stratum of this country, a sign, like some old Saurian, of an era that can never return; and I felt, that with the epoch which it represents, Washington city must pass away; pass into the fossil condition; be embedded with the past, so that upon its ruins we can lay the corner-stone of a free republic (applause). It seemed to me that its doom was written all over it and all around it. In Maryland, which borders Washington city, the spirit of the people, even of Unionists, is so determinedly pro-slavery, they do so hug to their hearts the viper that is stinging them to death, they are so resolved that harm shall not come to the dragon that devours them, that I fear they will have to pass along to their graves together.

Putting aside all rhetorical flourishes, Conway then gave a half-humorous, very informal account of his adventures in cutting the "red tape" of a nation at war and leading his family slaves to a new home. Only a patient president, straining to carry out the spirit of the Fugitive Slave Act despite the pressure of the abolitionists and the strain of military reverses, could have made it possible for Conway to succeed in his efforts. As he told his listeners:

> I was trying to get some negroes through Baltimore. It took me about two weeks to get those thirty-one negroes into Ohio, where I wished to take them. There they were in the District -- contrabands. If I had left them there, each of them would have had to receive an army ration from the government; each of them would have been in the hands of the government; so much money gone; and yet, so powerful was red tape, that nobody seemed to know who could give any permission to those contrabands to go North, or to go out of the District. Mr. Stanton scratched his head over it, and turned and twisted over it, and almost stood on his head over it (laughter), and he wanted to give some money to help get them off; but I would not take any money. I did not want his money; I wanted his authority. Well, he could not give it. And Mr. Lincoln, he unwound himself to a very great length (laughter), and then wound himself up again over it; he appreciated the

> State of the case a great deal, but did not seem to see what he could do about it. So we went from one to another.

Conway himself must have been struck by the patience and kindness of this harassed president who found time to attend to his problem. That was important, of course, because it was related to the larger problem of the fugitive slave. Conway continued:

> Finally, we had a consultation in Mr. Sumner's room, to try and devise some plan by which these contrabands could be got away, and everybody failed – even Mr. Sumner could not see the way clear. There was one man there – I forget his name – who sat very profoundly cogitating how we could get these negroes out to Ohio. The difficulty was to get them across Baltimore from one railroad to another, and so North, for the Baltimore railroads will not allow any negro to go over their roads unless he gives bonds to a fabulous extent. As I said, there was one man at Mr. Sumner's room, who sat cogitating over this subject; he did not say anything at first, but scratched his head and looked very profound; and we all began to feel that the man, when he spoke, would have a profound idea. We looked for it, we expected it, and finally we got a little nervous, as people will who expect a sharp flash of lightning, and it does not come. At last, the man raised his head and said -- "You want to take those negroes through Baltimore, through Maryland?" "Yes, that is what I desire." There is but one way to do it. You buy fifty feet of rope, and tie every buggar's hands behind him, and all Baltimore will bow down to you. They will be sure you are a big slaveholder, taking your slaves through Baltimore into Harford County, to keep them from being freed in Washington." That man hit the nail on the head. I did not have the courage to carry out his suggestion, but I have no doubt it illustrated the real feeling of Baltimore; for I felt, when I did at last get through that city, that nothing on earth but the signature of a Major-General, backed by the bayonets of Northern soldiers, kept the mob spirit from overwhelming us. We

went through that city for a mile and a half, and stopped at the depot for three hours, and nothing but that little bit of paper protected us from the muttering crowd around.

Frustrating as the whole experience was, Conway reflected, at least he had "got those people through Baltimore," with the help of "that name on a little bit of paper." "The time had come when at least thirty-one human beings could be carried straight through the heart of a slave State into liberty (applause); and although that did not reflect much glory on the government, or afford much prospect of its success, it did show, that despite the clouds with which weak men would blind us this is the Golden Hour for the land." However, said Conway, indulging in a bit of political prophesying,

Mr. Lincoln will never save this country. We shall be happy if we can, from month to month, keep ourselves from going to wreck under this Administration for a year or two, and then we shall know what we shall do. If we can succeed, though boldness, through moral courage, through stalwart determination and standing by our principles, in keeping the ship together for a year or so, then either we shall elect a Democratic President, who will put the nation under the heel of Jeff Davis, or we shall have Fremont in the Presidential chair, and Gen. Hunter will be Secretary of War (loud applause).[318] We must go one way or the other. We must elect one or the other. We are either to be saved or ruined. Garrison, critical of Lincoln as he was, had not joined the Emancipation League, of Boston (as had Conway) to agitate for immediate emancipation. Garrison, indeed, since the firing on Fort Sumter had slowly moved toward· support of Lincoln and war, reversing the position he had held for more than twenty years for a peaceful separation of North and South. In a two-hour speech recently made at the Cooper Institute, Garrison had declared, "I am now with the Government to enable it constitutionally to stop the further ravages of death and to extinguish the flames of hell forever." The "man of peace" had become the "man

> of war", in order to free the slaves by restoring the Union as soon as possible.

Phillips, who had supported Garrison throughout the long struggle, now showed signs of splitting with him. He went further than the old leader in his determination to destroy Southern society by confiscating the estates of the slave-holders. Not content with freeing the slave, he wished to rebuild the South on the foundation of the freed Negro, who, with the small farmer and the artisan, would annihilate the slave-holding oligarchy by means of the vote. Though Conway hardly realized it, Phillips was now the leader of the Radical Republicans who did not wish an end of war until the society in which slavery had flourished should be destroyed.

Conway could not, on that speech-making day in Abington, know the minds and hearts of the two men he so admired. Nor could they comprehend the final peroration of his speech. which carried him beyond the subject of "My father's Slaves" into a concept of the relation of slavery in the United States to world revolution. "Perhaps," said Conway, dropping entirely his somewhat humorous account of his experiences in Washington,

> looking at the case of the nation now, we are disposed to limit the great work of God. Perhaps we think so much of the United States alone, that we would be glad to limit this revolution. There are indications, my friends, that this revolution is to be world-wide before it is ended. There are indications that all nations are to be sucked into this maelstrom, and that when we are free the world will be free too (applause). I can interpret in no other way the ineffable stupidity of our rulers. I can in no other way interpret the fact, that in this great emergency we have a tortoise for President, except that, through the dreary length of a long war, gradually France, England, Russia, all monarchies and absolutisms are to be drawn into this controversy that sweeps over the land, the elements will melt with fervent heat, and the whole world be baptized with a fiery baptism and be redeemed. Let them come on! I say to the tyrants of the Old World, "What thou doest,

> do quickly!" I hope that England and France will intervene. Let them! It will only bring us shoulder to shoulder.

Thus, if the whole world were aroused, the "death-blow of the rebellion" would be struck at once, "for when slavery is struck, the rebellion lies dead." The implication of Conway's speech was probably not precisely understood by himself or his audience; his thoughts had flown to lofty visions of humanity redeemed from all forms of tyrannies. "We ought to remember," he said, "that there are other hearts that groan throughout the world, besides the slaves, that there are other beings, all through Europe, all through the North and the South, who groan under monarchies and despotisms, and that these, too, must be redeemed; and the signs of the times are that this revolution is to be world-wide, and that Humanity is to rejoice in the fruits thereof (applause)."

Conway, in the final paragraph of his speech, was expressing once more the thought he had been repeating from Washington to Boston and throughout the Middle West -- that slavery in the United States was only one aspect of the much larger problem of despotism of all sorts throughout the world. *The Rejected Stone* of Justice might still be used to rebuild the country if *The Golden Hour* were not allowed to pass -- the hour when Lincoln, by freeing the slaves, might have both saved the Union and avoided war. A second and third edition of Conway's earlier book came out in 1862, and *The Golden Hour* was on press when he addressed the Abington meeting.

Still hoping that the South might be spared and slavery eliminated, Conway had recognized in his book, and repeated in his speeches, that affairs had gone too far to avoid war. He feared that "over the eye of this nation Slavery has formed a hard cataract, so that it cannot see the peace and glory which are an arm's length before it, -- a cataract which only the painful surgery of the sword can remove." If this be so, he wrote, "we can only say, -- Bleed, poor country!" Conway perceived quite clearly that "Garrison, the old standard-bearer," had furled his banner of peaceful disunion, and that "the clear bugle of Phillips sounds the old martial call again," and he regretfully followed their leadership.[319]

Unlike Garrison and Phillips, however, Conway insisted that "there has been but one Satanic divider who had opened a chasm between us, -- Slavery." The South did not really hate the North, nor the North the South. Take away "the virus of Slavery" and men of good-will on both sides would recognize that they are of common Anglo-Saxon origin. [320] Conway was unable to measure the ignorance, hatred, and nobility that confused the minds of Garrison and Phillip. The eloquent young southerner's account of the resettlement of his father's slaves seemed to them only excellent propaganda material for further exploitation; his words on the relation of slavery in this country to the rest of the world might even prove useful.

In *The Golden Hour* Conway described himself as one who had come to understand both North and South and could throw aside his prejudices. Slavery itself was the "real foe of this Nation," he wrote.

> The writer of these pages was reared in the midst of hatred and contempt of the Northern people, and did himself hate and despise them cordially during all his early youth; he held it to be his highest ambition to assist in severing that section from the North. But fortune led him to a year's residence in a little Quaker settlement (Sandy Spring) where Slavery did not exist, and which consequently was an oasis upon a Slavery-wasted desert; and with this one step out of the atmosphere of Slavery, with the first glance of doubt toward that institution, a cloud of illusions cleared up, the antipathy to Northern men disappeared, and he experienced a revulsion in their favor which did them even more than justice.
>
> He knows, moreover, the leaders of the Southern Rebellion, many of them personally, all of them by character, and knows them to be very earnest madmen; he knows that the North can, by sealing up the one source of madness and disunion which has within a few years brought about this alienation, wither it up forever[321]

He added that, unfortunately, most northerners are not interested in curing this madness, for they profit by it. "I fear," wrote Conway, "the North is anxious to preserve Slavery for the cotton and sugar it brings: [and] anxious to have all the lands and political power, without which Slavery makes every white man as well as black man in the South a slave."[322] The abolitionists, he pointed out, had for years combatted the business interests of the North as well as the South in their tireless effort to eradicate slavery. "If this country is to be saved," wrote Conway, "the Abolitionists are to save it.,"

Conway's faith in the single-minded purpose of this spearhead group was unshaken when he made his long and outspoken address at Abington. He had yet to learn that Garrison and Phillips, the old leader of the abolitionists and the new leader, had in their change from a peace party to a war party become involved in a power struggle with the South that went far beyond emancipation of the Negroes to punishment of their masters. "What is an Abolitionist?" asked Conway in *The Golden Hour*. "He is simply a man who desires liberty for the entire family of man," was his answer to the question.[323] Conway defined the meaning he himself gave the term rather than that accepted by the leaders of the American Anti-Slavery Society.

Chapter XI
Concord and *The Commonwealth*

In September 1862, the Conways moved into a pretty little cottage in Concord, found for them by Emerson – the first house they had ever owned. Moncure, Ellen, and their two small boys, Eustace and Emerson, arrived in time to gather the apples that were sweetening the air in the large garden surrounding their new home. The new editor of *The Commonwealth* could not have been more happily situated.

Not only were the Conways living in a beautiful little village inhabited by such friends as the Emersons, the Alcotts, the Channings, the Thoreaus, with whom they had exchanged visits for years, but they were also breathing the somewhat heady air of the acknowledged center of abolitionist and transcendental thought. Conway's two books, *The Rejected Stone* and *The Golden Hour*, were read and discussed in the parlors of the Concord homes of Judge Ebenezer R. Hoar and Mrs. Horace Mann and others, for they were reviewed that autumn in the New York *Tribune* by Horace Greeley and in *The Atlantic Monthly* by the Rev. John Weiss.[324]

Conway was soon lecturing in the village lyceum on "the crisis," his simple theme being that "the war was a gigantic catastrophe and mistake, the only arm needed by Liberty being – Liberty." Conway was not slow to recognize that his experience in leading his father's slaves to Yellow Springs and settling them there was excellent material for a popular lecture, which he called "A Leaf from the History of To-day." As a Virginian who had fearlessly led his family slaves to freedom, Conway had not only a story to tell but also a chance to state again his case against Lincoln. Assuming that the nation was not at war, said Conway, Lincoln argued that he was merely trying to put down an insurrection of southern states and therefore had ordered that escaped slaves be returned to their "owners" in the South.

However, the nation obviously was at war; Virginia had been invaded. By not at once freeing the slaves, Lincoln had failed to make use of thousands of Negroes eager to help the northern army.

The events of the next few weeks, in fact, forced Lincoln to change his tactics. After General Robert E. Lee had been compelled to retreat at the Battle of Antietam, September 17, 1862, Lincoln believed that he was strong enough to add his second aim, the abolition of slavery, to his primary aim, the preservation of the Union. Up to that time he had hoped that gradual emancipation with compensation to slave-owners and the establishment of colonies for free Negroes outside the United States might prevent the conflagration of Civil War toward which the country had moved despite his efforts. On September 22, 1862, as the tide of war was changing, Lincoln issued a preliminary proclamation announcing that on January 1, 1863, he would declare all slaves "forever free" in the states that were still in arms against the United States.

Conway and his abolitionist friends felt that the president by this announcement was merely giving the slave-holders time to sell their slaves to harsher masters in the deep South; the intervening months would but serve to unify southern determination to withstand what seemed to them an infringement of states' rights. The fact that General McClellan failed to follow up his victory at Antietam, and that Lee was able to rally the Confederate forces after the command was given to General Ambrose. Everett Burnside, seemed to give support to Conway's view (and that of his fellow abolitionists), that the emancipation of the slaves was more important than ever as a war measure. The attempt to starve the South into submission by a blockade of the Atlantic coast from South Carolina to Florida had only meant the extension of the war to New Orleans and the Mississippi. The "crisis" for Conway was the crisis of slavery; he now feared that after the war for Union had been won; another war to abolish slavery would have to be fought at once.

These ideas Conway freely expressed in every issue of *The Commonwealth*, the responsibility of which he shared with Franklin B. Sanborn, one of the Harvard friends who had driven out to Concord with him one wintry night to hear Emerson speak. The first number of the weekly appeared on September 6, 1862; thousands of copies were printed and those that could not be sold were freely distributed to judges, legislators, and politicians, for this was a propaganda sheet with an avowed purpose, the emancipation of the slaves.[325]

The journal that Conway was asked to edit was, in fact, the descendant of an earlier publication that had been allowed to lapse. The original *Commonwealth* was the informal organ of the Commonwealth of Massachusetts, now headed by an anti-slavery governor, John A. Andrew, who had protested the use of soldiers of Massachusetts for the return of fugitive slaves. It was financed by a number of Republican leaders and gradually taken over by "The Frank Bird Club" to help fugitive slaves, to raise money for the Republican Party and to advise and encourage the activities of John Brown until his execution in 1859.[326]

Conway in his *Autobiography* made his only reference to this little-known but very influential group:

> A club of Republican leaders, formed around one of the best of men and called after his name "The Frank Bird Club," had arranged at one of their dinners for the new journal. Another admirable man was George L. Stearns of Medford. From him I received a note of July 31 [1862] saying, "I am ready to furnish the means for the present publication of a weekly newspaper which will fearlessly tell the truth about this war[327]

The Bird Club, the center of the anti-slavery political power in New England, worked secretly in support of John Brown.[328] In June 1862, members of the Bird Club, indignant at the quiet disregard of Senator Sumner among New Englanders, decided to revive their small campaign paper, discontinued after John Brown's death and the ensuing Senate investigation. Frank Preston Stearns, son of George Luther Stearns, described the circumstances of the revival of *The Commonwealth*:

> On the second Sunday in June Mr. Stearns drove to South Boston and held a long consultation with Dr. S. G. Howe. "There is not a newspaper in Boston" [he said] "that will publish one of Sumner's speeches, or say a good word for him." "Then," said Mr. Stearns, "we must have a paper of our own and I will put a thousand dollars into it as a sinking fund." "I cannot do that," replied Dr. Howe, "but

> I will give three hundred." It was arranged that the paper should be called the Commonwealth, and that James M. Stone, a rather high-minded politician of Charlestown, should be editor

Mr. Stone, however, did not have the desired touch. Who then could be engaged really to arouse his readers? By chance,

> Rev. Moncure D. Conway preached a sermon in Cincinnati at this time which struck the right key note and attracted general attention. "Launch out into the deep," he said to the administration, "and no longer drift among the shallows." Soon afterward he came to Boston, and Mr. Stearns arranged with him to assist Mr. Stone in editing the Commonwealth, while preaching and lecturing in Boston and vicinity.[329]

Conway, well-known throughout the East and the Middle West for his lectures and sermons against slavery, was just the man to exhort his readers into a realization of the religious implications of the slavery question.

While Conway had been freely asserting his views from his pulpit in Cincinnati, Franklin Sanborn had been quietly living in Concord, conspiring with George Luther Stearns and others of the Secret Six to further the plans of John Brown. When the attack on Harper's Ferry ended in national tragedy, several of these men, including Sanborn, had fled to Canada to avoid arrest. They soon returned, however, to face the Mason committee of the Senate, appointed to investigate the whole John Brown affair. No action was taken against any of them except for Frank Sanborn, whose arrest was ordered on February 16, 1860.[330]

Sanborn retreated again to Canada but was persuaded to return, refusing, however, to testify against those who had supported John Brown. The Senate gave several officers of the government from Boston the power to arrest Sanborn, then in Concord. He was apprehended by five officers on April 3, 1860, but released at once on a writ of *habeas corpus* issued by Judge Hoar. The officers were ejected from Concord by irate citizens, and the next day the Massachusetts Supreme Court, by a decision written by Chief Justice Shaw, ordered the discharge of Sanborn.[331]

By the time Conway encountered his friend again in the autumn of 1862, Sanborn had married and settled down as a school teacher in the town that had protected him. Whether these facts were clearly known to Conway before he undertook the editorship of *The Commonwealth* in collaboration with Sanborn is not certain. Since they were freely stated in several issues of the weekly, beginning with that of January 1, 1863, it is probable that he was aware of the position of his colleague and in sympathy with Sanborn, though he avoided references to past events.[332]

Conway wisely enlisted the pens of Amos Bronson Alcott's daughter, Louisa May Alcott, and Julia Ward Howe for the new publication, softening politics with literature.[333] He himself reviewed current books, penned editorials, clipped excerpts from other publications, and even ventured into poetry of his own. As the date approached for the promised Emancipation Proclamation, Conway attempted to link the dawn of a new day with the birth of the Christ-child, effectively cloaking politics with literature:

Now let the angel-song break forth!
For night shall nevermore be night!
A quenchless star climbs o'er the earth,
A torch lit up at God's own light.

There were the watching shepherds pressed,
Where Eastern seers bowed them low, -
From pole to pole, from east to west,
See the world's tidal pulses flow!
I saw the warrior on the plain
Pause in that light to sheathe his sword;
I saw that slave look up in pain, -
Chains melted in the fires it poured.

Thou God, who gavest our night this star,
Whose circling arm excludeth none,
Gather our treasures from afar
To the soul's monarch only born!

Kindle thy blessed sign again,

For the New World a Christ's new birth,
When to our cry, Good-will to men,
The heavens shall answer, Peace on earth![334]

Conway was convinced that the question of slavery was religious rather than political. Whether preaching a sermon, editing a journal, or addressing Congress, his style was rhetorical. The abolitionists who invited Conway to launch their weekly soon discovered that their editor was somewhat more vehement and independent than they had bargained for. Conway within a month announced that his name would be withdrawn from the masthead at his own request, explaining "the forces and persons which would naturally communicate with the public through this medium were in number and importance such as to make it improper to identify any single individual." Conway, in other words, wished to express his own views and not those of an editorial board, whose aims he only partially understood.

The new editor during the year of his incumbency also preached and lectured throughout the East, conferring with senators, ministers, newspapers editors, and, more than once, with President Lincoln himself. Conway threw himself with evangelical enthusiasm into the cause of immediate emancipation. That mission by no means precluded friendly association with his Concord neighbors, romps with his two little boys, scientific discussions in Boston with Dr. Holmes and concerts in the Music Hall. [335]

Entries in his diary reflect the vitality of this eminently social spirit. On December 19, 1862, soon after Robert E. Lee's victory over the Union troops at Fredericksburg, he wrote:

> Friday Dec. 19. Worked on my discourse "The Unrecognized Gift of God" from what Jesus said to the Woman at the Well "If thou knowest the gift etc." -- during the morning.
>
> -- Afternoon. Went with Mr. Austin & persuaded Mr. Sanborn to let his scholars out to go Skating. Sanborn wanted to go himself and let out. Went soon after to get Emerson girls. Found Mr. E's library full of little & big girls fixing skates etc. Asked him if he allowed that sort

> of thing to go in his study. Said "I was just wondering what good thing I had done that such a troop should enter." -- Had admirable Skate that night on Goose Creek. 20th. Went down to City. Thermometer at Zero. Heard Seward had resigned -- felt resigned myself. Called on Phillips who was much elated. Frank Bird met me Shouting 'Glory to God' like a Methodist. Went to J. T. Fields at 5. Una Hawthorne there. Called on [the Amos A.] Laurances – sic at Dr. Holmes' -- had long talk on Physiognomy.21st. Had a good deliverance at Music Hall [of "The Unrecognized Gift of God to America"]
>
> Dined & took tea with Dudleys, -- adorers of Emerson. -- Repaired to Fields' where Henry James & Mr. & Mrs. O. W. Holmes came in to spend evening. Dr. H. unusually pleasant -- had just heard of the safety of his son before Fredericksburg.[336]

The following day Conway again spent writing reviews for *The Commonwealth*, this time of the poetry of Adelaide Proctor and of the January 1863 issue of *The Atlantic Monthly*. In the afternoon he called on Emerson to arrange with him the Jubilee Concert for Emancipation, to be held in the Music Hall of Boston to celebrate the expected Emancipation Proclamation.[337] On his way home, Conway called on "poor Mrs. Thoreau," who had fallen down stairs and broken several bones. He spent the evening "making items for my paper, and writing up this Journal." Apparently, neighbors dropped in on the Conways for a chat during the evening, for Moncure added at the bottom of the page, "Much saddened by hearing tonight that Seward is still to be kept and the Cabinet not reconstructed. Not one should be left." After noting he had written for contributions to *The Commonwealth*, Conway closed the record for December 22 with the comment, "Thankful most today for good hours play with Eustace & Emerson."

Conway went off to Boston the next day, December 23, to talk over with his fellow editors an article he had written for *The Commonwealth* on Judge Conway's "resolutions" concerning immediate and unconditional emancipation, about to be presented in congress. Stone and Elizur Wright "objected," so the article became a "communication" to the Peabody Institute to deliver a lecture on "the crisis of the country" -- though Conway was warned that "a Literary Lecture" would be preferred.[338] On Christmas Eve, Conway lectured on the same subject at the Concord Lyceum and walked home with Judge Hoar, who took him to task for his remarks on the "Sewardism" of the American minister in London, Charles Francis Adams.

Home at last, Conway wrote up the events of the two days before Christmas and then observed, "The mellow light of Christmas is on us -- & wife moves about sly & mysterious & with stockings in her hands." On Christmas day, Conway took the family into Boston to enjoy a children's performance, "The Spectacle of Yellow Dwarf"; he then put them on "the cars" bound for Concord, while he dined with Judge Conway, G. S. Stearns, and others. Judge Conway was "all on fire with his theory of disunion for Freedom's Sake." Conway added, "He talks grandly, & I love him, & believe him to be essentially right." Before the year was out, on December 29, the Conways gave their first neighborhood party; Conway recorded in his journal of December 29, "Went to the City twice & returned to our Charade party which went off well, Wordsworth's Restoration (acted by Sanborn & Ellen Emerson etc.) and Transcendentalism which was very fine – Mr. Geo Bailure, Miss Alcott, Ellen Emerson, Edith E. Sanborn & myself acting."

On December 31, the day before emancipation took effect and all the slaves were freed by law, Conway was up before dawn to put a friend on the train to Boston, and then, observing the mounting snowdrifts on the road, resolved at once to set forth for Rochester, New York, where he had promised to lecture on January 2. By the time he reached Boston, however, the snow had abated. Instead of continuing on his way, he paused to visit friends and discuss once more the crisis in everyone's mind. As usual, Conway's anxiety concerning the morrow was relieved by the pleasantness of the moment. "Took tea with Judge Conway at Dr. Howe's," he wrote in his diary. "Judge C. still full of his Separation Theory -- which I approve of when we are sure we cannot get 34 States instead of 18 for Liberty. His error seems to me to lie in supposing Slavery a stronger thing than it is -- on its last legs I think."[339]

Later in the evening Conway found himself at the home of the Stephensons. Planning to go to "The African Church" to pray with them at midnight for the proclamation, the guests were glad to play charades. "Acted Transcendentalism again (Fanny Garrison, Slack, W L G Jr. & self)"[340] At eleven-thirty they arrived at the church and were recognized as friends. The only white people there, they were shown good seats though the church was crowded. The service opened with these words:

> *"Brethren and sisters, the President of the United States has promised that, if the Confederates do not lay down their arms, he will free all their slaves tomorrow. They have not laid down their arms. Tomorrow will be the day of liberty to the oppressed. But we all know that evil powers are around the President. While we sit here, they are trying to make him break his word. But we have come this Watch Night to watch and see that he does not break his word. Brethren, the bad influence near the President tonight is stronger than Copperheads. The old serpent is abroad tonight, with all his emissaries, in great power. His wrath is great, because he knows his hour is near. He will be in this church this evening. As midnight comes on we shall hear his rage. But, brethren and sisters, don't be alarmed. Our prayers will prevail. His head will be bruised. His back will be broke. He will go raging back to hell, and God Almighty's New Year will make the United States a true land of freedom."*[341]

The preacher was frequently interrupted by cries of "Glory." Just before midnight all were asked to kneel, and prayer followed prayer in a crescendo of rapturous excitement. Suddenly a long low hiss was heard and shouts arose, "He's here!" Hisses came from all comers of the church as the preacher's voice mounted to an incantation interrupted by cries of ecstasy. As midnight struck, the hisses died slowly away, and the congregation rose to sing with one voice the old Methodist "Year of Jubilee," so well known to Conway.

All joined hands as they shouted in the new era of freedom:

Blow ye the trumpets, blow
The gladly solemn sound:
Let all the nations know,
To earth's remotest bound,
The year of jubilee is come;
Return, ye ransom'd sinners, home!

Conway's voice broke with emotion as he joined in the triumphant hymn. The next morning, "New Year's Day, 1863," he wrote in his journal, "O What a glorious morning! Up early to glance at papers -- Alas no proclamation yet! It ought to have burst over the land with the morning Sun."

By 8:30 Conway was on the train for Rochester, ready to lecture and preach in various cities in New York and New England and eager to talk with old friends and new. He carried with him in his bag the sermon he had recently delivered with marked success, "The Unrecognized Gift of God," as well as his popular lecture on the escape of his father's slaves. He paused to go to the theater in Rochester – "rather rowdyish performance" -- and to visit Niagara Falls. On the second of January he recorded in his journal: "President's Edict at last -- such as it is. About as awkward as himself -- but still it liberates about 3,200,000 slaves! Spent the afternoon writing a discussion of it for my lecture. -- Lectured in the magnificent Corinthian Hall to about 1500 people After lecture many came up to speak to me." After the last handshake, Conway hurried to the theater "to hear the last half of The Marble Heart tolerably performed & and Poor Pillicaddy so-so." Five more days of lecturing, dining, sightseeing, and editorial-writing, then Conway wrote in his journal on January 8, "Left for home with merry heart," and on January 9, "Home Sweet Home. How can I ever leave it even for a night & day! All well, thank God."

Conway managed to stay in or near "home, sweet home" at least for the next two weeks. During this interval, he played with his children, skated on the Concord River, danced at Sanborn's school party, attended concerts, lectures and dinners, and he also preached on "Soul-Charity" ("No man cares for my Soul") to a "fine audience at Music Hall," wrote reviews, editorials, and essays for *The Commonwealth*, and worked on his lectures.

Conway's resilient nature enabled him to throw himself whole-heartedly into the demands of the moment – a conversation with "Miss Hardy" who wrote to him that she needed "Soul-Charity" and practical help in procuring support for her fatherless child, or a conference with Wendell Phillips, who had been invited to address the "old fogy Mercantile Library Assoc. of N. Y." Concerned though he was with events in Washington, Conway recorded in his journal, "Spent afternoon & tea at the Garrisons – delightful," and "Went with wife down to Alcotts to hear Miss Alcott's Letters from Georgetown Hospital--funny and pathetic." After attending a lecture on the English Navy on January 14, Conway completed the entries in his journal "and so woke up wife who slumbereth so peacefully over my 'Commonwealth'." As Sydney Howard Gay wrote of the abolitionists, "this handful of people, to the outside world a set of pestilent fanatics, were among themselves the most charming circle of cultivated men and women that it has ever been my lot to know."[342] In his circle of friends, the Conways found themselves perfectly at home.

The events of January 1863 show, however, that these charming and cultivated people were indeed "pestilent fanatics." Their serious concern with what seemed to them the ineffectiveness of the president's efforts to free the slaves soon became more outspoken. A "grand dinner at the Parker House" given for General Benjamin F. Butler, who had recently been superseded as military governor in New Orleans by General Nathaniel P. Banks, made many of the abolitionists doubt the sincerity of the government's position.[343] Though Butler professed to be anti-slavery, Conway was so convinced that his motives were merely political that, in disgust, he slipped away from the banquet table before he was to deliver his own speech and hastened to Medford to talk with George L. Stearns, recently returned from Washington, where he had been urging the recruiting of Negro troops. Stearns convinced him, though Butler was a "spoilsman," merely out to curry favor with the freed slaves, that Banks was worse and could be counted on to make only a pretense of enforcing the Emancipation Proclamation. "Shows what a fool Stanton is," Conway wrote in his Journal.

Conway's slogan, repeated in many of his speeches, was "Mercy to the South; Death to Slavery." He felt, therefore, that it was a tragic mistake for Lincoln to send pro-slavery generals into Virginia and North Carolina to enforce the Emancipation Proclamation. Like Stearns, Dr. Howe, and other members of the Bird Club, he considered John C. Frémont a better appointment than Banks, but he did not agree with these men that Negroes should be armed against their former masters. Unlike Garrison, Conway was "a man of peace."[344] Nor did he think, with the editor of *The Liberator*, that the work of the abolitionist was ended after the slaves were declared free. Like Phillips, he believed in civil rights for Negroes, but he did not wish to see the South crushed. The Emancipation Proclamation did not free the slaves but succeeded in spreading confusion among the abolitionists. The American Anti-Slavery Society was permanently split when the cause for which the society was organized was won.[345]

Conway's reply to a letter from Sydney Howard Gay, managing editor of the *Tribune* and ardent abolitionist, reflects his disagreement with the more militant wing of the group. Gay had suggested Negro insurrections in the South, perhaps with the thought of gaining the support of the editor of *The Commonwealth.*

Conway replied, on January 11, 1863, "MY dear Sir,"

> Your note is read. What assurance is there that if a Negro insurrection were to break forth thc Govt. at Washington and its Generals in the field wd. not be as much panic-striken as the rebels, -- and that the world wd. not see men held to bondage by the U.S. arms?
>
> We have the men ready to do the work which alone can save this country. If an assault shd. be made at Freds'bg .. and Segil & Fremont sent -- the one six miles above the other six below the city on the Rappahannock to cross & arm the Negroes -- to burn down a few houses & Haystacks, -- the army at Fred'bg wd. be worse than the dismemberment of the Union. You see Banks had actually stationed U.S. Soldiers about for the purpose of suppressing any stir on Jan. 1.-- the rotten-hearted scoundrel.

And the Govt. will cease this just so soon as the organs of public opinion -- the opinion of the real people not the 5 points swarms of maggots whom democrats call the people -- open on the rotten generals & leaders. Why cannot the Tribune & Post agree to open upon the miscreant (such as all know him to be) Banks? And Halleck -- the negro-hater, who said the other day to a friend of mine that "no country could be great without a servile class." And Burnside who proved himself incompetent at Fred'g is an idiot in saying that McClellan is the man to lead the army. And Seward.

If the leaders & representatives of the free & true North are as brave as they wish the Govt. to be we can force them to a true effort to be saved; if not, not.

It is a serious question whether this Slavery Corruption in the North has not gone a step too far. The cerebral tissue representing Commonsense seems to be eaten into.

Yours Cordially, M. D. Conway[346]

In Chapter XIII of *The Golden Hour* ("The Probabilities of Insurrection"), Conway had already given his answer to the question proposed by Gay. "We hear," he had written, "some talk of arming the slaves: would it not be well first to try the effect of doing them simple, unelaborate justice?" The instant the Negro should be declared free, and his freedom made valid by northern leaders who were in their hearts against slavery, then "Not insurrections, but stampedes to the banners of the Union Army would follow, and the war would be truly won."[347] These were the views Conway expressed before he undertook the editorship of *The Commonwealth*, and they remained unchanged after he became editor. He now found himself associated with men who responded in various ways to the problems that arose after the Emancipation Proclamation was promulgated on September 22, 1862, 100 days before becoming law on January 1, 1863.

On January 17, Conway dined in Boston with his friends of the Bird Club. Although never a member, as editor of *The*

Commonwealth he regularly attended their weekly collations in a private dining-room of the Parker House. Conway was also frequently included in the small, delightful dinners in the Stearns' home. Frank Stearns remembered that "during the autumn, [of 1862], Emerson, Wendell Phillips, and Moncure Conway dined together repeatedly at Mr. Stearns' house to discuss public affairs.' Encouraged by good food and wine, the conversation of these gentlemen was "very brilliant," wrote George Stearns' son. "When Emerson was animated the keenness of his criticism levelled all before it, and Conway's was more refreshing than the champagne."[348]

Though the meetings of the Bird Club were often gay and sociable, they had a serious political undertone. "The club never acted together consciously as a political body," wrote Stearns, "and yet when the leading members were of one mind it was a very powerful political machine. While Andrew was governor, the club was almost omnipotent in Massachusetts; and yet it never undertook to do politics for Massachusetts. It never became a clique or faction, nor the advocate of sectional interests. It had a truly national character and was as influential at Washington as at the statehouse."[349]

At one of these gatherings, Conway recorded in his journal, he talked with Governor Andrew. "Fremont is the only man who has shown ability to make a staff and his campaign plan is the only one which events have proved to be the very best," Andrew observed, for Frémont had demonstrated his sympathy for the cause of the Negro. During the summer and fall of 1862, the Bird Club was attempting to organize regiments to train Negro soldiers in the South. If General Stanley, the pro-slavery military governor of North Carolina, could be replaced by General Frémont , colored regiments might be trained. These liberated slaves would support the Union Army in the mountains of North Carolina, creating a diversion in the rear of General Lee's troops. Stearns was in "continual consultation" with Governor Andrew and also supplying loans to help launch the First Regiment of Massachusetts Volunteers, which was drilling near Stearns' house in Medford. Undiscouraged by the failure of John Brown, the Bird Club, led by Stearns and Higginson, was continuing the struggle.

Fired by the idealism of these men, Conway had written in *The Golden Hour*, "The side that first cries FREEDOM TO THE

SLAVE gains the day in this war," but he added that freedom was a farce if pro-slavery generals were appointed to delay the new order. Lincoln seemed to Conway and to many other abolitionists to lean toward the side of the pro-slavery element in the North as well as in the South in order to "preserve Slavery for the cotton and sugar it brings." But "as a Southerner I knew that negro insurrection was impossible," Conway insisted. The depth of his feeling for the South was probably not yet apparent either to himself or his northern friends.

The abolitionists of Boston decided to send a delegation to Washington to confer directly with the president "to bring a little radical influence to bear" on him.[350] Accordingly, on January 22, 1863, Conway, with Wendell Phillips, S. G. Howe, Francis W. Bird, George L. Stearns, J.H. Stephenson, Elizur Wright, and the Hon. Oakes Ames, set forth on their journey. They arrived on the evening of January 23, and Conway went at once to confer with William H. Channing, then chaplain of the Senate, to arrange with him to preach in the Senate Chamber on Sunday, January 25. Conway spent Saturday morning polishing his sermon, "The Unrecognized Gift of God to America," and sought out his old friends in Washington during the afternoon, among them a certain Nancy Parker, one of his father's slaves who had not gone with the others to Ohio. In the evening the delegation attempted to see the president, but Lincoln was called away by Stanton and the meeting was postponed until the following night.

Conway's sermon in the Senate chamber, delivered to about two thousand people, many of them old Unitarian friends, was greeted with several rounds of applause and then praised by Channing in a speech in which he pointed out that Conway was once "driven from the Capital for such Preaching." "It was the grandest opportunity of my life," wrote Conway in his journal, "& I was never so well satisfied with my performance." [351] News of the speech was wired to the New York *Tribune*, where it was given the caption, "The Negro, the Saviour of America." The label seemed to Conway "not unfair."

On the second evening, President Lincoln received the eight men of the Boston delegation together with Senator Henry Wilson of Massachusetts. The president entered the room laughing over a conversation he had just enjoyed with his little sons. "It was pathetic," Conway noted, "to see the change in the President's face when he resumed his burden."[352]

Senator Wilson arose to introduce the group individually, but Lincoln waved him aside, asking all to be seated, saying that he knew the men quite well. No doubt Lincoln knew not only his visitors but also their message concerning the proclamation. Wendell Phillips led the conversation by quietly asking the president how well the proclamation was working. Lincoln replied that he hoped something would come of it in time -- that he had not expected sudden results and so could not be disappointed.

To Phillips' reminder that the people in the North were largely anti-slavery and that they were more and more convinced that the generals appointed by the government to carry out the edict in the South were lax in their duties, to say the least, Lincoln replied with a certain dryness: "My own impression, Mr. Phillips, is that the masses of the country generally are only dissatisfied at our lack of military successes. Defeat and failure in the field make everything seem wrong." Phillips hinted that the president might be interested in assuring his reelection by considering northern sentiment in regard to slavery. The president broke in, "Oh, Mr. Phillips, I have ceased to have any personal feeling or expectation in that matter, -- I do not say I never had any, so abused and borne upon as I have been."

After his return to Concord on January 28, Conway hastily wrote in his Journal an account of the conference with Lincoln. "W. P. & I did most of the talking," Conway admitted. He and Phillips "plead hard" that Stanley be removed as Military Governor of North Carolina and that Frémont replace him. Lincoln assured them that he had heard no complaints against Stanley for the past three months. He then added, slowly, with a smile: "I have great respect for Fremont and his abilities, but the fact is the pioneer in any movement is not generally the best man to carry that movement to a successful issue. It was so in old times, wasn't it? Moses began the emancipation of the Jews, but didn't take Israel to the Promised Land after all. He had to make way for Joshua to complete the work. It looks as if the first reformer of a thing has to meet such hard opposition and gets so battered and bespattered, that afterwards, when people find they have to accept his reform, they will accept it more easily from another man."

Though Conway and his associates appreciated Lincoln's half-humorous remarks, they politely but persistently urged him to make a more vigorous effort immediately to enforce the Emancipation Proclamation. At last, the president, somewhat offended, said, "Well, gentlemen, I have got the responsibility of the thing & must keep it." Phillips responded, "Yes, Mr. President, but if you go down you carry us down also." Lincoln wearily reminded him that he had been elected by a minority of the people, and that he did not believe the country as a whole would have supported the edict at an earlier stage of the war. "All I can say now is that I believe the proclamation has knocked the bottom out of slavery, though at no time have I expected any sudden results from it."[353]

Conway then asked the president how he accounted for the fact that all the leading newspapers (the Cincinnati *Enquirer*, the *Chicago Times*, the *Boston Post*, the *New York Herald*) came out in enthusiastic support of Frémont's proclamation in Missouri. A burst of surprise came from the group when the president said he did not know that the papers had supported Frémont. Assured that files of the papers could easily be produced to prove the point, Lincoln "sank back in his chair in silence." The silence continued for a few moments, and then Phillips arose and thanked him for his courteous reception. The president bowed, shook hands with every one, remarking, "I must bear this load which the country has entrusted to me as well as I can, and do my best."

The account of this interview with Lincoln by Frank Preston Stearns, son of George Luther Stearns, gives a glimpse of the contribution of his father to the discussion. Since the organization of the first colored troops under General David Hunter in May 1862, the elder Stearns had been advocating the general enlistment of colored soldiers in Massachusetts.[354] Unlike Conway, who reluctantly agreed that war was sometimes unavoidable, Stearns did not hesitate to urge on Lincoln the importance of arming all men, white and black, who could carry a gun.

President Lincoln complimented Wendell Phillips on his fine oratory, according to Stearns. Mr. Phillips gracefully returned the compliment and explained the object of the conference. Lincoln objected at once to the appointment of Frémont, who he said was "too much bespattered with the mud of reform." Then

Bird took up the argument, proposing removal of the military governor of North Carolina on political grounds. Lincoln responded: “General Stanley called on me after I had written my proclamation of emancipation, and I showed it to him. He said he thought he could stand that.”

“Mr. President,” Conway was quoted as saying, “we don’t want a man who can stand it; but one who rejoices at it, who will enforce it, and make it a vital reality.” Lincoln countered, “Suppose I should put in the South these antislavery generals and governors, what could they do with the slaves that would come to them?” George Luther Stearns replied, “We would make Union soldiers of all who were capable of bearing arms.” Lincoln, however, was inexorable, and after some further discussion the company took their leave.[355]

Conway left this interview with the president -- the last time he was to see him -- with little hope for peace. He felt that Lincoln had assumed that the group was interested solely in the fate of the Negro, and that he did not fully comprehend that the delegation believed the enforcement of the Emancipation Proclamation should be used primarily as a military measure to stop the war. They suspected that Seward, as secretary of state, rather than Stanton, as secretary of war, had insisted on signing the proclamation only because he hoped the Supreme Court could be persuaded finally to set it aside. Conway visited the Senate the next day and found it “humdrum.” Judge Conway introduced him to “the Hon. Mr. Wadsworth of Kentucky,” who predicted “the abolitionists would all be hung as certainly as they had necks” and “Greeley is uneasy about his neck now.”[356]

Even a dinner given by Stearns for the senators and representatives from Massachusetts in the evening after the interview failed to lift from the shoulders of the delegation “the heavy weight of the gloomy present.[357] Several “eminent journalists” were there, among them Henry J. Raymond of *The New York Times,* as well as a number of anti-slavery members of Congress. None of them appeared to the men from Boston willing to offer clearly in public the criticism of the administration that they were uttering in private. As a result, the president “virtually acknowledged” that he was influenced by the pro-slavery faction and advised those who were against slavery to go out and convince the country, which was still lukewarm.

After an excellent dinner, Phillips "opened with a searching speech," expressing a "demand" that the men seated around the table "should not whisper in the ear of the President but speak boldly from their own places in the Capital." Speech after speech followed, including one from Conway. "There was much excited & warm discussion & after more supper we all retired," Conway wrote in his journal. They left Washington the next morning at an early hour, the object of their visit having been accomplished. But they were not happy; as Conway summarized their feeling later: "Our delegation returned to Boston to our 'Commonwealth' and our lectures and Bird Club talks, with a conviction that the President, with all his forensic ability and his personal virtues, was not competent to grapple with the tremendous combination of issues before him.[358] Lincoln refused, it seemed to them, to regard the freeing of the slaves as a moral rather than a political, issue.

Conway arrived in Boston at six o'clock on the morning of January 28 in time for a family breakfast in Concord. "All well," he wrote in his Journal. In the evening he returned to the city to deliver at the anniversary dinner of the American Anti-Slavery Society, a very dull, "cindery" speech, for he had not had a good night's sleep for a week. The next morning -- "the Birthday of the great & good Thomas Paine" -- Conway awoke to find that his face was badly swollen and that his old enemy, erysipelas, was "steaming down [his] cheek." "Wife doctored -- nursed -- read to me" from the famed journalist William Howard Russell's *Civil War: Private Diary and Letters*, which presented a picture of social conditions in the far South worse than anything the abolitionists of the North could imagine.[359] Sanborn came in during the evening and "conversed pleasantly" with the patient. By February 1 he felt "much better, and wrote a biographic & physiognomic sketch of McClellan."

The next day Conway was "nearly well" and debating whether or not he could keep his engagement to speak in the South. "Shall go," he wrote and did -- his "head muffled in red scarf, an astonishment to beholders." Conway turned down an invitation to a masquerade at the Sargents on February 3, staying home to work on his "physiognomical sketch of McClellan." The following day he was off again to speak in Beverly: "Fair audience in the coldest room I was ever in. Spoke in dread of erysipelas." Having spent the night with friends, he awakened to find a "hard rain" falling, then "home as fast as possible.

Conway's entry of February 7 gives the first suggestion that his editorship of *The Commonwealth* was drawing to a close. James Stone, the publisher of the weekly, had never been fully in sympathy with Conway's ideas. Now, apparently, tension had mounted: "Mr. Stone will leave Commonwealth," Conway wrote. "He cannot quite go with my radicalism & does not wish to be in the way….I propose Sanborne. -- Dined with the Bird Club. Many compliments for my McClellan Sketch."

Having missed the last train to Concord by three minutes, Conway stayed in town and went to the Philharmonic Concert - "very fine -- Garrisons & Stearnses there." He spent the night with the Stearnses but caught a cold in his chilly room. "Got the Stearnses to drive me up to Lexington," he wrote in his journal. "Walked seven miles to Concord -- Most dreadful. Emerson returned. Spent the evening at his house."

Frank Stearns suggests that his father began to look upon the editor he had chosen for his paper with some doubts:

> He gave a finer literary quality to the Commonwealth than any other journal in Boston could brag of, but Mr. Stearns soon discovered that M. D. Conway did not properly belong to his circle. He professed to be an Emersonian, but was really a disciple of Tom Paine; that is, he belonged to the eighteenth century, instead of the nineteenth; and besides this, he was continually running into extravagances of one kind or another.

Frank Stearns was probably reflecting in these remarks conversations he had heard in his home. Conway himself was unaware that:

> Mr. Stearns was not sorry when an opportunity occurred for sending M. D. Conway to England to represent the Union cause there as a native-born Virginian. Excepting

on the slavery question two men could not differ more widely than did M. D. Conway and George L. Stearns.[360]

An excerpt from the diary of Ellen Conway, written sometime in February, records the "opportunity" which occurred that relieved Conway of his editorship of *The Commonwealth*:

> Wendell Phillips came to me to ask if I would consent to my husband going to Europe to lecture and persuade the English that the North is right. Reluctantly I consented, feeling that as he was exempt from serving as a soldier I had no right to prevent his being of service in some other way. The proprietor of the 'Commonwealth' agreed to give him $1000 for two letters per week. Phillips, Stearns, Gerrit Smith, Thomas Mott, H. W. Longfellow, Edward Clarke, Mr. Barker, R. Hallowell, Elizur Wright, the (Parker) Fraternity, the new Bedford Society raised $700.[361]

The time had come, Conway felt -- his wife agreed -- for him to go to England for a few months "to represent the moral and political situation as viewed by American anti-slavery people." Phillips and Garrison were first asked by their anti-slavery friends in England to make the journey, but they both declined. Emerson, who never wholly identified himself with the abolitionists, did not wish Conway to undertake the mission. Perceiving that his younger friend was determined to go, however, he provided Conway with letters of introduction to Thomas Carlyle and other friends. George W. Curtis gave him a letter to Robert Browning, and Mr. and Mrs. Stearns presented him with a life-sized bust of John Brown to bestow upon Victor Hugo. William Lloyd Garrison armed him with many letters to anti-slavery leaders abroad. As for Conway himself, he entered into the plans with his usual vigor, as the following letter to Gerrit Smith indicates:[362]

Commonwealth Office

Boston Feb. 27, [1863]

Hon. Gerrit Smith

Dear Sir,

Mr. George L. Stearns has doubtless seen you and mentioned the movement that he and Mr. Phillips have united with me in thinking well of, -- to wit, that I should visit England at this juncture and bear an Anti-Slavery Virginian's testimony on the condition of their country. I am anxious to go. I have known personally many of the leaders in this rebellion-amongst others Mason. I long to tell all that I know about Slavery to them. Emerson, Longfellow and other friends would introduce me to many of the literary men who have not been particularly associated with the A. S. movement while the Abolitionists wd. introduce me to the Antislavery men there. The Editors of the Spectator are my friends personally though I have never been in Europe.

I have just been conversing with Phillips, Garrison and Ed and they all approve of my going. The time fixed is early in April so that I may be present at the May Anniversaries.

The means of going are -- that some gentlemen shall together advance $1000 -- half to be raised at once, the other to be drawn upon in England if needed. It is supposed that from admission to lectures enough may be gathered to repay this money when I return, but although I shall do my best to repay, I am too poor to bear the expense. Phillips and Stearns with their known generosity to the cause at once set themselves down for $100 a piece.

If you approve of the movement, you will perhaps help - as we have very few Antislavery men here who are able to help.

Mr. Garrison told me that he would write to you about it if I wished to, but advised me to do it myself, -- as it was nowise a personal matter with me. I shd. have left this to Mr. Stearns' mention, but I have not seen him since I saw Garrison, who gives his hearty approval to the plan ....

I am

Yours cordially,

MONCURE D. CONWAY

Apparently Gerrit Smith added his $100 to the fund. On March 11, Conway wrote enthusiastically to Longfellow, telling him that he now had $300 for his trip and would welcome more from him "if you could find it convenient to help this fund."[363]

On April 11, 1863, Conway sailed on the steamship "City of Washington." A sketch of his life and an announcement of his departure appeared in the *National Anti-Slavery Standard*: "The Rev. M. D. Conway, one of the editors of the Boston *Commonwealth*, is going to England in a few days with the purpose of spending the summer there lecturing in behalf of the anti-slavery and the Union cause in America. His expenses are paid by some friends, earnest anti-slavery loyalists of Boston...."[364] He left the country with a copy of *Les Miserables* and of John Stuart Mill's new book *On Liberty* in his bag -- and the feeling that he had the backing of the abolitionists.

Conway was justified in his understanding of his mission. Two days after he sailed, Garrison wrote to Alfred Paton of Glasgow heartily recommending his young friend to the well-known British abolitionist. Garrison had visited Paton in 1847 when he was sent to England on a similar expedition. Recalling the earlier struggles, Garrison wrote:

> Mr. Conway is on an anti-slavery mission to England, and cannot fail at this time to make something of a sensation when the particulars of his remarkable case are known. He is a native Virginian, the son of a large slave holder whose slaves the son has safely conveyed to a free State since the rebellion broke out, (the father adhering to the cause of the Southern Confederacy,) and related to some of the most prominent families in the Ancient Dominion. His abolitionism is of the strongest quality, and his zeal and enthusiasm, as well as his moral intrepidity, of the true heroic stamp. No such witness against slavery and the rebellion has yet appeared in England. Mr. Conway is a man of genius, a racy writer, and an interesting public speaker. I hope he may have a chance to be heard in Glasgow, and I have no doubt it will give you pleasure to do what you can to get up a meeting for him.[365]

More than once Conway's enthusiastic nature had caused him to be oblivious to "the cloud in the sky" presaging a coming storm. "Mr. Conway's Letters" opened on page one of *The Commonwealth* of May 15, 1863. The light-hearted three and a half columns describing "Our Voyage" give no hint of the rough waters ahead.

Chapter XII
The Conway-Mason Controversy

Leaving his wife and children in the small house in Concord, Conway departed for England in the spring of 1863, to be gone, he thought, until the following September. He did not return to America, except for brief visits, for more than twenty years. The "golden hour" for ending the war at once by the effectual emancipation of the Negroes had passed; so also had the moments almost gone by, it seemed to the abolitionists, when the sympathy of the British for the northern cause could be enlisted. "The leaden hour had come," wrote Conway, "we were compelled to support the war which the President had made our only hope of eradicating slavery, the root of discord."[366]

Conway went to England with the backing of Wendell Phillips, Garrison, Stearns and other members of the abolitionist group of Boston and Concord to lecture on slavery and the Civil War. He reported at once to Aubrey House, the comfortable London home of Peter Alfred Taylor, member of Parliament for Leicester, a leading spirit among the sympathizers in England and a friend of all the Boston abolitionists. Mr. and Mrs. Taylor had welcomed the new arrival warmly and had urged him to make their home his headquarters during his six-month's stay in England. In a cheerful state of mind Conway wrote to his wife on May 8, 1863, that he was delighted by the "sweet rest" of the Taylors' home, which was surrounded by a park, in which he could hear the cuckoos and nightingales singing at almost any time of the day. "I cannot imagine," he wrote to his wife, "that I am near a city of 3 millions of beings."[367]

Conway soon discovered that Aubrey House was the meeting place for ardent "ladies of high position" who were writing and circulating pamphlets concerned with the troubles in America. Most of them were fervid members of the American Anti-Slavery Society and the Aborigines Protection Society" and had accepted uncritically the picture of the South presented by *Uncle Tom's Cabin.*[368] Those who were lecturing in London for the cause of the North were, for the most part, non-conformist preachers like himself, addressing groups that already agreed with them.

Conway's first speech in London, on May 6 at Finsbury Chapel, drew "an immense audience," he wrote his wife. It was fully reported in *The Commonwealth* of June 5, 1863. The meeting opened with the following motion: "Resolved, that this Meeting, believing Slavery to be Anti-Christian, and opposed to every principle of justice and humanity, cordially approves the Emancipation Policy, now being triumphantly carried out by the Government of the United States, and offers to the Loyal States the assurance of its heartfelt sympathy in their present struggle against the despotism sought to be perpetuated and extended by the slaveholders Confederacy." Conway then said:

> To you, my fellow men of England, and you women of England, who are so nobly laboring for the cause of justice now undergoing its ordeal in America, I bring the cordial greeting of the friends of Freedom in America, -- that body of men who hold now, as they have always held, that the rights of man are above questions of Union or anything else. They are now not a small body of men: beginning with one man setting up a little paper in an attic with one negro boy to help him, they have now about twelve journals in the United States consecrated to Liberty, and they have voices in Congress and in the Legislature of every State. I could wish that some worthier representative of them could stand in my place tonight. I would wish that Wendell Phillips (loud applause) could wave over this crowd that wand of eloquence under whose magic all must bow. I could wish that the old pioneer himself (renewed applause) whose life is better than any oration, could stand before you, but to send them here at this juncture would be like sending Queen Victoria and Earl Russell to Boston for a season. My own claim to you depends chiefly on the fact that having been born in the South and for many years [having] sympathized with slavery and secession, I can speak with some authority concerning facts which it is important to know. It is as a Southerner that I speak to you; and here let me say that

> having years ago recoiled from the bad motto "Our country right or wrong" so far as to suffer exile from my own State, Virginia, because she was wrong, -- I will not today adhere to the Union or any other cause except as far as I believe it to be that of the right."

The speech of this young representative of Phillips and Garrison indeed held the audience spellbound, for Conway not only told the English how his views on slavery had changed and developed but also ended with a stirring analysis of the "responsibility" of the anti-slavery societies in England and in America. He then enlarged upon views more characteristic of himself than of those for whom he spoke:

> However comfortable it might be for us to let the South go, to recall our sons and brothers to the fireside; to build up the North into a great Republic; -- we are pledged to our posterity, to four millions of oppressed human beings, to Humanity in whose behalf we are entrusted with that new world which is its beacon and hope to prevent if possible the surrender to organized and powerful barbarism of 850,000 square miles of that Continent. Not to do so would be evading a responsibility which we ought to fulfil. It was come to us as a hard and heavy cross, but America has bowed her shoulders to it, and, by God's blessing, will bear it to the end!
>
> But can we prevent this? For our responsibility is limited by our ability. (Cries of "yes," with a few "noes.") Let the facts indicate: the census of 1860 gives the States in rebellion: Whites, 4,622,000; Slaves, 3,371,000. It gives the North, 23,462,000. Now I do not hesitate to say just here, what is notorious in America, that our Government has shrunk from striking the South with its full power. (Hear, hear.) It has been in the condition of a good-natured man, six feet high, weighing two hundred, who has to fight with a man three feet high, weighing one hundred. But the South has already run almost to the end of her resources whilst the North has scarcely begun upon hers. The price of gold in the two sections will indicate

this. Whilst in the North gold has only a premium of a half dollar, in the South the gold dollar costs five. Even then I am told that gold is a myth, -- and that it is found in Richmond only in Museums, labelled "an ancient and curious metal -- very rare!" (Laughter.)

But not only this; those 3,371,000 slaves we are lawfully and gradually, but surely transferring from the wrong side to the right, which will make our strength 26,833,000. (Applause.)

Remember, that of those 4,622,000 rebellious whites, 3,000,000 at least are of the wretched class known there as "poor whites." These are indescribably wretched; the serfs of the soil -- the miserable tenantry of the rich slaveholders. Scorned even by negroes; not one in a hundred able to read; suffering every discomfort, -- these men now arrayed against us we expect to conquer to our side, where they really belong, did they only know it. Without direct interest in slavery -- with every interest against it -- they will see that as we come in contact with them we bring them blessings instead of evils. They will have plenty instead of want -- education instead of ignorance. They will wake up and recognize their true friends and their actual foe.

And indeed we do not despair of conquering thus the entire South after a generation by giving her bloom and beauty -- wealth and education, the fruits of freedom, for the ashes and dust in which she is now clad." The South has sought our destruction, we will take a great revenge upon her -- we will heap her with plenty, with light which shall roll away her clouds of ignorance, with all the blessings which liberty alone can bestow.[369]

Later in May, Tom Hughes, correspondent for the New York *Tribune*, introduced Conway to a large audience in Exeter Hall as an "emissary" from America, the son of a slave-holder.[370] The audience, made up largely of the anti-slavery vanguard of the British working class led by John Bright, maintained a strong position against slavery. An undertone of excitement could be felt in the lecture room. Conway's ringing words made it clear, though a Virginian, he was also an abolitionist. William Lloyd Garrison and Wendell Phillips, rather than Lincoln, were the dramatic figures in the imagination of the English sympathizers with the anti-slavery cause.

Conway discovered that Englishmen in general felt no particular interest in saving a Union that many in America had assured them was not worth saving. Though impressed by Lincoln's Emancipation Proclamation and inclined toward the side of the North, they were also aware that the North, attempting to hold the South in the Union against its will, was inciting the Negroes to insurrections. Moreover, cheap cotton and the "Southern way of life" appealed to the English. At this "leaden hour" in history, just before the decisive victories of Vicksburg and Gettysburg, it seemed to Conway and to many of his English supporters that the sympathy of English was evenly balanced between North and the South. Conway suggested in a letter to *The Commonwealth* (May 22) that the scales seemed a little tipped in favor of the South.

Though the American ambassador in London, Charles Francis Adams, was scrupulous in maintaining a strict surveillance over the declared neutrality of England, it was evident to all that the Lord Palmerston ministry, supported by the London *Times*, was secretly in sympathy with the South. In his letter to *The Commonwealth* of May 22, on the subject of English neutrality, Conway declared that Adams was an unfortunate appointment, for his sentiments were not disinterested. Though recognition was never accorded the Confederate envoy, John M. Mason, by the British government, he was a man of great power in government circles. "The secessionists here are very active," Conway observed in a letter (May 29) to *The Commonwealth* (June 19). "Mason, Maury, and others who are here are leaving no stone unturned to accomplish their end -- the recognition of the South, and the raising of the blockade for the sake of cotton. They bribe bands and orchestras to play Dixie, a tune which is well known here, whereas no one has ever heard the 'John Brown song.' The other day I observed in the omnibuses a large placard with the English flag, and that of the Confederate States united."

Conway remembered Senator Mason well, for he had been a frequent visitor of his father's house when Moncure was a boy. Conway also remembered him as the author of the Fugitive Slave Act and the senator who had snubbed him when he was a young law clerk in Warrenton. Later, he knew him as chairman of the Senate committee that had investigated his friends of the Bird Club in connection with the raid of John Brown. Garrison had remarked, in his letter of introduction to Alfred Paton, that his protege would like nothing better than to meet Mason before a British audience. "But, of course," Garrison had added, "Mason will take good care never to take any such appeal to the people.

The problem was, how could Conway combat the subtle power of Mason, who, according to a traveler from "Dixie," was the sort of man the English like: "He is so manly, so straight forward, so truthful and bold. 'A fine old English gentleman,' according to Lord Russell." The writer continued, "Over here, whatever Mason does is right in his own eyes. He is above law."[371] Conway soon discovered that Mason was attempting to prove to the English that the real cause of the war was economic, not slavery, and abolitionists on both sides of the water were merely fanatics responsible for his removal with his colleague, John Slidell, from the British steamer Trent on November 8, 1861. An American commander had imprisoned the men in Boston until January 2, 1862, when the British were able to bring diplomatic pressure to bear for his release. With such an introduction to the English, Mason -- in collaboration with Matthew F. Maury, the well-known ship designer -- was just the man to encourage construction in British shipyards of cruisers to use against northern shipping in order to counteract the blockade of the southern coast and restore the shipping of cotton to England.

Fortunately for Conway, John M. Forbes, a wealthy Boston merchant and railroad magnate, was also in London for buying up, if possible, the ships under construction for the South. Forbes was not only a capitalist but also an abolitionist who had worked closely with Governor Andrew and other members of the Bird Club to put Massachusetts on a war basis. Recently, he had helped Higginson, Stearns, and others to organize Negro regiments and had been one of those urging Lincoln to arm the Negroes of the South. Alerted by their mutual friends, Forbes wrote to Conway at once that he was glad to learn that he was on hand, "as we need all the help our friends can give us to keep out of mischief, and your varied information about slavery will be most available." Conway records: "I was fortunate enough to see a good deal of him. We passed several evenings at the house of Fanny Kemble, where American affairs were talked over with reference to the Confederate intrigues in England."[372]

Forbes believed that such political figures as Prime Minister William Ewart Gladstone were too apathetic in their attitude toward the war. Conway, for his part, "felt keenly the silence concerning our conflict" after "several leading literary men" had left "our cause" in the hands of dissenting preachers.

Calling himself "Our Foreign Correspondent," Conway wrote to *The Commonwealth* (June 23) that he regretted to report that "literary men of England seem to me very much demoralized on the subject of Slavery.[373] More pro-slavery than pro-southern, most of the literati seemed to Conway to "talk Carlylese," reflecting the influence of the Scottish historian and essayist, Thomas Carlyle. Conway concluded:

> Mr. Carlyle's influence over the leading literary men here is immeasurable: they admire and gather about him with enthusiasm. He is a man of tremendous convictions, and they see all things as subjects of delineation and art. Their purpose ends with literature; Carlyle makes literature a means to a purpose. So he can overhear and coerce dozens of them. With each one he drew his knife and proclaimed war, and such as were not willing to fight it out would yield. And it is doubtful whether these who yield to his wrong views will ever really get so sacred a niche in his heart as he who fought him at every step. Emerson too, whom Carlyle now venerates more than any other man, proved no 'mush of concession.'

Conway had long been familiar with the wrong-headedness of Carlyle's ideas on slavery, for he had become acquainted with his "wonderful genius" many years earlier when he had had an opportunity to read freely in cousin John M. Daniel's library in Richmond. One of Carlyle's *Latter-Day Pamphlets,* "The Nigger Question," had appeared in the *Richmond Examiner*. Here Carlyle had expressed the idea, perfectly acceptable to Conway at that time, that slavery could be justified because the Negro was not, strictly speaking, a human being.[374] When, however, Conway made his first "Visit to Thomas Carlyle" (the title of his essay in *The Commonwealth* of June 5, 1863), he was swept from his familiar bearings by the impact of the great man himself. "In a modest old mansion, apart from the great whirl of fashion, resides the man to whose wonderful genius, more than to that of any other is to be attributed the intellectual and spiritual activity of the current generation," the article begins. Just as Conway's life was changed by his encounter with Emerson, so now he responded to Carlyle the moment he opened the door of his home. "A strange thrill passed over me," he wrote, "when I first stood face to face with those grand features, so heavily marked with Time and Fate." Invited to remain for dinner while another guest was present, he "had a good opportunity to study the characteristics of this remarkable man." Conway was fascinated:

> Tall and almost slender, contrary to my expectations, with a longish head, bent forward from somewhat stooping shoulders, with a magnificent brow overhanging a blue eye that suggests a tenderness which nowhere else appears in his manner or conversation, but which one can imagine were in the ascendant when the Life of Stirling was written; with a short beard and moustache giving an impression of granite on the lower face; with a light and ruddy color which overspread the face with deep flushes during conversation; with a voice which began and gently rose in a moment to a tornado; with a habit of bursting out into loud and almost convulsive laughter which often ended in a fit of coughing; with nervous movements of fingers and shoulders, hinting strongly of over-study; with a terrible undertone to all these -- most of all to the laughter -- of pain and grief; Carlyle seemed to me one of the most fearful and fascinating of all the men I have ever seen, and whilst in his presence, I remembered the weird impressions of mingled beauty and awe which I had when journeying through the Mammoth Cave.[375]

After dinner, Carlyle inquired for news of Emerson and eagerly displayed a photograph of his Concord friend that he compared with another that Conway carried with him. As the conversation swept on to larger subjects, Conway wrote:

> It is impossible with this great frank outspoken man not to enter at once upon the great social problems of the hour; though he seizes upon them and goes on from hour to hour in wonderful monologue, -- with as full and high pressure going with as against the current of the sentiment around him. It certainly was formidable to come face to face with a powerful Pessimist; and whilst he spoke I felt a dreary skepticism chilling me, and seemed to hear cries of despair coming out of the heart of nature. All was going wrong; our ballot-boxings, our negro emancipations, our cries for liberty, all showed nothing but that the nations were given over to believe a lie and be damned. Possibly, indeed, the only way to Paradise lay thus through hell; but what the people were seeking thus they would never obtain. Society was all wrong, and would go on getting worse. For such men as all this Liberty is producing, one may well be thankful that a good supply of powder and shot is preparing.

"Ballot-boxing!" exclaimed Carlyle, "Why we have tried that in England once or twice." He then overwhelmed his visitor by example after example of the evils of the ballot box. "As soon as it is opened, out springs the most whippable rascal that can be found," Carlyle concluded. "You know well that in America you have for years had your meanest man in the White House....But so they all go -- pell-mell." Conway remarked, in his essay, that to this mighty flow of language "there was no use for reply, had there been any chance for it, and there was not." He at last took his leave with a feeling that he was breaking away from "a depressing fascination" such as he had never before experienced.

> I found the firmament more necessary, and looked up to the stars for help. and all the way home this grand face was before me in its sublime solitude, resembling more than anything else the Old Man of the Mountain, up in our

Northern snows, ever looking out from his bleak height for the convulsion which shall bring him deliverance. But until the archangel is enthroned on earth, and the arch-fiend bound a thousand years, he will scorn all relief and pleasure.

Frequently, after this first encounter, Conway was invited to join Carlyle in his walks about London when he charmed his younger friend by the wealth and variety of his conversation. A talker himself, Conway was silenced by his companion. "It would be hard to give a right conception of the wealth with which he showers his visitor," he wrote.

> Between the great heavy boulders of his political views, -- conglomerate of worthy and unworthy substance, -- there are beautiful walks and swards, with which he restores and delights the soul he has just wounded. Sketches of history, of persons he has known, of Dr. (Samuel) Johnson, of London Suburbs -- all these are etched with the subtlety of Cruikshank and the sentiment of Darley. He once so described the 'loyal lady' of some hard but able man, that I felt a mist gathering in my eyes, as when I read, in the Flight of the Duchess.
>
> *"The little lady grew silent and thin,*
> *Paling and ever paling."*

Conway was baffled by the realization, though Carlyle was undoubtedly a mistaken conservative in many of his social views, he was loved and respected by the more radical thinkers both in England and America. As Conway noted:

> The radicals here are still his best friends, and they will not, and they cannot give him up. The man with all these faults does stand so grandly alone, in such absolute sincerity, in such sadness. He gains no princely chaplaincies or professorships by opposing us; he evermore scorns the rulers of those whom he wishes ruled. So the best young men here still love him; and I have observed the same feeling in America. Carlyle is

> now morbid; but he cannot undo the great work he has wrought, -- who waked up every sleeping mind in his generation, even as Emerson purged and uplifted those minds when they were awake. His morbidness is the result of solitude. He has thought too much, not purged his knowledge by daily use, and so is now "sicklied o'er with the pale cast of thought."

Conway wished for "an invisible cap, that [he] might draw near to [Carlyle] unperceived and whisper that perhaps were he to go out among the men and women within the city around him, he would learn that they were more than the rats and lice he now seems to think them." He himself spent many of his days in London walking the streets, studying shop windows, visiting churches and museums, gazing at the beggars whom he found on every hand with the horror at the hopelessness of the poor he had caught from Carlyle. They were indeed "the very vermin of the city, which one almost expects to see turn to rats and cockroaches and creep away into their holes."[376]

The worst of it was that Carlyle was so often right in his judgments: "All the worth you have put into your cause will be returned to you personally," Carlyle told him, "but the America for which you are hoping you will never see; and you will never see the whites and blacks in the South dwelling together as equals in peace."[377] Carlyle's casual remark made Conway realize that his own opinions -- or those which he had supposed were his own - were not so "thoroughly rooted" as he had thought.

Impressed as Conway was by "Carlyle's touchstone -- unbiased thought," he nevertheless became aware that his master's opinions were influenced by an unofficial Confederate from Virginia, John R. Thompson, formerly editor of Richmond's *Southern Literary Messenger*, in which some of Conway's early writing had appeared. Thompson's gentlemanly bearing and his gifts as a poet made him acceptable in London society; he was, however, disseminating a pro-slavery influence wherever he went. Thompson took special care not to encounter Conway at Carlyle's home, where he, too, was a welcome guest. Conway soon realized, when he visited Carlyle "there was now a Virginian at each ear."[378] The same was true of other literary men whose silence about America distressed him.[379]

During the next few weeks Conway discussed with many of these "literary men" their views of America and the Negro question. Leslie Stephen, a supporter of the Union cause, invited him to spend a week-end at Cambridge where "the general opinion" was averse to the North, partly owing to the "unwearied efforts of Rev. Charles Kingsley," who was lecturing at Cambridge on the side of "the Southern oppressors."[380] The poet Alfred Lord Tennyson explained his "silence" to Conway by showing him hundreds of clippings from newspapers sent him by his American friends, all unfriendly to England; the writer John Ruskin told him that he hated war for any cause and thus had nothing to say of the present struggle. Of all the men with whom Conway discussed the question, Robert Browning seemed the most informed. Browning told him, in a long conversation in his library, that English writers did not understand the issue of the war in America, which, they had been assured, was not really emancipation. "Scarcely were the greetings over," wrote Conway, "when Mr. Browning introduced the subject of our 'War with Slavery' -- for he appreciated it as such." Conway continued:

> Ah, how I wish that the Round Table Knights of Freedom in America could have been present to see the fervor and hear the eloquence with which he uttered his sympathy with our cause, and the almost passionate vehemence with which he denounced the Southern sympathizers in England. He holds our cause to be sacred beyond every other now undergoing its ordeal; and I have a (not very definite to be sure) hope that he will soon utter his sympathy from his own throne of Poetry.[381]

When Conway referred to Carlyle's latest diatribe against the Union cause, "Shooting Niagara," Browning said it was only "a grin through a horse-collar." He added that English writers were thoroughly confused by the issue between the North and the South because the North had never given clear evidence that its real aim was to emancipate the slaves.[382] The force exerted by the North to hold the South in the Union seemed to Browning to be justified only by upholding the Emancipation Proclamation so the slaves would actually be set free.

Conway assured Browning that the anti-slavery leaders in America, such as Wendell Phillips and Garrison, were known to be opposed to war and would not support the Civil War were it not for their determination to free four million black men from pro-slavery generals in the South. Pressure was exerted on Lincoln and his administration, Conway told him, to preserve slavery until Union should be achieved. English writers could serve the world by believing the American conflict to be between freedom and slavery and pointing out the war was part of "the world-wide struggle for liberty."[383]

Browning suggested that anti-slavery Americans themselves "should declare before the world that they had no desire to subjugate the South except for the liberation of the slave and the nation from long oppression." Then and there, Conway wrote in pencil his challenge to the Confederate envoy in London. He showed it to Browning and put it into the mail at once.

The letter reads as follows:

> Aubrey House, Notting Hill, London, W.
> June 10, 1863.
>
> Hon. J. M. Mason, Com'r, etc.
>
> Sir, -- I have authority to make the following proposition on behalf of the leading antislavery men of America, who have sent me to this country:
>
> If the States calling themselves "The Confederate States of America" will consent to emancipate the negro slaves in those States such emancipation to be guaranteed by a liberal European commission, the emancipation to be inaugurated at once and such time to be allowed for its completion as the commission shall adjudge to be necessary and just, and such emancipation once made to be irrevocable, - then the abolitionists and antislavery leaders of the Northern States shall immediately oppose the further prosecution of the war on the part of the United States government, and, since they hold the balance of power, will certainly cause the war to cease by the immediate withdrawal of every kind of support from it.

I know that the ultimate decision upon so grave a proposition may require some time; but meanwhile I beg to be informed at your early convenience whether you will personally lend your influence in favour of a restoration of peace and the independence of the South upon the simple basis of the emancipation of the slaves.

Any guarantee of my responsibility and my right to make this offer shall be forthcoming.

I am, sir, yours, etc., M. D. Conway[384]

Mason lost no time answering the challenge by demanding Conway's credentials:

24 Upper Seymour Street, Portman Square,
June 11, 1863.

Sir, -- I have your note of yesterday. The proposition it contains is certainly worthy of the gravest consideration, provided it is made a proper responsibility, -- yet you must be aware, that whilst you know fully the representative position I occupy, I have not the like assurance as regards yourself.

If you think proper, therefore, to communicate to me who those are, on whose behalf and authority you make the proposition referred to, with the evidence of your "right to make this offer," I will at once give you my reply, -- the character of which, however, must depend on what I may learn of your authority in the premises.

I am, sir, your obdt. serv., J. M. Mason.

Conway did not overlook the fact that Mason had written his full name on the envelope, "Moncure Daniel Conway," thus proving that he knew "the renegade Virginian" he was addressing. Conway thought over for a day or two the dilemma in which he found himself and then wrote:

Aubrey House, Notting Hill, London, W.
June 14, 1863.

Sir, -- Your note of the 11th has been received. I could easily give you the evidence that I represent the views of the leading abolitionists of America; but with regard to the special offer which I have made, I have concluded that it was best to write out to America and obtain the evidence of my right to make it in a form which will preclude any doubt as to its sufficiency.

I shall then address you again on the subject.[385]

I am, etc., M. D. Conway.

Just as Mason was penning his elaborate reply, news of the grand reception given for Conway appeared in the London *Times* of June 17. Mason's second letter in *The Times*, published two days later, set all London talking. It opened with the admission that Conway was not without authorization to speak for the abolitionists, as made clear in the introduction to Conway's lecture.

24 Upper Seymour Street, Portman Square,
June 17, 1863.

Sir, -- I have received your note of yesterday.

You need not write to America, to "obtain the evidence" of your right to treat on the matter it imports. Our correspondence closes with this reply -- it was your pleasure to commence it -- it is mine to terminate it.

I desired to know who they were, who were responsible for your mission to England, as you present it; and who were to confirm the treaty you proposed to make, for arresting the war in America, on the basis of a separation of the States, with or without, the sanction of their government. But such information is of the less value now, as I find from an advertisement in the journals of the day that you have brought to England letters of sufficient credit from those who sent you to invite a public meeting in London, under the sanction of a member of Parliament who was to preside, to hear an address from you on the subject of your mission, with the promise of a like address from him.

The public meeting to which Mason referred was held on the evening of June 16, in the London Tavern.[386] It was arranged by the Emancipation Society of England to initiate a series of lectures to be delivered in various parts of England by Conway, on the issues of the War in America. John Bright, who had not so far spoken out on the war, had consented to introduce Conway in order to state his own views. In his prepared remarks he pointed out, though the cotton interests of England had been hurt by the war, the industry would recover and improve if slavery were abolished. Bright then introduced Conway by reading aloud a letter from Garrison summarizing Conway's claim to speak on the subject of emancipation in terms similar to these he used in his letter to Alfred Paton. To Bright, Garrison wrote:

> Boston, April 10, 1863.
>
> You are such an attentive reader of the Liberator and Standard that the name and services of the bearer of this, Mr. Moncure D. Conway, author of The Golden Hour and The Rejected Stone, etc., must be familiar to you, so that he will need no special introduction. Allied by birth and relationship to the first families of Virginia, the son of a prominent slaveholder, brought up in the midst of slavery and all its pernicious influences, classically educated, he has for several years past been the brave, outspoken, fervid advocate of the antislavery cause, bringing to it all of Southern fire, resolution, energy, and persistency; and, consequently, had made himself an exile from his native home and commonwealth for an indefinite period, though as true to the honour, safety, wealth, and progress of Virginia "as to the pole." You will know how to appreciate such a moral here, and he will rejoice to make your personal acquaintance.

Bright's "introduction" lasted an hour, and was, no doubt, far more significant to the English audience than was Conway's speech, for Bright clarified the issue of cotton for thousands of British working-men, and helped them to see that their interests lay on the side of the North. Mason, who read the speech in *The Times*, recognized the impact of Bright's word on wavering

British sentiment and took measures to bring to public attention the political implications of Conway's "special offer" of negotiating a peace that he had rashly asserted he was "authorized" to make.

Mason's letter to Conway of June 17 concluded with the assertion that:

> This correspondence shall go to the public, and will find its way to the country -- a class of the citizens of which you claim to represent. It will, perhaps, interest the government, and the soi-disant "loyal men" there to know, under the sanction of your name, that the "leading antislavery men in America" are prepared to negotiate with the authorities of the Confederate States, for a restoration of peace, and the independence of the South, on a pledge that the "abolitionists and antislavery leaders of the Northern States shall immediately oppose the further prosecution of the war on the part of the United States government; and, since they hold the balance of power, will certainly cause the war to cease by the immediate withdrawal of every kind of support from it."

Conway realized at once that he had been cornered by a politician more adroit than himself; he saw that his second letter to Mason was an admission that he had erred in writing the first before consulting his supporters in America. Garrison, "the great chieftain" of the American Anti-Slavery Society, had for years advocated non-resistance and the separation of North and South. Conway did not realize that Garrison was now throwing his support to Lincoln and to the continuance of the war.

News of these matters did not reach Ellen Conway until she unfolded her *Commonwealth* of June 27, 1863, and read the following brief and disturbing article, entitled "Mr. Conway in England."

> A meeting was to be held at the London Tavern on the 16th, at which Mr. Bright was to preside, and Mr. Conway was to speak in answer to Mr. Roebuck's recognition speech, which he had already noticed in the Star. Mr. Conway will be urged to make some proposals to the

Confederate Commissioners on the subject of Emancipation. We cannot believe that any of our English friends, however unacquainted with the state of feeling here, can have persuaded him to such a course. Certainly, neither the *Commonwealth* nor any of the anti-slavery men in this country would for a moment sanction any proposition looking to a recognition of the Confederacy, or its very obnoxious Minister in England. Nor has Mr. Conway any authority (unless it be from the State Department,) from any person in America, to enter into any conference whatever, with any representative of the South, save in the way of public discussion, or to make any offers of any kind to any person whatsoever, or any of the questions of the day.

Mr. Conway was to leave England for Rome and Venice on the 18th, but only for a flying visit.

Ellen was at that time visiting the family of Conway's sister in Easton, Pennsylvania, where the Conway parents were also staying. The following letter, written on June 30, 1863, the result of a family consultation, could not have eased Moncure's mind when he received it in England.[387]

Dearest One,

Rec' Commonwealth yesterday with article down on your letter to Mason. It was the 1st l had heard of it - I felt it was true and though rash to do it without counting chickens after hatching it was a just view -- Your mother said it was a downright falsehood and you w'd never do it in the world -- Afternoon got your letter which I immediately remained to Phillips & could not help saying what I thought even to so great a man -- Rec'd also a letter from Sanborn stating the disapproval & worry of all anti-slavery people & the hope it was all given up. (I think you would find it worse than a church quarrel just now) People have got to loving war -- Even Pa. people are roused & going off to help -- Peace Democrats & Abolitionists will soon· be the most furious -- Hooker is removed in the face of the enemy & some general put in his place -- I am a good deal worried by this move of yours, though sure your feeling is right, but equally sure, at present you will have no support in it -- I shall leave Easton and go back to Concord in a day or two -- I feel now as if I ought to be nearer to deliver your letters instantly -- I have had Emerson till now and hastily write a few lines -- Just bought the Tribune & find something relative to your plan & send it to you. It is rather more kindly than the Commonwealth.[388] I rather think you & Sanborn will never agree perfectly again. He has had his way too long. & is looked upon in Concord by Brooks, Thoreau, Whiting as not a brave man since his arrest they say that frightened the spunk out of him -- A conservative better half is more or less contracting -- Hooker is removed & all speak well of Meade because they never heard of him -- I went down town with the children this morn. bought a pretty little carriage for Mildred's baby which I am to use while here -- I envied you seeing Tennyson, Ruskin & Browning - As soon as I reach Concord I shall go & see Emerson & see what he thinks of things -- I can hardly believe Garrison can be so strongly opposed to you -- Phillips may be possibly --

God bless you.

Ellen D. Conway

On July 1, before the actual correspondence between Conway and Mason was published in the New York *Tribune* of July 2, an editorial entitled "Conway's Folly" came out in that paper. In the same issue appeared a letter to the *Tribune* from Garrison (dated June 30), repudiating Conway's move about which he had read only a brief and garbled summary.[389] Wendell Phillips in a speech at Framingham, Massachusetts, on July 4, declared that he thought Conway's motives in the affair were "as honest as the midday sun is clear," and that his devotion to "The great cause of human liberty" was "single-hearted." Nonetheless, he wrote: "I know at the same time that he does not represent in that offer one single man on this side of the Atlantic. I do not say

I believe it, but I say -- my own knowledge joined to his -- I know it." Phillips then added these ambiguous words:

> Now I wish to say further that I entirely agree with the essence of that offer. The Union without liberty is to-day tenfold more accursed than it was any time the last quarter of a century. Union without liberty I spit upon ... But if the sun were forbidden ever again to rise and I could have sunrise again by asking Mason, I would remain in the dark forever rather than speak to the author of the Fugitive Slave Act.[390]

Though the approaching presidential campaign in the United States had divided Conway's old abolitionist friends, one faction following Garrison, who now supported Lincoln, and another following Phillips, who favored Frémont for president, neither side could afford to approve of Conway's proposal that the North should lay down its arms if the South would immediately emancipate the slaves. Conway's friends on *The Commonwealth*, refusing to go back on their former editor, declared that he was an "independent writer, who does not profess to belong to any party, except the radical Anti-Slavery party." The editorial, entitled "Mr. Conway and Mr. Mason," then went on to explain what this party, *The Commonwealth*, and "our corresponding Editor" stood for in terms that hardly reflected Conway's actual beliefs:[391]

> the Anti-slavery men of America go for a vigorous prosecution of the war, and no man more than Mr. Phillips, unless it be our corresponding Editor. *The Commonwealth* claims to be of this party, and we neither expect, nor desire to see peace until the last link of the slave's chain is broken, the whole slave-holding class stripped of their privileges, and their land divided among their former slaves, and the free emigrants from the North and from Europe. The journal which has done more than most others to set on foot a negro army cannot be accused of favoring "peace at any price." We believe that now, as therefore, Mr. Conway is heartily of our opinion, however he may have been misled by English influences, on one special point.

In misstating Conway's views as to the steps to take after the Emancipation Proclamation, The *Commonwealth* was attempting to bring their "Corresponding Editor" under the banner of Wendell Phillips, leader of the Radical Republicans and bitter opponent of Lincoln. Though Conway followed Phillips in his support of Frémont for president, he by no means envisaged the disenfranchisement of the southern slave-owners, the confiscation of their property, and the division of their land among the former slaves.[392] Sanborn, editor of *The Commonwealth* since Conway's departure, struggled to defend his friend in the face of the many articles, letters, and editorials concerning "Conway's Folly" in the American press.

Against the aspersions of the *Boston Advertiser*, for example, the editor wrote in *The Commonwealth* of July 17, 1863:

> The Advertiser speaks of the affair of Mr. Conway as "The Climax of his many follies." We admit that it was an unauthorized and injudicious act, but the "follies" of men like Mr. Conway are more to their credit than the stupid prudence of men who are young without enthusiasm, and old without wisdom; who flatter a crime so long as it is prosperous, and have been trained to look with as much horror on a word misspelled, as on the betrayal of a slave to his master, or the approaching ruin of a great nation. Mr. Conway's "follies" have cost him his inheritance, they have secured him banishment, obloquy, and the hatred of the mob. If we were editing a paper that had never raised its voice against a popular sin, nor uttered an opinion that the world did not make haste to forget, we should be slow to censure the generous mistakes of others. [393]

The Mason affair did result in Conway's self-imposed "banishment" for the next twenty years -- to a full and useful life as a Unitarian minister in London.[394]

Chapter XIII
In Search of a Country

The effect of the Conway-Mason controversy was milder in England than in America. Mason, in the last paragraph of his letter to Conway, of June 17, 1863, had stated in elaborately veiled language that the South had no intention of relinquishing its slaves no matter how the war ended. In this open letter to the London *Times*, Mason had written as "some reward" for Conway's "interesting disclosure" that the abolitionists of the North would use their influence to end the war if the southerners would free their slaves:

> ... your inquiry whether the Confederate States will consent to emancipation, on the terms stated, shall not go wholly unanswered. You may be assured, then, and perhaps it may be of value to your constituents to assure them, that the Northern States will never be in relations to put this question to the South. nor will the Southern States ever be in a position requiring them to give an answer.
>
> I am, sir, your obedient servant.[395]
>
> J.M. Mason.

After the first embarrassment felt by the Emancipation Society of England at Conway's audacious proposal, letters from various groups began to appear in the London papers pointing out that the agent for the Confederacy, who had hitherto insisted that the war had nothing to do with slavery, had at last shown his true colors. The Foreign Affairs Committee of Sheffield wrote a public letter to Mason taking him to task, though not condoning Conway's error of judgment: "Wholly disapproving of the improper committee confine their remarks to the last paragraph of your letter. You are aware that nothing could be more hideous, hateful, and loathsome to honest and true Englishmen than your audacious avowal of your determination to maintain slavery and your defiant prediction that you will succeed."[396]

The *Morning Star* even suggested that "honest, simple-minded Mr. Conway" might have been setting a trap for Mason by forcing him to make a public avowal of his attitude toward slavery.[397] The discussion was the more heated because it was well known that the eccentric, one-time liberal, John Arthur Roebuck, was to introduce in the House of Commons on June 29 a motion recommending that the Confederacy be recognized. It was to combat this rising sympathy for the cause of the South that Conway was sent by the Emancipation Society on a lecture tour arranged by Richard Cobden and John Bright, both political if not radical figures.

For this purpose, the Free Trade Hall of Manchester -- the largest such auditorium in England at that time – was engaged for Sunday afternoon, June 21, 1863. Mr. Potter, member of Parliament from Manchester, presided, and on the platform were preachers from all the churches in the city. Conway began his address to the large audience by exonerating the chairman and the Emancipation Society from any responsibility for his correspondence with Mason. Before he had gone far in his speech, he was stopped by a rush to the platform of about two hundred "gentlemen" who had been sitting quietly in the front rows of the hall until Conway should speak. Fortunately, the platform was five or six feet above the floor, and the preachers on the stage had no trouble in pushing back the Confederate agitators until the leaders were hurried out of the auditorium. They were unarmed and not "ruffianly"; their intent had been to seize the rostrum by force and to propose a resolution supporting Roebuck's motion to recognize the Confederacy.

Conway, meanwhile, stood quietly behind the rostrum. When the confusion subsided, he proceeded with his carefully prepared speech, which, the next day, was printed in a pamphlet and widely circulated.[398] Conway's address, and the near-riot that accompanied it, played a real part in the defeat of Roebuck's motion several days later. Soon afterward Mason left England, realizing that the cause of the Confederacy in England was lost forever.[399] Conway, on the other hand, could not return to his family in Concord, for his presence would only deepen the rift among his abolitionist friends, already divided by the coming election. All Conway could do to make his position clear to his readers, both in England and in America, was to write a long letter to the London *Times*, published on June 22, 1863. "I am ready to confess," he said, "that my inexperience in diplomatic and political affairs has led me to make a proposition, the form of which is objectionable."[400] Conway's ingenuous avowal won him friends in England if not in America.

The following day, June 23, "Our Foreign Correspondent" wrote a brief article for *The Commonwealth* in which he described "the terrific efforts" being made in England to carry the House of Commons for Mr. Roebuck's motion to recognize the South. "Singularly enough," Conway remarked, his controversy with Mason had startled the Confederate agent into "dropping his mask" and confessing that the South was fighting for Slavery and nothing else. "I think Mr. Roebuck will fail," he said – as indeed he did a week later.

Conway sent off a reassuring letter to his wife on June 23 (which must have crossed her letter of June 30), saying that he was sure that she and their American friends had been shocked by the garbled accounts of the Mason-Conway correspondence, and all the letters, articles and editorials that had followed. "But," he added cheerfully, "it has turned out that the friends of America here are in high glee over the result and think my explanation of it which I send you to be entirely satisfactory as to the means by which I obtained a confession from Mason which all think damages him."[401] Without mentioning the near-riot at the opening of his speech, Conway told Ellen of his success at Manchester. "When the meeting was over," he wrote, "the vast crowd collected at the door & gave me 3 cheers as I got into my carriage." Conway spoke again at Leicester, where the people were thinking of raising a fund to keep him in England. "I am beginning now to be much sought for to lecture," he wrote. "Invitations are pouring in," he added, but "I have gone through about as much excitement as I can stand."

In a final note at the end of the letter, Conway scrawled, "You must decide for me about the *Commonwealth* going on. I cannot." He must have convinced Ellen that she herself had to take command and reunite the family. Her house in Concord was already on the market; the note from Stearns, enclosed with Conway's letter, made her sure the sooner it was sold the better.

In brief, wrote Conway, "Stearnes says he will not be responsible for pay of Editor & Publisher after Sept. But will let us [Conway and Sanborn] have it with a bonus of $1000. You must decide." Conway added humbly, "I shall expect you to advise me in all matters & shall obey you."

The immediate decision to accept an invitation from William Dean Howells to visit him in Venice needed no further discussion. Howells had written:

> To tell you the truth, you and Mrs. Conway are two people whom we should very much like to see in Venice. The spring is coming on after the "slow, sweet" fashion of spring in southern lands; the Adriatic is warming up with the view of being bathed in; the sun is bringing out all that is brightest and loveliest in the city and embroidering the islands and the terra firma with flowers. Four weeks ago we gathered daisies on the Lido; and now the almond-trees are heavy with bloom and bees. Besides all this, we live in the old Palazzo Faliero (where Marino Faliero, according to all the gondoliers, was born,) and we have a piano, and a balcony on the Grand Canal, and the most delightful little breakfasts in Venice. You will come, won't you?[402]

On June 26, five days after Conway's speech in Manchester and three days before Roebuck's address in the House of Commons, Conway left London for the Continent. As he journeyed through France, envying the "simple and happy peasants" he saw from the train window, he wrote to his wife enclosing a letter to President Lincoln, which he asked her to mail for him if she approved of the contents.

> I had a long interview yesterday with Mr. Adams the American Minister in London. He says that the first letter was certainly a mistake; but that after that I did the very best thing I could, and that he regards my course as most honorable. He says no harm, and possibly some good, has been done in England by it; and he hopes no evil will result in America. He has no doubt that a note to Mr. Lincoln or Mr. Seward, declaring that the letter was

> written without proper reflection and was well meant, would cause me to stand as well as I could desire with them. Adams was very kind to me indeed. Just what next step in the matter should be I do not know; so I will take none as yet.[403]

He was looking forward to a needed rest in Venice, he wrote, adding, "If I could just now retire from the world I would like it much."

On July 6, Conway, in a letter to his wife ("something of a diary" of the trip) wrote: "Last night [Sunday] at about 11 o'clock, I arrived at the spot for which I have been yearning so long. The Howells rec'd me with open arms, and a kiss from both of them so warm that I feel it now. We had the most charming talk over a very nice supper, -- then a sound rest; and this morning I waked to the tremendous reality of being in Venice."[404]

Conway spent the greater part of his first week in Venice suffering from fever caused by a return of his old enemy, erysipelas, which only a letter from his wife, announcing the sale of the house and the date of her arrival in Liverpool in September, could cure. For the remainder of the summer Conway was Howells' companion as the consul gathered material in the canals and squares of the city for the essays afterwards called *Venetian Life*.[405] Often they arose at dawn to drink coffee in the great Piazza as the varied tints of morning suffused St. Mark's and the Campanile, and then strolled together through the vegetable and flower markets to breakfast at Casa Faliero.

While Howells was attending to his consular duties, Mrs. Howells took Conway into the art galleries and churches she and her husband had learned to know and love. After dinner they drank their coffee on the little balcony of Casa Faliero or sat for a while in one of the large cafes on the square, returning home early in the evening to listen to Howells read the latest chapter of a novelette he was writing in verse.[406] Not infrequently the three journeyed to a nearby town on a Sunday morning gathering material for Howells' essays, his wife busy with her sketch-book. While Conway was in his "sweet dream in Venice," Howells made a sketch of him that found a place in *Venetian Life*. Howells wrote, without naming Conway, "Upon my word, I have sat beside wandering editors in their gondolas and witnessed the expulsion of the newspaper from their nature, while, lulled by the fascination of the place, they were powerless to take their own journals from their pockets, and instead of politics talked some bewildering nonsense about coming back with their families next summer."[407] The Howellses accompanied their guest on several house-hunting jaunts, for Conway dreamed of meeting his family in Liverpool and then returning with them to Venice forever.

After one such happy day with the Howellses, Conway wrote his wife: "We have spent nearly the whole time at dinner conversing on the subject of our living here a year. The largest sum we can spend in Venice for a year is $1000. Now can we and shall we do it."[408] As usual, Conway added, "I shall rely upon your judgment in the matter." Before he closed his letter to "the dearest & best of wives," Conway clearly indicated his own inclination to remove himself from the American scene entirely. "I know it seems cowardly but I really do feel very little like entering the political arena again at present," he wrote. Aided by his solicitous hosts, and the warm sunshine of Venice, Conway was ready to agree that his "blunder in that Mason affair" was largely due to "the nervous and impatient state of mind" into which he had allowed himself to drift.

In another week, on July 14, Conway wrote Ellen that he had received from her "a letter so bright" that his eyes filled with tears at the sorrow he had caused her.[409] Now, he assured her, "I am preparing to meet the storm which I have been waiting for as bravely as I can." The day after the arrival of the cheerful letter from his wife, he told her, he learned "from Phillips & Sanborn first notes of the shrill blast of surprise and indignation which I know must come from America." Painful as these communications were, they cleared Conway's mind of any lingering impression that he might return to his country and his old position on *The Commonwealth.*

With renewed firmness, he now wrote:

> It seems to me certain that my public life there will now end by an utter loss of influence. Whether this be in itself a thing to grieve over I very much doubt. I now feel but too plainly that I have been wearing myself away by too much excitement of a political kind; and I doubt whether I shall be able even to trust myself hereafter even should

> others be willing to trust me. At times lately it has flitted across my mind that some Higher Power had something to do with my blunder; and that I must accept this as a chance for getting more entirely out of party politics, and dedicating myself more entirely to Literature for which I now have much material. I have had grievous days and nights of agony over this matter, and O how I have longed for you.

Now that word had come from those with whom Conway had worked most closely that his "blunder" was fully as disastrous as he had feared, his "darkest hour" was over and he was able to look about "for what is best." Sell the furniture, he wrote, auction off books (except for those Ellen must pack in the bottom of the big trunk), procure passage for the family on the best Cunard steamer, and "come over here as soon as you can." Conway enclosed a note of resignation from *The Commonwealth*, which Ellen had permission to hold for a while if she thought best. Stearns had sent word to the office that the journal "must not compromise him by criticizing the administration," Conway had heard. "You know very well that I could not work with any such cramps upon me. Come as soon as you wish, the sooner the better." Whenever she gave the word, "I shall rush to Liverpool to receive you. and we may yet be happy."

By the following week Conway had started on his long journey back to England. From Milan he wrote, as the day approached for a reunion with his family, his relief grew at having left behind him "the foolish and malignant clamor" of the Mason affair. Conway's disappointment in the attitude of. "the best of the Antislavery men" also became more articulate as he reviewed the controversy on both sides of the Atlantic.

"I never was so sick and tired of it," he wrote his wife:

> It entered into my mind as soon as I had written the letter that I had made a mistake in making any proposition to Mason; but it never entered into my mind that any leading Antislavery man cd. question the principle involved -- or wd. in any way support the War, simply for Conquest or Union. Whether Liberty were or were not involved the wholesale slaughter of men is vile enough

> anyway; but to slaughter them except for the Noblest Cause is worse than treason to any Govt. that does it. I for one wash my hands of it forever! -- The worst thing about the whole affair of mine is that it gives an occasion to all my enemies to make all sorts of attacks against me. All these things combine to give me an occasion which I mean to improve of getting out of the dirty ruts of politics forever, or at least until they get nobler.

Two days later, on July 24, Moncure began another long letter to Ellen in his hotel overlooking "the beautiful lake Lucerne." Here he sat by an open window and listened to the music in the street below that sang to him of his approaching meeting with his wife and children. The letter continued in Paris where Conway fell in love with the boulevards and the parks. "My latest idea," he wrote, "is that we shall find Paris in every way the cheapest most delightful place in which to reside & it is quite near enough the Literary Market." Dr. John McClintock, Conway's former professor of Greek at Dickinson College, was at the time in charge of the American church in Paris; a walk "in a beautiful park" with his old teacher, and dinner afterwards with McClintock's wife and daughter, made Conway feel that here he might quietly resume his life as a writer.[410]

Fortunately, Ellen had no opportunity to respond to this passing whim; the best she could do was to assemble the books and magazines Conway urged her to bring with her to England, to carry a few bottles of wine to Emerson, with Conway's love, and to deliver "kind adieux to all friends in Concord" from the husband whom she was about to follow into exile. She handed in Conway's resignation from *The Commonwealth* just before she sailed.[411]

When Conway found himself once more in London, on the first of August, 1863, his "latest idea" that he might make a home in Paris vanished as had the dream of Venice. For there in Aubrey House was not only a letter from his wife announcing that the family would arrive in Liverpool on September 16 but also a letter from Phillips, saying that the "momentary annoyance" of the Mason affair was forgotten and his letters to *The Commonwealth*, though controversial, were valued. There was also awaiting him an invitation to deliver a "discourse" in South

Place Chapel, Finsbury, on September 13, which his old friend, Peter Taylor, had secured for him. This dissenting society, founded by an American in Philadelphia in 1793, had for forty years flourished under William Johnson Fox, a member of Parliament, who had made it famous as a center of liberal thought. Since the retirement of Fox five years earlier, the society had searched in vain for a minister as rationalistic as Fox and as eloquent. But for Taylor's suggestion of Conway's name, the chapel would have closed its doors. The committee reported:

> Now we have a comparatively empty chapel; and it would be strange, indeed, in this age of free inquiry, and in this free church of ours, if it were not so, seeing that for the last five years we have had scarcely any other source of religion opened to us but records of the past as contained in the Bible. The daily heroisms of our own time, the martyrdoms of old, the great spirits of all countries and of all climes, have ceased to be called in to our assistance; and from our pulpit the rocks and the heavens no longer sing their grand hymn of devotion and praise.[412]

Conway's first "discourse" made the congregation of hardly more than seventy people realize that here perhaps was the man they sought. Several of the old radicals who had not been to the chapel for many months came to hear his next address. Conway, however, did not consider himself a candidate for the position, for he was still receiving letters from his friends on *The Commonwealth* consulting with him as to whether or not he should resume his editorship. Since the presidential campaign was already beginning, and since the American Anti-Slavery Society was expressing the views of Garrison and supporting the nomination of Lincoln, *The Commonwealth*, with Phillips as its voice, was backing Frémont. Conway realized, as the weeks went by, that his presence in his own country would only add to the bitterness of the controversy between his two old friends. Moreover, he had learned through *The Commonwealth*, and through letters from Sanborn and others, that Stearns and Higginson were recruiting Negroes to fight against their masters.

Conway at last grasped the full divergence of his views and those of the men in Boston whom he had so much admired. He was content to remain in London, rejoicing to learn that his wife had paid the three hundred dollars required to buy a substitute when he was drafted for military service.

When Ellen and the boys arrived in England later in the month, Conway felt that "the leaden hour" in his personal life at least had passed. The reception of his first "discourse" reminded him that he was, after all, a preacher and not a politician. Several days after he had established his family in pleasant rooms at 16 Lansdown Terrace, Regent's Park, a note arrived from the United States minister, requesting him to call at his office. Conway recorded the interview in the new journal he had just begun:

> Wednesday, Sept. 23: Went to call upon Minister Adams, 5 Upper Portland Place, in obedience to a note received yesterday from him. He told me that he had received a note from Secretary Seward concerning my Mason correspondence, -- in which he (Mr. S.) said that he had shown my letter, and one from Mr. Adams concerning it, to the President; and that the President said that as I had acted so frankly and honourably in the matter after it was done, he should not feel disposed to pursue the matter further.[413]

The tide of the war had changed, and with it the mood of Lincoln. The victories at Gettysburg and Vicksburg early in July 1863 had lessened the probability of England's recognition of the Confederacy. Lincoln, always willing to extend a friendly hand when the political situation made it possible, not wishing to humiliate Conway further, willingly accepted his apology for his part in the Mason affair. The rush of national events, between Lincoln's Gettysburg Address of November 1863 and the campaign the following autumn for his election for a second term left no room in Washington for serious concern for the London preacher. Conway, however, continued to think about Lincoln, and to express his views publicly.[414] Though he admired him as a man, he never altered his opinion of "the slow Kentuckian President" who put Union before Emancipation.

But Conway's thoughts were now more occupied by his personal affairs than by American politics. In February, 1864, Conway accepted the position offered him by the South Place

Chapel, after an exchange of letters with Phillips, Sanborn, Bird, and Stearns, his friends on *The Commonwealth*, which made him realize that his former relationships were weakened. Correspondence with his old associates in Sandy Spring, Maryland, showed him that even the Quakers were indignant with him for proposing to stop the war.[415] Conway remained in England for more than a decade without returning to America, for he perceived that his presence in the United States would only be a signal to reopen the old arguments. Henceforth, he was hardly more than a spectator of national events.

As one of those who had played a minor role in the effort to bring about passage of the Emancipation Proclamation, however, Conway had given his whole-hearted support to two great leaders, Garrison and Phillips. He was, therefore, more than a little interested in the news that reached him of the meeting of the American Anti-Slavery Society in the Spring of 1864. Here Garrison and Phillips fought out their differences as to the future of the society. Garrison's motion that the society should be dissolved now that emancipation had been achieved was defeated. Phillips, who insisted that nothing was really accomplished until the Negro should be granted the right to vote, was elected president of the society. He, however, was unable to gain control of the organ of the society, the *National Anti-Slavery Standard*. The editor, Oliver Johnson remained faithful to Garrison while urging him to take a firmer position in regard to the Negro's right to vote. Garrison was unconvinced; *The Liberator* was no longer dedicated to the cause of the Negro but rather to the election of Lincoln for a second term. *The Commonwealth* became the voice of Phillips and the Radical Republicans, with whom the members of the Bird Club soon identified.

Conway's close association with the New England abolitionists had ended when he crossed the Atlantic. His attempt to represent them to the English proved to him that both factions were in favor of continuing the war. "I had no faith that war could achieve any permanent benefit to white, or black, or to any nation, while the President and the people recognized only the military method of pacification and emancipation. There was no place for me in militant America."[416]

In a sense, Conway never recovered from the disillusioning experience of finding himself totally at odds with the men whom he thought he represented. Reflecting on the experience as a lonely old man several years before his death, Conway wrote:[417]

> The personal events that strike deepest in a man work out their effects slowly....The mysterious and indefinable lightening that touched the innermost life in me was the virtual outlawry I suffered in 1863 for having proposed to abandon the war against the Confederates on condition of a guaranteed emancipation of all their slaves. There were only two voices that came to me from America declaring that I was right, -- that of my wife and that of the Hon. Martin F. Conway, who had just lost his seat in Congress for opposing the war in the interest of justice to both black and white. Those whose friendship I valued much were not unfriendly. "We know you are sincere and your heart right, but we have a country now, we glory in the Union we once wished to destroy, we worship what we have burned, and we see that you are following a delusion!" Such in substance was what my old anti-slavery comrades said. That I had committed a mistake in supposing that they would not support a war merely for the sake of a political or territorial union it was easy to confess. For the sake of my family, I bent before the storm. But the work of the lurid flesh that came out of us could not be undone. I was driven -- yes, driven -- by every force of mind and heart into myself! It was compelled to the painful and humiliating certainly that the whole world was wrong. My heart and mind had no relation to a union that required a half million human sacrifices for its continuance.

Having achieved a pulpit in London, a large lecture audience, and a foothold in the British magazine world, Conway presented to his readers his views on many subjects other than slavery. Invited by *Harper's Monthlys* to write for the magazine an account of the Shakespeare tercentenary at Stratford, for example, he thoroughly enjoyed his trip to the old town where he sought out all the buildings associated with the Shakespeare legend.[418]

On his return to London, however, he found his younger son, Emerson, seriously ailing, and his wife disheartened. Doctors could not halt the undiagnosed illness that culminated in the death of the boy on August 4. The Conway family attempted to recover from their grief by a brief trip to the Continent and then moved to lodgings near Aubrey House. The death of Emerson and his burial in England made the family feel less inclined to return to America and unresolved disagreements with their friends.

Conway had scarcely become adjusted to his altered life, when he was reminded of the slavery controversy in all its fury by discovering on the front page of the *National Anti-Slavery Standard* (July 23, 1864) an exchange of letters between his British friend, Professor Francis Newman, and William Lloyd Garrison. Newman took Garrison to task for his support of Lincoln who, he said, was not truly interested in "striking off fetters from the slaves." The president, he wrote, countenanced pro-slavery generals such as N.P. Banks in order to prevent the Negroes of Louisiana from achieving the freedom promised them by the Emancipation Proclamation.[419] Garrison replied by commending Newman for his former support of the president and then by expressing his surprise at "the tone" of Newman's letter, which he felt could not have been spontaneously written; no doubt it "owes its birth to the promptings of certain ill-balanced, erratic American minds on your side of the Atlantic."

In fact, wrote Garrison,

> Mr. Conway's jaundiced views are so literally expressed in your letter, that I shall not do him or you any injustice in attributing its origin to him. And here let me say, that you will not find him a safe counsellor, or a reliable witness on public issues. Impulsive, eccentric, reckless, highly imaginative, and ambitious at this time for "radical" distinction, his flaming zeal is not always according to knowledge; and his vision is too apt to "magnify mole-hills into mountains," and to "give to an inch the importance of a mile," according to the mood of his mind. His extraordinary and unwarrantable correspondence with Mr. Mason, wherein he falsely assumed to be duly authorized by "the leading Abolitionists of America" to negotiate for the recognition

> of the independence of the Southern Confederacy, provided it would in some way abolish slavery (the sole cause of its inception and object of its existence!), should make our English friends cautious in giving credence to his representations concerning men and things in America, and admonish him that he is not specially competent to call in question the anti-slavery integrity of those whose lives have been devoted to the liberation of the fettered millions on our slavery-cursed soil. However fervent his zeal or praiseworthy his object, the cause he is pursuing is well calculated to damage the American government abroad, and to help faction and sedition at home.

Conway had for several years been on friendly terms with Newman.[420] Garrison, however, had no grounds for his assertion. In any case, *The Commonwealth*, which was now anti-Garrison as well as anti-Lincoln, defended Conway. The issue dated August 10 published Conway's half-humorous but firm denial that he had ever seen Newman's letter before it appeared in *The Standard*.

Conway was, in a measure, responsible for Garrison's angry attack, for he had frequently reverted to his unfortunate encounter with Mason in his letters to *The Commonwealth*, seeking both to justify himself and to discredit Lincoln by pointing out that the president no longer had the full support of the English. Conway's underlying disagreement with Garrison and with Lincoln was that neither seemed to him to have the cause of the Negro at heart. In his letter to Garrison, Newman had quoted "an American" as saying to him: "The North hates slavery; but it hates colored men still more; and it will rather break up the Union than admit them into real equality."

The person to whom Newman referred might well have been Conway, for to him it seemed that the war had only brought about a "new slavery." His old friends of the Bird Club advocated the organization of Negro troops separately from white troops; Garrison did not believe that the Negro should vote. Nor did Lincoln, who to placate the southern slaveholder appointed generals in the deep South such as Banks, who cared nothing for the rights of Negroes. Conway had become disillusioned with the cause for which he had supposed he had been sent to England. It was increasingly apparent to him, were he to return to America, he would stand alone. Instead, Conway continued to write for *The Commonwe*alth. His letters, which Phillips still considered invaluable, reflected his view of the political situation in England and the progress of events in America, concerning which he was sometimes ill-informed.

The election of Lincoln for a second term seemed to Conway to offer an opportunity to examine with more critical scrutiny the "new order." The lead article by Conway in *Fraser's Magazine* of January 1865, "President Lincoln," by "An American Abolitionist," contained not only an analysis of Lincoln, "the candidate of compromise," but also a statement of disillusionment with these abolitionists who had failed to maintain their original stand.[421] He reminded his readers:

> There are circumstances under which one must have a long spoon at supper. The abolitionists did not, perhaps, fully remember this when they undertook to sup with the cotton lords of the North, with Wall Street, and State Street; and so comes the singular fact that the pioneer of 'immediate and unconditional emancipation' is found to-day supporting the candidate to compromise, the President who has returned more fugitives to slavery than any of his predecessors, and even loudly applauding General Banks of the 'White Men Beware!' Platform above referred to!

James Anthony Froude, editor of *Fraser's*, published Conway's article exactly as the unnamed "American Abolitionist" had written it; however, he wrote him on December 23, 1865, that he personally agreed with Carlyle on the slave question more nearly than with Conway. "At least I look at it, and have all my life looked at it, as a thing to be allowed to wear itself gradually away as civilization advances. You cannot treat an institution as old as mankind as a crime to be put out by force."[422] To Conway, however, the Union army seemed to be exerting the "force" against slavery -- which might have been legislated out of existence had Lincoln acted sooner. The "pioneer" himself now supported the president.

The "pioneer" to whom Conway was referring was, of course Garrison, for the controversy between the old leader and Conway continued. A southerner at heart, Conway did not feel that the bloody battles fought under Generals Ulysses S. Grant and William Tecumseh Sherman after the fall of Richmond, and sanctioned by the once peace-loving Garrison, were in the interests of the slaves. "It were idle to say that the victories of the Union are now the victories of emancipation," he wrote.

> Sherman's progress through Georgia is traceable in burning towns, but not, so far as the world learns, in broken fetters. Few are the cries of joy from liberated slaves that mingle with the wailings of those whose homes are desolate. Are these the fine issues to which the spirits of American reformers have been finely touched?

Froude's comment to Conway in his letter of December 23, 1865, "If the sword is pressed into service beyond the common service of ordinary average men, it will kill the man that uses it," soon was fulfilled by the assassination of the president. Conway heard the news at "a grand dinner" in celebration of the victory in America given by Peter Taylor at Aubrey House. Before the party was over, the butler came in quietly and whispered the news to the host of the evening, who sprang to his feet just as the newsboys were shouting the murder of Lincoln. The entire company rushed to the streets to buy the papers.[423]

The world was shocked into a sudden realization that a chapter was closed and a new chapter begun. Conway had promised for the May issue of *The Fortnightly Review* his "Personal Recollections of President Lincoln," to which he added:

> … it is natural that in the presence of the grave, wherein questions of individual policy are buried, and on which traits of personal character bloom with fresh beauty, these critics of the President should be harshly judged. It should be remembered, however, that if the President had a heavy burden to bear, so had they who were set to watch the War in the special interest of emancipation.[424]

Conway then reviewed in his mind the article that had so recently appeared in *Fraser's*, and, at Froude's invitation, wrote another essay for the June issue. In "The Assassination of President Lincoln," he said, "I am unable to cancel any statement of fact in that article, "I am free to confess that, standing beside the grave into which he has been violently thrust -- not for his defects, but for his virtues -- I could wish that its tone had been more tender." In this long essay on Lincoln as "the average Man," Conway again reviewed the whole history of Lincoln's presidency and his own effort, through several conferences with Lincoln, to encourage him to consider the position of the abolitionists as they urged him to issue an Emancipation Proclamation as an initial step in restoring the Union. Lincoln had listened quietly, courteously, and meditatively. He had not been moved from his position, however, that a military victory must come first. Conway concluded that Lincoln was "indeed so representative of his country, that to quarrel with him was to quarrel with the nature of things, and the criticism of him was a confession of national shortcomings. Consequently, though a martyr, Mr. Lincoln was no hero. "[425]

"It has been my lot," he wrote a year later, "to be amongst those Americans who have been, in some degree, politically alienated from the President on account of what they considered his dangerous hesitation to hurl slavery, utterly and forever, into the pit which it had digged for The Union; and to me this has been very painful, because I had rarely seen and known a man whom I could more admire personally."[426] Few tributes to Lincoln can match the account that Conway gives in this reminiscent essay of his first glimpse of Lincoln when he spoke in Cincinnati and of his several talks with the president in the years that followed. Conway's disagreement with Lincoln on the matter of Emancipation was clear, unchanging; and impersonal.

Conway disagreed with Garrison and Phillips, and also with Lincoln, not just on the political issue of emancipation; basically, Conway disputed their interpretation of the place of the Negro in the family of races. The Negro was, as Conway had said on many earlier occasions, "God's Unrecognised Gift" to the world.

In *The Golden Hour* (Chapter IX) Conway had stated what was to him the essential idea of the struggle against slavery: "THE

NEGRO HAS AN IMPORTANT DESTINY TO FULFILL IN HUMAN SOCIETY," and must not be kept in a "depraved" condition. In spite of the "pressure of law and force" that has encouraged ignorance, superstition, and often servility, the Negro has "shown a vitality equal to that of the white race....and has often proved himself superior." What are we to do with the Negro after he is freed? He must remain with us, wrote Conway, not only because many square miles of untilled land need his strength, but also because he has brought with him "from the remote past and fervid East a sacred stream of vitality.... without which man in the New World could never fill out the outlines sketched for him by the Supreme Artist." (p. 127). In support of his concept of the place of the Negro in the family of races, Conway quoted still another abolitionist, Ralph Waldo Emerson, with whom he had often discussed the ideas of Agassiz, Linnaeus, and Darwin. Conway wrote that Emerson, celebrating emancipation of the slaves of the British West Indies in 1844, had esteemed

> the occasion of this jubilee to be the proud discovery that the black race can contend with the white; that, in the great anthem which we call History, a piece of many parts and vast compass, after playing a long time a very low and subdued accompaniment, they perceived the time arrived when they can strike in with effect, and take a master's part in the music.[427]

Though Emerson had seen something more of the South than had Garrison and Phillips, his image of the southerner was almost as unrealistic as that of his abolitionist friends. However, Emerson's more enlightened view of history and evolution gave Conway a philosophic framework into which he could fit his love for his father's slaves.

Conway's interest in evolution and anthropology, as well as his deep concern for the family "servants," had drawn him into the abolitionist group, the political involvements of which he underestimated. In an article for *The Atlantic Monthly* (April 1863) on Benjamin Banneker, the Negro astronomer, Conway remarked that "this war is utterly inexplicable except as the historic method of delivering the African race in America from slavery, and this nation from the crime and curse inevitably linked therewith in the counsels of God, which are the laws of Nature." [428] The story of the struggles of Banneker, "the most original intellect which the South has yet produced," Conway wrote, was a study of effort of the Negro to find his place in "the family of races." Indeed, no inquiries "can be more suitable to our times than those that recognise his special capacity." These questions concerning the Negro seemed to Conway far more important than the military questions of the moment.

Having made his views on the Negro known in London, Conway was invited to become a member of the newly-formed Anthropological Society. Here he discovered to his surprise that the meetings were influenced by a few "ingenious gentlemen" who were chiefly interested in proving the inferiority of the Negro. The president of the society, Dr. James Hunt, published a small pamphlet, 'The Negro's Place in Nature," that Conway, after consultation with the anthropologist Thomas Huxley, undertook to answer in a series of speeches before the society.[429] Finding that Hunt's views were more generally accepted by the English than he had supposed, he issued his *Testimonies Concerning Slavery* in a small book in 1864. The book was widely discussed in England and reprinted in 1865 but never published in the United States.[430] Indeed, it would hardly have found sympathetic readers in either the North or the South.

Far in advance of any ideas as to the potential powers of the Negro expressed by even the more liberal abolitionists, Conway stated his belief in the equality of the Negro with the white man, intellectually, physically, and morally. Conway, in this pamphlet addressed to the English, also advocated racial inter-marriage.[431] As a member of the "Young Virginia" group of racists, he had announced unhesitatingly his belief in the superiority of the white race. How far he had traveled since then! Through his contact with the leaders of the anti-slavery movement in America and in England, he had learned to grasp an entirely new idea, "namely, the right of every man to himself," a concept that had carried him beyond the boundaries of nationality, race, or class -- well beyond the teaching of his former leaders.

To Conway, the struggle for the emancipation of the Negro was not merely a political one; it was "the romance of our age." As a child, he had listened to the Negroes' tales and songs in their log cabins, gone with them to their camp-meetings on the edge of the forest, and watched their hymn-singing baptismal rites by the Rappahannock River. He never forgot the special gifts of imagination and expression of the colored people. The *Testimony* he brought to the English was that they were not only equal to the white race but in some areas superior. "Negro sermons, fables, and descriptions are in the highest degree pictorial," he wrote. "My belief is, that there is a vast deal of high art yet to come out of that people in America. Their songs and hymns are the only original melodies we have." Freedom from slavery and the right to vote were important chiefly for aiding the Negro in evolving in the human race. "The evening-star of the epoch of separate races is the morning-star of Human Unity. Men we have; but not yet Man."[432]

Chapter XIV
"The Interpreter" at South Place Chapel

"It was a relief," wrote Conway, "after so many weary years of strife and polemics in America to have no further need to preach about slavery and dogma."[433] Now that the Civil War was over and the Mason affair more or less forgotten, Conway found that he was "not in an aggressive spirit." He was content to pursue his duties at South Place Chapel, occasionally preaching to the right-wing Unitarians of London. England had offered Conway what his native land had not, "a field for the exercise of the ministry for which [his] strange pilgrimage from slaveholding Virginia and Methodism to freedom and rationalism had trained [him]."[434]

The cause in which he was interested was "liberty," Conway discovered, and not merely the emancipation of the Negro. For years he had been so much absorbed in an effort to help avert war by freeing the Negroes that he had not been able to study the books on his own shelf, much less mingle with enlightened men and women in other fields of art, literature, theology, and science. As an "Interpreter" of current ideas to a congregation that might include John Stuart Mill, Robert Browning, Thomas Carlyle, or Sir Charles Lyell, Conway wandered far afield. The new minister from Virginia was able in his "discourses" to reflect on Man himself and see the Negro as one aspect of the long evolutionary process of civilization. "Freedom of thought," Conway wrote later, "had gradually taken the place in my religion which freedom of the slave occupied before it was secured," and "freedom of thought" for Conway covered a wide area.[435] As minister of South Place, he necessarily began with certain innovations in the services.

William Johnson Fox, Conway's predecessor at South Place, had already relegated the old sacramental vessels to a shelf in the vestry and established the custom of using the communion table only for flowers.[436] Conway, with a smile, laid aside Fox's handsome old gown, which he had left for the use of the new incumbent. The decanter of port or sherry always placed in the pleasant vestry for the refreshment of the preacher was a reminder to him that the "veteran radicals" of South Place were a different breed from the abolitionists of Boston. Conway soon learned that this new congregation was not only more liberal in its observance of ritual but also more liberal in thought. James Watson, who had been sent to prison for selling the works of Thomas Paine, and William Lovett, an elderly Chartist crusading for the rights of ordinary people, were both members of Conway's congregation.[437]

Fox, "the chief orator of the Corn Law agitation," too old to attend the services, became to Conway a link with the Unitarian tradition he had known in Boston and Concord. Fox was an uncompromising radical in opposing any particular wrong like slavery or the Corn Laws, enacted to ensure steep prices for food grown locally by imposing high tariffs on imports. He belonged to no party but "thought for himself," wrote Conway, who spent many evenings in "the elegant drawing room" of this picturesque personage. A social-minded minister, for twenty years "the most famous orator in England," Fox was also a musician who had made his chapel well known for fine music. His love of beauty, Conway noticed, had "educated Unitarians out of their lingering notion that godliness was akin to ugliness." This fine old white-haired minister, garbed in a velvet coat that harmonized with his armchair, spoke with admiration of Emerson, Margaret Fuller, Theodore Parker, and Longfellow, all of whom had come to hear him at South Place, and had visited him and his wife in their home near Regent's Park. Not infrequently Moncure and Ellen, the Taylors and other friends would gather in the drawing-room for a game of whist or the reading of a Shakespeare play or an evening with Browning.[438] After Fox died on June 3, 1864, Conway delivered a "discourse" at the memorial service for this "beautiful and gracious old man." Having known his predecessor at the outset of his own career at South Place, Conway felt connected with "the intimate history of this chapel."[439]

After difficulty finding a replacement for Fox, the congregation of South Place eagerly encouraged Conway to carry on the chapel's tradition of liberalism. The chapel committee, struggling under a heavy debt when Conway became minister, was able to pay him only a small salary but gave him "freedom -- not grudgingly, but with enthusiasm."[440]

"Literature as well as religion, science, art, philosophy, sociology, history -- the boundless continent of human interest" was his, Conway wrote with delight. "Here I could freely, fully pour out my soul. What joy was that!" [441] Sometimes Conway's thought was expressed in plays and tableaux in which the congregation took part. When he substituted a portion of a Persian prayer for the Second Lesson of the bible, no one was disturbed. Nor was the chapel committee displeased when he requested permission to offer no more prayers to an "abstract God." Instead, Conway proposed to make use of a "devotional reading," composed either by himself or "some eminent writer," frequently from the East. Conway's congregation was well pleased with their choice of a minister as recorded in the chapel minutes at the close of his first year: "A more earnest, interesting, instructive, and eloquent series of Services than Mr. Conway has presented to the Congregation throughout the year could scarcely have been hoped for by the most sanguine among us, reviving, in the opinion of many, in their deep philosophy, in their nobleness of thought, and in their stimulus to upright and useful conduct, the best memories of the Finsbury pulpit."[442]

Conway's known sympathies for the Orient, expressed in his devotional readings, brought many Hindus and Buddhists to South Place, especially when he announced that his Christmas "discourse" would be the birth-legends of Jesus and Buddha. After one such discourse, Conway records, a visiting Hindu scholar arose, walked up the aisle, and silently grasped the hand of the minister. "I felt," wrote Conway, "the warm heart of all India in that extended hand, answering again to the heart of South Place Chapel."[443]

Conway's study of Oriental literature began, he tells us, in Emerson's library in 1853.[444] There he wrote down extracts in his notebook, extended versions of which he later printed in *The Dial* in 1860. After he became minister in South Place, Conway added to his selections for readings and even employed several Hindus and Persians to search out and translate "Eastern flowerets," hitherto inaccessible to him. Conway's custom of reading from the works of Buddha, Zoroaster, and Confucius, as well as from the Bible, was much commented upon and finally led to the publication in 1874, of *The Sacred Anthology, a Book of Ethical Scriptures*.[445] Prepared for "the thoughtful reader," rather than for "the eminent scholar," Conway's book was praised on all sides. It went through many editions and was adopted for pulpit reading in the more liberal Unitarian churches in England, Scotland and America.[446]

The purpose of *The Sacred Anthology*, declared in the preface, was "simply moral." "The editor has believed," wrote Conway, "that it would be useful for moral and religious culture if the sympathy of Religion could be more generally made known, and the converging testimonies of ages and faces to the great principles more widely appreciated." If Conway's earlier attempt to prove that the question of slavery was essentially a religious one had not been altogether successful, his later insistence that true religion, freed from "the rust of superstition and the dross of ritual," embraced all members of the human family, including the Negro, was welcomed by scientists and theologians, by poets and members of Parliament. Letters of congratulation poured in from Tennyson, the Irish physicist John Tyndall, Harriet Martineau, the German orientalist Max Müller, and many others. Dean Stanley quoted from *The Sacred Anthology* in Westminster Abbey, and Sir Charles Lyell invited Conway to address the British Association for the Advancement of Science. "In my ministry Theology was naturally replaced by Anthropology," wrote Conway, but since all such studies proved the brotherhood of Man and the fatherhood of God, Conway's Anthropology frequently seems to the modern reader very like Theology.[447]

Conway's interpretation of the problem of the Negro was enlarged by his study of the interrelation of races. His growing congregation at South Place listened to his sermons with rapt attention. They were, however, less willing to accept Conway's presentation of the political scene in America during reconstruction days. Conway found that his efforts to justify the granting of civil rights to Negroes in America after the war met with unexpected opposition. John Stuart Mill, for example, was not prepared to follow Wendell Phillips and the Radical Republicans in insisting on the enfranchisement of the Negro as an essential corollary to emancipation. To put the question clearly before Mill, then in France, Conway mailed to him several speeches by Phillips, which Mill found "cheering and auspicious."[448] Mill wished to have his "warmest thanks" expressed to Phillips, correcting his "unintentional misrepresentation of the Abolitionists," whom, he wrote, he considered "the elite of their country, not to say of their age."

Mill then expressed reservations as to the wisdom of granting the Negro the right to vote without certain qualifications. Mill wrote that he had not been convinced by Phillips' argument against an educational qualification. "It is very true," he said, "that intelligence, and even a high order of it, may be formed by other means than reading, and even (though, I think, rarely) without the aid of reading: but not, I think, intelligence of public affairs." At the moment, however, "the securing of equal political rights to the negro is paramount to all other considerations," and Phillips was correct in trying to convince Congress that it should not pass a compromise bill "admitting negroes on an educational qualification common to them with the whites." Mill, though a supporter of the Union cause throughout the war, did not wholeheartedly agree with either Conway or Phillips on Negro enfranchisement.

As spokesman for the abolitionists in England, Conway had already discovered that interpretations of the Negro question varied in Britain as in the United States.[449] Those who believed in emancipation did not necessarily believe in giving the vote to the Negro after the war. Carlyle's well-known views on slavery, widely quoted in London, sometimes forced Conway to defend his position more vehemently than he intended. One Sunday evening, Conway was taken by Tom Hughes to the room of the English publisher, Macmillan. Here the conversation turned to "the American situation," and Conway was sharply criticized for his views. Hughes spoke up against Conway's assailant "with a severity from which the company could not recover." Herbert Spencer, seated near Conway, leaned over and said to him in a low voice, "A good many intelligent people do not hold the same views of the negro and his position as those of the abolitionists."[450]

Conway found support for his interpretation of American politics among the liberal thinkers who visited Aubrey House and frequently attended his services at South Place. Francis Newman, whose book on *The Soul: her Sorrows and her Aspirations* was to Conway "a spiritual pasture....not hedged by dogmatic thorns," soon became an intimate friend with whom Conway discussed politics as well as religion. Emeritus professor of Latin from the University of London, now in retirement, Newman cordially welcomed the young man who had so recklessly thrown himself into public controversy on slavery. Newman subscribed to *The Commonwealth*, *The Liberator* and the *National Anti-Slavery Standard*; he talked with Conway "about the intimate discussions and differences among our abolitionists as if he were one of the Frank Bird Club." When the Mason affair became public, Newman urged Conway to leave his case in the hands of his English friends and risk the wrath of Garrison by expressing his views in the *National Anti-Slavery Standard*. "No American could follow the vicissitudes of our struggle with more poignant anxiety," wrote Conway of this retired teacher of Latin whose vehement support of the radical Republican program in the United States helped Conway to formulate the views he expressed in British and American journals.[451]

Busy as the new minister was with his duties at South Place, he nevertheless took his seat in the reporters' galleries of the House of Lords and the House of Commons, listening to speeches by Gladstone, Benjamin Disraeli, John Bright, Richard Cobden, and many others, who, after the defeat of the Chartists in 1848 and the repeal of the Com Laws were looking forward to a new era of liberal thought.[452] The outcome of the Civil War in America encouraged the Liberal Party, and Conway was seen mingling with members of both houses. "At the table of the Duke and Duchess of Argyll, at Argyll Lodge, Kensington, I first met a number of lords who, like themselves, were deeply interested in the antislavery cause," Conway wrote. "Afterwards I met other aristocratic families, several members of which came to South Place chapel."[453]

Richard Cobden, however, was Conway's "ideal of a parliament leader." Cobden's dignity and graciousness, as well as his idealism, impressed him. "I used to watch him from my seat in the Speaker's gallery while discussions were going on, such as those involving the United States,"[454] Conway remembered. Before long Conway was breakfasting with Cobden in his rooms near Westminster Hall, marveling at "the extent of his knowledge of our affairs in America." Conway contributed an essay to *The Atlantic Monthly* (June, 1865) in which he described the scene in the House of Commons when Cobden's death was announced. America, he pointed out, had "lost one of her truest friends," for Cobden's celebrated speech in favor of the Union cause had helped to turn the tide of British sympathy "at the time when the busy Southerner" was trying to prove free trade, not slavery, was the issue of the war.

John Elliot Cairnes, professor of political economy in University College, London, proved to be Conway's constant advisor in his articles on changing events in the United States. "This admirable man was thoroughly instructed in America affairs," wrote Conway. "He knew our constitutional history, and the causes of the anomalies and compromises which had led to the war. He was well acquainted with all the legal, economic, and international questions involved, and being withal a man of sweetness as well as light, I could consult him about all my articles written for either country."[455] Conway had read and commented upon the book on which Cairnes' reputation rested, *Slave Power: its character, career and probable design, being an attempt to explain the real issues involved in the American contest* (1862). Though written before the end of the Civil War, the book clearly stated that the real issue was slavery and the North would be victorious. "How is the conquered South to be governed?" Cairnes asked in his concluding chapter. The answer: "I can see but one way in which this can be affected -- by the overthrow of representative institutions in the Southern States, and the substitution of a centralized despotism wielded by the Federal government." In making this statement, however, Cairnes recognized the latent dangers of centralized power, adding, "If the new government were only equal to its task of reconstructing Southern society, its advent would be wholly a blessing."[456]

To Conway's satisfaction, Mr. and Mrs. Cairnes engaged the only other apartment in "the pleasant lodgings at 28 Notting Hill Square," thus supplying Moncure with an advisor and friend and Ellen with the companionship of the "witty and cheerful Mrs. Cairnes." John Stuart Mill and Professor Henry Fawcett were the intimate friends of the Cairneses, and now and then the Conways were included in small dinner parties given by Mill and his stepdaughter, Helen Taylor.[457]

Conway's unflagging sociability, as well as his many-sided interests, drew him into the stream of London society, enabling him to converse with men and women of many different groups. Nor did this minister of South Place Chapel, also a journalist, ever willingly miss an opportunity to mingle with the great and famous. On April 30, 1866, for example, Conway rushed a note to a friend, inviting him to "a rich treat" on May 2 -- "Nothing less than an invitation and ticket to the great Literary Dinner at Willis' rooms." Froude had given Conway two tickets, which, he hoped, included a free dinner. "But," he wrote, "the great men you will see and hear wd. be worth ten guineas even to poor men like ourselves -- Lord Houghton's friends and Kingsley's, Hughes's, Dickenses', and the like will be plentiful as blackberries are not in these days. Wit and fun will be lying around loose....Be in evening dress at the door of Willis' Room, St. James, Wednesday before 6 P.M."

Behind this gaiety was Conway's instinct that made him sense opportunities in such gatherings. He was soon writing to the pastor, professor and historian Moses Coit Tyler, that "Hughes had resigned the [New York] *Tribune* and I am now regular Correspondent there." In the same letter Conway wrote, "I am getting radicaler and radicaler every day, and if I live here much longer under this Tory govt -- shall assuredly 'bust.' We have been having fine prospects of a general smash on the Continent, but now things are looking horribly peaceful over there. War is hateful I know, but then people had better die than by tyrannized over -- especially other people than you and me, don't you think so?"[458] Neither Conway's congregation at South Place nor the readers of the *Tribune* objected to his liberal views. Conway became, indeed, an interesting "personality" both in pulpit and press.

George Henry Lewes, in his newly launched *Fortnightly Review*, welcomed Conway's radical views of reconstruction in the South. A friend and disciple of John Stuart Mill and leader of the British Positivists, Lewes made *The Fortnightly* the mouthpiece of the Liberal Party.[459] Though the chief subject of his editorials were reform of the franchise in England, the modernizing of British education and the disestablishment of the Church, the newly freed Negroes of the South remained a subject of major concern to readers of *The Fortnightly*. Not only was slavery an issue to the British Liberal, so also was the question of classes in America. The party of reform felt that the South had found support among upper-class gentry and cotton manufacturers of England. The assassination of Lincoln the month before publication of the first issue of the *Fortnightly* redoubled interest in "the task of reconstructing Southern society" by the new government under President Andrew Johnson.

Conway, like Cairnes, had at first high hopes that Johnson "might prove a better President to carry out emancipation than Lincoln."[460] However, it soon became apparent to Conway that this Democrat from Tennessee, elected on the Republican ticket with Lincoln in 1864, by granting amnesty to former Confederates opposed the party that elected him. Northern Republicans, Conway pointed out in *The Fortnightly* of January, 1866, bitterly opposed "return of the Southern States with their governments still committed exclusively to the whites."[461] Provided that the provisional governments of the South ratify the Thirteenth Amendment against chattel slavery, they would then be free to establish a system of Negro serfdom against which the North could not act except by declaring another war. Conway insisted, unless the Negro were granted the vote at once, the country would be doomed to the same agitation and dissension that began a generation before the Civil War. Lincoln, wrote Conway, foresaw this issue and planned to demand equal voting rights for the Negro in the states reentering the Union. "But President Johnson is a very different man," he said in an essay that appeared just before passage of the Fourteenth Amendment penalizing states that deprived the Negro of the ballot.

"The plaudits of educated Englishmen are mingled with those of the mobs of New York and Washington," wrote Conway in his next *Fortnightly* essay (May 15, 1866).[462] He discussed with disdain the stubborn adherence of the English to the ex-slaveholder and the "almost universal applause" of Johnson's veto of the measures taken by Congress to protect the Negroes' right to vote. Let thoughtful Englishmen consider the crisis at which the United States has arrived after several generations of bitter agitation ending in a bloody war. If this "dreary experience has taught the country anything," he wrote, it is that there can be no internal peace, and consequently no real advancement in America so long as there is a negro agitation in it."

Moreover, Conway predicted, it was certain that this agitation would continue "so long as the negro is deprived of the rights and immunities awarded to the lowest and most ignorant of all other races." By denial of the principle of equality set forth in the Declaration of Independence, "the chain which was around the negro's neck was gradually fastened about that of the nation, and of every man in the nation." Conway was voicing the views of the Radical Republicans, who, the following autumn, won an overwhelming victory at the polls.[463]

The "Reign of the Radicals" was inaugurated by passage of the Reconstruction Acts on March 2, 1867, over the veto of the president. Conway heartily endorsed the program of reconstruction in his next *Fortnightly* essay, "American Prospects."[464] Much as Conway deplored the suffering of the South, he rejoiced in what seemed to him a moral victory achieved by the Radical Republicans despite the hesitation of the president. "Very slowly the President came around to their view," wrote Conway, "and he is now reluctantly carrying into effect a policy infinitely more radical than that which he might have followed at an earlier period, but which he rejected with indignation." Just as the cause of the abolitionists had seemed to Conway defensible on solely moral grounds, so now the position of the Radical Republicans seemed to him essentially moral. That the program contributed to the financial and business interests of the North did not seem to him a consideration.

"There can be no question that the result [of the passage of the Reconstruction Acts] is the triumph of a purely moral conviction in the mind of people," he wrote.

> There was hardly a man in America who would not have immediately benefitted by the restoration of the South to equal power in Congress on its own terms, for under the uncertainty and agitation the financial depression affected everybody. But the issue before the people was very plain: 'Is it just that we, having liberated the negroes when it served our purpose to do so, and received from them an aid which has excited against them the anger of the masters they helped to humiliate, should now abandon them to the unchecked control of those masters? Many interests said, 'Yes;' but conscience said, 'No,' and prevailed.

Conway's clear conclusion was that of a man who had been far from home for more than five years. A letter to Tyler on March 14, 1868, announcing the birth of a daughter, suggests that

Conway was so busy and so prosperous that the situation of his Virginia family seemed somewhat remote to him. "I am, -- saving to-day -- jogging along in the same old way, writing hard, with more work opening before me than I can manage. I have charge in addition to South Place, of an evening appointment with a new and fine liberal congregation at Camden Town. South Place gives me - 250 pounds,[465] and Camden Town - 100 pounds per annum - one sermon doing for both. I made - 800 pounds last year and shall easily make - 1000 pounds this." Moreover, the Conways new home at 14 Milbourne Grove, West Brampton, was very comfortable. "We like housekeeping," Conway wrote, "have excellent servants; and if you and Mrs. T. will drop in at six will give you as neatly up a dinner as if you were in Paris - whence both our servants (mother and daughter) come."

In spite of Conway's defense of Congress in his articles for *The Fortnightly*, the "patient English public" still seemed to favor the President who wished to allow the rebellious states to return to the Union with their "original forms of organization unimpaired," except for their right to buy and sell Negroes. Conway's analysis of "The Internal Conflict of America" appeared in *The Fortnightly* of March, 1868, only a few days before the trial of the president opened in Washington. The fact that Johnson "had recalled from the South all post-war officers who intended to uphold the Reconstruction Acts, and finally removed Edwin M. Stanton as Secretary of War," seemed to Conway to presage the virtual re-establishment of slavery in the South. Without visiting to hear of the acquittal of the President, Conway expressed no doubt that Congress would convict Johnson and believed that "the only hope remaining to the President was to appeal to the Supreme Court to declare unconstitutional the Reconstruction Acts passed by Congress." The new legislature of Ohio had already voted to rescind its ratification of the Fourteenth Amendment and to support a proposal that government bonds be paid in greenbacks rather than in gold.

The overwhelming victory of General Grant, the following autumn, justified, Conway believed, Wendell Phillips' determination to continue the struggle until the Negro should become enfranchised. Writing for *The Fortnightly Review* of June 1, 1870, Conway celebrated the passage of the Fifteenth Amendment in an article on his old friend and leader, now

President of the American Anti-Slavery Society.[466] Not only had Phillips, as one of the most tireless of the Radical Republicans, persisted in his struggle for the enfranchisement of the Negro; he had tirelessly combatted the "reasonable" action of President Johnson, and supported the campaign of Grant by helping to organize the Negro vote responsible for his overwhelming success in the election of 1868.

"The Abolitionists have hardly had fiercer battles to wage than those which followed between the accession of President Johnson and the election of Grant," wrote Conway. Wendell Phillips, he declared, was "the leading orator of the movement" which had come to a triumphant conclusion. Just as Garrison had announced that the work of the American Anti-Slavery Society had been achieved when the Emancipation Proclamation was issued, so now Phillips considered that the granting of the vote to every citizen, without regard to "race, color or previous condition of servitude," marked the end of the battle for the negro. By nature a reformer, Phillips proposed to turn the journal of the American Anti-Slavery Society into *The Standard* which would "devote itself to do for law, woman, labour, temperance, and free thought, what it had done for the negro. Thus, said Conway, the Anti-Slavery flag was unfurled anew "in the interest of all those movements for reform which were really awakened by the agitation it was originally raised to represent."

Before embarking on a full and eloquent account of his hero, Wendell Phillips, Conway summed up in several pages the career of the "faithful and fearless pioneer of emancipation." William Lloyd Garrison, in terms which serve as a just interpretation of the "great cause" as well as "the ordinary man" who served it.[467] A "mad printer" of little education and no eloquence, Garrison had been "as a pane of glass through which the plain light of moral sentiment passed freely to expose and judge the immorality of African slavery," wrote Conway, overlooking his personal conflicts of a later date.

The sight of Garrison being dragged through the streets of Boston with a rope around his neck by "an infuriated mob of roughs" turned a young Harvard law student from the path he was quietly pursuing to become the "tongue of flame" which fired the Anti-Slavery movement. Wendell Phillips "found it a vulgar street agitation, with only poor and unlettered men supporting it; he gave it his position, his wealth, his scholarship and eloquence, and won for it the hearts of the young men who could not be kept from crowding every hall where he was to speak.... He rivalled the theatres with his audiences, he drew the professors, he excited the young authors; it began to be 'the thing' to profess some interest in the anti-slavery movement. Longfellow, Lowell, Whittier began to sing of it. Emerson, Parker, Margaret Fuller began to adorn it with their philosophy."

Into this movement Conway himself had been swept as a young Divinity School student in Cambridge. In tracing Phillips' career--his attack on Daniel Webster in 1851, his efforts to protect the Negroes who escaped to Boston, his oratory in defense of John Brown--Conway was recapitulating his own contact with "the grandest crusade which the world has seen since the days of Luther." Unaware--or unmindful--of the chaos brought about in the South by the Reconstruction Acts of 1867, which placed the "unreconstructed states" of the former Confederacy under military rule until they should ratify the Fourteenth Amendment, Conway held to the position he had adopted many years earlier in regard to the fundamental human rights of the negro.

An idealist rather than a politician, Conway disregarded the corruption and extravagance which followed in the wake of Northern "carpetbaggers" and Southern "scalawags" who controlled the vote of politically inexperienced Negroes. "A purely moral conviction" of the right made Conway an eloquent supporter of Wendell Phillips and the Radical Republicans during the dark after the close of the War. Though Virginia was not readmitted into the Union until 1870, Conway remained firm in his belief that the signing of the Fifteenth Amendment was the only means by which the South could begin to rebuild itself on a sound basis, in spite of the "Warning," by Phillips, published in the *Cincinnati Commercial* for April 11, 1870. Since Conway, too, was writing for this same paper a weekly letter from London, it is probable that he read "Phillips' account of "violence and blood" throughout the South, against which Phillips was warning his readers. Unwilling to put into effect the Fifteenth Amendment giving the Negro the vote, "defiant Legislatures" and Governors were calling for more Federal troops to quell the angry mobs which they could not or would not control. As long as Union officers were daily threatened in the streets, "how mad is the cry for universal amnesty," until the South should acknowledge defeat and accept the new order, military rule must prevail.

In spite of newspaper accounts of violence in the South, the American scene was slowly receding from Conway's imagination. Re-established at 28 Notting Hill Square after the death of his son, Emerson, Conway flung himself into the life of a free-lance journalist as well as into that of a preacher and lecturer. Trips to the Continent to cover the Paris Exposition, to see the Passion Play at Oberammergau, or to study the myths of Germany, jaunts to the South of England with fellow anthropologists, a journey to Scotland to witness the installation of Carlyle as Rector of the University of Edinburgh - all these excursions and many more made excellent copy for the numerous articles Conway was writing for *The Atlantic Monthly. Harper's Monthly, The Round Table*, and *Cincinnati Commercial*, and New York *Tribune, Fraser's Magazine. The Fortnightly Review*, and other publications.

The birth of two more children, Dana and Mildred, explains in part Conway's efforts to augment his salary as a minister. His inquisitive, sociable, experimental, and restless temperament, however, impelled him to participate fully in the world around him. Conway's unshakable belief in the equality of the Negro with the white man and his staunch insistence that the Civil War could not be considered won until the Negro gained the vote continued to find expression through articles and lectures in England; his field of vision was simply enlarged so that the story of the Negro took its place in the new scientific, literary, and political thought which opened up about him.

When he was himself an elderly man, Conway's son, Eustace, looked back over these London days, and recalled his extraordinary father in a delightful little booklet, entitled *A Boy's Eye View of Mid-Victorian Times* (1936). Moncure D. Conway, his son wrote, gave what he liked to call "discourses" to a large London congregation, predominantly middle-class, for more than thirty years. Eustace remembered that "a favorite role of his was that of interpreter, like Bunyan."

> He took the great works of the leading scientific, literary and artistic leaders of the day, and wove a simple account of their different views and works into his

sermons. For instance, J.M.W. Turner's Slave Ship, Dante Gabriel Rossetti's Mary Magdalene, Robert Browning's Sordello and John Tyndall's Belfast lecture were among his subjects.[468]

To the boy it seemed that these "eminent men of literature, art and science" all loved "the people," but only at a distance; in his father they found "a sympathetic interpreter of their ideas" who was able by the magic of his oratory to bring poetry, science, art, as well as religion, to all classes of people. "Accordingly," Eustace reported, "a multitude of friends in the circles I have mentioned often came to our house and took walks with my father and talked, I many times tagging along."

Self-exiled in England though he was, Conway became "an interpreter" of American thought to the English, and of British and European ideas to the Americans, for his articles and letters never ceased to flow back across *The Atlantic* during his more than thirty years abroad. The "multitude of friends," remembered by Eustace many years later, included John Stuart Mill, Charles Darwin, Giuseppe Mazzini, Harriet Martineau, Edwin Abbey, and many others. Diverse though these personalities were, all of them were aware of the liberal thought which had flowed through South Place Chapel many years before Conway became its minister. Having come to England as spokesman for the Abolitionists, he became the "interpreter" of a world movement of which the Civil War in America was only a phase. Backed by the liberal men and women whom Conway met at Aubrey House and among the members of his congregation at South Place, the minister in his role of journalist, and lecturer, as well as preacher expressed views on American politics that seemed to some to relate the Civil War to the larger revolutionary movements of Europe.

At Aubrey House, where the Taylors maintained a *salon* for writers, artists, liberals and visitors from foreign lands, Conway met Mazzini, Garibaldi, Venturi, Louis Blanc, and many other refugees from the 1848 revolutions on the Continent, who spent their evenings in the beautiful home of the Taylors. The personality of the aging Mazzini especially exercised a particular charm, gifted as he was with a fine intelligence, as well as extraordinary beauty. A Dante scholar and a lover of music, and a distinguished gentleman, Mazzini lived almost in squalor in a lodging house in London, for he gave not only his time and thought to the ideal of a unified Italy, but also all the money he could spare. To Conway's inquiry as to the right of the Negro to vote, he had replied, "Can you doubt it? As God is one, ... so the stamp of mankind is one."[469] Mazzini's views, however, were those of a man experienced in revolution, who dreamed of uniting the struggles of all nations into one: "A nation has a task to fulfill in the world for the good of all," he wrote Conway on May 25, 1865. Each nation has "a flag to hoist in the giant battle to which all local battles are episodes ... To abstain is to deny the oneness of God and of mankind."

Conway might have responded to the impetuous urging of Mazzini, contained in a letter of May 5, 1865, to exhort his countrymen to make common cause with Europe, had he not become aware of the fact that Mazzini was proposing a "scheme for European conflagration, with the United States to participant" Conway showed his letter to no one, publishing it for the first time in his *Autobiography*.[470] When Mazzini died in 1872, however, Conway held a Memorial Service[471] in his honor at South Place Chapel, where he was universally loved and considered "a sort of high priest of the religion" of the "divine Republic" where all men are free and equal. "Poor Mazzini"-- as Carlyle called him--was entangled in what seemed to him "hopeless visions," though he was "a very religious soul."

Conway discovered, when "the odious epoch of reconstruction arrived," that his own conviction that the Negro cause was only half won by the War was not shared by either Carlyle or Froude, the editor of *Fraser's Magazine*. Froude was willing, however, to publish an article "By an American Abolitionist" just before the assassination of Lincoln, and another after his death, though he did not share Conway's views. Froude urged on Conway, "when peace broke out," the impossibility of enfranchising the Negroes, who would certainly remain devoted to their old masters no matter what steps the northerners might take to destroy the slaveholders of the South. "That you have killed slavery is certain enough," wrote Froude. "That the negroes will remain devoted to their old masters ... that the poor whites will cast their lot with them to whom they have always looked up, seems to be equally clear. The masters may accept the results of the war and return quietly to the Union under such conditions as they can get, but that they will never forgive New England and will watch for the time to be revenged under the forms of the Constitution flows necessarily from the common laws of humanity. Do what you will, the whole South will be Democrat."[472]

When Conway returned to the United States for a lecture tour in 1875, he found that Froude's prediction was substantially fulfilled. Virginia had, indeed, ratified the Fifteenth Amendment, forbidding any state to deny suffrage on the grounds of "race, color, or previous condition of servitude," and thus had returned to the Union in 1870. But the Enforcements Acts of 1870-72, implementing the Fourteenth and the Fifteenth Amendments, did not prevent the South from quietly reasserting white supremacy, as Froude had predicted, and becoming the Solid South, in opposition to the northern Republicans.

Conway cradling one of his babies.

Chapter XV
Pilgrim's Return

"I am thinking of coming over to America for a six months visit a year from now, bringing with me a few lectures, in order to pay expenses and if possible make a little besides. What think you?" Conway wrote to Moses Coit Tyler in 1869.[473] He continued gaily, "Would all lecture committees speak at once; should I have to hire, charter, express trains; should I be in a position to tear up the proposition of any Committee for less than $1000 and throw it in their faces? Or does Hope tell an over-flattering tale in these suggestions?" On March 31, 1870, he wrote to Tyler again to say that he had concluded that he must give up the trip that year because of pressure of work and limitation of time. He saw that he could make 1000 pounds per annum in England "quite easily." He was at that time working on two books, *The Earthward Pilgrimage* and *The Natural History of the Devil.*

Put off by Conway's growing family obligations and writing and speaking commitments, the long-projected trip did not take place until late August 1875. His extensive lecture tour, through all the large cities of the East and as far West as Chicago, would not commence until October. Conway went at once to Fredericksburg, Virginia, where his old parents were living with his brother, Peter. Conway House, in Falmouth, he found, was the home of working people from the North; after the occupation of the mansion by Union troops, the terraces and gardens had never been restored. "The footprint of war was everywhere traceable in desolation."[474]

Conway's two-week visit with family and friends proved to him, despite the obvious signs of poverty and destruction, that his part of the South, at least, was beginning to mend. If the Negroes were being deprived of their right to vote, he saw no visible sign of threat or intimidation. Nor did he feel in the warm welcome he received on every side from both whites and blacks anything of the harshness of the last visit he had made to Falmouth and Fredericksburg in 1859. Giuseppe Mazzini's idea of World

Revolution seemed remote, for now he was again in the familiar Virginia countryside among people who did not regard him with suspicion or sorrow. Neither politics nor religion was discussed. His father, after inquiring for his son's health, looked at him affectionately and said nothing; his mother entertained him with "curious old family romances." His brother, Peter, recounted "queer stories of his career as a soldier."

"The cordiality with which I am recd. is far beyond my expectation, and gives my parents great pleasure," Conway wrote on September 14 to his wife, who remained with the children in London: "Old friends pour in and the neighbors congratulate me by sending huge baskets of flowers, &c. Three magnificent baskets have just come in all at once. A deputation waited on me to lecture. I am invited out on all sides. The drawing room (a very pretty one) is filled with young men, lawyers, physicians &c every evening. The weather is charming; everything in bloom; fireflies darting about every evening. Peter has a good horse always at my service. I am enjoying deep rest; sleeping 8 hours every night; eating all manner of luxuries. Pa is most affectionate to me and to all. His business is good and he enjoys it."[475] In short, the Old Dominion was still there. "It is odd to find so much that is wonderful and exciting in this quiet little village, but I don't believe a voyage round the world would be so interesting."

Conway was invited to speak in churches in Fredericksburg, honored at a dinner given by the mayor, and driven about the countryside to see for himself the effects of the war. "The war has done the people good." he wrote Ellen. "Instead of the old sharpness & feuds between families there is universal friendliness, all drawn together. None are more beloved than our family. Ma has acquired a sort of "saintly reputation by her devotion to everybody except herself... They are imploring pa to be Mayor but he resolutely refuses." Moncure observed that the elder Conway now read his son's books and was quite willing to forget the anxiety he had caused for so many years. As a man of forty-three, with a home and a position in England, Conway himself could listen more reflectively to his father's stories of simple neighborhood events during the melancholy years of war.

When Virginia seceded in 1861, Walker Conway told him, the governor had announced that all white farmers and their families in sympathy with the Union must leave the State by a certain date, and a long procession had passed through Fredericksburg to the river where they found boats to take them to Baltimore. Conway's father watched the refugees pass; he remembered them well. He told his son:

> *They were poor countryfolk, travelling in wagons with wives and children, -- some on foot, -- all moving on in silence, gloomy and frightened. Everybody crowded to see them and some near me began to jeer; but I moved away from these with disgust. I was touched by the sight of these humble people sacrificing their homes and solemnly following their old flag.*[476]

From other men in Fredericksburg, Conway learned that the Negroes of Fredericksburg, after the war was over, had unanimously elected Walker Peyton Conway as their official representative on the local reconstruction board, set up after the Constitutional Convention of 1870. Walker Conway served without salary; his first remark when he took his place on the board was: "Gentlemen, henceforth I know neither white man nor blacks," and to this resolution he remained loyal in his difficult position. "The two races were getting on pleasantly together, in 1875, in northern Virginia," Conway observed. Neither his father nor any other white man that Conway encountered wished to return to pre-war conditions; they were relieved no longer to have the responsibility of clothing and feeding their Negroes.

Moncure's father told him an amusing story of a farmer from a remote area of the state who came to Fredericksburg six months after the war to buy clothes for his slaves. Not having heard that they had been declared free, he would not believe the news when he learned it from the salesman but came to the elder Conway to find out the truth. "They tell me down the streets that the servants are all free," he began. "I suppose they are making fun at me. My hands are working down there just the same as for the twenty years." The elder Conway was able to enlighten the farmer -- perhaps to the chagrin of "the hands" themselves who, Conway suspected, preferred to work for their old master rather than risk the dangers of their new freedom.

Though Walker Peyton Conway had lost not only his slaves, his home, two farms, and a fortune of about $100,000 when Virginia seceded from the Union, his son found him more prosperous in his old age than he could have expected. "I think his [banking] business amounts to about $3,000 a year," he wrote Ellen, "and he has about 500 acres of land."[477]

Before secession, Conway learned, his father had been forced to accept a warehouse full of cotton at Mobile in return for a debt he could not collect. Noticing that the price of cotton was rising, he ordered it shipped to New York, stored and insured at war value. A few days later the warehouse containing Conway's cotton went up in flames, but the insurance company refused to pay the insurance to a Confederate. The elder Conway concluded that he would never be able to collect. However, his brother-in-law, Richard Cassius Lee Moncure, now chief justice of Virginia, insisted that Conway keep trying even after a lapse of four or five years. The insurance company took the case through every court but eventually had to pay the full sum -- and thus repair the fortunes of the Conway family. Judge Conway, holding court some miles away, had "just sent word to me not to go out of the country without seeing him," Moncure wrote Ellen. "He is the great man of the South."[478]

One beautiful morning in mid-September, Peter and Conway rode ten miles into Stafford County to old Aquia Church where a cousin, the Reverend John Moncure, was to preach from the high pulpit near the tomb of the original John Moncure, the great-great-great grandfather of the Conway brothers. Together, Peter and Moncure strolled through the family graveyard after the service and read over the names of the fifty or more descendants of the first John Moncure, the Episcopal minister who had come to the new world in the mid-eighteenth century and had built Aquia Church. Here Union soldiers had camped, but all was in order again -- and looked as Conway remembered it as a boy.

In a letter of September 19, 1875, Conway described to his wife the delights of this trip:[479]

> On Friday morning, a bright day, Peter and I started on horseback for Stafford Court House, 10 miles away. It was glorious to go over the old road once more. I seemed to recognize old friends in every fish-trap in the river and every tree & bush by the road side. I stopped at the very bushes where I gathered chinquapins when a little boy.

> The little nuts were just peeping like black eyes through their burrs. I gathered & ate some, the first after 25 years. We were riding on horses that were easy and good looking. I met an old farmer I had known in early life named Honey; he gave me two fine peaches sweet as his name. I met old fellows who remembered me afar off; passed by the house of Charles Lawson, a man partly negro who used to quarrel a good deal, & whenever he did make haste to call his antagonist a "damned nigger" so as to anticipate the epithet which wd. be aimed at himself. He was sitting at his door extremely aged. Saw two Stafford snakes on the way, much to my delight. When we arrived at the Court House stopped to read on its walls the names left there by Northern soldiers during the war. The same houses (half a dozen in all) stood in the same places, though much dilapidated with age. Went into the Clerk's Office where my grandfather had sat writing for half a century.

From the Court House, Conway and Peter rode up to their Grandfather's old home, "Erleslie," where they were met at the garden gate by Aunt Margaret and Aunt Fanny. Aunt Margaret, who lived in the house alone, told her nephews that "Erleslie" had been entered a number of times by burglars. They, however, had become tired of breaking in, having discovered that there was nothing in the house worth stealing. Dr. Valentine Conway, their father's elder brother, was also waiting with his sisters to greet the nephews. Conway had last seen this uncle in 1859 when he had become "very angry" because his young nephew had "warned him that Slavery was doomed & that all who adhered to it would be ruined." "He now quoted my words," Conway wrote Ellen, "and pointed to the dilapidation & poverty all around as the fulfillment." As Conway and Peter sat talking with their aunts and uncle, another uncle came in, "and we had an old-time dinner party with a great deal of cordiality & fun." "Uncle George," Conway wrote, "is rather under a cloud in society, but I have found him one of the best fellows here."

> In earlier life he met with a disappointment in a love affair & has never married. He was and is very poor. He found

> a coloured woman whom he liked & had lived with her ever since, and has several children by her. She was a slave, and by law the children followed the mother's condition and were slaves also. But uncle George worked day & night with his hands, and earned money enough to buy the woman & her children. The law did not & does not yet permit him to marry her. But he treats her as his wife, lives with her in a good house, stands by her in all cases, and by his fidelity to her has gradually conquered the prejudices around him. Even my father declares that he is the best-hearted of the family. Uncle George was devoted to me, as indeed were all the rest.

After the noon-time, and the visiting that followed, "we all went to take tea at Dr. Conway's." Here Uncle Valentine urged Conway to smoke "an old silver-mounted corn-cobb pipe which was the last [his] grandfather smoked, & which he had smoked 20 years before his death." Aunt Fanny gave Conway five Indian arrowheads, and Aunt Margaret found for him a sixth which her grandfather had picked up. They insisted that Conway was as good a Methodist as ever and they would go to his church every Sunday if he should "set up a church" in Stafford. They had never believed a word against him, they insisted, and urged him to tell them something of his lectures in England. "So I told them some of my devil & oriental & London stories," wrote Conway.

Peter and Conway spent the night at the home of Aunt Fanny. The next morning "We drove off in fine spirits" to visit the Moncures at Glencairne where they were received "with open arms and kisses." After this round of country visits in Stafford County, Conway concluded:

> My relations in Stafford -- the Conways especially -- are very poor. They live in respectable houses, and own one or two cows & horses, and their gardens support them. They gave me good dinners & breakfasts -- melons, fruits, vegetables, chicken, ham, etc. But they cannot get much money. Labour is scarce. Negroes hate to live in the country, & flock to Richmond & Fred'sb'g. But they (relations) all seem serene & cheerful in their poverty, and all glad to be rid of Slavery....Those whom I left as lovely

> young girls are now crowned with gray & have grown up daughters sweet & gentle as they used to be & bearing the same names.

Conway brought his long letter to Ellen to a close on Sunday after a dinner of "old Va. oysters!" enhanced by "a beautiful bouquet" presented by "the negro housemaid." She had gathered them from the cemetery "where lie the bodies of the Northern soldiers who fell in the battle of Freds'b'g." Conway outlined his itinerary for the next six months for his wife – "Boston, Cincinnati, Pittsburgh, Philadelphia, New York, then West again." He closed, "My own home (in London) never looked to me so beautiful as at this moment" but added that he hoped before returning to England to visit once more the Virginia family that had given him such a warm welcome.[480]

Conway found an equally warm welcome when he arrived at Yellow Springs, Ohio, to visit the family Negroes who now formed a flourishing community.[481] Dunmore and Eliza Gwinn were living in a good house on a well-stocked five-acre farm. Still the leaders of the group, they gave a prolonged banquet in honor of their visitor. The tables were heaped again and again with the food of old Virginia. All the preachers from all the Methodist and Baptist churches together with their families were invited in groups to the banquet. The ceremony began at one o'clock and continued through the afternoon. Conway solved the problem of uttering a succession of "graccs" by passing the honor to the most patriarchal preacher in every new set of guests. Called upon to lead the prayers at the evening meeting, he recited what he could remember of an ancient Persian hymn, which elicited the customary "Amens" from the gathering of friends old and new.

At the end of the evening, Conway was abashed by the eloquent address to the company made by Dunmore Gwinn, describing the heroic part Moncure had played in the events of more than twenty years ago when he had been threatened by the youths of Falmouth and forced to leave the State. "I was pictured," Moncure reports,

> standing in the centre of Falmouth with the whole village raging around me, and pointing to a poor negro and crying, 'That woolly-head has in him an immortal soul;

> he is a child of God; he has the same right to freedom as any of you have,' and so forth; for the speech was long and admirable. Still more graphic was Dunmore's description of how the mob was cowed by my eloquence, and the blacks encouraged. For there were visions and prophecies and manifestations.

In sober truth, Moncure remarked in his *Autobiography*, no speech was made and no Negro was present. He could not, however, humiliate his host by disclaiming the illegitimate honors heaped upon him.[482]

While in Yellow Springs, Conway was invited to lecture on one of his favorite topics, demonology, before the faculty and students of Antioch College. Behind the rostrum to illustrate his talk were large drawings of dragons, demons, and a variety of devils which he had assembled on his trips on the Continent.[483] To his surprise, he observed as he took his place on the platform that the front rows of the gallery were filled with his Negro friends -- the section occupied in Europe by royalty -- and they were grandly arrayed for the occasion. Conway tried as best he could to toss in as many anecdotes as possible to make his speech, which was, of course, scientific, acceptable to the attentive listeners in the gallery. When he raised his pointer to his drawing of the devil, remarking, "This is the only known representation of Satan," Eliza shouted from the gallery, "Give it to him, honey! Give it to the old devil hot and heavy!" The laughter of the audience greet-ng this interruption did not deter further responses from the gallery ("Right too!" "Ain't it good!" "True's gospel!"). The last word on the new inquiry into demonology was good Methodist doctrine.

In talking with his Negro friends the next day, Moncure perceived that his lecture had seemed to them very acceptable; they were aware of no heresy in his presentation of biblical myths. The preacher from London (now a Universalist) listened with "philosophic attentiveness" to their account of the trials and temptations of their own lives and felt a rekindling of the religion of his youth. Conway spoke that morning to his father's former valet, James Parker, a fine-looking mulatto, once scornful of Methodist piety but recently "converted." Conway had learned while in Fredericksburg that Parker in 1862 had attempted to return through Union lines to the service of the elder Conway but was told that he must accept freedom. He would still like to live with the Conways, he said, for he had never been happy since leaving them. All the Negroes present, proud of their independent, self-respecting community, inquired affectionately for the family they had parted with so many years ago.

This was Conway's last glimpse of the colony he had founded in Ohio.[484] He had, in fact, stopped off at Yellow Springs primarily to lecture on "Demons and Devils" before touring the country from the western states to Maine and then returning to his London pulpit after three times turning down an invitation to assume the ministry of the Parker Memorial Hall in Boston.[485] On each occasion he put the question to Ellen, who wisely warned him against accepting the offer; she remembered too well her husband's propensity for both charming and antagonizing his congregation. Conway himself was overwhelmed by the reception he received, which he described to his wife in a letter of December 6, 1875:

> Yesterday morning when I went over to preach in the Parker Memorial Hall I was met in the anteroom by John Weiss, Sam Longfellow, Lyd. Morse, Ricketson (New Bedford) and a number of others who overwhelmed me with the enthusiasm of their welcome...There were 20 people in the anteroom & my entrance was signal for an uproar. The Hall was crowded with an admirable audience -- over 1000. I preached my sermon on the 'New Testament' which you wanted me to preach at Collyer's. It excited even more enthusiasm than in London. At the close there was a sound of applause. Many have begged me to give it for my lecture at the Horticultural Hall (for the Free Relig-Assoc.) & many have asked for its publication. The Parkerites wish me to take every Sunday at their Hall while I am in the country at $30 a sermon. They are very enthusiastic. About 60 people stopped to shake hands yesterday.[486]

Moncure wrote the letter to his wife while visiting Willam Dean Howells and his wife "at their pretty home" in Cambridge, where he had arrived "in good time -- 6 ½ -- for a pleasant dinner tea and charming talk with my two friends. They are most loving-hearty-delightful." However, Conway confessed, London in comparison to Cambridge looked to him more pleasant and comfortable. "Unless people have fortunes here," he wrote, "They get their noses to the grindstone & it isn't easy to get them up again." Howells could save nothing on his $5,000 a year and his house was only half paid for.[487]

Conway returned to London in the spring of 1876, having delivered his lectures on "Demons and Devils," "St. George and the Dragon," "London Men of Science," "Oriental Religions," and other subjects from Maine to Chicago, from Boston to St. Louis, meeting new and interesting people and renewing old acquaintances. In New Haven he stayed at the home of Professor Whitney, where he enjoyed "oscillating between fun and philology." He even found time to return to Sandy Spring, Maryland. According to *The Annals of Sandy Spring,* written by the neighborhood historian, William Henry Farquhar, "February 25th, Moncure D. Conway gave us a lecture on London, which is too fresh in our recollection to require comment."[488]

Whitlaw Reid presided over a dinner in his honor at the Lotus Club in New York; "the venerable poet [William Cullen] Bryant" chaired a breakfast given to Lord Houghton and Conway at the Century Club; newspapers carried laudatory notices; there were many requests to lecture that he could not fulfill. Conway was sure, at the end of his five-month tour, that he had succeeded as a popular lecturer and journalist.[489] He cleared far less money than he had expected but let his congregation at South Place know that he had been urged to "accept the place left open by the death of Theodore Parker" at a considerable increase in salary. "The facts had to be submitted to this Society, with an admonition that if they desired my return it would be necessary to give me a larger pecuniary support," Conway wrote in *The Centenary History of South Place Society* (1894), adding, "They desired my return, and met me with a grand reception (March 27, 1876) and an illuminated address."[490]

On the last night of 1876, Conway wrote a long and loving letter from England, addressed to his mother, but intended for both of his parents, from whom he had been separated by distance as well as thought for so many years.[491] His recent visit to Virginia had reinstated the "pilgrim" in the hearts of family and neighbors; now he could again send his New Year greeting with the assurance that it would be welcome:

> Midnight has just passed, and I now wish you -- and all near and dear to you -- a happy and peaceful New Year!
>
> --Since writing the above we have all had refreshing sleep and waked up to a beautiful day. The air is balmy -- the sky blue -- the birds in full choir in our old elms. The winter here has been so mild that the strawberries and roses have been showing some blossoms at Christmas time, and yesterday Mildred brought in some flowering jasmines. Dana celebrates his New Year Day by visiting the South Kensington Museum -- Mildred by playing new themes on her piano -- Ellen prepares to receive her usual Monday callers -- Eustace and I (who now occupy the same study) set to work again with our work. So we begin the year as pleasantly as ever, and with grateful trust in the Eternal Love.

Conway's eagerness to be loved by his parents, if not understood, is apparent in this letter written from his London home after an especially happy family Christmas. Perhaps he had already written too fulsomely. "This letter, my dear parents," he wrote,

> would seem very egotistical were it written by any but a son to his father and mother. But to you I hope it will only appear as a budget of home-gossip about matters which are a part of your own interest. I own that I am very anxious that my doings and affairs shall be put in their best light to those I love. I crave only that you shall believe in my heart as being right with your hearts, whatever may be the different intellectual conclusions at which we have arrived.

In the expansive mood of New Year's Eve, Conway could even imagine that the difficult problem of the place of the Negro in the reconstructed Dominion might magically dissolve. "I feel deeply concerned at the news of political troubles in America, knowing as I do how deeply they involve the feeling of my friends in Virginia," he wrote. "But I trust that all will go well. I do hope the negro will somehow disappear from American politics, and that Virginia especially will continue to see that the safe and true way is to deal with that race in such a wise and friendly spirit that they may become a source of comfort and a restoring element in society." Looking out his study window in the early hours of January 1, 1877, he ended, "With greetings and best wishes to Richard & his family -- to Peter and his wife -- to my relatives -- I am your devotedly attached son."

Conway remained at South Place for "eight more happy and harmonious years."[492] Then, aged fifty-two, he "desired to leave the pulpit," his simple explanation being, "I had been in that kind of work since I was nineteen, my twenty-one years at South Place chapel had enabled me to deliver my religious and ethical convictions with a certain completeness, and I had several works in view that demanded literary leisure. So we sold our house in Bedford Park, and on July 27 the last of my seven 'Farewell Discourses' (part-listed 1884) was given." He dedicated his Discourses "to my South Place Society, whose minister I have been for 21 years, and whose unwearied sympathy and support, now passing into memories, sweeten the sorrows of parting."

Conway and his beloved wife, Ellen

Paine-ful Postscript

One of the "works" that Conway had in view was a life of Thomas Paine, the Quaker youth who, led by his "inner light" and by "reason," had found himself deeply involved in two revolutions. Conway, in passing through a Quaker neighborhood as a lad of nineteen, had received Paine's *Age of Reason* from Roger Brooke -- who also armed him with arguments against Paine, "the atheist." Later in life, Conway had been swept into national events to which he had responded with an unshakable belief in "the rights of man," as defined by Paine.

The philosophical ideas of Paine had never left Conway since he had read his works seriously and discussed them with his friends in their Cincinnati days. When he learned in 1860 that the city of Philadelphia had refused to accept a proffered portrait of Paine to be hung in Independence Hall, Conway had celebrated Paine's birthday by giving an address.[493] Visiting the Philadelphia Exposition of 1876, Conway was reminded once more that the name of Paine was anathema when he discovered that a bust of Paine had been refused a place in the gallery. The author of *Common Sense* and *The American Crisis*, and friend of Washington and Jefferson, was still regarded as a civic danger by the Exposition Committee. Conway reviewed again "the myth of Paine's ideas and character" in an article for *The Fortnightly Review* (March, 1879).[494] In his essay, "Thomas Paine," Conway told his English readers:

> The late Hon. Jared Sparks, while President of Harvard University, showed me some letters which passed between Jefferson and Paine on religious subjects. I believe they are still withheld from the public, and no doubt more for the sake of the great Virginian's reputation than for that of Paine, who, as I remember, was by no means the more unorthodox of the two.

Conway then quoted Paine's own statement of his religious views -- which were clearly those shared by Conway and many another deist of the time: "I believe in one God, and no more, and I hope for happiness beyond this life. I believe in the equality of men; and I believe that religious duties consist in doing justice, loving mercy, and endeavoring to make our fellow-creatures happy." Such seemingly innocuous views in times of political upheaval have a meaning that shapes events. Paine was soon attacked by both Federalists and slave-holders: "The Federalists of the North, who wished to make the United States another England, and hated everything French, dreaded him; the slaveholders of the South had been alarmed at his having written about the abolition of slavery -- 'We must push that matter farther on your side of the water! [Paine had written]. 'I wish that a few well-instructed negroes could be sent among their brothers in bondage; for, until they are enabled to take their own part, nothing will be done.'" Conway realized that these attitudes had changed but little between the days of the Revolution and the Civil War.

When Conway withdrew from South Place in 1884, he was already embarked on *The Life of Thomas Paine*. This "large and arduous task" took him not only through the archives of America and Europe but on explorations of the neighborhoods where Paine had lived in London, Paris, and Bordentown, New Jersey.[495] The book, published in 1892, was recognized at once as the first genuine study of a much-maligned patriot.[496]

In 1893, Conway was persuaded to return to his ministry at South Place, where, in 1894, the Paine material that he had collected over the years was displayed.[497] In the same year appeared Conway's four-volume edition of *The Writing of Thomas Paine*, the first essay in Volume I being "African Slavery in America."[498] "So far as I can discover," wrote Conway in his "Prefatory Note," to "Thomas Paine belongs the honor of being the first American Abolitionist." In 1895, *The Rights of Man* was separately printed with introduction and notes by Conway. Paine's essay, Conway asserted, was "the earliest complete statement of republican principles." These principles were accepted by Thomas Jefferson, James Madison and Andrew Jackson as basic to the American Republic. They were evolved, Conway claimed, from Paine's early Quakerism, which taught him "that every human soul was the child of God" whose rights must be defended not only against privilege and rank but also against the majority.[499]

Conway had already discussed Paine's views on slavery in his *Life of Thomas Paine*; there he had concluded, after five years of research and contemplation, that the failure to heed Paine's prophetic words against the African slave trade at the time of the Revolution was the cause of the Civil War. "The two wars were branches of the same poisonous tree," he wrote. In Paine's "First Essay" (on Slavery), Conway pointed out, "Every argument and appeal, moral, religious, military, economic, familiar in our subsequent antislavery struggle, is here found stated with eloquence and clarity." Conway added:

> Paine's paper is as thorough as Garrison himself could have made it. And, indeed, it is remarkable that Garrison, at a time when he shared the common prejudices against Paine, printed at the head of his *Liberator* a motto closely resembling Paine's. The motto of Paine was: "The world is my country, my religion is to do good"; that of the *Liberator*: "Our country is the world, our countrymen are all mankind."[500]

In his "Prefatory Note" to *The Writings of Thomas Paine*, Conway pointed out that the first American Anti-slavery Society was organized in Philadelphia at the Sun Tavern, Second Street, April 14, 1775, under the title, "The Society for the Relief of Free Negroes, unlawfully held in bondage." Conway suggested that Paine was one of the founders, for he, with others, drafted and signed the Act of Pennsylvania abolishing slavery, March 1, 1780, which Conway claimed was "the first legislative measure of negro-emancipation in Christendom."

The illness of his wife in May 1896 persuaded Conway to return to the United States, thus ending his official connection with South Place Chapel where he had for so many years put in a larger framework the problem of the Negro, only one aspect, he believed, of the problem of Man. After the death of Ellen, in December 1897, Conway left for Europe, "broken by personal bereavement, filled with horror by the reign of terror suffered by negroes in the South, alienated from my countrymen by what seemed to me a mere lynching of Spain -- my youthful visions turned to illusions."[501]

Pausing in London to deliver several "discourses" to his old congregation at South Place, Conway then hastened to Paris. He settled into the Hotel de Strasbourg, 50 Rue de Richelieu, which, he soon discovered, was in the neighborhood where Paine had lived and worked. Of still greater importance, he learned that six articles on his *Life of Thomas Paine* had appeared in a Parisian journal, *La Revolution Française*, and there was now a desire for a French translation of his book. Felix Rabbe, the reviewer of *The Life of Thomas Paine*, called on Conway and at once made plans for a fruitful collaboration. Many a happy morning was spent by the two old scholars in the courtyard of the hotel. "I sit here at my table from morning till 5:30 or 6," Conway wrote to an old friend in London,[502]

> Then I promenade till 7; then dine (for this is not an eating hotel, save cafe) at some restaurant; then go to some amusement. In this way I am getting on fairly well, -- and have been especially lifted out of my sense of loneliness by the happy prospect of having my book translated by an eminent man, and by absorption in congenial work. I haven't time to mope.

The "Preface de L'Auteur" of the French edition of *The Life pf Thomas Paine*, published in 1900, may serve as the conclusion to this study of Conway as an abolitionist.[503] Here he rehearsed once more the struggle to understand the complex problem of the Negro's effort to take his place in what he called the "family of races." Bereft of his wife, disheartened by the Spanish-American War in America, and the threat of the Boer War in South Africa, Conway reviewed the story of the pilgrimage he had made, extending over a long life, from his home in Falmouth, Virginia, to a small hotel in Paris, where he completed his monumental work on America's unappreciated abolitionist.

Paine was the philosopher who helped Conway deal rationally with the vision of his father's slaves that haunted him all his life. In his *Farewell Discourses*, in characteristically poetic and religious terms, he told his congregation that

> among the earliest recollections of my childhood is the recurring scene of baptism in the river that ran by our

home. Those baptized were mainly African slaves, to whom an ancient slave, by the sabboth [sic] he instituted, still brought a little weekly exodos [sic] from their land of bondage. On such a Sunday their dark forms, arrayed in robes of cotton (their Pharaoh's livery), moved in procession to the bank of the Rappahannock, and there, in crystal waters beneath our blue Virginia sky, were immersed. Time and fate have not dimmed that scene. Still do I hear, in memory, the singing of those lowly believers coming out of the water, oftimes mingling with notes of the dove, which no doubt brought to their hearts a message from heaven.[504]

Moncure Daniel Conway reading a bible.

Selective Bibliography of the Writings of Moncure Daniel Conway on Slavery

Three efforts have been made to compile "selective bibliographies" of Moncure D. Conway's printed work (not including Conway's articles in dozens of newspapers, magazines and journals, both in this country and in England). The first, entitled *A Sketch and an Appreciation of Moncure Daniel Conway, Freethinker and Humanitarian* was by Edwin C. Walker, published by Walker himself in 1908 at 244 W. 43rd Street, New York City. The second was included in a volume entitled *Addresses and Reprints*, 1850-1907, "Published and Unpublished Work Representing the Literary and Philosophic Life of the Author," The Riverside Press, 1909. The third, and most extensive, is included in the study of *Moncure Conway, 1832-1907*, by Mary Elizabeth Burtis, Rutgers University Press, 1952. The Selective Bibliography of the writings of Moncure D. Conway accompanying this study is limited to the books, essays, sermons, and speeches bearing upon slavery. No attempt has been made to assemble a bibliography of the abolitionist movement. References to abolitionist writing will be found in the notes. (Since Clara Marburg Kirk's death in 1976, there have been two studies by John d'Entremont, *Moncure Conway, 1832-1907: American Abolitionist, Spiritual Architect of 'South Place', Author of 'The Life of Thomas Paine,'* published by South Place Ethical Society, London, 1977, and *Southern Emancipator Moncure Conway, the American Years 1832-1865,* Oxford University Press, New York, 1987. -- DK)

1850 *Free-Schools in Virginia: A plea of Education Virtue, and Thrift, vs. Ignorance, Vice and Poverty.* Recorder Print, Fredericksburg, Virginia, October, 1850. Reprinted in *Addresses and Reprints.*

1856 *The One Path: or, the Duties of the North and South*, Washington, D.C.: Buell and Blanchard. Reprinted in *Tracts for To-day*, 1858, 176-194.

1856 *Spiritual Liberty*. A Discourse Delivered in the Unitarian Church, Washington, D. C., on Sunday, February 17, 1856. Published by request of members of The Society. Washington, D.C.: Buell and Blanchard, 1856.

1856 *Virtue vs. Defeat*. A Discourse Preached on November 9, 1856, in the Unitarian Church, Cincinnati, Ohio. Published by request of the congregation, printed by the Cincinnati Gazette Company, 1856.

1858 *Tracts for To-day*. Truman and Spofford, Fifteen sermons of this early period.

1859 *East and West*. An Inaugural Discourse, Delivered in the First Congregational Church, Cincinnati, Ohio. May 1, 1859. Published by request, Cincinnati.

1860 *The Dial*: A monthly Magazine for Literature, Philosophy and Religion. 1860, Volume I, Cincinnati.

1860 *Thomas Paine: A Celebration*, delivered in the First Congregational Church, Cincinnati, Ohio -- January 28, 1860.

1861 *The Rejected Stone: or Insurrection vs. Resurrection in America*. By a native of Virginia. Boston: Walker, Wise and Company, 1861. Second, third editions, 1862.

1862 "Then and Now in the Old Dominion," *Atlantic Monthly*. IX, April 1862.

1862 *The Golden Hour*. Boston: Tichnor and Fields 1862. Reviewed in *The Atlantic Monthly*, X, November 1862, 644-646.

1862 *The Commonwealth*. Published weekly by James M. Stone, at No. 22 Bromfield Street, Boston.

1864 (Address on John Brown) printed without title in *The Martyrdom of John Brown*. The Proceedings of a Public Meeting held in London on the 2nd December, 1863, to Commemorate the Fourth Anniversary of John Brown's Death. London: The Emancipation Society, pp. 4-14.

1864 *Benjamin Banneker, The Negro Astronomer*. Tract No. 9. London: printed and published for the Ladies' London Emancipation Society, by Emily Faithful, Victoria Press ... Hanover Sq. This article first appeared in *The Commonwealth*, December 27, 1862. and later in *The Atlantic Monthly*. XI, April 1863, 79-84.

1864 *Testimonies Concerning Slavery*. London: Chapman and Hall, 1864. An article in *The Westminster Review*, XXVIII, n.s., July 1865, 43-47, is based in part on the second edition of *Testimonies Concerning Slavery*. published in 1865.

1865 "Mr. Lincoln," by an American Abolitionist. *Fraser's Magazine*, LXXI, January 1, 1865, 1-21. "Personal Recollections of President Lincoln," Moncure D. Conway. *The Fortnightly Review*, I, May 15, 1865, 56-65. "The Assassination of President Lincoln," by an American Abolitionist. *Fraser's Magazine*, LXXI, June 1865, 791-806.

1866 "America, France, and England," Moncure D. Conway. *The Fortnightly Review*, III (Jan. 1, 1866), 442-459. "The President's Defense," Moncure D. Conway. *The Fortnightly Review*, V (May 15, 1866), 98-106. "Russia and America," Moncure D. Conway. *The Fortnightly Review*, VI, November, 1866, 659-665.

1867 "American Prospects," Moncure D. Conway. *The Fortnightly Review*, I, n.s., June 1, 1867, 748-753.
"Theodore Parker," Moncure D. Conway. *The Fortnightly Review*, VIII, August 1, 1867, 143-52.

1868 The "Internal Conflict in America," Moncure D. Conway. *The Fortnightly Review*, III n.s., March 1, 1868, 311-318.

1870 "Wendell Phillips," Moncure D. Conway. *The Fortnightly Review*, XIV (June 1, 1870), 59-73.

1876 "Our Cause and Its Claim Upon Us," Moncure D. Conway. A Discourse Delivered at South Place Chapel, Finsbury. (Printed for private circulation. London: G. Levey & Co.

1882 "Ralph Waldo Emerson," by Moncure D. Conway. *The Fortnightly Review*, XXXVII, June 1882, 747-770.

1887 *Pine and Palm* (a novel) 2 vols. London, Chatto and Winders.

1892 *The Life of Thomas Paine*. 2 vols, New York & London: Putnam & Son.

1904 *Autobiography: Memories and Experiences of Moncure Daniel Conway*. 2 vols. Boston & New York, Houghton, Mifflin & Co. The Riverside Press.

Notes

Chapter I: Conway House

[1] Middletown, Stafford County, Va.
[2] Often spelled "Gaskins."
[3] *Testimonies Concerning Slavery*, by M. D. Conway. London, 1864, 15-18.
[4] Ibid., 19-21. See also *Anthony Burns, A History*, Charles Stevens, 1856, 158-160.
[5] *Testimonies*, 4-6.
[6] lbid., 119-122. See also "Then and Now in the Old Dominion," by M. D. Conway:

> It gives but a poor description of the "poor-white trash" to say that they cannot read. The very slaves cannot endure to be classed on their level. They are inconceivably wretched and degraded. For every rich slave-owner there are some eight or ten families of these miserable tenants. Both sexes are almost always drunk. There is no better man than the Anglo-Saxon man who labors; there is no worse animal than the same man when bred to habits of idleness. When Watts wrote:
>
> "Satan finds some mischief still
> For idle handle to do,"
>
> he wrote what is much truer of his own race than of any other. This law has been the Nemesis of the young Virginia. His descent demands excitement and activity; and unless he becomes emasculated into a clay-eater, he obtains the excitement that his ancestors got in war, and the New-Englander gets in work, in gaming, horse-racing, and all manner of dissipation. His life verifies the proverb, that the idle brain is the Devil's workshop. He is trained to despise labor, for it puts him on a level with his father's slaves.

(*The Atlantic Monthly*, IX, April 1862, 500.)
[7] *Autobiography*. I 6 n.
[8] Ibid., 20.
[9] As a Justice, Walker Peyton had to ask his wife to suspend the lessons.
[10] Peter Humstead, a brother of Charles.
[11] *Autobiography*. I, 26.
[12] *Testimonies*, 52-53
[13] *Autobiography*, I, 33-34.
[14] See *Dictionary of American Biography*, 1943.
[15] *Testimonies*, 54-55.
[16] *Autobiography*, I, 42.

[17] Texas was annexed by a joint resolution of Congress, passed by a narrow margin, on February 27, 1845.

Chapter II: Dickinson College and After

[18] *Autobiography*, I, p. 48.
[19] *Testimonies*, p. 27. John McClintock was editor of *The Methodist Quarterly Review.*
[20] *Autobiography*, I, p. 51.
[21] Ibid., I, p. 52.
[22] Ibid., p. 53.
[23] Ibid., p. 56.
[24] The diary is entitled "A Glance at 1848". Pp. 66-67 are in the Conway manuscripts. Special Collections. Columbia University Library.
[25] T. E. Bond, "The Methodist Episcopal Church, South," *The Methodist Quarterly Review*, I, 4th Series (April, 1849), 282-302. III, 4th Series (July, 1851), 399-409.
[26] *Autobiography*, I, p. 58.
[27] Ibid., Pp. 59-60. Many references to Norval Wilson are found in "a glance at 1848."
[28] See "Then and Now in the Old Dominion," p. 498.
[29] For the views of John M. Daniel on the emancipation of the slave, see *Autobiography*, II, 4n.
[30] The Negro in Carlisle," *The Examiner,* II, December 15, 1848, no. 12, signed "M. C." "Christmas at Carlisle," Ibid., January 12, 1849, no. 20, signed "Virginiensis."
[31] *Autobiography*. I, 68.
[32] Moncure D. Conway is considered one of Dickinson's outstanding graduates. In 1904, Andrew Carnegie contributed funds to Dickinson College for the construction of a building to be called Conway Hall "In honor of Dr. Moncure D. Conway, a distinguished alumnus of the college, in recognition of his great services in the realm of letters, of reform, and of humanitarian efforts." This building was replaced by a library in 1965. See "The Hall and the Man; Conway," Walter E. Beach. *The Dickinson Alumnus*, Winter, 1965, 4-6.
[33] *Autobiography*, I, 72. See Testimonies, 30.
[34] *Testimonies*, 28-29.
[35] *Autobiography*, I., 75.
[36] The views of Daniel and Parker were akin because both were followers of Agassiz.

> Mr. Parker would respect intellectual honesty wherever he found it. There was an editor in the State of Virginia who boldly maintained slavery on grounds which were then regarded in the South as subversive of many orthodox views, but which Parker believed were the only grounds upon which an intelligent man could base any honest attempt to defend; that institution. So he subscribed for the paper and always read it carefully; and indeed such faith had he in the

honesty of that editor, that when they both were in Europe, the one as a \yU'charge d'affaires, the other as an invalid, he did not hesitate to make (though he was not in_ need of friends) a personal request to this very fiery Southerner. Moncure D. Conway, "The Transcendentalists of Concord," *Fraser's Magazine*, LXX, August 1864, 261.

[37] *Autobiography*, I, 77.

[38] *Blackwood's Edinburgh Magazine*, No. CCCLXXXVI, December 1847, LXII, 643-657.

[39] Quoted incorrectly in *Autobiography*, I, p. 78. Years later Conway told this anecdote of his first acquaintance with Emerson to John Stuart Mill. Mill paused and then remarked, "'That is something that should be engraved on a man's tomb."' *Autobiography*. II, 16. See also "The Transcendentalists," 255-256. After the death of Emerson in 1882, Conway remembered:

> The secret nook near my Virginian home, to whose crystal fount and flowers my eighteenth spring carried a wintry heart. Near that wooded slope the Rappahannock spread silvery in the sunshine, placid after its falls foam-white in the distance, streaming past its margin of meadows to the peaceful homes and spires of Fredericksburg. Fresh from college, now from every career planned by parent or friend I had recoiled: some indefinable impediment barred each usual path: the last shadow settled around me when the law-book was closed to be opened no more. Utterly miserable, self-accused amid sorrowful faces, with no outlook but to be fettered master of slaves, I was then wont to shun the world, with gun for apology, and pass hours in this retreat. So came I on a day, and reclined on the grass, reading in a magazine casually brought. The laugh and chatter of negroes, pushing their flat-boats loaded with grain, the song of birds, the sound of church-bells across the river, all smote upon a heart discordant with them at discord with itself. Nature had no meaning, life no promise and no aim. Listlessly turning the printed page, one sentence caught my eye and held it; one sentence quoted from Emerson, which changed the world and me. A sentence only! I do not repeat it: it might not bear to others what it bore to me: its searching subtle revelation defies any analysis I can make of its words. All I know is that it was the touch of flame I needed. That day my gun was laid aside to be resumed no more. *Emerson at Home and Abroad*, 1882, 3-4.

[40] *Autobiography*, I, 79. Conway repeated this story in "Then and Now in the Old Dominion," 498.

[41] *Autobiography*. I, 80.

[42] *Autobiography*, I, p. 83.

[43] Ibid., p. 84.

Chapter III: "Free Schools in Virginia"

[44] *Testimonies*, p. 31.

[45] For the part Hunter and Mason played in the Senate at this time, see Henry Harrison Sims, *The Life of Robert M.T. Hunter, A Study in Sectionalism and Secession*, 1935.
[46] "Lecture on the North and the South," Cincinnati, 1849.
[47] *Free Schools in Virginia, Addresses and Reprints by Moncure D. Conway*, (1850-1907), 1909. 27.
[48] See "Then and Now in the Old Dominion," 500.
[49] *Autobiography*, I, 84.
[50] A copy of this pamphlet is in the Alderman L. Library, University of Virginia, Charlottesville.
[51] *Autobiography*, 85.
[52] *Testimonies*, 33. In "Then and Now in the Old Dominion," Conway wrote that, "It was at an early period as manifest as now that a slave population implied and rendered necessary a large poor-white population."
[53] *Autobiography*, I, 85.
[54] *Free Schools in Virginia*, 27.
[55]*Autobiography*. I, 88.
[56] G.B.E., "Agassiz's Tour of Lake Superior", *The Christian Examiner*, July 1850, 9. Louis Agassiz, "The Diversity of Origin of the Human Race". Reviewed unfavorably in *The Methodist Quarterly Review*, III, 4th Series, July 1851, 366-77.
[57] This essay is among the Conway papers at Columbia University. "Diversity of Origin of Races", Warrenton, Va. Dec. 1850. The opening sentence is "The Great Evil Spirit of the Earth is Conservatism." The essay is written in a fine hand on both sides of four double sheets (folded)
[58] For a description of the Methodist "Style of Preaching," see T. E. Bond, "What is Methodism," *The Methodist Quarterly Review*, I, 4th Series, October 1848, 503-04.
[59] *Autobiography*. I. 93.
[60] Ibid., 93-94.

Chapter IV: Methodist Circuit Rider

[61] *Autobiography*. I, 94.
[62] Ibid., 97
[63] Ibid., 79.
[64] Ibid., 94-95
[65] Ibid., 101.
[66] *Testimonies*, 36-39. See also *Annals of Sandy Spring, Maryland* (1884), I, 62, and Ibid. (1887-1888), II, 113, 147. Also Warren Sylvester Smith, "Moncure Conway at Sandy Spring," *Quaker History*, Spring 1863, 19-26.
[67] *Autobiography*, I. 106. Roger Brooke's remark was not strictly true. The Brookes were slaveholders from pre-Revolutionary days, when James Brooke first settled in Sandy Spring in 1728. He, a Roman Catholic from Calvert County, married Deborah Snowden, a Sandy Spring Quaker. Slaves were given up in Sandy Spring at the end of the eighteenth century. It is probable that there was a station of an "underground railroad" for fugitive slaves in Sandy Spring

or in the neighborhood during the Civil War. Rebecca T. Miller, "Legends and Traditions," *Centennial of Sandy Spring Meeting House, 1817-1917*, 18-28.
[68] Ibid., 108.
[69] Fair HiIl School is described by Mary Coffin Brooke in *Memoirs of Eighty Years* (New York, 1916), Chapters V and VI. Miss Coffin, later Mrs. William S. Brooke, went to Fair Hill School as a teacher in 1854. She was met in Baltimore by William Henry Farquhar and she writes, 42-43:

> As we were leaving the station in Baltimore, a young man appeared at our car window, and, handling a book to my companion, called out: "You must read these, they are fine." The young man was Moncure D. Conway, who was later known in America and England as a Unitarian minister of decided ability

[70] *Autobiography*, I, 108.
[71] Mrs. Sarah Farquhar (Sarah Brooke) was Mrs. Charles Farquhar, sister-in-law of William Henry Farquhar. The letter is in the Conway Collection, Dickinson College, Carlisle, Pennsylvania.
[72] *Testimonies*, 38-39. See also "Apologia," *Farewell Discourses* (1884), 157-160. Here Conway states that the Hicksites were called infidels by the Methodists and hated by the politicians because they were opposed to slavery. "My eyes were opened to the great wrong of my native country. As I rode my lonely circuit I saw, for the first time with human recognition - men, women, and children, toiling in ignorance and hopelessness." The Rev. T.E. Bond contrasts the attitude of the Methodists and the Quakers toward slavery in "The Methodist Episcopal Church, South, "*The Methodist Quarterly Review*, I, 4th Series, April 1849, 300.
[73] *Testimonies*, 39.
[74] *Annals of Sandy Spring*, 1884, 62.
[75] *Farewell Discourses*, 130.
[76] "Apologia," 158-59.
[77] *Autobiography*. I, 102.
[78] *Testimonies*, 39.
[79] *Autobiography*, I. 109.
[80] Apologia," 161.
[81] *Autobiography*, I, 109-10. Holograph letter of Emerson to Conway, November 13, 1851, is in the Berg Collection, New York City Public Library.
[82] Moncure D. Conway, *Emerson At Home and Abroad*, 1882, 6.
[83] *Autobiography*, I. 110.
[84] W. H. Farquhar?
[85] Ms. letter. Special Collections, Library, Columbia University.
[86] *Autobiography*. I, 110-111. Kossuth spoke in Concord in the course of his American tour. He addressed Emerson personally at an open meeting: "You, sir, are a philosopher. Lend me, I pray you, the aid of your philosophical analysis." T. W. Higginson, *Contemporaries*, 1899, 15. Emerson responded to this request by writing an essay on Kossuth. See *Miscellanies*, 1932.
[87] Ibid., 113.
[88] Ibid., 115.
[89] Ibid., 116.

[90] Ibid., 119. A contrast between the views of the Methodists and the Unitarians in a review of *The Memoirs of William Ellery Channing. The Methodist Quarterly Review*, I, 4th Series, January 1849, 50-75.
[91] Ibid., 118.
[92] Ibid., 119. Published in seven installments in "Christian Advocate and Journal."
[93] *Testimonies*, 41.
[94] *Autobiography*. I, 125.
[95] The Methodist Church had split at the General Conference of 1844.
[96] "Mr. Hawthorne was the only literary man in America who had not given his voice against slavery." "The Transcendentalists," 252.
[97] *Autobiography*. I, 127-128. The young lady was Fanny Dulaney Tomlin, who was the younger sister of the wife of Eustace Conway. She married John Conway Moncure, the oldest son of Richard Cassius Lee Moncure. Gisela Stirling was the character in *Pine and Palm* which was based on the character of Fanny Tomlin Moncure.
[98] Ms. letter. Special Collections, Library, Columbia University.
[99] For a reflection of the training of Methodists, see T. E. Bond, "What is Methodism?" *The Methodist Quarterly Review*, I, 4th Series, October 1848, 485-504. See also the Rev. S. Olin, "Young Men of the Church," *The Methodist Quarterly Review*, 111, 4th Series, April 1851, 86-114.
[100] *Autobiography*, I. 128.
[101] Ms. letter. Special Collections, Library, Columbia University.

Chapter V: Harvard Divinity School

[102] Benjamin did not belong to the Conway family.
[103] *Autobiography* I, 133.
[104] Ibid., 129.
[105] Manuscript letter. March 2, 1853. Special Collections, Library, Columbia University.
[106] Ibid. See also *Autobiography*, I, 54.
[107] Dr. Furness was a graduate of Harvard, 1820, and of the Divinity School, 1823. For an account of his relationship with Emerson, see *Records of a Lifelong Friendship* (1910), edited by his son, Howard Horace Furness.
[108] Parker was installed as minister of the 28th Congregational Society of Boston in 1845. Conway enlarged upon the controversy between Parker and the Unitarian Church in a later essay, "Theodore Parker," *The Fortnightly Review*, VIII, August 1, 1867, 143-152.
[109] *Autobiography*, 130-31. See "The Transcendentalists", 260.
[110] Ibid., 260. See also *Autobiography* I, 162.
[111] *Autobiography* I, 131.
[112] Ibid., 132.
[113] "Theodore Parker," 143.
[114] *Emerson at Home and Abroad*, M.D. Conway, 1883, 142-47. See also "The Transcendentalists", 259-62.

[115] *Autobiography*, I, 133. See also "Theodore Parker," 150. See also *The Dial* (July, 1860), 444-53. See also "The Transcendentalists", 259-62. As a member of the Vigilance Committee, Parker had rescued two fugitive slaves, William and Ellen Craft, in 1850, and had attempted to save Thomas Sims, in 1851. On October 31, 1852, a week after the death of Daniel Webster, Parker had delivered a sermon against Webster's espousal of the Fugitive Slave Act.
[116] *Autobiography*, I, 156-57. See also T. W. Higginson, *Cheerful Yesterdays*, Boston & New York, 1898, Chapter IV, 100-131, for an account of the Divinity School.
[117] Ibid., 158-59.
[118] *Autobiography*, I, 149-50. See also "The Transcendentalists", 262-63.
[119] *Autobiography*, I, 134. See also Moncure D. Conway, "Ralph Waldo Emerson," *Fortnightly Review*, June 1882, 768-69, and "The Transcendentalists," 258.
[120] Manuscript letter. An account of the visit is also found in *Autobiography*, I, 134-39. See also "The Transcendentalists", 256-58, and *Emerson at Home and Abroad*, 6.
[121] Conway here should have written "3rd." See *Autobiography* I, 134.
[122] Mrs. Longfellow wrote to Samuel Longfellow:

> May 26, 1853
>
> .... I believe I wrote you of Mr. [Moncure D.] Conway, a Virginian youth of the Divinity School, and a warm hater of slavery--refreshing to know from a slave state--a very agreeable, excellent fellow. I wish you could know him. He made a reverential pilgrimage to Emerson and got him to promise the school a visit. He was amused with Thoreau, who, asking what they studied and he replying, "The Scriptures," asked, "Which? The Chaldea, Hindoo, or Jewish?'

-- *Selected Letters and Journals of Fanny Appleton Longfellow* (1817-1881), ed. By Edward Wagenknecht, London, 198.
[123] *Autobiography*, 1, 139.
[124] Hillside," on Ponkatasset Hill, where William Ellery Channing once lived. *Autobiography*, I., 140.
[125] *Autobiography*, I, 134-135. See also "The Transcendentalists," 250-252.
[126] Ibid., 141.
[127] *Autobiography*, I. 141-43.
[128] Ibid., 143. See also "The Transcendentalists," 259.
[129] *Emerson at Home and Abroad*, 246.
[130] Autobiography, I, 146. "Transcendentalists," 264.
[131] Ibid., 152-53. See also "The Transcendentalists", 262-63. See also "Ralph Waldo Emerson," 747-70. In this essay, p. 765, Conway summarized the argument between Emerson and Agassiz as follows:

> Emerson, at the beginning of his career had assumed the truth of evolution in nature. More and more this idea became fruitful to him. His friend Agassiz, on the appearance of *The Vestiges of Creation*, had committed himself warmly against it, but Emerson felt certain that the

future of science belonged to that principle which he had reached by his poetic intuition.

[132] *Autobiography* I, 164.

[133] Ibid., 166-169. "The Transcendentalists", 258. Here the date is 1852.

[134] This essay was considered too controversial to be published at that time. It finally appeared in *Letters and Social Aims*, 1876. See *Emerson At Home and Abroad*, 128-30.

[135] See M. D. Conway. "Emerson and his View of Nature." This lecture was delivered at the Royal Institute of London, February 9, 1883. *Autobiography*, I, 168.

[136] "Ralph Waldo Emerson," 765-66. See also "The Transcendentalists", 258-59, and "Apologia," 165.

[137] Manuscript letter. Special Collections, Library, Columbia University.

[138] "The Transcendentalists", 261. The story of the rescue of Ellen and William Craft in 1850 is retold in "Theodore Parker," 149-50.

[139] Ibid., 262. See also *Autobiography*, I, 163.

[140] "Ralph Waldo Emerson," 760. *Emerson At Home and Abroad*, 142-148.

[141] The Transcendentalists," 262.

[142] Manuscript letter January 17, 1854.

[143] *Autobiography*, I, 171.

Chapter VI: The Anthony Burns Affair

[144] Manuscript letter. Special Collections, Library, Columbia University.

[145] Conway retold this story in *Testimonies*, 43-47.

[146] It was against the acceptance by Massachusetts of the Compromise Bill of 1850, which included the Fugitive Slave Act, that Thoreau had written *Civil Disobedience* in 1849. The Bill was passed by the Massachusetts legislature in 1851.

[147] Charles Emery Stevens, *Anthony Burns*, A History (Boston, 1856). See also William I. Bowditch, *The Rendition of Anthony Burns* (Boston, 1854), and "The Case of Anthony Burns," *Annual Report*, American Anti-Slavery Society (New York, 1855), 23-40. See also Henry Steele Commager, *Theodore Parker* (1936), 23-47

[148] Stevens, op. cit., 24-25.

[149] Moncure D. Conway, "Wendell Phillips," *Fortnightly Review*, XIV June 1870, 59-73. See also *Testimonies*, 83-84.

[150] Stevens, op. cit., 28.

[151] *Cheerful Yesterdays*, 149-50.

[152] Stevens, op. cit., 61-79.

[153] Ibid., 60.

[154] *Autobiography*. I, 176.

[155] "Virtue vs. Defect," a Discourse Preached on November 9, 1856. (First Sunday After the Presidential Election) in the Unitarian Church, Cincinnati, Ohio. By Moncure D. Conway, 1856. 16-17.

[156] For the subsequent history of Burns, see Stevens, Op. Cit. The death of Burns on July 27, 1862, is commented upon in *The Commonwealth*, September 27,

1862, 1. 13. For the subsequent history of Burns, see Stevens, op. cit., The death of Burns on July 27, 1862 is commented upon in *The Commonwealth*, September 27, 1862, 1

[157] Thoreau said: "You have my sympathy: it is all I have to give you, but you may find it important to you." This anecdote is repeated in *Emerson At Home and Abroad*, 234. The entire speech was first printed in the *Liberator*, July 21, 1854, under the title, "Slavery in Massachusetts."

[158] *Autobiography*, I. p. 185-86.

[159] See "The Fugitive Slave Law and Its Victims," 1856. *American Anti-Slavery Society Pamphlet* IX, p. 18.

[160] Moorfield Storey, *Charles Sumner*, Boston & New York, 1890, 108.

[161] Ibid., 108-121.

[162] Ibid., 122-30.

[163] Quoted by Mary Elizabeth Burtis, *Moncure Conway, 1832-1907* (New Brunswick, 1952), 46. From transcript draft, *Autobiography*, Ch. XV.

[164] *Autobiography*. I. 188.

[165] Ibid., 189.

[166] William Henry Channing, nephew of William Ellery Channing.

[167] Manuscript letter. Special Collections, Library, Columbia University.

[168] See Jennie W. Scudder, *A Century of Unitarianism in the National Capital, 1821-1921* (1922)

[169] See "A Discourse on the Life and Character of the Hon. William Cranch, LL.D.; Late Chief Justice of the District of Columbia," by Moncure D. Conway. Delivered in the Unitarian Church, Washington City, October 7, 1855. Published by Vote of the Society. *Autobiography*, I, 201.

[170] *Autobiography*, I. p. 190.

[171] Ibid., 191n.

[172] Reprinted in *Tracts for To-Day*, M. D. Conway (1851), 137-60.

[173] *Autobiography*, I, 193-94. See also "Then and Now in the Old Dominion," 301, See also *The Golden Hours*, 49.

[174] *Autobiography*, I, 225. See also *Testimonies*, 49-50.

[175] *Testimonies*, 46.

[176] *Autobiography*, I, 223.

Chapter VII: Unitarian Minister in Washington

[177] Whitman had sent *Leaves of Grass* to Emerson in July, 1855. Emerson's famous letter of appreciation was written on July 21, 1855.

[178] *Autobiography*, I. 215. Conway says that he visited Whitman in the summers of 1855 and 1857. Ibid., 215, 218, 264.

[179] *Autobiography*, I. 216.

[180] Ibid., 217.

[181] Ibid., 218-219.

[182] In his essay, "Walt Whitman", *The Fortnightly Review*, VI (October 15, 1866), 538-548, Conway describes his two visits but does not give the dates of either. Instead, he treats the visit of 1855 and of 1857 as though they were one occasion rather than two. After stating that he sought out Whitman soon after the

appearance of *Leaves of Grass* (1855), Conway then describes the "Sunday in midsummer" (1857) when he journeyed out to Paumanok only to be told by Walt's mother that he was not at home. Following Mrs. Whitman's directions, Conway soon discovered the poet stretched upon his back on the top of a small hill, gazing directly at the hot summer sun, composing, as he said, a poem. Whitman then led Conway to his small room where they had a long literary talk before going for a ramble on the beach which ended in a swim in the sound.

In his *Autobiography* (I, 217-218), Conway introduced the subject with the sentence, "On my second visit, during the summer of 1857, he was not at home, but I found him on the top of a hill near by lying on his back and gazing at the sky." He then touched more briefly than in his essay on his visit to Whitman's room, their walk on the beach and their swim in the bay. Apparently, Conway's second visit with Whitman's took place after he had given up his ministry of the First Unitarian Church in Washington. In a letter to his mother, November 13, 1866, Whitman wrote, concerning Conway's *Fortnightly* article, "It was meant well but a good deal of it is most ridiculous." *Walt Whitman: The Correspondence*, ed. by Edwin H. Miller, 2 vols. I, 294. See also I, 287.

[183] *Autobiography* I, 219-20.

[184] The True and the False in Prevalent Theories of Divine Dispensation." With a Preface. September 21, 1855. See *Autobiography*. I, 197. A copy of this Discourse is in the Medical Library, Rochester University. "Pharisaism and Fasting, A Discourse Delivered in the Unitarian Church, Washington City," September 30, 1855. See *Autobiography*. I, 198.

[185] *Autobiography*, I, 198.

[186] Ibid., 200.

[187] Ibid., 223.

[188] *Emerson At Home and Abroad*, 249-50.

[189] In this view of the question of slavery or the Union, Conway was merely following the platform of the *American Anti-Slavery Society*. founded in Philadelphia in 1833. See "What is Meant By Immediate Abolition," *First Report*, The New York Anti-Slavery Society {1853), pp. 25-27. See also *Testimonies*, 79.

[190] *Tracts for To-day* (Cincinnati, 1858), 174-194. Perhaps Conway derived his title form a speech by Wendell Phillips (January 27, 1853), in which he said, "None but a New Englander can appreciate the power which Church organizations wield over all who share the blood of the Puritans ....The Abolitionists early saw that, for a moral question like theirs, only two paths lay open: to work through the church--that failing, to join battle with it." M. D. Conway, "Wendell Phillips," 69. Charles Sumner, in 1855, gave an anti-slavery lecture in Boston, entitled "The Anti-slavery Enterprise, its Necessity, Practicality, and Dignity, with Glances at the Special Duties of the North." Sumner's argument was that the issue was moral rather than political. Storey, 127.

Theodore Parker took the same position. See *The Abolitionists. A Collection of their Writings*, Louis Ruchames, editor, (1963), 199-208.

[191] *Tracts for To-day*, 184.

[192] In an address delivered before the New England Anti-Slavery Society, May 31, 1848, Theodore Parker made it clear that he thought the people of

Massachusetts desired slavery to be continued because of the commercial advantages to the North. *The Collected Works of Theodore Parker*, ed. by Frances Power Cobbe (London, 1863), 5 vols., V, 93-102.
[193] *Tracts for To-day*, 186-88.
[194] *Autobiography*. I, 235.
[195] Idem.
[196] "Apologia," 165.
[197] His apprehension, however, is evident from a letter Conway wrote on March 1 to Miss Mytilla Miner, the principal of a girls' school in Washington to whom Conway was lecturing on "the origin and use of words." Because of the excitement and annoyance" occasioned him by a "disaffected congregation," these pleasant afternoons at the school would have to be discontinued. He further explained to Miss Miner that "My sermon has awakened reproach which I had no idea would ever come from my congregation to me, or I surely would never have accepted the call to be their minister. But now I feel as if I were called to remain here preaching to those who stand by me as long as I can." Conway added, "I am having many visits and much correspondence on the subject," and therefore found himself unable to help her in the "noble and self-sacrificing design of preserving an oasis in the sad desert through which the colored race have to pass." Holograph letter at Syracuse University. Photostat at Dickinson College, Carlisle, Pennsylvania.
[198] *Autobiography*, I, 236.
[199] Pennsylvania Yearly Meeting of Progressive Friends," The New York *Daily Tribune*, May 29, 1856, 8.
[200] Storey, 145-48. More than a million copies of the speech were distributed in a few weeks after its delivery.
[201] Sumner's attack on the Kansas-Nebraska Act (which he called a swindle) brought forth a violent exchange of personal insults between Sumner and Douglas, as well as between Sumner and Brooks.
[202] Conway was aware of the fact that his associates reflected many conflicting views. He wrote in 1864:

> This party, the Republican, is the child of the Anti-Slavery movement. When I first became attracted to the ranks of the Abolitionist, about twelve years ago, I found that there were many varieties of opinion among them as to method. Gerritt Smith, Foster, and others, believed that Congress had the right to abolish Slavery. Mr. Seward and Mr. Sumner believed that the Government was to be so reformed that it would be administered in the interest of Freedom, and that this would finally give such an anti-Slavery education to the people, that at length a Convention would be called, which with the requisite majority of three-fourths of the States, would amend the Constitution with a clause abolishing Slavery. Theodore Parker firmly believed that Slavery would go down in blood, and that the North should prepare for war. In 1853, I heard him prophesy that the second presidential election from the time would be followed by war. The Abolitionists of the Garrison school were convinced that the Union should and would be divided. *Testimonies*, 84-85.

[203] Storey, 151.
[204] *Autobiography*. I, 244.
[205] Manuscript letter, Special Collections, Library, Columbia University.
[206] *Autobiography*, I, 239-40.
[207] Ibid., 246-47.
[208] For comment on the relation of the churches to slavery, see "The American Tract Society," *Annual Report*, American Anti-Slavery Society (1856), 21-24. See also the views of Theodore Parker and of Wendell Phillips on the subject. *The Abolitionists*, 209-44.
[209] *Autobiography*, I, 242.
[210] Ibid., 245.
[211] October 7, 1856. Manuscript letter. Special Collections, Library. Columbia University.
[212] Possibly spread by William Henry Channing for he was Minister of the First Unitarian Church in Cincinnati (1838-39).
[213] *Tracts for To-day*, 167-75. Channing did not at that time accept the invitation sent him by the Church. See also *Testimonies*, 46-47.
[214] Conway found no difficulty in making his Unitarian sermons acceptable to the Congregationalists. See "The Minister," *Tracts for To-day. Autobiography*. I, 254-55.
[215] *Autobiography*, I, 249-50. The original of this letter (July 10, 1857) is in Special Collections. Columbia University Library. 40. "*Apologia*," 163.
[216] "Apologia," 163.
[217] *Autobiography*, I, 269.

Chapter VIII: Cincinnati and *The Dial*

[218] *Autobiography*, I, 269. See "Virtue vs. Defeat," A Discourse Preached on November 9, 1856. Cincinnati, 1856. 8-20.
[219] *The Letters of Ralph Waldo Emerson*, edited by Ralph L. Rusk, 6 vols. (New York, 1939), V, 60-61.
[220] *Autobiography*. I, 251.
[221] Later minister to Russia where Conway visited him.
[222] "The Dred Scott Case," *Annual Report*, American Anti-Slavery Society (New York, 1855), 58-76; Taney's decision was declared unconstitutional, 69-73.
[223] At least four branches of the underground railroad radiated from Cincinnati after 1847. Wilbur H. Siebart, *The Underground Railroad From Slavery to Freedom*, 1899. See also "The Story of 'Uncle Tom's Cabin,' by Harriet Beecher Stowe," 1878. *Old South Leaflets*, IV, No. 82. Boston [no date]. This essay gives a description of conditions in Cincinnati, Ohio, when slaves were escaping from Kentucky on their way to Canada.
[224] *Autobiography*, I, 252.
[225] Ibid., 274.
[226] "The Church," *Annual Report*, op. cit, 83-84. See David M. Reimars, White Protestantism and the Negro (Oxford University Press, 1965).
[227] *Autobiography*, I, 262-64.

[228] Conway's visit was described in *The Dial* (May 1860) in a review of *The Land of Hope*: a work written on the gospel of Free Love; *Esperanze*, by T.L. Nichols. A portion of this essay was reprinted in *Autobiography*, I, 262-263.
[229] Apologia," *Farewell Addresses* (1884), 165-66.
[230] *Autobiography*, I, 258. "The Theater". A Discourse Delivered June 7, 1857. Cincinnati, 1857.
[231] Ibid., 290-91.
[232] Ibid., 281. See also Ibid., 168n; also *The Dial* (October 1860). Conway discussed these ideas with Huxley and Tyndall in 1883. See Conway, "Emerson and His Views of Nature" (London, 1883).
[233] "Sermon by Rev. M.D. Conway,· preached December 4, 1859. *Echoes of Harper's Ferry*. ed., James Redpath (Boston, 1860), 350.
[234] *Autobiography*, I, 274-75. Conway used this sermon for many years, both in England and in America.
[235] "East and West," An Inaugural Address, Delivered in the First Congregational Church, Cincinnati, OH. May 1, 1859. Published by request. A copy of this pamphlet is in the Alderman Library, University of Virginia. For an account of the separation of the church, see *Autobiography*. I, 306n. The congregations were reunited by Conway on his visit of 1875 when he preached "First Love Again."
[236] *Autobiography*, I, 297. Conway preached a sermon on the subject, "The Nemesis of Unitarianism," Ibid., 299. See also "Theodore Parker, A Discourse," M.D. Conway, *The Dial*, July 1860, 444-53.
[237] *Autobiography*, I, 299. In 1892 a statue dedicated to Theodore Parker was erected in Florence, Italy. A short life of Parker, by Moncure D. Conway, was read aloud at the unveiling. Conway, who was not present, wrote, "Every great principle that he affirmed amid persecution has prevailed. The slave for whom he pleaded is free; the oppressions of women which he pointed out are removed; and the free and tolerant religion which he proclaimed, is now that of the leading preachers of nearly all churches in America." *Magazine of American History*, XXVII, January-June 1892, 130.
[238] Ibid. See "Letter From Theodore Parker to Francis Jackson," Rome, November 24, 1859. *Echoes of Harper's Ferry*, 73-87.
[239] Quoted by Conway, *Emerson At Home and Abroad*, 251.
[240] "A Plea For John Brown," Concord, Massachusetts, October 30, 1859. *Echoes of Harper's Ferry*. 41.
[241] Ibid., 43-66.
[242] Ibid., 305-09. "The Mob Revival," *Annual Report*, 175-91.
[243] Theodore Parker," *Dictionary of American Biography*, 1943. See also *Cheerful Yesterdays*, 220-23. See also Franklin B. Sanborn, *Recollections of Seventy Years*, 2 vols. (Boston, 1909.) In Chapter V, Sanborn describes the secret committee and listed the members. They were George L. Stearns, Dr. Samuel G. Howe, Thomas Wentworth Higginson, Theodore Parker, Gerritt Smith and himself. Martin F. Conway, Congressman from Kansas, was the representative of this committee in Kansas. He was not a relative of Moncure D. Conway, though the two men were friends. Moncure D. Conway's name was never mentioned in Sanborn's *Recollections* in connection with the conspiracy. Nor was his name mentioned by a later historian Oswald Garrison Villard, who, in

John Brown, 1800-1859 (Boston and New York, 1911), gave the fullest account of these events. For a description of the members of the secret committee supporting John Brown, see especially 271-345 of Villard's study. See also George M. Fredrickson, *The Inner Civil War* (New York, 1965), Ch. Ill, "The Impending Crisis."

[244] *Echoes of Harper's Ferry*, 353. Memorial services were held for John Brown on December 2, 1859 in Concord. Neither Emerson nor Thoreau knew anything at that time of the Potawatomi massacre in Kansas. See Gilman Ostrander, "Emerson, Thoreau and John Brown," *Mississippi Valley Historical Review* XXXIV (1953), 719. W.D. Howells contributed "Old Brown" to *Echoes of Harper's Ferry*. Like Conway, he later learned that he had admired Brown without knowing all the facts. *Years of My Youth* (1916), 138.

[245] Quoted from *The Dial*, March, 1860. See *Autobiography* I, 302. Redpath dedicated this book to "Wendell Phillips, Ralph Waldo Emerson and Henry D. Thoreau, Defender of the Faithful, who, when the mob shouted, 'Madam!' said 'Saint.'"

[246] *Autobiography*, I, 303. In 1887, Conway attempted to resolve the problem of John Brown in an unsuccessful novel, *Pine and Palm*. (Conway perhaps borrowed the title of the novel from a weekly newspaper, *The Pine and Palm*, published in Boston by James Redpath, between May 1861 and October 1862.) In Conway's novel, John Brown was presented as Gideon, of whom one of the characters observed, "He strikes me as suffering a sort of sane insanity." (246) That Conway had learned of the support Brown had received from the secret committee when he wrote the novel is evident. See the letter supposedly written by Brown and the letter from "A Friend," warning Stirling [Conway] of the plot (329-331).

Twenty years later, Conway remarked in his *Autobiography*. "In my novel, *Pine and Palm* (1887) Captain Brown (alias Gideon) figures in a light that could not please his admirers, but it is better than I could find for him now, when, reading his career by the light of subsequent history, I am convinced that few men ever wrought so much evil." (302-303.)

A glance through the speeches, sermons, letter and poems assembled by James Redpath in *Echoes of Harper's Ferry* shows the justice of Conway's remark. Wendell Phillips wrote, "Harper's Ferry is the Lexington of to-day." (53); Theodore Parker, "Brown will die, I think, like a martyr, and also like a saint." (87). "All the grand institutions of America ... come from the Puritan stock." (91); Emerson spoke of Brown as a part of "the great Puritan faith." (68).

[247] *Autobiography*, I, 303-304.

[248] Ibid., 281-282.

[249] With the exception of Jared Sparks, historian and President of Harvard when Conway was in the Divinity School. Sparks, Conway wrote, "repeated to me a suggestion of Thomas Paine to Jefferson, that Christ and his disciples were modelled on the sun and zodiac. Indeed, it was from Jared Sparks that I first learned that Thomas Paine was to be respected." *Autobiography*, I, 155. Conway did not forget that Roger Brooke had previously given him a volume of Thomas Paine. He had, however, expressed his disapproval of the book. *Autobiography*. I, 123.

Conway wrote and thought about Paine for the rest of his life. He began to collect material for his *Life of Paine*, 1890. *Autobiography*, II, 433-34 (note). Conway sold his "large collection of Paine editions" to "the National Library at Washington," retaining for himself an oil portrait of Paine painted during his life by an unknown artist.

[250] *Autobiography*, I, 304-05.

[251] Ibid., 312.

[252] Emerson's "Address" appeared in two number of *The Dial*, November and December, 1860. Conway appended a note: "We publish the request this Address which is not included in its author's collected works."

[253] Theodore Parker," a Discourse by Moncure D. Conway. *The Dial* (July, 1860). "The Views of Theodore Parker." *The Dial* (October, 1860). Conway also discussed Parker in an essay entitled "The Nemesis of Unitarianism," (June, 1860).

[254] *The Dial*, February 1860, 118-29. In a long note (129-30), Conway announced that he was not responsible for the views of his contributors.

[255] *Autobiography*, I, 315.

[256] Reprinted in *The Commonwealth*, December 27, 1862, 1.

[257] See Howells' account of a meeting with Conway in Columbus, Ohio, soon after this review appeared. *Year of My Youth* (1916), Appendix V. Howells and Conway discussed over lunch the poetry of the West and the East, and Conway carried away with him a poem by Howells to be published in *The Dial.*

[258] 307-308. See Frank Luther Mott, *History of American Magazines, 1850-1865* (Boston, 1957). Mott wrote that "the only new Western magazine of distinction was Moncure D. Conway's *Dial*, of Cincinnati which, though it published only twelve numbers of 1860, was so infused with the vigorous and original character of young Conway that it set a high standard. Politics, theology, belles-lettres, and criticism were *The Di*al's menu; Emerson was its most notable contributor."

[259] 316. Reviewed in *The Dial*, June 1860.

[260] The child was named Eustace.

[261] *Autobiography*, I, 312.

Chapter IX: *The Golden Hour*

[262] *Autobiography*, I, 317-318. Conway described this first sight of Lincoln in several articles, "Personal Recollections of President Lincoln," *Fortnightly Review*, I, May 15, 1865, 56-65; "Mr. Lincoln," *Fraser's Magazine*, LXXI, January 1865, 1-21; "The Assassination of President Lincoln," Idem., June 1865, 791-806.

[263] 1n "Critical Notes," *The Dial*, July 1860, 455, Conway wrote:

> we have come to the conclusion that Mr. Lincoln would, if elected, do the country almost as much good as another democratic administration. The democratic administration would probably settle the slavery question sooner, but it would do it by bringing on dissolution, or, perhaps, war. Mr. Lincoln's method is suggested in the following paragraph from his speech in this city, last fall - a speech, by the way, which we had the good fortune to hear, and a more able one we may live long and not hear:

"I think we want and must have a national policy, in regard to the institution of slavery, that acknowledges and deals with that institutions as being wrong. Whoever desires the prevention of the spread of slavery, and the naturalization of that institution, yield all when he yields to any policy that either recognizes slavery as being right, or as being as indifferent thing. Nothing will make you successful but setting up a policy which shall treat the thing as being wrong. When I say this, I do not mean to say that this General Government is charged with the duty of redressing or preventing all the wrongs in the world, but I do think it is charged with the duty of preventing and redressing all wrongs which are wrongs to itself. The Government is expressly charged with the duty of providing for the general welfare. We believe that the spreading out AND PERPETUITY of the institution of slavery impairs the general welfare."

It is obvious that an administration in accordance with this strongly-put principle, would do all that any policy which retained the Union at all could do, for the abolition of slavery - that is, the whole animus of the country would be for freedom; the tide of official and popular influence would set that way. A spirit must seek its appropriate body; and the spirit of the country being for freedom, it could not be long before it would organize itself into a free government. We think Mr. Lincoln sees all this; if not, he is "building better than he knows." Surely, it is something to look forward to the inauguration of a President who has said, "There is no reason in the world why the negro is not entitled to all the natural rights enumerated in the Declaration of Independence -the right to life, liberty and the pursuit of happiness. I hold that he is as much entitled to these as the white man."

[264] *Testimonies*, 79.

[265] *Autobiography*. I, 320.

[266] Ibid., 321.

[267] Ibid., 319.

[268] *Testimonies*, 86-87.

[269] *Autobiography*, I, 326.

[270] Conway analyzed Seward's position in "Critical Notices," *The Dial*, July 1860, 455. thus:

The politicians have underrated the anti-slavery feeling of this country. Mr. Seward, before his return from Europe was the inevitable Chicago nominee: and why? Because his name had become associated with the two finest watch-words of the great struggle in America, to-wit: "Higher Law," and "Irrepressible Conflict." These watch-words would have nominated him and carried him on to freedom; but when he returned he showed that he was himself not up to them: he made a forcible-feeble speech at Washington, in which he belied his heart by saying that John Brown had been justly hung. Then the tide of the only real heart in the political mass ebbed away, and left him high and dry on the shore of his enemies.

[271] *Autobiography*, I. 328.

[272] Ibid., 353. See also letter to his wife [n.d.]. Special Collections, Library, Columbia University.
[273] Ibid., 330.
[274] Conway's report of the conversation with her brother is in "Nomadic Letter III," signed "Here and There." Burtis, 78-79. Conway later found that his mother exaggerated, and he modified his statement. *Autobiography*. I, 332-333.
[275] It is possible that Conway talked with George Luther Stearns about the editorship of *The Commonwealth* at this time. Frank Preston Stearns, *The Life and Public Services of George Luther Stearns*, (Philadelphia and London, 1907), 263-264.
[276] *Autobiography*, I. 335.
[277] Ibid., 337.
[278] Ibid., 338.
[279] Ibid., 340. See James Redpath, ed., *Echoes of Harper's Ferry*, Introduction.
[280] *The Rejected Stone*, October 1861, 29. The Vice-President of the Confederate States had made use of the metaphor of "the rejected stone" in a speech delivered on March 21, 1861. He, however, equated the stone with slavery. See Frances Ann Kemble, *Journal of a Residence on a Georgian Plantation*. Frontispiece. New York, 1863.
[281] Ibid., 27-28.
[282] Ibid., 25-26.
[283] Ibid., 89. "There is no President of the United States - only a President of Kentucky," Conway wrote Sumner, September 17, 1861. The Sumner Papers, Harvard. Quoted by Frederickson, 9n, 253.
[284] "personal Recollections," 64.
[285] Houghton Library, Harvard University.
[286] The second son, born in October, 1861, was named "Emerson," after Ralph Waldo Emerson. On October 6, Emerson wrote from Concord:

> MY DEAR SIR AND MY DEAR LADY, -- I have your note, and give you joy of the happy event you announce to me in the birth of your son. Who is rich or happy but the parent of a son? Life is all preface until we have children; then it is deep and solid. You would think me a child again if I should tell you how much joy I have owed, and daily owe, to my children; and you have already known the early chapters of this experience in your own house. My best thanks are due to you both for the great good will you show me in thinking of my name for the boy. If there is room for choice still, I hesitate a good deal at allowing a rusty old name, beaten with Heaven knows how much time and fate, to be flung hazardously on this new adventurer in his snow-white robes. I have never encountered such a risk out of my own house, and for the boy's sake, if there be time, must dissuade. But I shall watch the career of this young American with special interest, born as he in under stars and omens so extraordinary, and opening the gates of a new and fairer age. With all hopes and all thanks, and with affectionate sympathies from my wife,
>
> Yours ever, R. W. EMERSON
>
> (My wife declares that name or no name her spoon shall go.)

See Emerson letter, *Autobiography*, I, 354-355. See also *Emerson at Home and Abroad*, 12-13.
[287] *Autobiography*. I, 344-345.
[288] Special Collections, Library, Columbia University.
[289] *Autobiography*, I, 345-346.
[290] Ibid., 346. Published by Tichnor and Fields, 1862. *The Rejected Stone* and *The Golden Hour* were both reviewed by John Weiss in *The Atlantic Monthly*, X, November 1862, 644-646.
[291] January 22, 1862, Special Collections, Library, Columbia University.
[292] Special Collections, Library, Columbia University.
[293] Idem. Letters to his wife from July 16 to July 26 indicate that Conway was at that time contributing letters to *The Tribune*.
[294] Idem.
[295] *Autobiography*. I, 351.
[296] Special Collections, Library, Columbia University.
[297] *Autobiography*, I, 354.
[298] Ibid. For an account of similar attacks on Phillips in Boston at that time, see Higginson, *Cheerful Yesterdays*, 246-247.
[299] *Autobiography*, I, 302.
[300] *Autobiography*. I, 354.
[301] *Atlantic Monthly*, X, April 1862, See *Autobiography*, I, 348-49.
[302] Ibid., 508-509.
[303] Ibid., 510.
[304] *Autobiography*, I, 349.
[305] 53-55.
[306] Ibid., 61. See also *Emerson at Home and Abroad*, 254, and "The Assassination of President Lincoln," 796-797.

Chapter X: "My Father's Slaves"

[307] *Autobiography*, I, 355. In *Testimonies*, 103, Conway says that the note was from his sister.
[308] Conway noted that "After the lapse of fourteen years I revisited Cincinnati, and after my lecture in the Opera House, Dr. Meredith challenged me to finish the game which had been interrupted at Yellow Springs. He had taken down the situation, and now in the presence of an invited company the game was won by me, and published in the papers next day." *Autobiography*, I, 355n.
[309] *Testimonies*, 105.
[310] *Autobiography*, I, 356.
[311] Described by Whitman:

> Falmouth, Va., opposite Fredericksburgh, December 21, 1862. Begin my visits among the camp hospitals in the army of the Potomac. Spend a good part of the day in a large brick mansion on the bank of the Rappahannock, used as a hospital since the battle - seems to have receiv'd only the worst cases. Out doors, at the foot of a tree, within ten yards of the front of the house, I notice a heap of amputated feet,

legs, arms, hands, etc., a full load for a one-horse cart. Several dead bodies lie near, each cover'd with its brown woollen blanket. In the dooryard, toward the river, are fresh graves, mostly of officers, their names on pieces of barrel staves or broken boards, stuck in the dirt. (Most of these bodies were subsequently taken up and transported north to their friends. The large mansion is quite crowded upstairs and down, everything impromptu, no system, all bad enough, but I have no doubt the best that can be done; all the wounds pretty bad, some frightful, the men in their old clothes, unclean and bloody. Some of the wounded are rebel soldiers and officers, prisoners. One, a Mississippian, a captain, hit badly in leg, I talk'd with some time; he ask'd me for papers, which I gave him. (I saw him three months afterward in Washington, with his leg amputated, doing well.) I went through the rooms, downstairs and up. Some of the men were dying. I had nothing to give at that visit, but wrote a few letters to home folks, mothers, etc. Also talk'd to three or four, who seem'd most susceptible to it, and needing it.

Specimen Days, Floyd Stoval, editor (New York, 1963), 32. Conway, noting that the mansion described was the Conway home, cited this passage in a footnote to an 'essay, "Hunting a Mythical Pall-bearer," *Harper's Monthly Magazine*, LXXII, January 1886, 211.

[312] In a letter to his wife, July 15, 1862, Conway wrote that he had just arrived in Washington after a difficult trip. He then added, "Contrabands have not been found yet but will be. We were prevented by a severe storm this afternoon. Think we'll try this evening. I am staying at Mrs. Johnson's and writing in Mr. Channing's Library. It is doubtful how soon I can leave - not before Friday, I fear; but much depends on the results of my search this evening and tomorrow." Special Collections, Library, Columbia University.

[313] The description of the journey is taken from *Testimonies*, 106-112, and from *Autobiography*. I, 358-362.

[314] In *Autobiography*, I, 363-364, Conway quotes the poem as follows:

Tell me, master, am I free?
From the prison-land I come,
From a wrecked humanity,
From the fable of a home,-

From the market where my wife,
With my baby at her breast,
Faded from my narrow life,
Rudely bartered and possest.

Masters, ye are fighting long,
Well your trumpet-blast we know:
Are ye come to right a wrong?
Do we call you friend or foe?

Will ye keep me, for my faith,
From the hound that scents my track
From the riotous, drunken breath,
From the murder at my back?

God must come, for whom we pray,
Knowing his deliverance true;
Shall our men be left to say,
He must work it free of you?

Links of an unsighted chain
Bound the spirit of our braves;
Waiting for the nobler strain,
Silence told him we were slaves.

This poem appeared in *Later Lyrics*, by Julia Ward Howe (Boston, 1866). Several words and phrases were altered in the printed version. The third and fourth stanzas were reversed.

[315] Oliver Johnson became editor of *The Standard* in 1844 and remained editor until *The Standard* went out of existence in 1865. He was author of *William Lloyd Garrison and His Times* (1880).

[316] A note by the editor said that Mr. Phillips' speech had been received too late to include it in that issue of *The Standard* and would be deferred until the next.

[317] T. W. Higginson quotes Garrison as follows: "For myself, I hold no fellowship with slaveowners. I will not make a truce with them even for a single hour. I blush for them as countrymen. I know they are not Christians; and the higher they raise their profession of patriotism or piety, the stronger is my detestation of their hypocrisy. They are dishonest and cruel – and God and the angels and devils and the universe know that they are without excuse." *Contemporaries*, 253

[318] General David Hunter was the first Union general to sanction raising a Negro regiment (the 1st of South Carolina) in 1862.

[319] 58.

[320] 62.

[321] 63-64.

[322] 84.

[323] 137.

Chapter XI: Concord and *The Commonwealth*

[324] *Autobiography*, I, 366. In *The Atlantic Monthly*, November 1862, the Rev. John Weiss praised *The Rejected Stone* and *The Golden Hour* in a three-page review. Though himself a leading abolitionist of New England, Weiss congratulated Conway on not advocating colonization of Negroes as a solution, for thus "the only men in the South who know how to labor" would escape. "Let no cotton-grower ever budge," he wrote. "We want the cotton labor even more extensively diffused, to conquer John Bull with bales, as at New Orleans."

[325] The first number of the [reorganized] *Commonwealth* appeared early in September 1862, boldly advocating the emancipation of the slaves as a war measure, the removal of General McClellan as an incompetent commander, and the replacement of Andrew and Sumner. Strange to relate, these three objects were accomplished within the next four months; although it is not to be presumed that the Commonwealth exercised much influence on the two former. Thousands of copies were printed, and those which could not be sold were distributed to members of the legislature, country judges, and the like. -- Stearns, 268-269. See also *Autobiography*. I, 369.

For the part these abolitionists played in encouraging and in financing John Brown, see Oswald Garrison Villard, *John Brown 1800-1859, A Biography of Fifty Years After* (New York and Boston, 1911), 271-345.

[326] The Republican Party originated in various parts of the country at approximately the same time. It arose as a Northern protest against the Kansas• Nebraska Bill (1854), and was a coalition of interests opposed to slavery and secession.

> In 1854 Frank W. Bird, Dr. S. G. Howe, and others supported a campaign paper called the Commonwealth, of which Elizur Wright was editor; and this brought him into the ring. Sumner attended their meetings whenever he was in Boston, and as the Republican party developed the club increased in numbers. In 1855 Parker built his marble hotel on School Street - quite a novelty in its time - and the club engaged a private dining room there, which they retained until 1863. At the time of Lincoln's election the club numbered among its members the governor of the state, both senators, four or five representatives to Congress, and two of three ex-governors. There were other members of the club, important in their way, who either held offices or wanted offices. --Stearns, 156-157.

[327] *Autobiography*. I, 364

[328] The Bird Club originated circa 1850 when the Free Soil party met together in Boston on Saturday afternoons for dinner and political discussions. The "Secret Six," who attempted to aid John Brown, were members of this group. By 1862, Parker had died; Gerritt Smith had joined another group; and George L. Stearns, a wealthy Boston lead-pipe manufacturer, supplied most of the money and the enthusiasm. He was supported by Samuel G. Howe, famous for his work among the blind, and by T. W. Higginson and Frank Sanborn, as well as by Senators Sumner and Wilson, Governor John Andrew, Frank Bird and others. See Martin Duberman, *The Antislavery Vanguard* (Princeton, 1965), 6-7. Frank Preston Stearns writes that his father was first invited

> to the Bird Club in the spring of 1858, although at that time it could hardly be called a club at all. Mr. Bird himself could not remember exactly when the club originated. Like all permanent and effective organizations it had a natural and spontaneous origin.
>
> .... Long before the election of President Pierce, Frank W. Bird, John A. Andrew, and a few other Free-soilers were accustomed to dine together on Saturdays to discuss political affairs. There was no formal

organization, and how the name of Bird Club came to be attached to their meetings, they never could tell. If would seem to have originated with their political opponents.

In 1854 Frank W. Bird, Dr. S. G. Howe, and others supported a campaign paper called the Commonwealth, of which Elizur Wright was editor; and this brought him into the ring. Sumner attended their meetings whenever he was in Boston, and as the Republican party developed the club increased in numbers. In 1855 Parker built his marble hotel on School Street - quite a novelty in its time - and the club engaged a private dining room there, which they retained until 1863. At the time of Lincoln's election the club numbered among its members the governor of the state, both senators, four or five representatives to Congress, and two or three ex-governors. There were other members of the club, important in their way, who either held offices or wanted offices. -- Stearns, 156-157. See also *Five Years' Progress of the Slave Power*; a series of papers, first published in the Boston "Commonwealth." July, August, September, 1851 (Boston, 1852).

[329] Ibid., 263-64.

[330] See Ch. VII, entitled "Kansas and John Brown," in *Cheerful Yesterdays*, by T.W. Higginson. See also "A Visit to John Brown's Household," in *Contemporaries*, by the same author. See also "Mr. Stearns and Jeff Davis," *The Commonwealth* (May, 1863), 1.

[331] The story is told by Stearns, 215-217. It is told also by Villard, 533-534, and again by Sanborn in *Hawthorne and His Friends* (1908), 8.

[332] See *The Commonwealth*, February 22, 1863. In an article by Sanborn, entitled "War and Peace, A Sermon" these facts were set forth. They were presented again in *The Commonwealth*, July 10, 1863, by "M.F.C." (Martin F. Conway), in an article, entitled "Kansan Recollections." A full account of the whole senatorial investigation was given in *The Commonwealth*, May 1, 1863, "Mr. Stearns and Jefferson Davis."

[333] M. L." by Louisa M. louisa, *The Commonwealth*, Jan. 24-Feb. 21, 1863. This story is reproduced in its entirety in the Appendix of *Anti-Slavery Sentiment in American Literature Prior to 1865*, by Lovengo Dow Turner. "Hospital Sketches" opened in *The Commonwealth* of May 21, 1863.

[334] "Hymn to a New Advent," Autobiography. 1, 370-71.

[335] Special Collections, Library, Columbia University.

[336] Conway's notion of the Negro as a special gift to the white man was a reflection of Garrison's editorial in *The Liberator* of August 7, 1861, against deportation as a solution of the slavery questions. Garrison wrote: "Before God, I do not see how the nation can be really civilized and Christianized if you go. You are needed to make us Christians, to make us understand what Christianity means." Quoted by John L. Thomas, *The Liberator: William Lloyd Garrison* (1963), 416.

[337] See also Stearns, 275-276.

[338] Conway's views were somewhat too outspoken for his public. See *Autobiography*, I, 376. The account of his differences with his editors given

here is a repetition of a portion of his Journal. Elizur Wright, former secretary of the American Anti-Slavery Society, was a follower of Garrison from Ohio, with whom he finally broke.

[339] Sanborn wrote of this occasion, "At one period during the War, I should say in 1862, a staunch anti-slavery Marylander, who had settled in Kansas before 1856 and was the first Congressman from the state, Martin Conway, made a speech which surprised his old friends, of whom I was one, because he advocated peace and the recognition of the Southern Confederacy." *Hawthorne and His Friends*, 60.

[340] Stearns gives the following account of Slack:

> Charles W. Slack, a member of the Bird Club, was highly useful at this time in preserving the organization of Theodore Parker's society. With this body as a nucleus, Boston Music Hall was filled every Sunday by an audience for which Mr. Slack obtained the ablest speakers and preachers. These Sunday gatherings could hardly be called religious services, for politics and negro philanthropy were the universal theme. The orthodox James H. Manning was followed by Lucretia Mott, a Quaker preacher of Philadelphia. It was a free political church, and more than once Wendell Phillips was obliged to enter it surrounded by a body• guard of his younger friends. Mr. and Mrs. Stearns attended these meetings whenever the weather permitted and usually had seats on the platform. When springtime came they often invited the speaker with other friends to their house to dinner. There was no small table-talk on such occasions; for these feasts were more like Platonic symposia of art and literature, in which both Phillips and Garrison were as much at home as they were in forensic discussions.
> --Stearns, 260-61.

[341] *Autobiography*, I, 372. Conway described this episode once more in "The Demons of the Shadow," *Fraser's Magazine*, November, 1870, 70.

[342] *Dictionary of American Biography*. 1931-1960.

[343] General Banks replaced General Butler in New Orleans in May, 1861. Butler was a Massachusetts Democrat who fought for the Union. He was a ruthless and dishonest Military Governor of New Orleans and later became an active member of the Radical Republicans in Washington. Banks was Governor of Massachusetts before Andrew, and, as Military Governor of New Orleans, was as thoroughly hated as Butler had been.

[344] In a speech on November 2, 1859, Garrison said, "As a peace man, I am prepared to say 'success to every slave insurrection in the South."' Quoted by John L. Thomas, *The Liberator*, William Lloyd Garrison (Boston, 1963), 398.

[345] See M. D. Conway, "Wendell Phillips," *The Fortnightly Review*, June 1870, 59-73.

[346] Special Collections, Library, Columbia University.

[347] *The Golden Hour*, 80.

[348] Stearns, 224.

[349] Idem., 150.

[350] Idem., 276.

[351] It was estimated that nearly two thousand were present in the Senate chamber on Sunday morning, January 25." *Autobiography*, I, 377.
[352] *Autobiography*, I, 378.
[353] Idem., 381. In his Journal, Conway quoted President Lincoln as saying, "knocks the bottom out of the tub for Slavery."
[354] The order was upheld by Congress. Lincoln annulled General David Hunter's order liberating the slaves in the Department of the South.
[355] Stearns, 278-279. See also *Autobiography*, I, 383. For a later account, see Idem., II, 87-88. See also the Conway Journal. George Luther Stearns, as a Major in the Army, worked with T. W. Higginson in recruiting and training negroes. See F. P. Stearns, Chapter VIII, "The Colored Regiments." Higginson writes that Howe and his group thought of "taking a hint from John Brown and putting a guerilla party instantly into Virginia; thus saving Washington by kindling a back fire. The steps promptly taken in recruiting troops prevented this project from being carried farther, but it was precisely the scheme to suit Dr. Howe." T.W. Higginson, *Contemporaries* (Boston, 1899), 300.
[356] Conway Journal. Special Collections, Library, Columbia University.
[357] *Autobiography*, I, 382. See also Stearns, 280.
[358] *Autobiography*, I, 383. The trip to Washington was described *in The Commonwealth*, January 31, 1863, "Things at the Capital."
[359] Sir William Howard Russell, *Pictures of Southern Life; Social, Political, and Military*, New York, 1861. Russell was special correspondent of the London *Times*. He also wrote *The Civil War in America* (Boston, 1861). Here he said "The South will never go back into the Union." 9. He also observed that Southerners believed "that England is in absolute dependence on cotton for their material existence." 175.
[360] Stearns, 194-95.
[361] *Autobiography*. I, 388-89.
[362] Holograph letter. Dickinson College Library.
[363] Houghton Library. Harvard University. The letter to Longfellow reads:

Commonwealth Ohio

March 11 [18632]

Mr. H. W. Longfellow,
Dear Sir,

It has been agreed between certain friends of Liberty and Union here and in England, that if, just at this juncture, an antislavery Virginian (like myself) should appear at some of their meetings in England, to be put on the witness stand as to Slavery as it is in the South, to confront other disloyal Southerners there, it would have a good effect. I shall go over there with letters from Emerson & other well known persons guaranteeing my good faith.

It is generally thought that my lectures concerning the South & Slavery over there will pay their way, but, as I am not able to venture a trip on my own purse, it is proposed to raise a fund - the money to be repaid as far as admission fees can do it.

Some three hundred dollars have been already raised.

My plan is to work at once - leaving here Apl. 1 in the Europa and returning in Sept.

If you could find it convenient to help this fund (which I hope to refund in English gold) I should be glad; but whether that be convenient or not, may I not hope for one or two letters of Introduction to persons such as I wd. wish to know?

With love to brother Samuel,

Yours cordially.
Moncure D. Conway

I will come & get the Letters, if my plan suits you, & make my adieux. I shall want some advice about England also - having never been abroad.

[364] Reprinted from the New York *Tribune* in *The National Anti-Slavery Standard*, April 11, 1863, 2.

[365] Holograph letter. Dickinson College Library.

Chapter XII: The Conway-Mason Controversy

[366] *Autobiography*, I, 388.

[367] Conway to his wife, May 4, 1863. Ellen's letter of May 15, showed that she was lonely and unhappy in Concord. She wrote that the children were ill; that she had had no letters from Conway; that it was raining, and that the people of Concord were unfriendly. "You must send me letters so I will get one every week or else I will be found in the insane asylum when you return," she wrote. Ellen continued, "I would not live in Concord if I had to sell for $3,000 - They have got up a French class & never invited me. Mrs. Sanborn, Alcotts or Emersons have never called but once then on errands & would not come in-". Special Collections, Library, Columbia University.

[368] *The Commonwealth*, July 17, 1863. In a brief article, entitled "Our Foreign Correspondent," and dated June 16, Conway listed these ladies and remarked, "These women meet and toil nobly. They have already distributed over eight thousand pamphlets on the American struggle...They also intend to have a series of lectures." The British and Foreign Anti-Slavery Society was founded in England in 1823. In 1829 its name was changed to the Anti-Slavery Society. *Encyclopedia of the Social Sciences.*

[369] *Testimonies Concerning Slavery*, 1864. See "Thomas Hughes," *The Commonwealth*. Signed M.D.C., June 12, 1863, 1-2.

[370] *Autobiography*, I, 392.

[371] *A Diary From Dixie*, Mary Boykin Chestnut. Edited by Isabella D. Martin and Myrta Lockett. London, 1909. 117. See also 116 and 125.

[372] *Autobiography*. I, 408. Conway described his visit with Forbes in *The Commonwealth*, May 29, 1863.

[373] *The Commonwealth*, July 17, 1863.

[374] *Autobiography*. I, 61.

[375] *The Life of Stirling*. by Thomas Carlyle.

[376] "Walks About London," *The Commonwealth*, June 19, 1863. See also description of a walk with Carlyle in "Cambridge University." first page of the same issue. See Moncure D. Conway, *Thomas Carlyle* (1881) for an account of these conversations.
[377] *Autobiography*. I, 401.
[378] Ibid., 410.
[379] Ibid., 406-07. There was also "an enthusiastic Southern lady" who visited Carlyle frequently and convinced him that prosperity was springing up in the South in spite of the blockade. 93-94.
[380] The Commonwealth, June 19, 1863. Dateline, May 26, 1863. See also Autobiography, 1, 392-93.
[381] "A Visit to Robert Browning," *The Commonwealth*, May 29, 1863.
[382] *Autobiography*, I, 412.
[383] Idem.
[384] Ibid., 413-18, or this letter and those that follow. These letters appeared in the London *Times*, June 18, 1863. Reprinted in *The Commonwealth*, July 10, 1863. In the same issue were reprinted from *The Spectator* of June 20, as editorial comment, "Conway-Mason Letters," and from The Star of June 17, a two-column article, "Mr. Conway's Speech at the London Terrace."
[385] Original in Special Collections, Library, Columbia University.
[386] The article that appeared on June 17 in the London *Times*, 5, was entitled, "Mr. Bright on the War in America." After a summary of Bright's remarks, the reader is told, "Mr. Bright then introduced to the meeting Mr. Conway, a gentleman from Eastern Virginia, who gave an account of his experiences both in the South and North." This speech was published in full in *The Commonwealth*, July 10 and 17, 1863.
[387] Special Collections, Library, Columbia University.
[388] *The Tribune* of June 3, 1863, stated the case in a ten-line article. See *Autobiography* I, 424. In the same issue of *The Tribune* appeared a humorous statement of the case, entitled "Conway-Mason." The anonymous contributor writes:

> Mr. James M. Mason is an old Virginia gentleman, having his residence near Winchester, whence his slaves run away a year or more ago, but he is temporarily lodging at London, where he hopes to be one day received as Embassador from the man-stealer's Confederacy. Mr. Moncure D. Conway is a young and ardent Virginian, though also of an old family, born and reared Fredericksburg in old Virginia ideas, but perverted by a Harvard education into an Abolitionist, Transcendentalist, and all sorts of a "fanatic," as they are called; though he doesn't believe in anything he can't bite.
>
> Mr. Mason having gone to London as an unacknowledged Embassador, Mr. Conway followed as an amateur in the same line, and has been spending some time in England in that capacity. And, as neither he nor Mason had any recognized function as a negotiator, the bright thought appears to have struck him that, though they could not negotiate with anybody else, they readily might with each other. So he

> set about it. And in order to have a power behind him, Mr. C. introduced himself to Mr. M. as representative of the Abolitionists just as Mr. Mason is of the insurgent slaveholders.
>
> Unlike all but very green diplomatists, Mr. C. played his best card first. If Mr. Mason would get the Rebels to abolish Slavery, Mr. Conway would undertake to make the Abolitionists oppose the further prosecution of the War for the Union and favor the recognition of the Confederacy! The bait was large and tempting but Mason is a shy old fish, and don't bite at the showiest fly. He wanted to know what authority Mr. C. had to speak for the Abolitionists! That was a staggerer; and Mr. Conway could only say in reply that he would send over to America and get it. Fancy an Embassador sending three thousand miles for his credentials! So here the matter dropped, and Mr. Mason sent the correspondence at once to The Times, hoping to make some capital for his master out of it. We guess it will amount to little more than a demonstration that the old Virginian is a little craftier than the young one.

[389] The title was "Mr. Mason and Mr. Conway."
[390] *The Commonwealth*, July 10, 1863.
[391] Ibid., July 3, 1863.
[392] Phillips expressed the views of the Bird Club. Frank Stearns writes in life of his father, George Luther Stearns:

> About the middle of January, Garrison surprised his former friends and supporters by publishing an editorial in the Liberator congratulating the abolitionists on the success of their long effort, but also presuming that their work was nearly at an end, and that the future of the freedmen could be safely intrusted to President Lincoln and his Cabinet. The Boston Advertiser praised this confession of the veteran philanthropist, but Mr. Stearns, Frank Bird, and Dr. Howe did not like it at all. Mr. Bird attributed it to Senator Wilson's influence, and his growing jealousy of General Butler; and Mr. Stearns said that Garrison evidently seemed to think that the negroes were already liberated, although the greater part of them still remained in slavery, and would continue so unless the rebellion could be suppressed; and this was not yet certain.

[393] Ibid., July 3, 1863.
[394] By 1875, Conway called himself a "Universalist," rather than a "Unitarian."

Chapter XIII: In Search of a Country

[395] *Autobiography*. I, 415.
[396] Ibid., 418.
[397] Conway at once sent a letter to *The Commonwealth*, published June 17, 1863, in a small article entitled "Mr. Conway's Explanation." Conway wrote that Mason's letter of June 17, 1863 (*The Times*, London, June 19, 1863) "is regarded

here, by our friends, as a complete unmasking of Mason. So think the Star, Spectator, etc.,--and there is no doubt that the Confederates here are much enraged at it. My letter was well meant, and it turned out well by reason of Mason being as much over crafty as I was under crafty."

[398] Reprinted in *The Commonwealth*, July 17, 1863, from *The Manchester Examiner*, June 24, 1863.

[399] Mason remained in Canada for three years, fearing that he would be arrested by federal agents for his activities against the United States in London. In 1868 he returned to a home near Alexandria, where he died in 1871.

[400] The letter was written on June 22, 1863, and reprinted in *The Commonwealth*, July 10, 1863. See also *Autobiography*. I, 423.

[401] Special Collections, Library, Columbia University.

[402] Idem. See also *Autobiography*, I, 426. In the midst of his troubles, Conway had received, early in May, this letter from W. D. Howells, then consul in Venice. The letter, enclosing several poems for publication in *The Commonwealth*, had been written on March 24, and addressed to Conway in Boston. Howells knew nothing of Conway's mission to England when he invited him and his wife to visit the Howellses in Venice. Conway copied Howells' letter and mailed it to his wife on May 8. In his letter to Ellen of June 23, he wrote, "I have gotten another warm letter from Howells." For Howells' account of Conway's visit, see Appendix II.

[403] *Autobiography*. I, 427.

[404] Special Collections, Library, Columbia University

[405] Conway says that he furthered the publication of *Venetian Life* in England, and that he wrote the first review of the book, published in *The Fortnightly Review*, VI, May 1866, 126-127. See *Autobiography*. I, 429.

[406] "No Love Lost, A Romance of Travel." 1869. Presentation copy signed by Howells and dated 1875, is in the Rare Book Room, University of Texas Library, Austin.

[407] *Venetian Life*, I, 163. Reprinted in *Autobiography*, I, 430. Conway wrote "Venice," and "Milan Diary," *The Commonwealth*, July 10 and 22, 1863.

[408] July 6, 1863. Special Collections, Library, Columbia University.

[409] Special Collections, Library, Columbia University.

[410] Idem. Conway always loved Paris. In 1867, asked by *Harper's* to write up the Exposition of Paris, he began his article with a meditation on the city: "The Chief delight of Paris is, perhaps, the feeling of being there. With what an experience of gentle ecstasy does one wander through these fascinating streets and boulevards, these parks whose trees are singing fountains, where earth, sky, and human life are a romance into which each newcomer feels himself easily woven!" "The Great Show at Paris," *Harper's* XXXV, July, 1867, 238.

[411] Idem. Conway remarked in his letter of July 24, 1863, written to his wife from Lucerne, "I am sorry that I did not know sooner about remaining on the Commonwealth until Sept., and I hope that you may have availed yourself of the liberty given you of withholding it. The fact is that I have been able to write for it very little indeed. I shall try & send more the next week to make up for defects." Conway continued as editor of *The Commonwealth*, in name, until his resignation on August 28, 1863. His letters to the journal appeared until

September 14, 1867. They were usually signed "M.D.C.," but several were unsigned and one was signed "Aubrey."

[412] *Autobiography*, I, 435. See also Moncure D. Conway, *Centenary of the South Place Society*. London, 1894. 100. See also *Autobiography*. II, 53-56.

[413] *Autobiography*, I, 434.

[414] A letter to Moses Coit Tyler of December 19, 1863 asks Tyler to pick up for him on his way to the Conway house a copy of *The Standard* of the 12th, 13th, or 14th, "containing an attack on me by name in an editorial (leader, I heard) for being at the Exeter Hall meeting." Cornell University Library. Tyler had recently resigned his ministry in the Congregational Church and come to England as a journalist and lecturer.

[415] *Autobiography*, I, 437-38. See John L. Thomas, *The Liberator* (1963), 421-41. See Horace Greeley's letter to Conway, *Autobiography*, II, 44-45.

[416] *Autobiography*, II, 45.

[417] *My Pilgrimage to the Wise Men of the East.* (1906) 25.

[418] "Mr. William Shakespeare at Home," *Harper's*, XXIX, August 1864, 337.

[419] Nathaniel P. Banks came to New Orleans in December, 1863. He arranged to have Negroes returned to work on plantations for planters who had taken the oath of allegiance. Abolitionists denounced Banks. Sydney Gay said in a New York *Tribune* editorial that Banks' labor system was little better than the former serfdom. Radical Republicans agreed. Lincoln supported Banks, as did Garrison. James M. McPherson, *The Struggle for Equality* (1964), 287-289.

[420] *Autobiography*, I, 441-45. The question of the Newman-Conway relationship is discussed in Chapter XIV, 7-8.

[421] See Conway's English "Diary," September 1863-November 1870. Special Collections. Columbia University. Library. In an entry of October 25 [1864] Conway described an afternoon visit to Froude, when the editor engaged Conway "to write six articles for Fraser beginning Jan. 1865." In the evening Conway called on Carlyle. Conway recorded their conversation in his "Diary." Said Carlyle:

> I have recd. a letter from Emerson since I saw you. It is a strange letter--1 will show it to you. He says that the battle of Humanity is waging in America. Wonders that there is no eye in England able to look to the middle of the thing & see what it really is. Seems to think that I take my view because of some eccentricity or disposition to repel disagreeable people. It is the first letter I have had from Emerson for years--and surely it fills me with astonishment. That the clearest mind now living--for I don't know Emerson's equal upon earth for perception--should write so is quasi-miraculous. I have tried to look into the middle of the thing & I have seen nothing but a people cutting throats indefinitely to put the nigger into a position for which all experience shows him unfit.

In the course of the conversation, Conway reported in his "Diary," "I said New England had indeed loved him and it seemed to me a very great proof of his sincerity that he could have recently inflicted upon his friends there the deep pain that had been inflicted by his position about Slavery. He ran up, suddenly

& I thought was about to be angry: but he said--"Let us now take a walk." It was 10 and he went with me nearly to the Old Exhibition buildings." The letter from Emerson to Carlyle was written on September 26, 1864. It was reprinted by Conway in his essay "Ralph Waldo Emerson," *Fortnightly Review*, XXXVII, January 1882, 747-770.

[422] *Autobiography*, II, 204.

[423] Idem. 86. 323

[424] Conway's article appeared in the first issue of the *Fortnightly Review*, May 1, 1865, 56-59. This journal was founded by George Henry Lewes as "a platform for the free expression of the individual opinions... of the best writers on Literature, Art, Science, Philosophy. Finance, and Politics generally." Quoted from the prospectus of the *Fortnightly Review*, which appeared in the *Saturday Review* of March 25, 1865. Reprinted by Edwin Mallard Everett in *The Party of Humanity. The Fortnightly Review and its Contributors, 1865-1875.* Chapel Hill. 1939, 331-332. Conway's personal sorrow at the death of Lincoln is reflected in a letter he wrote to Dr. McClintock on May 4, 1865, in which he said, "I have scarcely yet recovered from the stunning bolt that fell from the clear sky in America. Though in political feeling I was to some extent alienated from the President (and not so much the last month or so of his administration as before) yet personally I regarded him as a most admirable and loveable man, and I have felt as if I had heard of the violent death of my father." Special Collections, Library, Columbia University.

[425] Ibid., 793-94.

[426] "The President's Defense," *The Fortnightly Review*, V, May 15, 1866, 98-106.

[427] Conway had published this essay in *The Dial*, November and December, 1860.

[428] printed by the Ladies Emancipation Society. London, 1864.

[429] printed by Anti-Abolitionist Society, New York, Tract No. 4.

[430] Conway circulated *Testimonies* among his friends in England. See letter to J. Emory McClintock, July 21, 1863. Dickinson College Library. Moncure D. Conway to J. Emory McClintock, 1840 - Class of 1858.

29 Cannon Place
Brighton. July 21. (1863)

Dear Emory,

Your kind letter about my little book has been read. I am glad you think well of it, & hope with you that it may accomplish some good.

I own myself disappointment in Fremont's friends certainly - & somewhat in him. But if we "swallow Old Abe," as you say, you fellows must serve him up with a new sauce. He certainly is slow; and though I like him I cannot swallow the Banks policy in Louisiana.

If you think of purchasing some copies of my "Testimonies," & have not already written to the Publishers about it, allow me selfishly to say that if you order them of me I get much more than if you order of the publisher.

Yours very cordially
M. D. Conway.

P.S. Give my love to your father when you write. My eyes have always followed him, and will.
(Emory McClintock was a son of John McClintock, Professor of Greek and Latin, Dickinson College, 1840-1848. He was U.S. Consul at Bradford, England, 1863-1866.)
[431] "I, for one," wrote Conway, "am firmly persuaded that the mixture of the blacks and whites is good; that the person as produced is, under ordinarily favourable circumstances, healthy, handsome, and intelligent. Under the best circumstances, I believe that such a combination would evolve a more complete character than the unmitigated Anglo-Saxon." *Testimonies*, 76.
[432] Ibid., 76.

Chapter XIV: The "Interpreter" at South Place Chapel

[433] *Autobiography*, II, 49-50.
[434] Ibid., 45.
[435] Moncure D. Conway, "Apologia," in *Farewell Discourses*, delivered at South Place Chapel, Finsbury, London, 1884, 168.
[436] Frequently referred to as "South Place Ethical Society," often as "South Place Society," sometimes as "South Place Unitarian Chapel." The group was, in fact, a liberal wing of the Unitarian Church. As usual, Conway was not in accord with the more orthodox members of the church: "The Unitarians of London never liked us," Conway wrote in *Farewell Discourses* (1894), "Apologia," 176. See also C.W. Marshall, 'The Future of South Place Ethical Society," *The Ethical Record*, January 1966. Published by South Place Ethical Society, Conway Hall, Humanist Centre, Red Lion Square, London WC1.
[437] Moncure D. Conway, *Centenary History of the South Place Society* (London, 1894), 104n.
[438] Ibid., 71.
[439] Ibid., Appendix I, "The Service in Commemoration of William Johnson Fox, late M.P. for Oldham and Minister at South Place. Finsbury Chapel." Sunday morning, June 12, 1864.
[440] In 1865 Conway's salary was fixed at 150 pounds a year, and it remained there for the next eight years. Ibid., 102.
[441] Ibid., 106.
[442] Mark E. Marsden, "General Minutes, Finsbury Chapel, South Place," January 29, 1865. Manuscript in South Place Ethical Society, Red Lion Square, London. Quoted by Lloyd D. Easton, *Hegel's First American Followers* (Ohio, 1966), 151.
[443] *Centenary History*, 112.
[444] *Autobiography*, I, 328.
[445] In the same year an American edition was brought out and reviewed in *The Nation*, XIX, July 9, 1874. Five editions appeared in England and five in America before 1889. The Library of Congress owns a presentation copy to "Professor Weber, 11 signed by Moncure D. Conway.
[446] *Autobiography*. II, 330.
[447] Ibid., 333.

[448] John Stuart Mill & Moncure D. Conway, Avignon, France, October 23, 1865. Reproduced in *Autobiography*. II, 16-17.
[449] *Autobiography*. I, 406-407.
[450] Ibid., II, 1.
[451] Ibid., I, 441-444.
[452] Conway wrote essays on all four of these men: "Gladstone, as Leader of the Commons," *Harper's*, XXXIII, June 1866, 61-64; "Disraeli," *Harper's*, XXXIV, May 1867, 753-758; "John Bright," *Harper's*, XXXIV, December 1866, 94-99; "Richard Cobden," *Atlantic Monthly*. XV, June 1865, 724-729.
[453] *Autobiography*, II, 74.
[454] Ibid., 83.
[455] Ibid., 15.
[456] *The Commonwealth*, July 19, 1863, 157-58.
[457] Conway admired John Stuart Mill, as did the men and women of South Place Chapel. See Conway's articles: "The Great Westminster Canvass," Harper's, XXXI, November 1865, 732-745." *In Memoriam*. A Memorial Discourse in Honor of John Stuart Mill. South Place Chapel, Finsbury, May 25, 1873. "John Stuart Mill," *Harper's*, XLVII, September 1873, 528-534.
[458] To Moses Coit Tyler. are Book Room, University of Cornell. Moses Coit Taylor (1835-1900), & congregational minister, resigned his position in 1862, and came to England in 1862, to lecture on various subjects, among them the Union code.
[459] For a statement of Lewes' position as a Positivist, see "The Reign of Law," *Fortnightly Review*, II, n.s., July 1867, 96-110. This is a review of a book by that name, written by the Duke of Argyll. See also Lloyd D. Easton, *Hegel's First American Followers*. In Chapter V, "Religious Naturalism and reform in the Thought of Moncure Conway," Easton's chapter suggests many sources for Conway's positivist leanings. He overlooked, however, Conway's own statement on the subject of Positivism and the "Religion of Humanity" (*Autobiography*. II, 379-384). This "religion" he thought both unappealing and philosophical untenable. See also "Apologia," *Farewell Discourses*, 1894. Here Conway says that he was closely associated with those who did find a resolution to religion in Positivism, which, however, he could not accept. Conway admired their scientific realism, and observed that the Positivists "look in the right direction." "Our excellent friends, the Positivists," in deifying Humanity, forget that "their brave opinions on war, etc., are not consistent with Humanity as it is." 175-77.
[460] *Autobiography*, II, 87.
[461] "America, France, and England," *The Fortnightly Review*, III, January 1, 1866, 442-459.
[462] "The President's Defense," *The Fortnightly Review*, V, May 15, 1866, 748-753.
[463] See the letters from Charles Sumner to Conway, July 30 and August 15, 1865. In the letter of July 30, Sumner wrote, "I thank you for your vigilant testimony to the good cause, which has suffered infinitely, first, through the terrible tergiversation of the President, and secondly, through the imbecility of Congress, which shrank from a contest on principle. If Congress had willed it, we could have carried a bill for political rights as well as for civil rights and on precisely

the same arguments, - that it was needful in the enforcement of the prohibition of slavery." *Autobiography*. II, 89.
[464] *The Fortnightly Review*, VII, June 1867, 748-753.
[465] Holograph letter in the Library of Cornell University, are Book Room.
[466] *The Fortnightly Review*, XIV, June 1, 1870, 59-73.
[467] See Chapter X of *Testimonies* for an earlier comparison of Garrison and Phillips. Here Conway stated that the Abolitionists, in spite of their differences, "unanimously recognize in this war purely a struggle between Slavery and Freedom." He added, "little heed need be given to those who speak of other issues."
[468] 4.
[469] *Autobiography*, II, 63.
[470] Ibid., 61-63.
[471] *Mazzini: A Discourse Given in South Place Chapel, Finsbury*. March 17, 1872.
[472] *Autobiography*, II, 207.

Chapter XV: Pilgrim's Return

[473] October 28, 1869. Rare Book Room, Library, Cornell University.
[474] *Autobiography*, II, 299.
[475] Letter from Conway to Ellen, September 14, 1875. Special Collections, Library, Columbia University.
[476] *Autobiography*. II, 300.
[477] Conway reported in his *Autobiography*, II, 300, that his father had about $100,000 at the outbreak of the War, "in addition to Conway House and gardens and his two farms stocked with negroes." After talking the family affairs over with his father in 1875, Conway wrote to his wife: "When the War broke out he had besides negroes (whose money value was $50,000) $70,000 in gold. The whole was swept away except $300. Of this he gave Peter $100 and had $200 to begin anew. When he got a little he had to lend money to impoverished relatives, - $200 to Judge Moncure, and several other two hundreds. He works hard and prays hard, gives and saves, and so it will be to the last." Walker Peyton Conway was a partner in the banking house of Conway, Gordon and Garnett.
[478] See *Dictionary of American Biography* for account of the career of Richard Cassius Lee Moncure, before and after the Civil War.
[479] Holograph letter. Dickinson College Library. Rare Book Room.
[480] Ellen Conway's reply of 1st [October] 1875 to her husband's letters is in the Dickinson College Library. Ellen's suggests that her views on the Virginia family were not entirely in harmony with those of Moncure. After thanking him for his letters, she wrote,

> We are all very angry at your giving two best lectures in Virginia 1st & for nothing & to Baptists & Methodists .... There is no use in my racking myself with anxiety & loneliness for people who never did us anything but harm. If you want to give why not make them pay for the lecture & give the money to Richard's wife or the negroes. It is nothing

> but Virginia pride and I've no patience with it. Now I've screamed & grunted I feel better -- I only wish I was one of those Baptist or Methodist ministers to see & hear you for nothing & pocket the proceeds of others paying. Why did not you use part of your time in taking your Mother to Richmond, Baltimore & Easton & also to see Mr. Farquhar. I am so eager for you to get through & come home. I feel as if I could not wait. Now having scolded enough I will be sweet & kiss you 1000 times & tell you I have not coughed for 8 or 10 days until your letter arrived offering 4 d each to chicks I was instantly seized with violent fit of coughing ... You certainly need your fox with you to be up to the world. Those Southerners are right, except for me, you never would have saved a farthing. You vowed in your letters to me from England you would never let that ocean be between us again but you have not kept it. If I get a chance I shall make a vow & keep it. You can guess what it is. In the meantime I would like to skin all ministers & all reporters. Love, ever so much from all
>
> Your own
> Ellen D. Con

Conway's reply to Ellen's letter was written from the Cooper Institute, New York, on October 16, 1895. Special Collections, Library, Columbia University. Moncure writes that he has received her "screed" of October 1 and then remarks:

> I hope you will think it enough to vent your vexation on paper without then venting the paper on me. They have sent me (Baptist & Methods. together) $55, which is pretty fair for an utterly poverty stricken place. The Wesley lecture was free. It is provoking that it shd. be published & how it happened I cannot tell. You are mistaken in thinking the Freds'b'g people "never did me anything but harm"--ludicrously so.

Conway closes his long letter on his recent adventures with the comment:

> It is raining hard, the sky strongly resembling your green letter just recd. I think you wd write sweeter on white paper.

[481] A small notebook describing the trip of 1875 to Yellow Springs, Ohio, is in Special Collections, Columbia University Library. It is written in pencil in Conway's hand.

[482] *Autobiography*, II, 302-303. Conway had written *The Natural History of the Devil* in 1859. In 1869, "A Hunt after Devils" appeared in *Harper's* XXXVII, March, 1869, 540-549. See also "The Demons of the Shadow," *Scribner's*, V, November 1870; December, 1872), 63-77, 233-250; see also *Fraser's Magazine*, (86) 596; 697.

[483] Conway was lecturing from the material he had gathered in his "merry hunt for devils" in the old towns of Germany, France, and Russia in 1871. See Appendix II. Conway subsequently delivered four lectures on Demonology before the Royal Institute of London, *Autobiography*. II, 256. *Demonology and Devil-Lore*, Moncure D. Conway, was published in 1879 in New York and London.

[484] After the deaths of Eliza and Dunmore Gwinn, the so-called "Conway Colony" disappeared, or was absorbed in the urbanized area of Yellow Springs. Conway sent Dunmore a larger check than usual the Christmas after the death of his wife. Dunmore used the money to return to Fredericksburg to visit his former master, Walker Peyton Conway, and died soon after his return to Ohio. *Autobiography*. II, 304-305n.

[485] Conway wrote to his friend, Murat Halstead, January 15, 1876: "I shall have an important letter to write you from Mark Twain's when I get there (Tuesday) about the invitation the congregation of the late Theodore Parker have given me to settle with them permanently; but now the Lotus Club gathers and I am their special guest this evening. Ever yours M. D. Conway" Pennsylvania Historical Society. Philadelphia, Pennsylvania. See also *Autobiography*, I, 306n.

[486] Special Collections, Library, Columbia University.

[487] Idem.

[488] Vol. III.

[489] *Autobiography*. II, 306.

[490] 116.

[491] Dickinson College Library. Rare Book Room.

[492] Autobiography. II, 416.

Paine-ful Postscript

[493] On the 123rd anniversary of the birth of Paine, Conway delivered an address which was published at the request of his congregation. *Thomas Paine, A Celebration.* Delivered in the First Congregational Church, Cincinnati, Ohio, January 29, 1860. By M. D. Conway, Minister of the Church, Cincinnati, 1860.

[494] *Fortnightly Review*, March 1879, 397-416. In the same year, Conway published an article on Paine, "Modern Thinkers," in the April 19 issue of the *Chicago Times*; and another in the May 17 issue of the *Chicago Tribune*, appeared another article by Conway, "Thomas Paine, a Friendly Sketch of the Remarkable Career of a Remarkable Man." See also *A Vindication of Thomas Paine*, Robert G. Ingersoll, and *Thomas Paine, A Criticism*, Moncure D. Conway (Chicago, 1879). Conway here said that, though the bust of Paine was refused by the International Exposition at Philadelphia, Paine's portrait had at last been hung in Independence Hall -- 'near that of George III."

[495] Alfred Owen Aldridge, *Man of Reason, The Life of Thomas Paine* (Philadelphia and New York, 1959). Aldridge said of Conway's *Life of Paine* that he was the only biographer up to that time to study the original documents concerning Paine's French period. He writes: "There have been a number of biographies since Conway's, but not a single one adds anything of importance concerning Paine's French period, and very few contain new factual material of any kind." Conway's *Life*, he adds, is somewhat "impaired by prejudices in Paine's favor," especially in his portrayal of Gouverneur Morris as a villain, who plotted to keep Paine in prison in France.

[496] The alumni of Dickinson College invited Conway to give their annual address in 1892, and Dickinson College conferred on him the degree of L.H.D. *Autobiography*. II, 434. Conway's letter of thanks is at Dickinson College:

Dear Professor Himes,

Material

I have your favor notifying me of the degree L.H.D. conferred on me by the authorities of Dickinson College. I assure you that no other honor could give me so much pleasure and satisfaction as this recognition by my Alma Mater of my literary labors during the forty years that have elapsed since I received my M.A. at her hands.

Yours very truly

Moncure D. Conway

Wianno, Barnstable County, Massachusetts, July 8, 1892.

Also at Dickinson College is the manuscript of an article by Conway on Thomas Paine and his theory of government, 1892.

[497] A copy of the Catalogue of this exhibition is in the Public Library, New York. On the cover in Conway's handwriting is written "Merry Christmas from Mr. and Mrs. Conway. 1894." See also *Rights of Man; Being an Answer to Mr. Burke's Attack on the French Revolution*, by Thomas Paine. Edited with Introduction and Notes by Moncure Daniel Conway (Part I). New York: G. P. Putnam's Sons, 1895. Reprinted from *The Writings of Thomas Paine*, Vol. 2. See also *Autobiography*. II, 434n. Here Conway tells the reader that:

> My large collection of Paine editions was some years ago purchased by the National Library at Washington. I possess still an oil portrait of Paine printed during the life (artist unknown), but my most curious relic is a bit of Paine's brain, removed and preserved by Benjamin Tilly, the English agent of Cobbett who carried the body from New Rochelle to England in 1819. I paid £ pound for this in London to stop its being hawked about.

[498] See appendix II of this book.

[499] *My Pilgrimage to the Wise Men of the East*. 1906. "What was it," asked Conway, "that in 1776 enabled two colonies - South Carolina and Georgia - to set aside the anti-slavery feeling of elevin colonies, and compel Jefferson to cancel the denunciation of slave in Declaration of Independence? War.. .It was that black mark persistent in the war between the North and South which slew half a million."

[500] *The Life of Thomas Paine*, II, p. 152. See *Autobiography*, II, 368, for Conway's account of Garrison's last visit to England in June, 1877. On June 8, 1879, Conway preached a sermon on Garrison at his memorial service in South Place Chapel. Special Collections. Columbia University Library.

[501] *Autobiography*, II, 438.

[502] The letter of December 16, 1898, is addressed to Mrs. Alexander Tweedie. See *Autobiography*, II, 160. Manuscript at Dickinson College.

[503] See appendix IV of this book.

[504] "A Gnostic's Apology," *Farewell Discourses*, 3-4.

Index

www.ingramcontent.com/pod-product-compliance
Lightning Source LLC
LaVergne TN
LVHW020526100826
845148LV00010B/1356